Praise for Harald Jähner's

AFTERMATH

"[Jähner] does double duty in this fascinating book . . . elegantly marshaling a plethora of facts while also using his critical skills to wry effect, parsing a country's stubborn inclination toward willful delusion. Even though *Aftermath* covers historical ground, its narrative is intimate, filled with first-person accounts from articles and diaries."
—*The New York Times*

"The national psyche is the principal protagonist in Harald Jähner's subtle, perceptive and beautifully written *Aftermath*. . . . [It] is a revelatory, remarkably wide-ranging book crammed with material, much of which will, I imagine, be new to an international audience." —Andrew Stuttaford, *The Wall Street Journal*

"Harald Jähner's highly readable account of how Germans went about leaving Nazism behind. *Aftermath* is about the price and the accomplishment of a new beginning when the aggressive war the Germans had waged was reversed to utter defeat in 1945. . . . Jähner is counterintuitive but thoughtful." —*The New York Times Book Review*

"Jähner . . . sets out to complicate our picture of those tumultuous times. . . . [An] often intriguing social and cultural history."
—*Forward*

"This is an important addition to the library of Holocaust literature." —*New York Journal of Books*

"Harald Jähner's *Aftermath* is a transfixing account and subtle analysis of Germany after the Second World War has ended. A scrupulous investigation of the past, it reads, constantly, like a prelude to what is still unfolding." —*The New Statesman*

"Important, exemplary. . . . This is the kind of book few writers possess the clarity of vision to write."   —*The Sunday Times* (London)

"Many consider the years before 1945 to be the most crucial in understanding Germany and the Germans. Wait until you have read this book."   —Norman Ohler, author of
Blitzed: Drugs in the Third Reich

"What does total defeat mean? Germany 1945–55. Ten years of poverty, ruins, fear, violence, black markets, manic hard work, inventive sex—and always, always, silence about the murdered millions of the Third Reich. A fascinating read."   —Neil MacGregor, author of
Germany: Memories of a Nation

"Harald Jähner claims to have discovered a hole in the heart of modern German history. This book triumphantly proves him right. It is absolutely extraordinary. Every page stops you dead with insight and revelation."   —James Hawes, author of
The Shortest History of Germany

"For those who want to understand the Germans, *Aftermath* is essential reading. . . . Anyone with even the slightest interest in history and the human condition should read this book."
—Julia Boyd, author of
Travelers in the Third Reich

"Extraordinary. . . . One of the most evocative pieces of carefully researched history that I have ever read. It's a remarkable piece of work."   —Misha Glenny, author of
McMafia and The Balkans

Harald Jähner

AFTERMATH

Harald Jähner is a cultural journalist and former editor of *The Berlin Times*. He has been an honorary professor of cultural journalism at Berlin University of the Arts since 2011. *Aftermath*, his first book, won the Leipzig Book Fair Prize in 2019.

Shaun Whiteside is a translator of French, Dutch, German, and Italian literature. He has translated many works of nonfiction and novels, including *Manituana* and *Altai* by Wu Ming, *The Weekend* by Bernhard Schlink, *Serotonin* by Michel Houellebecq, and *Magdalena the Sinner* by Lilian Faschinger, which won him the Schlegel-Tieck Prize for German translation in 1997.

AFTERMATH

AFTERMATH

LIFE IN THE FALLOUT OF THE THIRD REICH
1945–1955

HARALD JÄHNER

Translated by Shaun Whiteside

VINTAGE BOOKS
A Division of Penguin Random House LLC
New York

The translation of this work was supported by a grant from the Goethe-Institut.

Grateful acknowledgment is made to the following for permission to reprint previously published material: Günter Eich: Inventur, from idem., Gesammelte Werke in vier Bänden. Band I: Die Gedichte. Die Maulwürfe. © Suhrkamp Verlag, Frankfurt am Main 1991. All rights Suhrkamp Verlag Berlin. Elisabeth Langgässer: Kalte Reise in die Fassenacht, in: Merian, Städte und Landschaften, Mainz. Vol. 2, 1949, No. 3. Erich Kästner: Marschlied 1945, from: idem., Der tägliche Kram. © Atrium Verlag AGs Zürich 1948, and Thomas Kästner.

The Library of Congress has cataloged the Knopf edition as follows:
Names: Jähner, Harald, [date] author. | Whiteside, Shaun, translator.
Title: Aftermath : life in the fallout of the Third Reich, 1945–1955 / Harald Jähner ; translated by Shaun Whiteside.
Other titles: Wolfszeit. English | Life in the fallout of the Third Reich, 1945–1955
Description: First edition. | New York : Alfred A. Knopf, 2022. | Includes bibliographic references and index.
Identifiers: LCCN 2021020610 (print) | LCCN 2021020611 (ebook)
Subjects: LCSH: Germany—History—1945–1955. | Germany—Social conditions—1945–1955. | Germany—Intellectual life—20th century. | Germans—Social life and customs—20th century.
Classification: LCC DD257.2 .J3513 2022 (print) | LCC DD257.2 (ebook) | DDC 943.087/5—dc23
LC record available at https://lccn.loc.gov/2021020610
LC ebook record available at https://lccn.loc.gov/2021020611

Vintage Books Trade Paperback ISBN: 978-0-593-31393-0
eBook ISBN: 978-0-593-31974-1

Author photograph © Barbara Dietl

vintagebooks.com

Printed in the United States of America
10 9 8 7 6 5 4 3 2

Contents

Preface

On 18 March 1952 the *Neue Zeitung* published an article by the author and editor Kurt Kusenberg entitled NOTHING CAN BE TAKEN FOR GRANTED: PRAISE FOR A TIME OF MISERY. Only seven years on, the author yearned for the weeks of confusion that had followed the end of the Second World War in Germany. Even though nothing had worked at the time—not the postal service, the railways, public transport—in spite of the homelessness, the hunger and the occasional corpse that still lay buried under the rubble, in retrospect those weeks struck him as having been a good time. "Like children," he wrote, people after war had begun "to mend the torn net of human relationships." His choice of words is unusual and perhaps a little disconcerting . . . "Like children"?

Kusenberg urgently recommended that his readers imagine themselves back into the "starving, tattered, shivering, poverty-stricken, dangerous time" when, in the absence of state order, morality and social connections were redefined among the scattered people:

> Respectability did not exclude resourcefulness and cunning—not even the petty theft of food. But in this semi-larcenous life there was an honour among thieves that was perhaps more moral than today's cast-iron conscience.

It is a strange nostalgia. Was there really supposed to have been so much adventure immediately after the war, so much "honour among thieves"? So much innocence? The unifying force that had held the Germans together until the end of the war had been—fortunately—completely ruptured. The old order was gone, a new one was written in the stars, and for now the Allies supplied the basic necessities needed to maintain the population. The 75 million or so people collected on what remained of German soil in the summer of 1945 hardly merited the name of a society. People talked about "no man's time," the "time of the wolves" in which "man had become a wolf towards his fellow man." The ethos of everyone caring only for themselves or their wolf-pack shaped the country's national identity until deep into the 1950s, by which point conditions had been improving for some time and yet despite this people still stubbornly withdrew into their families as self-contained refuges.

After the war over half the population of Germany was neither where they belonged nor wanted to be, including 9 million bombed-out people and evacuees, 14 million refugees and exiles, 10 million released forced labourers and prisoners, and countless millions of slowly returning prisoners of war. How was this horde of ragged, displaced, impoverished and leftover people broken up and reassembled? And how did former "national comrades" (Volksgenossen), as German nationals were known under Nazism, gradually become ordinary citizens again?

These are questions that threaten to disappear under the weight of momentous historical events. The most important changes were played out in everyday life, in the organisation of food, for example, in looting, money-changing, shopping. And also in love, as a wave of sexual adventurousness followed the war. There was some keen disappointment when much-missed husbands failed to return home, but, equally, many Germans now saw things with different eyes, they wanted to start everything afresh, and divorce rates leapt.

The collective memory of the post-war age in Germany is shaped by a few images that have etched their way deeply into people's minds: the Russian soldier pulling a woman's bicycle out of her hands; dim black-market figures clustering around a few eggs; the temporary Nissen huts housing refugees and people whose houses had been bombed; the women questioningly holding up photographs of their missing husbands to the returning prisoners of war. These few pictures are so visually powerful that they imprinted on the German public memory of the first post-war years like an unchanging silent film—although, it must be said, half of life ends up on the cutting-room floor.

While memory usually bathes the past in a softer light with the passing years, the reverse is true for the post-war period in Germany. In hindsight it became increasingly dark. One reason for that lies in the widespread need among Germans who had not been persecuted by the Nazi regime to see themselves, nevertheless, as victims. Many people clearly felt that the grimmer the accounts of the genuinely terrible starving winters of 1946 and 1947, the more their guilt was diminished. But if we listen carefully we can also hear laughter. A spontaneous Rosenmontag (Rose Monday) carnival procession passed through a terribly depopulated Cologne as early as 1946. The journalist Margret Boveri remembered the feeling of life being "enormously enhanced by the approaching nearness of death." In the years when there was nothing to buy she had been so happy that she later decided not to undertake any major purchases even when times improved.

Misery cannot be understood without the pleasure that it provokes. Escaping death drove some into apathy, others into a passionate love of life. The old order of things had gone off the rails, families had been torn apart, connections lost—but people were starting to mingle again, and anyone young and spirited saw the chaos as a playground in which they had to seek their joy anew each day.

*

The Holocaust played a shockingly small part in the consciousness of most Germans in the post-war period. Some were aware of the crimes on the Eastern Front, and a certain fundamental guilt at having started the war in the first place was acknowledged, but there was no room in many people's thoughts and feelings for the murder of millions of German and European Jews. Only a very few individuals, such as the philosopher Karl Jaspers, addressed the issue publicly. The Jews were not even explicitly mentioned in the much-debated admissions of guilt by the Protestant and Catholic Churches in August 1945.

In a perfidious way the unthinkability of the Holocaust also extended to the nation that had perpetrated it. The crimes had an enormity which banished them from the collective consciousness even while they were happening. The fact that even well-intentioned people refused to think about what would happen to their deported neighbours has left trust in the human species severely shaken even into the present day. And the majority of Germans at the time were guilty of this.

The hushing-up of the extermination camps continued after the end of the war, even though the Allies tried to forcibly confront the defeated German people with evidence of Nazi crimes. Post-war Chancellor Helmut Kohl used the sardonic phrase "the blessing of late birth" to suggest that the younger generation had no right to feel quite so superior to the one that came before. But there was also the blessing of the experience of terror. The nights of bombing raids, the harsh starvation winters of the first post-war years and the sheer struggle for survival under anarchic everyday conditions kept many Germans from thinking about the past. They saw themselves as the victims, and thus had the dubious good fortune of not having to think about the real ones. Because, had they still been halfway decent after all that had happened, had they been aware of the systematic mass murder committed in their name, with their tacit support and thanks to their willingness to turn a blind eye, they would hardly have been able to summon the courage and energy required to live through the post-war years.

The survival instinct shuts out feelings of guilt—a collective phenomenon that can be studied in the years after 1945 and must be deeply unsettling to anyone with faith in humanity. But how the two societies of East and West Germany, both anti-fascist in their different ways, could both be founded on repression and distortion is a mystery that this book seeks to address by immersing itself in the extreme challenges and curious lifestyles of the post-war years.

Even though books like Anne Frank's *Diary* or Eugen Kogon's *SS-State* disrupted the process of repression, it was only with the Auschwitz trials beginning in 1963 that many Germans began to reckon with the crimes that had been committed in their name. In the eyes of the younger generation the Germans had brought extreme dishonour upon themselves by postponing the trials, even though in purely material terms they had profited considerably from their parents' capacity for repression. Seldom in history has a generational conflict been waged with more bitterness, rage and self-righteousness than that of the young German people of 1968 against their parents.

Today, the German people's overall impression of the post-war years has been shaped by the perspective of those who were young at the time. The anti-authoritarian fury the children felt towards their parents' generation—a generation that had not made itself easy to love—was so intense, their criticism so eloquent, that the myth of a suffocating layer of fustiness that needed to be eliminated still dominates the image of the 1950s held by most Germans, in spite of more sophisticated historical research. The generation born around 1950 enjoyed the role of having made the Federal Republic of Germany (West Germany) inhabitable and having given democracy a heart, and this generation continues to promulgate that picture. In reality, though, there remained a strong presence of the old Nazi elite in the offices of the Federal Republic during this time, which was a source of revulsion for many, as was the readiness with which Nazi criminals were granted amnesties. However, the post-war era in Germany was more exciting, its sense of life more open, its intellectuals more critical, its spectrum of opinion broader, its art more innovative, and its everyday life more contradictory than the impressions that have prevailed from 1968 until the present day might suggest. It is something that research for this book has revealed time and again.

There is another reason why the first four post-war years in Germany represent a relative blind spot in historical memory. Between the big chapters and research headings of history they form a kind of no-man's-time for which, loosely speaking, no one is really responsible. One major chapter in German school history deals with the Nazi regime, ending with the capitulation of the German Wehrmacht, while the next, which begins in 1949, tells the story of the Federal Republic of Germany (West Germany) and the German Democratic Republic (East Germany) and is concentrated at best on currency reform and the Berlin blockade as a backstory to the foundation of the two states. The years between the end of the war and the currency reform, the economic Big Bang of the Federal Republic, are in a sense a lost time for historiography, because they lack an institutional subject. German history-writing is essentially still structured as a national history, which places the state as a political subject at its centre. But from 1945 four political centres were responsible for German history: Washington, Moscow, London and Paris, each exercising authority over their designated occupation zone—hardly ideal conditions to construct a national history.

The classroom appraisal of the crimes perpetrated against the Jews and forced labourers also ends, as a rule, with the happy liberation of the survivors by Allied soldiers. But what happened to them after that? What about the 10 million or so starving prisoners, already dragged from their homelands and now dumped unsupervised in the land of their torturers and murderers? How did they react? The way the Allied soldiers, the vanquished Germans and the liberated forced labourers behaved towards one another is one of the saddest, but also one of the most fascinating, aspects of the post-war years.

Over the course of this book the focus shifts from the societal aspects of everyday life—from clearing up, making love, stealing and shopping—to the cultural features: the life of the mind and the efflorescence of a radical new visual aesthetic. Here, questions of conscience, guilt and repression are asked more pointedly. Instances of denazification, which also had its aesthetic side, are treated with appropriate care. The fact that the arts (broadly taken to mean architecture, painting, etc.) of the 1950s found such lasting fame may be traced back to one surprising factor: by altering their surroundings the Germans changed themselves. But was it really the Germans who so radically transformed the shape of their world? A fight broke out around concepts of design and abstract art, in which the occupying powers of America, Britain, France and Russia all pulled strings; it concerned the aesthetic decoration of the two German republics, pitting the socialist realism of the East against the abstract art of the West, and would define the sense of beauty during the Cold War. Even the CIA was involved.

Even more than is the case today, German people tended to present themselves as refined, sophisticated and tirelessly involved in serious discussions, as if it were possible to pick up seamlessly from the manners of the nineteenth century, which had been transformed into "the good old days." Today we know a great deal about the Holocaust. What we know less about is how life in Germany continued under the shadow it cast across the country's future. How does a nation in whose name many millions of people were murdered talk about culture and morality? Would it be better, for decency's sake, to avoid talking about decency altogether? To let one's children find out for themselves what is good and what is evil? In the years immediately following the war analysts in the media were working overtime, along with other institutions, to take part in the reconstruction of society. Everybody was talking about a "hunger for meaning." Philosophising on "the ruins of existence" meant searching for meaning, just as many were reduced to searching for scraps among the rubble.

AFTERMATH

AFTERMATH

I

Zero Hour?

Never before was there so much beginning. And never so much end

The theatre critic Friedrich Luft experienced the end of the war in a basement. Down in a villa near Nollendorfplatz in Berlin, he had sat out the last few days of the final battle with a few other local people amidst the "smell of smoke, blood, sweat and gunpowder." It was safer in the basement than in the apartments, exposed as they were to crossfire between the Red Army and the Wehrmacht. Luft recalled the day that the Red Army arrived in Berlin:

> It was an inferno outside. If you peered out you saw a helpless German tank pushing its way through the blazing rows of houses, stopping, firing, turning round. Every now and again a civilian, darting from shelter to shelter, stumbled along badly bombed streets. A mother with her pram rushed from a bullet-riddled, burning house towards the nearest bunker.[1]

An old man who had been crouching near the basement window was shredded by shrapnel. On one occasion a few soldiers from an office in Wehrmacht Supreme Command drifted in, "irritated, discouraged, sick fellows." Each of them carried a cardboard box of civilian clothing, so that they could disappear "in an emergency," as they said. How much emergency was still to come? "Just clear off," the inhabitants of the basement hissed. No one wanted to be near them as the end approached. At one point, the corpse of the feared local Nazi block warden was carried past in a wheelbarrow; he had thrown himself out of a window.

Suddenly it occurred to someone that there was a pile of swastika flags and pictures of Hitler stored in the house opposite. A few brave people went over to burn everything, to get rid of it before the Russians came. When the gunfire suddenly grew louder again and the theatre critic looked cautiously out of the basement door, he saw an SS patrol also peering over a remnant of wall. The men were still combing the area in search of shirkers that they could take with them to their deaths.

> Then it became quieter. As we carefully climbed the narrow steps towards an eternity of listening and waiting, it rained softly. On houses beyond Nollendorfplatz we saw white flags gleaming. We wrapped white rags around our arms. Then two Russians climbed over the same low wall over which the SS men had come so menacingly just a few moments before. We raised our arms, we pointed at our armbands. They waved us away. They were smiling. The war was over.

For Friedrich Luft the end of the war, later to be called Zero Hour by some, had struck on 30 April. In Aachen, 640 kilometres west of Berlin, the war had already been over for six months; it had been the first German city to be taken by the Americans in October 1944. In Duisburg the war had been over in the districts to the west of the Rhine since 28 March, but on the east of the Rhine it raged for another 16 days. There are even three dates for the official capitulation of Germany. Generaloberst Alfred Jodl signed the unconditional surrender on 7 May in Reims in the headquarters of US General Dwight D. Eisenhower. Even though the document expressly acknowledged the Western Allies and the Red Army as the victors, Joseph Stalin insisted that the ceremony be repeated, so on 9 May Germany capitulated again; this time Generalfeldmarschall Wilhelm Keitel signed the document in the Soviet headquarters in Berlin-Karlshorst. And for the history books, the victorious powers agreed on the day in between, 8 May, on which nothing had actually happened at all.[2]

For Walter Eiling, Zero Hour still hadn't arrived four years later, at which time he was still in Ziegenhain Prison for "Crimes against the Ordinance on Antisocial Parasites." The waiter from Hesse had been arrested in 1942 for buying a goose, three chickens and ten pounds of salted meat at Christmas. A special Nazi court had sentenced him to eight years of imprisonment followed by preventive detention for "Violation of the War Economy Regulations." After the end of the war Walter Eiling and his family had believed that he would be swiftly released. But it didn't even occur to the legal authorities to review his case. When the justice minister of the region of Greater Hesse, under American military supervision, finally rescinded the absurdly severe punishment, his office insisted that the imprisonment had been repealed but not the preventive detention. Walter Eiling remained in prison. Later applications for release were rejected on the grounds that the prisoner was unstable, inclined towards arrogance, and not yet capable of returning to work.

In Eiling's cell the rule of the Nazi regime lived on, even beyond the creation of the Federal Republic of Germany.[3] Fates such as his were the reason why the concept of the end of the war being a "Zero Hour," a fresh start, was later violently disputed. In the corporate head offices, courts and offices of the Federal Republic most of the Nazi elite cheerfully carried on. Such continuities were concealed by talk of Zero Hour, which served to emphasise the desire for a new beginning and stress a clear normative watershed between the old state and the new, even though life, of course, carried on and dragged any amount of Third Reich legacy with it. However, the idea of Zero Hour was emblematic of the elemental break that Germany had experienced and not only does the concept remain useful, but in academic history it is even enjoying a renaissance.[4]

Elsewhere, every form of public order was collapsing. Police officers looked helplessly at one another, uncertain whether they still held their posts. Anyone who had a uniform preferred to take it off and burn it, or maybe dye it a different colour. Senior officials poisoned themselves, lower-ranking civil servants threw themselves out of the window or slit their wrists. It was the start of no-man's-time; laws had been overruled, yet no one was responsible for anything. Nothing belonged to anyone anymore, unless they were sitting on it. No one was responsible, no one was ensured protection. The old power had run away, the new one hadn't yet arrived; only the noise of artillery suggested that it would come eventually. Even the most sophisticated people engaged in looting. In little hordes they broke into food stores and roamed through abandoned apartments in search of food and a place to sleep.

In Berlin, journalist Ruth Andreas-Friedrich, doctor Walter Seitz, actor Fred Denger, and German-Russian musical conductor Leo Borchard discovered a white ox in the middle of the disputed capital. The group had just sought cover in a nearby house from a low-flying air raid, when suddenly the animal was standing in front of them,

Survival techniques in the city: a Berliner collecting firewood in the remains of the Tiergarten park.

unharmed and gentle-eyed, a surreal sight in the smoking scene of horror. They surrounded it and gently manoeuvred it by the horns, managing to lure it carefully into the backyard of the house. But what were they to do next? How do four urbane, cultivated citizens slaughter a cow? The conductor, who had a command of Russian, plucked up the courage to speak to a Soviet soldier outside the house. The soldier helped them to kill the animal with two pistol shots. The friends now hesitantly went to work on the dead creature with kitchen knifes. They weren't alone with their booty for long. "Suddenly, as if the underworld had been spying on them, a noisy crowd gathered around the dead ox," Ruth Andreas-Friedrich later recorded in her diary. "They crept from a hundred basements. Women, men, children. Were they lured by the smell of blood?" And within minutes everyone was tussling for the scraps of meat. Five blood-smeared fists ripped the ox's tongue from its throat. "So this is what the hour of liberation looks like. The moment we have spent twelve years waiting for?" she wrote.[5]

*

After the white ox had been carved up and torn to pieces, the four friends climbed into a bombed-out apartment and rummaged through the cupboards. Instead of food they found only large amounts of sherbet, which they laughingly crammed into their mouths. When, still joking, they tried on some of the unknown residents' clothes, they were suddenly horrified by their own brazenness. Their boldness subsided and the four anxiously lay down in the marriage bed of the unknown inhabitants, who, according to their doorbell, were called Machulke. HOME SWEET HOME, read the embroidered words above the bed.

It was 11 days after they first crossed Berlin's boundary at Malchow before the Red Army had advanced to the last inner-city districts. So even here, in the capital, the end of the war didn't happen everywhere at the same time. Marta Hillers, who was a journalist in Berlin and later wrote under the pen name Anonyma, didn't dare ride her bicycle through the ruined city until 7 May, when, curious, she cycled a few kilometres south from Berlin-Tempelhof. That evening she recorded in her diary:

> In this part of town the war ended one day earlier than where we are. You can see civilians sweeping the streets. Two women are pushing and pulling a mobile operating unit, sterile lamps ablaze, probably recovered from the rubble. An old woman is lying on top of the unit under a woollen blanket, her face white, but she's still alive. The farther south I ride the further the war recedes. Here you can even see whole groups of Germans standing around and chatting. People don't dare do that where we live.[6]

The next day Ruth Andreas-Friedrich set off through the city and tried to make her first contact with colleagues, friends and relatives. Like everyone else she was eager for news, progress reports, general assessments. Only a few days later, life in Berlin had calmed down to such an extent that she was able to move back into her severely battered apartment. On the balcony she made a makeshift stove of stones that had been lying about, trying to warm herself up a little— a Robinson Crusoe camp in the middle of the city. Gas and electricity were out of the question.

She recorded sudden mood swings in her diary. Hitler was dead, summer was coming, and she wanted to make something of her life at last. She couldn't wait to go back to work, to use her gift for observation, her talent as a writer. Only two months had passed since the end of the war, and she wrote in a moment of euphoria:

> The whole city is living in a frenzy of expectation. People are willing to tear themselves apart just to get back to work. They wish they had a thousand hands and a thousand brains. The Americans are here. The English, the Russians. The French are supposed to be on their way. [. . .] All that matters is that we are at the centre of the action. That the world powers are meeting in our rubble, and that we can prove to the representatives of those world powers how serious we are about our

eagerness, how infinitely serious we are about our efforts to make amends and rise again. Berlin is working full blast. If people understand and forgive us now, we will do everything for them. Everything! We will renounce National Socialism in favour of something new, we will work and we will be fundamentally good-willed. Never have we been so ripe for redemption.[7]

We might assume that Berliners felt the way their city looked: beaten, defeated, due for demolition. Instead, the 44-year-old diarist experienced a "frenzy of expectation," and not only within herself. She saw the whole city as being ready to get to work at full steam. Ruth Andreas-Friedrich had, along with her boyfriend Leo Borchard, been a founding member of the small "Onkel Emil" resistance group. At the Yad Vashem memorial in Jerusalem she is honoured as "Righteous Among the Nations." So it wasn't just hard-hearted Germans who wanted to plunge themselves into work, it wasn't just those incapable of mourning. Hitler's suicide was only two months in the past, and already Berlin—in Ruth's words—wanted to be back "at the centre of the action," it wanted to revive, and it wanted to be forgiven.

Behind that wild yearning for a new start lies the end of an inferno of which many had witnessed only a tiny part. Meanwhile the next generation of historians was already at work, trying to make the extent of the horrors halfway comprehensible. They remained unimaginable. No one can grasp the meaning of 60 million war-dead, but there are ways of making the scale more comprehensible. During the bombings in the summer of 1943, 40,000 people died in the Hamburg firestorm—a hell that buried itself deep in the nation's memory because of its savagery. It took the lives of about 3 per cent of the city's population. As terrible as these events were, the overall percentage of victims across Europe was more than twice as high. The war cost 6 per cent of all Europeans their lives. The scale of the catastrophe that befell Hamburg applied twice as much to Europe as a whole. In Poland a sixth of the population was killed, some 6 million people. Jews suffered the worst; in their families they counted not the dead but the survivors.

The historian Keith Lowe writes:

> Even those who experienced the war, who witnessed massacres, who
> saw fields full of dead bodies and mass graves brimming with corpses
> are unable to comprehend the true scale of the killing that took place
> in Europe across the war.[8]

That much was certainly true immediately after the end of the
war. The chaos that citizens discovered as they emerged from their
air-raid shelters with their arms raised was already quite enough to
bear. How could anything come out of this calamity, particularly in
Germany, which was to blame for it all?

But 26-year-old Wolfgang Borchert, who would be known to pos-
terity as a dark master of lamentation, tried to turn the burden of
survival into an emphatic manifesto of his generation. Borchert had
been conscripted into the Wehrmacht in 1941 and sent to the Eastern
Front. There he had been punished several times for "statements sub-
versive of national defence." Severely traumatised by his experiences
at the front and in prison, and by liver disease that went untreated, he
returned from Frankfurt to his home city of Hamburg in 1945, having
escaped transportation to a prisoner-of-war camp, walking a total of
600 kilometres. There he wrote the short essay "Generation without
Farewell." In it, with wild resolution, he sang of the arrival of a generation whose past had been literally blown to pieces. That past
was—and this is the meaning of the title—no longer available to the
psyche, whether because it was unimaginable, or because of trauma-
tisation or repression. "Generation without Farewell" is a manifesto
of Zero Hour:

> We are the generation without ties and without depth. Our depth is
> an abyss. We are the generation without happiness, without a home
> and without farewell. Our sun is narrow, our love cruel, and our youth
> is without youth.[9]

Borchert's rhapsodic text, hammering monotonously on, is powerfully disorienting. Not without a certain pride, he stylises a disposition

of wayward coldness. This young generation, he suggests, has bidden farewell to the dead too often to be able to respond emotionally to a farewell anymore; in fact those farewells are "legion." The last lines of the text are an account of the strength that even this fatally ill young man imagined he could summon for the future:

> We are a generation without a homecoming, because we have nothing that we could come home to. But we are a generation of arrival. Perhaps we are a generation filled with arrival on a new star, in a new life. Filled with arrival under a new sun, to new hearts. Perhaps we are filled with arrival to a new life, to a new laughter, a new God. We are a generation without farewell, but we know that all arrival belongs to us.

"Generation without Farewell" is the poetic declaration of a generation who felt themselves to be superfluous. In it, the shocking refusal of many Germans to wonder how it could all have happened is elevated to a movement. The slate of experience is wiped clean, freed up for a new style of writing, "a new God." An arrival on a new star. The word "repression" would be an understatement here—it is a conscious refusal. It is an emphatic new beginning, marking a bitter end with the past. Of course, Wolfgang Borchert was well aware that the *tabula rasa* is an illusion. He didn't need anyone to explain to him how tormenting memories can be. Forgetting was the utopia of the moment.

The poem "Inventory" by Günter Eich, written late in 1945, became famous in Germany and assumed the status of a manifesto for Zero Hour. In it a man lists his possessions, his equipment for the new beginning.

> This is my cap,
> this is my coat,
> here are my shaving things
> in their linen case.
> . . . .

In the bread bin are
a pair of woollen socks
and some things that I
will reveal to no one.

. . . .

This is my notebook,
this my strip of canvas,
this my towel,
this is my thread.

"Inventory" became the watchword for post-war literature because of its provocatively laconic quality. The "clear-cutting" writers, as they called themselves, opposed florid prose because they felt betrayed by it, having once used it themselves. Their capacity for enthusiasm lay in ruins as well. From now on they planned to keep things as simple

Don't turn around, look straight ahead. A small family gazes towards the future. Behind them the remains of Munich.

as possible, and to stick to intimate, private subjects, to the things they could spread out on the table—a lyrical proclamation for which the sociologist Helmut Schelsky would, in 1957, coin the phrase "the sceptical generation."[10] Günter Eich's poetic inventory avoids memory: with only mistrust, as well as a coat, notebook and thread (and something "that I will reveal to no one"—a phrase admitting deliberate repression that is perhaps the key to the whole poem), he enters his new life.

Marta Hillers also drew up an inventory in her diary. It has become famous because of the clear-eyed openness with which she describes the wave of rapes that followed the arrival of the Red Army. She experienced Zero Hour as a regime of sexual violence that lasted for days. When it was finally over, on 13 May, she took stock:

> On the one hand things are good for me. I'm fresh and healthy. I have not suffered any physical harm. I have the feeling that I am excellently equipped for life, as if I had webbed feet for the mud. I am adapted to the world, I'm not delicate. [. . .] On the other side there are only minuses. I no longer know what I'm supposed to do in the world. I'm indispensable to no one. I'm just standing around, waiting, I can see neither goal nor task before me.

She runs through a number of possibilities: going to Moscow, becoming a Communist, becoming an artist. She rejects everything.

> Love? Lies trampled on the ground. Perhaps art [. . .]? Yes, for those who have the calling, but I don't. I'm just an ordinary labourer, I have to be satisfied with that. All I can do is connect with my small circle and be a good friend. What's left is just to wait for the end. Still, the dark and amazing adventure of life beckons. I'll stick around, out of curiosity, and because I enjoy breathing and stretching my healthy limbs.[11]

And Friedrich Luft? The theatre critic who climbed out of the basement at the end of April with his white armband and walked towards the Russian soldiers was still in Berlin too, his curiosity unsated. He wrote regular pieces for the magazine section of the Berlin *Tagesspie-gel,* founded in September 1945. He wrote about the stimulating flow of the city, the fine spring clothes collections, the tension of waiting for the postman's arrival in the morning. Luft became the "voice of criticism" at RIAS Radio in West Berlin. Between February 1946 and October 1990, just before his death, he ended each of his weekly broadcasts with words that dripped like honey into the souls of his audience, promising dependability: "We'll talk again in a week. As always. Same time, same band, same place."

Luft spent many more years living with his wife, a draughtswoman, in the house from whose basement he had climbed in 1945. In the early seventies Heide Luft often took herself to a bar on Winterfeldt-platz, not far from their house. The bar was called Ruin. And it wasn't just in name, it was one: the front of the building was bombed out, but parts of the foundation were still standing, forming a bizarre little beer garden within their jagged walls. The bar was in the building to the rear and was always full to the rafters. A tree grew out of the rubble-covered basement in the front building, and a few lanterns hung from its branches. In the early seventies the bar was a meeting point for people who wanted to be poets. Most of them were students. It still looked as if the war had just ended. While her husband sat at home working on his reviews for the radio, Frau Luft sat in her elegant fur coat among the long-haired people, chatting a little, always bright and non-committal, occasionally buying a round. She was one of many who liked to go back to Zero Hour, each in their own way.

II

In Ruins

Who's going to clear all that up again?
Rubble clearance strategies

The war had left about 500 million cubic metres of rubble behind. To help people visualise the amount, they undertook all kinds of calculations. The *Nürnberger Nachrichten* took the Zeppelin field at the Reich Party rally grounds as its benchmark. Piled up in that space, 300 metres by 300, the rubble would have produced a mountain 4,000 metres high, topped with perpetual snow. Others imagined the Berlin ruins, calculated as having a volume of 55 million cubic metres, as a wall 30 metres wide and 5 metres high and stretching westwards, reaching all the way to Cologne. These were the sort of notions used to help people grasp the enormous quantities of debris that needed to be cleared away. No one who stood in cities such as Dresden, Berlin, Hamburg, Kiel, Duisburg or Frankfurt, whole districts of which had been completely destroyed, could possibly have imagined how the detritus could ever be removed, let alone the cities reconstructed. There were 40 cubic metres of rubble for each surviving resident of Dresden.

Of course the rubble didn't appear in such a compact form; the wreckage spread in city-wide expanses in the form of fragile and precarious ruins. Anyone who lived amidst them, often with only three out of four walls remaining and the roof open to the sky, first had to crawl through high piles of rubble and risk venturing through the free-standing remains of walls to get home. Individual walls were often the height of the façade, without supporting side walls, and threatened to collapse at any moment. Masonry swayed overhead on twisted iron girders and whole concrete floors protruded from a single wall, while children played below.

There was, in fact, every reason to despair, but most Germans couldn't afford even a brief moment of despondency. On 23 April 1945, before the war was even officially over, the municipal bulletin for the south-western city of Mannheim already published its proclamation: WE ARE REBUILDING.

We can only do this quite modestly for the time being, because mountains of rubble need to be removed before we can locate land to build on. The best thing to do is to start removing the rubble, and, as the old saying goes, to start outside your own front door. We will manage. It will be hard when someone lucky enough to have come home stands outside his shattered dwelling, which he would once more like to make his home. In that case much hammering and carpentry will need to be done, using skills acquired over many years, before the place is habitable once again. [. . .] Self-help is only a possibility when one has access to roofing felt and tiles. If as many people as possible are to be helped as quickly as possible, anyone who still has roofing material left over from previous work will have to deposit these at the appropriate district construction office forthwith. [. . .] In this way we want to rebuild very modestly at first, step by step, so that windows and roofs are closed up again, and then we will see what happens next.[1]

Huge quantities of British bombs had rained down on Mannheim, destroying half of the city's houses, but thanks to an effective system of basement air-raid shelters only 0.5 per cent of the population had perished. This may perhaps explain the strange glee with which hammering and carpentry are depicted, almost as an idyllic bout of DIY. But in other cities, too, people set about clearing things up with an enthusiasm that might have appeared macabre to outsiders.

"*Erst mal wieder Grund reinbringen*"—First re-establish your foundations—was the motto; literally, the phrase means "find a piece of land." Surprisingly quickly, an initial order was created amidst the chaos of the ruins. Narrow passages were cleared, where people could make their way easily through the rubble. In the collapsed cities a new topography of beaten paths came into being. Cleared oases appeared in the deserts of rubble. In some places people had cleaned the streets so conscientiously that the cobblestones gleamed as if they were brand new, while on other pavements pieces of rubble were stacked on top of one another, meticulously sorted by size. In Freiburg, in Baden, south-west Germany, which always had a reputation for being spick and span—"Freiburg city / Is nice and clean and pretty," as the nineteenth-century author Johann Peter Hebel had it— the loose rubble was piled so carefully at the feet of the ruins that the apocalyptic setting almost started looking habitable again.

A photograph taken by Werner Bischof in 1945 shows a man walking alone through this cleanly swept hell. He is wearing his Sunday best, we see him from behind, a black hat pushed back onto the back of his neck, his jodhpurs stuffed into his knee-high boots, which in combination with his elegant jacket gives him the appearance of a cavalry captain. He is carrying a wicker basket in his hand, as if he is strolling to the shops, which earned the picture the unofficial title "Man in Search of Something Edible." His gait is practically impudent; his posture suggests optimism and resolve, and together with the attentively upward-looking angle of his head, curiously taking in the surrounding area, gives a poignant sense of someone who has ended up in the wrong film.

The Germans had had a lot of time to get used to the devastation. Since the first bombing raids in 1940 they had been forced to clear their cities after repeated attacks, and patch them up as best they could. But then they had masses of POWs and forced labourers at their disposal, whom they deployed for the hard labour under inhuman conditions. In the last months of the war no one counted precisely how many had died in the process. But after the end of the war the Germans had to do that work themselves for the first time.

What better solution than to enlist the very people who had instigated the disaster in the first place? In the first weeks after the war ended, so-called "Party Member deployments" were organised; former Nazi Party members were pressed to work to help remove the rubble. In Duisburg in early May posters announced that ex-Party members were ordered to "clear away street obstacles." "They must be removed immediately by Party members, friends and sponsors of the Nazi clique. Those summoned to comply must provide their own suitable tools."² The summons was accompanied by the threat: "If you fail to appear, freed political prisoners will make sure that you do."

These enlistment orders had not been issued by the British military occupying authority nor by the mayor of Duisburg. The signatory was a "Reconstruction Action Committee," a front for a so-called "Anti-Fascist Committee," a coalition of anti-Nazis who wanted to take denazification and reconstruction into their own hands in a non-bureaucratic way. Unlike in many cities, where the Anti-Fascist Committees initially worked in collaboration with the city administrations, the mayor of Duisburg saw the punitive action by the citizens' committee as an illegitimate assumption of power. He tried to cancel the labour deployments with posters of his own, but was thwarted by the confusion of events: the self-appointed "Reconstruction Action Committee" actually managed to conscript a considerable number of former Nazi Party members for their repeated Sunday forced labour campaigns.

While such punishments imposed by citizens' committees on former Nazi Party members might not have been the rule, the example of Duisburg shows that Germans were quite capable of taking matters of justice and retribution into their own hands, and were not the stubborn and homogeneous mass of some later accounts. But more importantly, the process was typical of the administrative chaos of the first post-war months. As soon as they had conquered a region, the Allies automatically removed the existing mayors from office and quickly appointed new ones in order to maintain a minimum of order. Ideally, they tried to find the people who had occupied the post prior to 1933, or brought in former Social Democrats. Sometimes German citizens volunteered, for a great variety of reasons, some of them idealistic. Often these individuals only remained in the post for a few days before objections were raised by the recently constituted offices dealing with denazification.

In Frankfurt the journalist Wilhelm Hollbach held the job of mayor for a comparatively long time: 99 days. He had reached the top of the city administration by pure chance; immediately after Germany's capitulation he called on American headquarters in the city to request permission to found a newspaper. The sooner the better, he had thought. Hollbach was not granted that authorisation, but, fortunately for the city of Frankfurt, the military instead offered him the city's highest office. They had been racking their brains trying to think of somebody for the role when Hollbach had burst in. As soon as he was in office he carefully laid the basis for a rubble recycling corporation, which, though it started relatively late, was all the more efficient for it.

The writer Hans Fallada—famed for novels such as *Alone in Berlin* and *Little Man, What Now?*—who was fast-tracked into the mayoral office in the small lakeside town of Feldberg in the northern state of Mecklenburg, was not so lucky. Initially the Russians had wanted to lock him up or even shoot him because someone had discarded an SS uniform in his garden. But under questioning he, somehow, seemed like exactly the right person to get the village's businesses running. So, at just a moment's notice, the notorious drinker and morphine addict Fallada found himself responsible for resolving disputes between farmers, villagers and occupiers. In most cases this involved the confiscation of provisions and the organisation of work details. After four months he collapsed under the burden of these thankless tasks, was put in hospital in Neustrelitz and, particularly since his underlings had in the meantime looted his house, never went back to Feldberg.[3]

While the wartime mayors and other administrative heads were initially dismissed, mid- and low-ranking clerks and officials generally remained in their positions. This meant that the Allied military

administrations were able to rely on established administrative practices. Chaos and routine were kept in balance. While it remained
unclear how Germany would evolve, at least officials knew what pro-
cedures to follow.

The depth of the devastation felt by these officials contrasted
strangely with the efficiency of their administrative abilities. The
offices concerned with clear-up operations, with names like "Office
for Large-Scale Clearance," "Rubble Office," "Clearance Office" or
"Rebuilding Office,"[4] were no different to those in place before the
end of the war. They operated according to the principle: if there
were forced labourers only yesterday, there will be new ones again
today, we just need to requisition them. Somebody has to get rid of
this rubbish, after all. This time the rubble-clearers weren't Russian
prisoners of war or Jewish forced labourers, but rather German ex-
soldiers—which didn't matter much to the officials who were
concerned only with the end result. So they no longer enlisted their
workforce from the SS, as they had done previously, but from American or British military offices, who willingly handed over their
German prisoners of war.[5] How must those officials have felt? Were
they indifferent? Did they suffer pangs of conscience? There was no
reason for them to be guilt-stricken, because as difficult as life in the
Allied internment camps might have been, the German prisoners of
war there were not maltreated as the Russians and Jews had been
under the SS. Their deaths had certainly not been factored in, or
indeed turned into the whole point of the exercise, as had been the
case in the Nazi concentration camps.

As elsewhere, in the gigantic mountains of rubble in Berlin, clearance became a form of punishment. In the very first days after the
invasion, volunteers had been recruited with the promise of a plate
of soup after work. But soon the labour was made compulsory for
ex–Nazi Party members. These were easy to find, because Berlin's
Nazi district office had only interrupted its work for a few days during
the final battle for the city. The clerks and officials in Berlin were over-
seen by the "Ulbricht Group," a group of exiled members of the
Communist Party of Germany, led by future German Democratic

Republic (GDR) leader Walter Ulbricht, and other returning communist emigrants who had arrived with the Red Army to reorganise city life and reinforce confidence in the Russian administration. They were aided in tracking down Party members by a system of house and street representatives that was installed in the first days of the occupation. For example, the district offices organised "voluntary" work details. "Anyone who doesn't come and shovel will get no ration cards!" The house and street representatives were told to "ensure that everyone has an occupation, nobody can stand around and the work has to be done quickly so that the workers don't catch cold." In Berlin-Mitte there are said to have been 13,000 such people, in Friedrichshain 8,000 and in Weissensee 3,000.

Among the first draftees was the 18-year-old secretary Brigitte Eicke. A former member of the League of German Girls (the girls' wing of the Nazi youth movement), Brigitte had joined the Party just before the collapse of the regime, and for that reason she was made to join the "Nazi Special Operation." On 10 June 1945 she recorded in her diary:

We had to turn up at Esmarchstrasse at 6:30 in the morning. I'm always surprised that our leaders and the girls from our district who were also in the Party, like Helga Debeaux, are never here, and they seem to know how to duck out of things. The unfairness is appalling. We had to go to Weissensee station, but it was already far too crowded there, so they marched us back to the promenade. It's full of rubble and dirt to above our heads. We even found human bones in it. We shovelled there until midday, then lunch until two, then working again. And today the weather is so glorious, everyone is taking a walk and going past us. [. . .] We were supposed to go on working until 10 o'clock at night. It's a terribly long time, particularly when you're on display like that. We always kept our backs turned to the street so that we couldn't see the smirking faces. Sometimes you would have wanted to cry, if there weren't always some people there who managed to keep their sense of humour and managed to make others laugh.[6]

Of course it was clear to both the Berlin building authorities and the military administration that 55 million cubic metres of rubble couldn't be shifted with punishment operations alone, and construction companies were brought in to professionalise the rubble clearance. According to their political affiliation they were either conscripted or commissioned for hire. All four occupied zones employed building labourers who toiled away in the stony deserts in return for a small wage, but most importantly for the much sought after hard-labour food coupons.

The *Trümmerfrauen*—the "rubble women"—developed into a kind of post-war fairy tale. Contrary to what is generally believed today, they were not nearly as prevalent outside of Berlin, but in the capital city hard labour was predominantly women's work.[7] At the height of the clearance work in Berlin 26,000 women were working, and only 9,000 men. After hundreds of thousands of soldiers had fallen or been taken prisoner, the shortage of men was more noticeable in Berlin than elsewhere, even though before the war Berlin had been Germany's capital city for single women. They had fled from the constrictions of the provinces into the big city to breathe the smell of petrol and freedom, and to be able to live independently in new women's professions. Now working as a building labourer was the only way to get hold of something better than the minimum food coupon that barely kept a person from starvation with its seven daily grams of fat.

In the west of the country, by contrast, fewer women were employed in rubble clearance and typically only as punishment, as part of de-nazification or disciplinary measures against "degenerate girls and women with frequently changing sexual partners." That the rubble women would later be remembered in Germany as mythical heroines of reconstruction, despite their pasts, is due to the inspirational sight of them in the fields of ruins. If the devastation was already photogenic, the rubble women made it even more so. In the frequently published photographs we see the women standing in long rows on the mountains of rubble. Some of them wear aprons, some dresses with hefty working boots poking out beneath them. Often they wear headscarves, knotted at the front in tractor-driver style.

Trümmerfrauen *became mythical figures of the post-war era, not least because they were so photogenic. Here they are working in front of the Yenidze cigarette factory in Dresden.*

Standing like this they formed bucket chains, passing the rubble from hand to hand, clearing it from the ruins onto the street, where it was sorted and cleaned by children.

These images etched themselves into people's minds because the bucket brigades offered an excellent visual metaphor for the sense of solidarity that the broken-down German society urgently needed. What a contrast: here the crumbled ruins, there the cohesion of the bucket chain. Thus, the reconstruction was given a heroic aspect with which many Germans could gratefully identify, and which they felt they could be proud of in spite of the defeat.

Some rubble women stuck out their tongues defiantly at the photographers, or turned their noses up at the cameramen. The fact that some of them wore strikingly elegant dresses which, with their white collars and light floral fabrics, were completely unsuited to dirty work, was usually down to the fact that these were the only items of clothing they had. Anyone who had gone down to the air-raid shelter or been evacuated had always taken their best clothes with them. The women who had saved their finest dresses right to the end now found themselves clearing rubble in them.

In other cases, the displaced charm of the dresses had to do with the fact that the photographs were staged. In some newsreel scenes the women throw the rubble to one another as elegantly and accurately as if they were in a gym. It looks great, but it was also unbelievable and pointless. The shots amidst the Hamburg ruins, some of which were taken during the war on the orders of Goebbels, are completely fraudulent. In these, the supposed "rubble women" look so playfully at the camera as they throw their bricks that one would have to be completely credulous to think they were real. In fact they were actresses.[8]

The American photojournalist Margaret Bourke-White cast an unsentimental and pitiless eye on her fellow women as they toiled in the dust. In Berlin, in 1945, she wrote for a travel piece:

> These women, forming one of the many human conveyor belts which were organized to clean up the city, passed their pails of broken bricks from hand to hand with such studied slow motion that I felt they had calculated the minimum speed at which they could work and still draw their 72 pfennigs an hour.[9]

It was true that the first uncoordinated rubble clearance operations were not especially effective. Often the rubble clearers had simply thrown the rubble into the nearest underground train ventilation shaft, from which it later had to be removed again with great difficulty. In August 1945 the Berlin magistrate addressed the district offices and ordered them to disband the "unchecked bucket chains." "Primitive clearance operations" were to be brought to an end; from now on the work had to be performed professionally and under the supervision of the building department.

"Professional large-scale rubble clearance," as it was known in the building trade, required the establishment of an effective transport system by which the rubble could be conveyed from the inner cities out to the rubbish heaps. Agricultural light railways were used: small locomotives that pulled tiny carriages along temporary tracks. Seven such narrow-gauge lines were laid in Dresden; the T1, for example, led from the "city centre clearance area" to Ostragehege dump. Forty locomotives were employed, all bearing women's names. Because the tracks were makeshift installations, derailments were frequent, but by and large the operation ran smoothly, with main lines and branch lines, railway yards, extraction and dumping sites. A staff of 5,000 operated this strange railway, which ran through the scorched remains of Dresden as if through a ghostly dreamland. The last train ran in 1958, the official end of rubble clearance in Dresden. Even by then, however, by no means all areas of the city had been cleared. Even though, by as early as 1946, broad swathes of the city centre had been swept so clean that the author Erich Kästner described how he could walk for three quarters of an hour without passing a single house,[10] it was not until 1977, 35 years after the end of the war, that the last rubble clearance brigade in Dresden was able to lay down its tools.[11]

The piles of rubble altered the topography of the cities. Wartime moraines formed in Berlin, echoing the natural hills around the city. For 22 years up to 800 lorries a day unloaded so much rubble in the grounds of the former Factory of Armaments Technology that the resulting mountain, later quite appropriately called the Teufelsberg, or Devil's Mountain, grew to become West Berlin's highest elevation.

The way cities tackled the issue of rubble had an influence on their future economic development. That Frankfurt would not, as hoped, become the capital of the Federal Republic in 1949 but would instead become known as the capital of the economic miracle was due in part to the manner in which they addressed rubble clearance. The Frankfurters showed that there was money to be made from rubble— though this got off to a slow start; while other cities ordered their residents to start straight away, shovel in hand, Frankfurt's administration approached the matter scientifically. It analysed, brooded and experimented. Citizens began to grumble that their city was lying passively in chaos. Elsewhere, whole armies were doing the clearing, they argued, while in Frankfurt nothing was happening at all "to give the appearance of the city a friendlier character," as a petition from

the trade unions complained. But soon the wait proved advanta-
geous. Frankfurt's chemists discovered that by heating the rubble
they could produce plaster, which could be broken down into sul-
phur dioxide and calcium oxide. At the end of the process they were
left with sintered pumice, which was eminently saleable as an aggre-
gate for cement.

Together with the Philipp Holzmann construction company the
city founded the TVG, the *Trümmerverwertungsgesellschaft*, or Rubble
Recycling Corporation, which undertook the clearance of the city—
after some delay, but all the more effectively for it. With the construction of a large rubble reprocessing plant even the fine rubble which
had been piled up in mountains in other cities could be made usable
for reconstruction. By setting up what today we would call a public–
private partnership, Frankfurt managed to keep rebuilding costs
lower than in all other cities, and at the same time to make a handsome profit: the TVG was in the black from 1952.[12] The city's prosperity, clearly visible today in its skyline, sprang from the ruins of old
Frankfurt.

But it was only when the reconstruction process assumed the
appearance of furious activity that it fired the imagination of many
Germans and frequently drew comparisons with anthills. On Whit
Monday 1945 the mayor of the medieval city of Magdeburg, west of
Berlin, summoned the residents to take part in an unpaid clearance
operation—the opposite model to the Frankfurt action. He first
reminded them of the complete destruction of the city in the Thirty
Years' War, three centuries previously, before addressing the tasks at
hand:

> The people of Magdeburg must prove their civic spirit, which is also a
> community spirit, through their practical work. [. . .] No city in Ger-
> many that has been so touched by fate as Magdeburg would be in a
> position to free itself unpaid from the rubble that the war has left
> behind. The value that has already been gained through communal
> work, when the bricks have been removed from the heaps of rubble
> and sorted, can be simply calculated thus: 8,000 bricks are used for a

Part of the professional large-scale rubble clearance was the construction of a transport system. The rubble railway from Dresden ran along seven narrow-gauge lines with 40 small locomotives, all of which were given women's names.

normal apartment; if many thousands of industrious hands collected a million bricks one Sunday, there would be enough building material for 120 apartments. [. . .] The city administration calls and every citizen, every youth, every man should follow! Fateful hours in a moment of truth have come for the people of Magdeburg. They must not fail their city.[13]

They were to turn up at seven o'clock in the morning without previously having formed into groups, in rows of four, not staggered. Participation was obligatory, and each person was to free 100 stones from mortar so that they could be re-used. On the first appointed day 4,500 men showed up, and twice as many for the next few Sundays. Whether such operations remained joyless torment to be endured, or whether they were carried out with a certain verve, varied from city to city. The response to these labour appeals also varied. In Nuremberg just 610 men out of 50,000 answered the call.

The cleaned bricks were neatly stacked into rectangular columns, 200 at a time, on the edge of the rubble field. As a sign that they had been counted precisely one of the bricks at the top was placed upright. By the end, in Hamburg alone, 182 million bricks had been collected, cleaned, counted and stacked.

In the 1947 film *Und über uns der Himmel* (*And the Heavens Above Us*) Hans Albers, one of the most popular German actors of the twentieth century, strolls through the ruins of Berlin. Offscreen, he sings, "The wind blows from the North, it blows us hither and thither. What are we now? A pile of sand on the shore." The camera pans over a dusty desert of rubble. A small crowd is working away in the ruins. More and more people join them. Everywhere there is hammering, sorting, stones being tapped, the rubble train being loaded. "The storm sweeps the grain of sand that our life is like. It sweeps us off the ladder, we are as light as dust." With surging orchestral backing the choir joins in: "It must go on, we'll start over." "Oh," Hans Albers goes on, more shouting than singing, "Oh, let the wind blow!" Another pan over the field of rubble, and we see, in a quick sequence of edits, smiling people giving their shattered world a spring clean. The film ends with the Lord's Prayer: "And forgive us our debts, as we forgive our debtors. And lead us not into temptation, but deliver us from evil."

And the Heavens Above Us is one of the so-called *Trümmerfilme*, "rubble films," a style that became popular among filmmakers in Italy, Eastern Europe and Germany after the war. In its main section it presents realistic accounts of the Berlin setting, showing bitter poverty and the new wealth of the black-market profiteers. But its conclusion is an apotheosis of reconstruction—stirring, tear-jerking, creating a sense of community, a gigantic feat of labour, a mythical community of heroism, a superhuman task. All the heroic cinematic rhetoric deployed by the UFA film company in the 1930s, previously harnessed to the support of the Nazi regime, is revived here and used to a harmless purpose. "We had never been so ripe for redemption," Ruth Andreas-Friedrich had rejoiced in her diary.

Some, although not many, were uncomfortable with the bombastic style of the film. While the film was popular with audiences and broadly praised, the *Filmpost* critic was reminded of a kind of propaganda that he didn't want to see again:

> The improbable chorus of construction that lies heavily over the scene [a reference to the choral singing on the soundtrack]—a questionable reminiscence of the films of Veit Harlan [a leading anti-Semitic propaganda director under Goebbels]—vies in unbelievability with the inauthentic closing scene of the 1946 film *Irgendwo in Berlin* (*Somewhere in Berlin*), in which a group of young people perform Reich Labour Service exercises. No, we don't want to see that ever again![14]

Ruined beauty and rubble tourism

There was a simple reason for the popularity of the rubble films: the devastated cityscapes presented a staggering spectacle. It would be wrong to claim that it was only a shocking one. Some people couldn't get enough of the sight of the ruins. They experienced them as a reflection of their own internal state; for some, the ruined cityscapes gave physical expression to the way the world had been even before the war. They walked in the ruins, they brooded in the wreckage of the cities like Dürer's Melencolia over her various implements and pondered the hidden inner connections that could have led to this universal collapse.

The architect Otto Bartning, for example, saw the ruined landscape as "the image of a creeping disease suddenly exposed by war," and now clearly visible for the first time:

> . . . the ruins surround us, staring in silence, not as if they had collapsed in the roar of exploding shells, but as if they had fallen in on themselves for some internal cause. Can we, do we want to, rebuild the whole cruelly unmasked machinery of our mechanized existence, with all its stress and haste, thoughtlessness and demonic possession? No, the inner voice says.[15]

Many people had a sense that the ruins showed the true face of the world. They went out into the fields of rubble with cameras and took *Mahnbilder* (images of admonition); everything that lay in ruins fell under that heading. Of course they all wanted to depict the horror that they felt at the sight of what lay before them. But even such a horrific scenario as the crushed and fire-blackened Dresden did not diminish their ambition to extract even more from the disaster than it already presented. By chance, a skeleton used as a model for drawing and study was found in the shattered ruins of Dresden Art Academy, where it looked unusually apt. It was particularly unnerving because it was adjustable and could, for example, be set up to look as though it were walking bent over a stick, or with one leg stretched out, appearing to be running energetically as if it were being chased by the devil.

The photographer Edmund Kesting arranged the skeleton in such a way that it seemed to be dancing among the baroque ruins. His colleague Richard Peter spread its arms and legs dramatically until it looked as if Death were roaming through Dresden to collect corpses. Of course both photographers knew that the oppressive scenery did not really need such intensification. But the shocking sight of Dresden didn't stop the professionals from trying to outdo it with a bit of hocus-pocus.

Richard Peter's *Blick auf Dresden vom Rathausturm* (*View of Dresden from the Rathaus Tower*) became the German rubble picture par excellence. The photograph is often also called *Eine Skulptur klagt an* (*A Sculpture Accuses*). It shows the ruined city from a bird's-eye view. In the right-hand foreground a stone angel stands and points despairingly across the devastated city. It is a three-metre figure, shot from behind, standing at a dizzying height above the Rathaus Tower arcade. It took the photographer several attempts to frame the sculpture in the picture so that it overlooked the whole expanse of the ruined city. He found a four-metre ladder so that he could look down on the figure through a window in the tower. It was worth the effort:

> After 2 days I took a Rolleiflex and climbed the endless tower steps for the third time, and that way I got the photograph with the stone

figure's lamenting gesture—after a week of struggle and a lot of running about. The picture became iconic, it brought me in a lot of decent royalties, it was stolen countless times and also copied on a few occasions.[16]

The angel, as it is often described, isn't an angel, incidentally, but rather an allegorical representation of Goodness by August Schreitmüller. Of all things.

Peter's Western competitor, the Cologne photographer Hermann Claasen, wasn't shy about ratcheting up the impact of the rubble scenery with artificial interventions. In late May 1945 he photographed the first post-war Corpus Christi procession. It's an incredible picture: passing in front of the silhouette of the bombed-out city, whose ruins jut jaggedly into the sky, a karstic lunar landscape of pulverised concrete, is a procession of people wearing headscarves. They look like a ghostly cortège of penitents, a stream of lost souls drifting along against the setting of their now uninhabitable city. To heighten the effect still further, Claasen performed a simple trick. For his volume of photographs, *Gesang im Feuerofen* (*Singing in the Furnace*— its title is a reference to the Old Testament tale of Shadrach, Meshach and Abednego surviving the flames of Nebuchadnezzar's fiery furnace), first published in 1947, he extended the panorama by using the central part of the crowded image twice and splicing it together side by side. Cologne's disaster was, so to speak, doubled. You have to look very closely before you can see the doctoring.

The ruined cities were a great source of emotive visual symbolism. Fallen Christ figures lay, arms outstretched, in the rubble, sheep grazed among toppled columns, and potato stalks sprouted in front of the Brandenburg Gate. Soon photographic courses were on offer; amateurs clambered through the mountains of rubble and learned how to create striking images from these strange subjects—far more exciting than a photo-safari across the moors. The view through broken windows created an effect of depth, collapsing ceilings provided a hint of drama and twisted wire fencing made for rhythm and structure. Such images lingered in the mind for a long time. Sixty years later, Kassel

photographer Walter Thieme's career was commemorated in the
regional press with the headline RUBBLE PHOTOGRAPHER DIES.[17]

Children, romantic couples and, of course, fashion all looked good
set against rubble. While some people were still living in the ruins,
others were using them to display evening dresses for the first post-
war couture season. The fashion photographer Regina Relang showed
a wonderful white taffeta dress in the completely destroyed Café
Annast in Munich; the raffia sofa in the foreground was torn and the
model looked up at the ceiling as if it might fall in at any moment.
That uneasy look was the *pièce de résistance* of rubble-chic perfection.

With its comprehensive catalogue of images of *vanitas* (still lifes
featuring images of death), the ruined city revived an aesthetic familiar from the baroque rhetoric of many Catholic cities. In the preface
to Hermann Claasen's photography collection *Singing in the Furnace*,
the author Franz A. Hoyer wrote of ruined Cologne:

Prolonged horror: Hermann Claasen's Corpus Christi Procession, Cologne 1945. *If we look carefully we can see the trick; the central area of the photograph has been duplicated.*

And it sounds almost nonsensical to say that beauty previously unseen became visible in that destruction. The beauty of some architectural forms, for example. This seems to be the reason why some torsos reveal more form and formal opulence than anyone had noticed when viewing the whole sculpture. What, for example, does the Madonna of the Church of St. Kolumba effectively "gain" from her new state? Did the artist who made her hundreds of years ago not create her with a degree of perfection which—it might seem to us today—had a subtly dubious quality about it?[18]

Just imagine, in the middle of a landscape that shocked many hardened soldiers (as reports by members of the British and American armies from Cologne reveal), someone is philosophising about the

The ruins suit her. In 1946 the fashion photographer Regina Relang asked her model to stand in the ruins of the Annast Café in Munich.

fact that the perfectionism of gothic sculpture might have "a subtly dubious quality." It is the judgement of history itself, Hoyer argues, that has powerfully corrected and erased the sculpture, as if the perfect sculpture by an assiduous medieval stonemason now somehow deservedly lay in the dirt:

> So much presumptuous building and sculpting had overwhelmed the existing authentic, organic building and sculpture with an often pompous Babel-like grandiloquence, and only now is the authentic approach hidden beneath becoming visible once again![19]

Hoyer walked through the ruins of Cologne and was delighted that after the elimination of the embellishments the authentic had come to the fore. Was it a rampant hunger for meaning that led to this reading of catastrophe? Was it a chance to relativise German guilt and make the "Babel-like grandiloquence" the guilty party? Or was it just that the professional in him was still at work, the finely tuned responses of the art historian, untouched by the many dead, who could still be delighted by the way that the statue of the Madonna improved in the rubble?

In support of the latter we might quote a remark from the art historian Eberhard Hempel, who also reflected in the *Zeitschrift für Kunst* on the "beauty of ruins."[20] Many are struck by the depressing sense of something having been irreplaceably lost, Hempel admits, but "an eye that remains open to artistic impressions" will soon discern that the greater unity produced by the "emergence of the core structure" often gives buildings a beauty which they previously lacked because of the "variously decorated daubs and many inessential details." The effect is further intensified when the remaining walls succumb to the forces of nature.

This perception also expresses something else: the modern hatred of the ornamental was seen as a sign of a dissolute past that led with false promises and hollow phrases to the very catastrophe that they now faced. The dislike of any sort of decoration, which had been practised by the New Objectivity movement and had been further endorsed by fascism, lived on after the end of the war and led to a strange phenomenon known as *Entstuckung*, literally "the removal of stucco"; superfluous ornaments were hacked away so that buildings appeared stripped down and "somehow more true." Often safety aspects were invoked, because here and there stucco still fell from damaged houses, but the real reason was a revulsion against anything superfluous. Ornament—not cherished again until the present day—was enthusiastically hammered away from late nineteenth-century buildings, and presented the "purged" cube of the building as an aesthetic norm in accordance with the times. Many cities even paid *Entstuckung* bonuses.

Elisabeth Langgässer, a highly educated and politically alert author, wrote beautiful and lyrically delicate poems about the ruination of the cities. The devout Catholic daughter of a Jew who had converted to Catholicism returned to her home in Rhine-Hesse in 1947. There, in Mainz, she enthusiastically celebrated the city's famous carnival, *Fassenacht*, and began to appreciate the magic of the rubble-strewn city. She wrote an article about it, published in the Berlin *Tagesspiegel* on 16 March 1947 under the title "Cold Journey into *Fassenacht*," stating that it was not until she had tasted the '45 Domthal, "which still has a mild, fruity aftertaste, and only fully develops over the next five or six years," that she fully appreciated the magic of rubble-strewn Mainz.

Ravaged charm: no Capitol looks more ancient, no temple more graceful, no façade has greater power. But if other cities in the Reich, modern big cities [. . .] are nothing more than simply ravaged—mighty tooth-stumps their ruins, open mouths of old amphibians and broken spines—the dignity and the significance, the human scale and the intellectual freedom of a baroque Catholic city such as this one only fully returns in its downfall; it reveals its foundation and the core from which it grew; the organic and the lapidary; the seed-corn and the stone. How clearly the curved, empty gables stand out against the sky, how lightly rise the windowless walls, with nothing behind them! Here a delicate acanthus has been preserved, there a harmonious frieze, and when the river climbs over stones it seems to reveal a little spring, an obol from the depths of the grave, the smile of the *penates*. Nothing now seems to inhabit these ruins but dream and memory. A very deep and unscathed, petrified memory: flat brick-lined arches that line the path, passable or otherwise, like Roman aqueducts. What power! Laid bare like the power of colossi and at the same time toppled and vanquished like the old race of giants. What will it look like here once the moon pours out its enchanted rays, the lunar light of Hecate? When in the spring the burial field sprouts grass and weeds, the blue liverwort, the pimpernel and the flat rosette of the plantago, and a snail-shell sticks as if forgotten to a column, before once more following the curve of the volutes as it pursues its spiral trail; both sweeter and stronger than a drawing by one such as Rodin, when his stylus scurries across the page to capture a bas-relief.

The photographic group of the Krupp Cultural Association searching for subjects amidst the ruins.

   This text needs to be read several times if one is to savour all the facets of the intellectual flora that the field of rubble allows to flourish in the author's imagination. It is precisely constructed, but it is also hard to stomach the cultural-historical connoisseurship as she interweaves horror with the ramifications of mythology and toasts the fallen walls with another glass of '45 Domthal.

   If even the poet Langgässer could view the ruins of her hometown with such serenity, it can hardly come as a surprise that architects in the ravaged cities felt much cause for joy. They didn't linger long on shock and horror, but openly celebrated the greenfield opportunities for construction created by the bombs. Basel architect Hans Schmidt was excited about the "massive gaps in the organism of the city," and saw them as the vision for the future. Visiting Berlin he noted:

The pile of stones [. . .] has brought air and space. The individual buildings have an undreamt-of three-dimensionality. Should it not be possible, when a city is rebuilt, to maintain this size and spatiality, this depth and expanse of the sky that is opened up above it?[21]

Hans Scharoun, appointed head of Berlin's municipal planning and building control office for reconstruction in 1945, saw the destruction principally as a way of saving on demolition costs: "The mechanical loosening by bombing raids and the final battle now gives us the possibility of a generous, organic and functional renewal."[22]

The ruins were probably most productively effective in the work of the Berlin painter Werner Heldt. In the late 1920s Heldt had painted melancholy cityscapes. He started with the streets immediately around him and turned them into an imaginary urban space entirely free of advertising, ornament and, for the most part, of people. Returning from war and imprisonment, Heldt now experienced a Berlin that had come eerily closer to his pre-war visions. Even before the war, Heldt had imagined landlocked Berlin as a grey city by the sea, when he was overwhelmed by what he called his "Husum moods," after the small town of Husum on the North Sea coast of Germany. In the poem "My Home," written in 1932, he wrote:

And a hundred thousand pale houses stand brooding. With dead eyes they dream of the distant sea. And rigid grief lies on their far-off gables over which a pale sky arcs so heavily.[23]

In 1946 Heldt walked through the bombed city and found his fantasy brought to life: "Now Berlin really is a city by the sea!" Ocean-sized expanses of waste ground lay between the houses. Those streets that were still standing were like the seafront of a harbour town. Heldt, the son of a vicar, had lived with paralysing depression throughout his life, but the destruction of the city was not one of the causes that provoked despondency in him.[24] "Come to our Berlin, which has gained much from the ruins," he wrote to his friend Werner Gilles in Stuttgart.[25]

Werner Heldt, Ruins, 1947. "Now Berlin really is a city by the sea," the painter exulted, and wrote to his friend Werner Gilles in Stuttgart: "Come to our Berlin, which has gained a lot from the ruins."

The post-war years became Heldt's most productive time. He gave several works from around the same time the title "Berlin by the Sea." In them, the sand sloshed in waves through the rows of houses; in some works a fishing vessel even sails through the city, past a war memorial. Until his death in 1954 Heldt continued to paint an increasingly abstract image of the city in which the houses are reduced to their basic cuboid shapes and huddle together as if in still lifes. Sometimes the houses seem to rock on waves, sometimes they are crammed into a fan like playing cards. The bare walls are brightened by areas of colour, either dabbed or trowelled on, making them look like wood or textured marble. It is a strangely topsy-turvy Berlin that becomes a dream of itself in which, tellingly, no real ruins are ever shown, only great collections of gaps.

These urban still lifes may not, in their visionary other-worldliness, be exactly cheerful, but they convey the image of a devastated city in a tragic beauty that goes to the viewer's heart. Heldt became one of Berlin's most sought-after painters. In the Rosen Gallery, which had opened on the Kurfürstendamm on 9 August 1945, he was one of the most saleable artists. Here Werner Heldt delivered a talk on "Berlin by the Sea,"[26] in which he explained:

> Beneath the asphalt paving of Berlin there is always the sand of the Marches. And that was once the bottom of the sea. But human work is also part of nature. Houses appear on shores, they fade and rot. [. . .] Children like to play with water and with sand; they may still sense what such a city was made of.[27]

"Under the pavement, the beach"—that dreamlike political slogan from the May 1968 protests in Paris could equally appropriately be applied in 1946. In the bomb craters of Berlin Heldt saw the sand of the former seabed and the gravel of crushed rubble. Both reminded him of the dust that the city came from and to which it would one day return. But until then the houses danced on the sand, for now they rocked and remained upright.

III

The Great Migration

In the summer of 1945 about 75 million people lived in the four occupied zones of Germany. Some 40 million, far more than half of them, were not where they belonged or wanted to be. The war had acted as a powerful mobilisation, dispersal and abduction machine. Anyone who had survived had been spat out by it, somewhere far from what had once been their home.

This enormous number of 40 million displaced persons included the majority of the German soldiers who had become prisoners of war, who numbered over 10 million.[1] Most of them were released in stages between the middle of May 1945 and the end of 1946, apart from the 3.5 million prisoners of war who had been interned in the Soviet Union, and the 750,000 or so prisoners who had been taken to France. German prisoners of war were stuck in camps all over Europe and the USA, but several million had only been recently imprisoned as the British and the Americans advanced on German soil in 1945. Most of them had voluntarily surrendered.

In addition, there were 9 million city-dwellers who, for fear of air raids or because they had already been bombed out, had been evacuated to the countryside. Most of them yearned to return to the cities, particularly since the rural population generally hadn't given them an especially warm welcome. Given disruption to traffic networks, however, it was extremely difficult, and in many cases impossible, for them to return. Suitcases were among the most sought-after possessions. There was no point trying to buy them, since in the months of constant back-and-forth between apartment and air-raid cellar they had become scarce commodities.

There were also between 8 and 10 million prisoners who had been torn from their homelands and forced into the concentration and labour camps within Germany, from which they had now been liberated. Most of them had only the clothes on their backs. Their release did not assure the prisoners a homecoming, even if their homes still existed. Some had had the good fortune to be provided with food by Allied soldiers immediately after liberation and returned to their homeland shortly afterwards. Those who were less fortunate were left to wander through the defeated country whose inhabitants had recently enslaved them and in many cases murdered their families. But most people waited, weak and dispirited, in new camps or even old ones, to see what fate had in store for them. A further 12.5 million people drifted through Germany in groups of various sizes, exiles from the eastern territories that were now no longer German, mostly passing through regions that were unfamiliar to them and in which it was made very clear that they were not welcome. They had no choice but to find a place where they could stay.

On the day of Germany's capitulation, responsibility for all these people fell formally to the four Allied powers—a total of 40 million people uprooted in one way or another in the four occupied zones: refugees, abductees, deserters, the homeless and stranded—it was forced relocation on an unimaginable scale. That is not to say that everyone was actually in motion. Most people stayed right where they were, holding out in camps and only moving on painfully slowly or with significant delays. Some had to be returned home as quickly as possible, while others first had to be placed in custodial care. They all needed to be fed—a gigantic logistical effort at a time when even the barest necessities could not be sourced. The number of German prisoners of war needing to be interned temporarily was so great from April 1945 onwards that the Allies saw no other possibility but to fence in about a million of them in the so-called *Rheinwiesenlager* (Rhine meadow camps), forcing them to spend many weeks behind barbed wire and beneath the open sky. It was only over the course of

Behind barbed wire. During the advance of Allied troops millions of German soldiers became prisoners of war. The picture shows one of the "Rhine meadow camps" near Remagen in April 1945.

June 1945 that most of the 23 camps received latrines, kitchens with roofs and infirmaries. By September 1945 the last of these mass camps was dissolved after most of the inmates had been questioned and released or else distributed among smaller prisoner-of-war camps and former forced labour camps.

These soldiers, often crammed together in the hundreds of thousands, squatting on the ground and exposed to the elements, offered a shocking symbol of the sheer indistinguishable human mass to which the Nazi regime and the war had reduced society. Many living outside the fences didn't fare much better. Anyone who travelled during this time would have seen wandering people in the streets, on station platforms and in waiting rooms. The journalist Ursula von Kardorff saw the misery in Halle railway station in September 1945:

Terrible images. Rubble, amongst which wander creatures that seem no longer to be of this world. Homecomers in ragged, wadded uniforms, covered with boils, creeping along on makeshift crutches. Living corpses.[2]

Forty-five per cent of all dwellings were destroyed. In the cities millions of people were homeless and moved from one temporary habitation to the next. They slept in allotment plots, with relatives in cramped apartments, in bunkers or outside on any park benches that had not been broken up for firewood. Others simply lay down just off the road, often in basement doorways or under bridges, or found shelter in the rubble despite the threat of collapse from the ruined buildings. All of them were easy prey for criminals. The police statistics for crimes of theft leapt by 800 per cent; because people saw little point in reporting crimes the real numbers will likely have been much higher.

Many people in the big cities adapted to the black market. In Cologne, British soldiers happened upon a group of 60 people who had formed a criminal gang. They had accessed enough food for several months from the basement of a department store and stored it in the city's labyrinth of catacombs; they did a vigorous underground trade with the surplus. In Munich, a number of resourceful people had opened up the staff area in the basement of the ruined Regina Hotel to use as an emergency shelter. All around the former swimming pool there were changing cabins with white-covered loungers. Running water still came from the taps and even the showers worked. The group met up for breakfast in the former ironing room and devoured whatever had been scavenged on trips through the city the previous day.[3]

Others were stuck in less comfortable accommodation. Station waiting rooms were notorious collecting tanks. Sooner or later even the most affluent travellers were bound to share sleeping spaces on the floor with the people who lived there, because the few trains running were often delayed for days. Everyone was out in the streets all the time, not least in search of news. Without a working postal and telephone service, all communication had to be done on foot. In the anxious chaos of the post-war months, news was a vitally important commodity. If you wanted to find out who was alive and who was still missing, what goods could be got hold of and where, you had to go out and look. The situation was far from clear—the supply chains were broken—so it was of vital importance to leave messages about one's whereabouts, and let others know one was still alive. Anyone who moved house wrote their new address on the doors of the abandoned ruin: "Heinz Siebert is living in Wedding, at 98 Soldiner Str., with the Winzer family." People hungry for any kind of tips or information paid visit after visit, swapping tales and experiences. Getting hold of the barest necessities involved long journeys through every part of town.

Documentary footage from the summer of 1945 in Berlin shows everyone charging about in all directions: Russian and American soldiers, German police, gangs of youths, families dragging their belongings through streets on handcarts, scruffy homecomers, invalids on crutches, smart-suited men, cyclists in collar and tie, women with empty rucksacks, women with full rucksacks, and certainly many more women than men. Some stroll about, others hurry along single-mindedly, clearly seeking to make contact, urgently in need of food or a roof over their heads. For some, their normal everyday life seems to have been barely affected, while others wander distractedly through the streets, still searching for a place to stay. The social differences are vast: while scattered groups cook scraps of food on little flickering fires on pavements beneath the open sky, before squatting on the kerb to eat them, only five weeks after the end of the war others are sitting at cafe terraces on the Kurfürstendamm watching people strolling along the boulevard as they always have done. The first trams are running again, black limousines, military jeeps and horse-drawn carriages detour around the people. Certain street corners are packed, with people craving contact with others, as they stand around and jostle one another. Though some relish contact, others are repelled by the closeness required by the conspiratorial proximity of the black market. "At night in Wusterhausen, you can do some good de-lousin'," sang Bully Buhlan in his hit song "Kötzschenbroda Express," to the tune of Glenn Miller's "Chattanooga Choo Choo."[4]

The widespread notion that the German countryside was empty and silent after the end of the war is quite false. Of course there were areas that were deserted, idyllic settings where light and greenery flourished in early summer as they always had done, but uprooted people were also drifting through the areas that had been outwardly untouched by the war. In his novel *Off Limits*, published to great success in Germany in 1955 and almost entirely forgotten today, Hans Habe, a Jewish Hungarian-American journalist who served in the US Army during the war after becoming a citizen in 1941, describes, using the language of the time, meeting both the defeated and the liberated on country roads in 1945.

> Mixed up with them were convoys of trucks carrying deportees back to their homes: women and children, complete with bedding and booty. The trucks were driven by Negroes from Alabama and Georgia and Mississippi, driving back towards Warsaw. These columns were moving eastwards. And in the opposite direction, towards the west, travelled the liberated French prisoners-of-war, aboard second-class US Army trucks, waving tricolours.
>
> It was a world on wheels: military vehicles and gypsy caravans, tanks and circuses, victory and misery, everything motorized. And in between, like a narrow stream, trickled the other world, the world on foot, the German world. Men and women roaming the pitted highroads. Some were looking for a crust of bread, others for their children. Some cursed the conquerors, others did business with them. Whenever a convoy stopped the pedestrians stopped. Here and there a loaf of bread was handed out from a truck or a tank. [. . .] Women stood wedged between the tanks which issued blasts of hot air, as if they were burning inside, and the trucks that were loaded with prisoners-of-war. Should they give a smile to the conquerors or to the vanquished?[5]

Freed forced labourers and wandering prisoners—homeless forever

The trek consisted largely of two very different groups: the non-German "displaced persons" (*Verschleppte*) and the ethnic German "expellees" (*Vertriebene*) who were expelled or had fled from their homes in the eastern and central European annexed territories at the end of the war. "Displaced persons" (DPs) was the term used by the Western Allies for those foreign nationals dragged from their homes by the Nazi state, who were still in Germany after being freed from the camps, and whose fate was therefore in the hands of the occupying troops. *Displaced* might have been linguistically inelegant, but its German translation, *entheimatet*—de-homed, or expatriated—was apposite enough. The term worked, because it assigned the blame for their precarious situation not on the displaced people themselves, but on those who had displaced them. Among Germans, however, the word *heimatlos*—homeless—was more current, and was often followed by *Gesindel*, or rabble. Most Germans, however, simply called the DPs *Ausländer*—"foreigners."[6]

Over the course of the war Germany had transported about 7 million foreign nationals as forced labourers, including POWs, to the Reich territory, to replace the huge numbers of workers who had been sent to the front. These slave labourers had experienced an intensified form of hell during the last few weeks of the war, when they were ruthlessly maltreated more than ever before. The forced labourers still toiling in the factories were viewed with mounting concern by the Nazi regime. The more uncertain the situation grew the more fearful the German authorities became of an uprising among their slaves. The regime had always been more afraid of this than of the German resistance, but now that feeling turned into panic. When, towards the end of the war, it seemed as if the forced labourers were unlikely to be of any further use, German law enforcement officers simply killed them en masse.[7] Some of the massacres were perpetrated for fear of the prisoners' revenge, but some were the product of an "apocalyptic habit."[8] The security forces wanted to take as many "enemies" as possible with them into death, even if their victims were defenceless and unarmed. Those forced labourers who survived were left to wander the country like outlaws. They too, like the German civilians, had lived through the Allied bombs. Now they trekked through the woods or lay low in the cities. Occasional glimpses of their lives prompted a paranoid reaction among many Germans.

Given the way they had been treated, the fear that the forced labourers might revolt was not entirely unjustified. French and Polish forced labourers in particular had begun to organise themselves into a resistance force weeks before the end of the war, and secretly made improvised knives and machetes, which they had sometimes already put to use. And their violence was not only directed at the people who had been directly involved in their enslavement. The cruelties of life in the camp had in many cases brutalised the prisoners themselves. The mass murders of their companions had produced hatred and a thirst for revenge. In some cases groups of them attacked villages and isolated houses, murdering and looting.[9] Arrested by Allied soldiers, they were surprised to be held to account for their actions. When questioned, the perpetrators, mostly Russian, Polish or Hungarian, were honestly convinced that they had been acting within the law; they had assumed that the Germans were now fair game, just as they themselves had been under Nazi rule.[10] Many of them had been taken prisoner on the streets in so-called "capture operations" in Eastern European cities, and carted off. In many cases the occupying Germans hadn't even bothered to give a reason for the arrests, let alone inform the families of the deportees of their whereabouts.

One particularly brutal attack occurred near Bremen on 20 November 1945. A group of Polish DPs from the relatively well-appointed Tirpitz Camp invaded a house where a family of 13 people were staying that night, including children and young adults. After the residents had handed over their food and their few valuable objects, they were taken to the basement and shot.[11] Only the 43-year-old Wilhelm Hamelmann survived by playing dead. He later attracted considerable attention by publicly forgiving the perpetrators and pleading for them to be pardoned, despite the fact that they had killed his wife and children.

The Allies hadn't reckoned with the DPs becoming such a problem for what remained of public order. At first the Americans were completely overwhelmed by them, because all their resources were still directed at fighting and gaining ground. A staff officer in the US Army even thought the "hordes" of DPs were a new Nazi weapon

Start of a long journey. American soldiers bringing liberated forced labourers home from a collection camp. Up to 100,000 per day were "repatriated."

designed to sow confusion.[12] When the Americans took Frankfurt, they had deployed a team of just 21 soldiers to look after the 45,000 prisoners of war interned there. Again and again they came upon huge groups of helpless prisoners whose guards had fled. Near a factory that had manufactured aeroplane parts, for example, they were suddenly faced with 3,000 French forced labourers who didn't speak a word of English. No one knew where they were supposed to go, or who was going to feed them. The spreading confusion could not be dispelled. Some workers remained voluntarily in the hated barracks of the armaments factory, while others wandered off in different directions with no real destination in mind.[13]

Disoriented people collected in the streets in ever greater numbers, defending themselves against starvation through a mixture of cunning and brute force. One British observer reported on an overnight change from bondage to vagabondage:

You can see the vagabonds drifting alone along the roads, sometimes
in groups of up to a dozen, with all their possessions in a handcart;
some in rags, others in the shabby uniforms of a dozen armies.[14]

In the confusion before and after the capitulation it was some time
before the Allies managed to find anything like acceptable accommodation for the DPs, and when they did there was often friction and
outright conflict. The army's attitude towards the liberated forced
labourers went through various phases. Immediately after their liberation, the DPs received generous support as victims of the
vanquished enemy, wherever it could be provided. They were, on
Allied orders, to receive preferential treatment in shops, and this led
to disquiet and hatred on the part of the Germans, since provisions
were in extremely short supply and were strictly rationed. The DPs'
entitlement to adequate housing also caused much discontent. Such
a great mass of people could be accommodated only by the application of strict measures. Not only were factories and hospitals
requisitioned but entire terraced housing estates were comman-
deered without prior notice. The residents, generally factory workers,
had to leave their homes at a moment's notice, to make room for the
"foreigners." When the military administration ordered the DPs to
move out again a few months later, into newly erected camps, in
some cases the DPs rioted and wrecked the furniture and fittings.
Sometimes they even set the buildings on fire.

Years of slavery in the camps had induced severe behavioural problems among many DPs. Their trauma manifested itself in outbreaks
of violence, aggression and rebellion, even directed at people who
were trying to help them. Because of this destructive behaviour,
Allied soldiers often lost their respect and sympathy for the DPs. One
shocking case that occurred in liberated France clearly shows the
extent to which the prisoners had been brutalised. Early in 1945 3,500
Soviet DPs were placed in a camp in Châlons-sur-Marne. When the
camp was evacuated with the help of American troops, there were
repeated altercations in one of the trains deployed for the purpose.
Even before they set off, the Russian DPs had reduced their camp to

ruins and they continued their disputes throughout the journey. They caused frequent stops by pulling the train's emergency brake, during which they embarked on looting expeditions through the surrounding area and engaged in skirmishes with local French people. In the end the chief Soviet liaison officer, General Dragun, was informed of the situation at the Supreme Headquarters of Allied Expeditionary Force in Paris. He arrived on the spot, selected ten DPs at random and had them taken out and shot. He treated them as they had become used to being treated. The methods of dehumanisation pursued by the Nazi regime in the camps continued just as much in the behaviour of the exhausted victors.[15]

After the war there were between 8 and 10 million forced labourers to be returned to their homelands. These were unimaginable mass transports in which the lives of individuals were once again put at risk. There were long freight trains in which the liberated people travelled home cheering and singing, but also many in which they sat dispirited and depressed, in the certainty that the home they had once known no longer existed. The number of displaced persons was so high that their repatriation was calculated in daily rates. In the "best times," in May 1945, Allied forces managed to return 107,000 people per day.

What made this repatriation rate—as it was referred to at the time—all the more astonishing as an achievement was that it was executed in a devastated Europe with blown-up bridges, twisted train tracks and a bombed-out fleet of rolling stock. Westbound transport was also carried out by plane and truck, but railway wagons were usually deployed for those travelling eastwards, like the ones that had also gone to Auschwitz. The war had crippled the railway network. Often the trains stopped unexpectedly because the locomotives failed or the tracks had been destroyed. When that happened over a thousand inmates had to be fed without preparation in the open countryside. Journeys often took six days in trains with no heating or sanitation.

In September 1945 the number of repatriations dropped by 90 per cent, not least because by then many DPs objected to being sent back. The halting of the process was a cause of great concern to the military administration and the relevant refugee organisation, UNRRA (United Nations Relief and Rehabilitation Administration), since there were still over a million DPs in camps in Germany and the approach of winter would drastically complicate the situation.

Meanwhile, in the camps, the attitude of the Allied soldiers towards the DPs was becoming progressively more harsh and impatient. Increasingly they saw themselves less as caregivers and more as wardens. The fences grew higher and were often secured with barbed wire, while the gates were closed and guarded by sentries. Anyone who wanted to leave had to have a "good reason." The German POWs, dispirited, disciplined and dutiful to the point of submissiveness, had made life surprisingly easy for the occupying soldiers, while their displaced victims were, understandably, more agitated and rebellious. This led to bizarre alliances between Allied and German law enforcers; raids on the camps in search of weapons and stolen or black-market goods were often carried out by Allied soldiers and German police working together, which the DPs of course saw as an intolerable provocation. Stones flew, truncheons were swung, rage and bitterness rose on both sides.

The treatment of the DPs only improved after the publication of what became known as the Harrison Report. On the orders of the American president, Harry S. Truman, the former immigration commissioner Earl G. Harrison travelled to Germany in July 1945 to check in particular on the situation of Jewish survivors who had not been released on the day of their liberation. Most of them had to remain in the camps at first due to lack of alternative accommodation, though many of them were so mentally broken and physically debilitated by the end that they simply could not be transported. If they were lucky they were at least allowed to move into the houses of their former guards. On 24 August Harrison, along with other inspectors from international human rights organisations, prepared a report that shocked readers across the United States. This wasn't at all how they had imagined victory.

Many Jewish displaced persons and other possibly non-repatriables are living under guard behind barbed-wire fences, in camps of several descriptions (built by the Germans for slave-laborers and Jews), including some of the most notorious of the concentration camps, amidst crowded, frequently unsanitary and generally grim conditions, in complete idleness, with no opportunity, except surreptitiously, to communicate with the outside world, waiting, hoping for some word of encouragement and action in their behalf. [. . .] Many of the Jewish displaced persons, late in July, had no clothing other than their concentration camp garb—a rather hideous striped pajama effect—while others, to their chagrin, were obliged to wear German S.S. uniforms. It is questionable which clothing they hate the more. [. . .] In many camps, the 2,000 calories included 1,250 calories of a black, wet and extremely unappetizing bread. I received the distinct impression and considerable substantiating information that large numbers of the German population—again principally in the rural areas—have a more varied and palatable diet than is the case with the displaced persons.[16]

Harrison's report culminated in the revelation that his compatriots were not behaving much better than the Germans:

We appear to be treating the Jews as the Nazis treated them except that we do not exterminate them. They are in concentration camps in large numbers under our military guard instead of S.S. troops. One is led to wonder whether the German people, seeing this, are not supposing that we are following or at least condoning Nazi policy.[17]

The report led to a number of improvements; perhaps the most significant of these was that Jewish survivors were to be assigned their own camps and separated once again from non-Jewish Poles or Ukrainians. Harrison had for a long time hesitated to comply with that demand from the Jewish survivors. He was uneasy about separating the Jews again, but since many of them were subject to anti-Semitic attacks from their Eastern European compatriots in the ethnically mixed camps, he ordered the establishment of specifically

Jewish camps. Since "Jews as Jews (not as members of their national-ity groups) have been more severely victimized [by the Nazis] than the non-Jewish members of the same or other nationalities," they should now be privileged in the opposite manner.

The tense situation in the camps was exacerbated by the fact that from the summer of 1945, while the Allied military administration was currently doing its best to repatriate as many DPs as possible, new ones were arriving from the other direction: from Eastern Europe, and particularly Poland, more than 100,000 Jewish refugees flowed into Germany—a migration that nobody had expected. Of all places Munich, the birthplace of the Nazi movement, became the transit point for a mass-exodus of Jews from liberated Eastern Europe. They did not want to stay in Germany in the long term—their actual goal was America or Palestine. However, to them American-occupied Bavaria seemed to be a kind of American exclave in Europe, from which it would be easier to organise further travel to the promised land. And, at least while they waited, they felt considerably safer in American-controlled Germany than in Poland where, in the summer of 1945, two months after the end of the war, several pogroms had left the Jews extremely shaken.

As if they hadn't already suffered enough horrors, the few Polish Jews who had survived the Nazis had once again fallen victim to cruel persecution—this time at the hands of the Poles. Having evaded arrest by the Germans, a small number of Jews had hidden them-selves in forests in Poland, as well as in hiding-places in Russia and underground in Ukraine. Others had been liberated from the concen-tration camps by the advancing Red Army. They had returned to their Galician or Lithuanian places of origin, which in the meantime had become part of Poland/Soviet Union, only to discover they could no longer call those places home. Their families and friends had been murdered by the Germans, their towns destroyed. The returning Jews met with a hostile reception from many Poles, whipped up by bruised Polish national pride and anti-Semitism.

In Kielce, 180 kilometres south of Warsaw, terrible atrocities were carried out against the Jews a year after the end of the war. Of the original 25,000 Jewish inhabitants only 200 survivors had returned—less than 1 per cent. But even that was too many for some. In July 1946 anti-Semites forced a young boy to declare that he had been abducted and abused by Jews. A furious mob then killed 40 Jews and seriously injured another 80. For most Jewish survivors in Poland the Kielce pogrom was the final sign that they no longer had any prospect of a life there. A third of them fled to occupied Germany and struggled onwards—some on their own initiative, others with the help of agents from Jewish aid organisations—via various routes to Munich.

So while millions of Polish DPs returned to their homes, their Jewish compatriots were coming in the opposite direction and taking the places in the camps that they had just vacated. The exodus of the Polish Jews was actively supported by both the Polish government in exile in London, for the Jews' own protection, and the Jewish emigration organisation Bricha (meaning "escape" or "flight" in Hebrew). The intention of this movement was, by encouraging the greatest possible influx of Jewish DPs who wanted to emigrate to Palestine, to encourage the Americans to pressure the British to lift the ban on resettlement there.[18]

The escape of the Polish Jews to Germany is one of the most shattering migrations of this time of exile and deportation. Having to seek refuge in the land of the Nazis, of all places, required a great struggle on the part of many Jews; they could only justify it by considering occupied Bavaria to be no longer German but American. In spite of this, the Eastern Europeans survived remarkably well in the country of their defeated persecutors. They set up their central camp in the Munich district of Bogenhausen. Möhlstrasse saw the emergence not only of a black market but also a retail village of wooden booths, which reminded some observers of the vanished bazaar district around Nalewki Street in Warsaw.[19] Those booths—over a hundred in all—traded in chocolate, ladies' stockings, morphine and all kinds of preserves—almost all from Allied supplies. The residents of Munich were both delighted and annoyed; they haggled as best they could, and exploited every advantage, and yet, as with every other black market, they still felt outsmarted.

There were also Greek, Hungarian and Czech black-marketeers on Möhlstrasse, but for the Germans it was always about the Jews from Poland. They were held responsible for everything even slightly inconvenient. The men with their kaftans and sidelocks, previously known to the people of Munich only from Nazi caricatures, did not find a particularly warm welcome. One eyewitness remembered, "The Jews from the old days were really, how can I put it, very intelligent, polite and unusually friendly and elegant people. And of course the ones who turned up after the war included all sorts."[20] The Jews "from the old days," then, were the "good" Jews, the people one would have liked to see again, while the new Jews were the "bad" ones that one was reluctant to put up with. "These were not people who had been persecuted," one Munich citizen wrote to his newspaper. In fact they were "the sputum, the yeast and the scum of elements who were never deported but, to avoid regular work, came here from the eastern states, in many cases completely illegally, and are now spreading themselves raggedly about the place."[21]

But this time the Jewish refugees and DPs were able to defend themselves. After the publication of another reader's racist letter in the *Süddeutsche Zeitung* in August 1949 several hundred of them marched on the paper's offices. The letter did not in fact reflect the attitude of the newspaper, but such details no longer mattered now. When the police attempted to disperse the demonstrators there was a bitter street battle in which 20 officers were injured by blows from sticks and stones, and three DPs had to go to hospital with bullet wounds.

Many surviving German Jews, however, also felt uneasy about the behaviour of their Eastern European brethren. The author Wolfgang Hildesheimer wrote to his parents about the riot: "There can be no doubt that there is still a great deal of anti-Semitism here, but unfortunately it is also stirred up repeatedly by the activities of the DPs. There is nothing to be done about it."[22] The Jews of Munich viewed the Eastern Europeans with mounting suspicion—and vice versa.

Of Munich's 11,000-strong Jewish community before 1933, fewer than 400 had survived. Most of these were baptised Jews, or Jews in so-called mixed marriages, some of whom had been spared deportation. There were also 160 Munich Jews who had returned from

Theresienstadt concentration camp. Most members of this small community were Jews "who had tended to live on the fringes of the Jewish religion even before 1933,"[23] and who felt they belonged to a modern, secularised world; the Jewish DPs from Eastern Europe, with their traditional shtetl manners, were almost as alien to them as they were to non-Jewish Munich residents. The Munich Jews were afraid of being pushed to the margins by the Jews from the East. As well as being strong in numbers, they brought with them a religious fervour. The Eastern European Jews were not only more devout, but also had a powerful determination to emigrate to the Promised Land, which in the eyes of many in the international Jewish community made them better Jews.

The Orthodox Jews from the East in turn distrusted the Munich Jews for their worldly leanings and their "Germanness," which rendered them indistinguishable from Bavarians. They did not recognise them as "real Jews." They accused them of betraying Judaism by wanting to stay in the land of their murderers. In the eyes of the Munich Jews this dispute became particularly menacing because it also affected their claims for restitution. In the view of the Eastern European Jews—which coincided with that of international Jewish organisations—the so-called heirless property, the property stolen by the Nazis that had once belonged to the largely eradicated Jewish communities, could be claimed by Jewish people all over the world, and not just by the survivors in Germany.[24]

Of special significance were the millions of historical books that the Nazis had stolen from Jewish communities and transferred to German libraries and museums. Various Jewish organisations were set up, mostly with American support, to identify what remained of destroyed Jewish culture, and to claim it back from the German state and manage it. The philosopher Hannah Arendt, for example, as director of the Jewish Cultural Reconstruction organisation, travelled to Germany on one such mission and found herself embroiled in considerable quarrels with the two Jewish communities that had only just survived genocide. The disputes touched upon issues of Jewish identity and integrity that had a dramatic depth for both sides. Many of the Jews of Munich wanted to see the Eastern European Orthodox Jews travelling on to Palestine as soon as possible, even though in some respects they also benefited from their presence as black market traders and even as spiritual mentors in some rare cases.

In many ways it would have been a relief to the American authorities to get rid of the Jewish DPs from Poland who had been placed under their protection as soon as possible. Feeding and lodging them was a considerable expense. But the British blocked their emigration to Mandatory Palestine in the Middle East (the territories of Palestine and Transjordan, where the British administration had been given the responsibility for creating a Jewish national homeland), lest they increase the ethnic tensions there between the Jewish and Palestinian Arab communities. The prevailing policy of rapid homeward repatriation could not be pursued for the Eastern European Jews, because from a realistic political point of view, no home now existed for them.

At the Tehran Conference in 1943 and the subsequent conferences in Yalta and Potsdam in 1945, the Western Allies and the Soviet Union had decided that the state of Poland should be reconstituted but its borders changed. Eastern Poland would become part of the Soviet Union; in the west, on the other hand, Poland was granted the German territories east of the Oder-Neisse line. The German population had to leave the territory that now belonged to Poland, while the Poles had to leave the majority Russian-speaking east—a forced resettlement on an enormous scale, which affected both Germans and Poles. This division meant that the part of Poland from which most of the Jews came was now Russian. If they were deported to their place of origin they would remain displaced, because eastern Poland no longer existed. They were consequently homeless forever. And the more the tensions grew between the Western Allies and the Soviet Union as the Cold War developed, the less inclined the Americans were to deport the Jewish DPs eastward. For now, then, they were stuck where they were. In camps set up by the UN in Germany they waited to be relocated to a place where no one would be trying to kill them.

Screened off by high fences or walls, and often quite remote, enclaves of eastern Jewish life cropped up across Germany. The best known of these was Föhrenwald camp, an estate of terraced houses belonging to the German chemical and pharmaceutical conglomerate IG Farben at Wolfratshausen, near Munich, where 3,200 workers from munitions factories, half of them Germans and half foreign workers, had lived during the war. Populated after the end of the war with DPs of various origins, the camp was cleared of other ethnic groups in September 1945 and declared an exclusively Jewish DP camp. Föhrenwald had fifteen streets, with such names as Kentucky Street, New York Street and Missouri Street. The buildings had been constructed as a model estate by the Nazi regime in a style that was unadorned and monotonous but had central heating and adequate sanitation. Behind a two-metre fence, "a regular Eastern Jewish shtetl life came into being, with its own administration, political parties, police, camp law-court, religious institutions such as synagogues, a mikvah and a kosher kitchen, a health service, professional training facilities, schools, kindergartens, theatre groups, orchestras, sporting associations and much else besides."[25]

Local Yiddish-language newspapers were published in Föhrenwald and some other camps. The Föhrenwald paper was called *Bamidbar, Wochncajtung fun di befrajte Jidn* (Bamidbar, weekly newspaper of the liberated Jews). It came out every Wednesday, under the editorship of Menachem Sztajer. "Bamidbar" means "In the Desert" and referred to the Biblical story of Moses and the Israelites wandering in the desert after the exodus from Egypt. But "Bamidbar" also represented the German desert of Bavaria, and the wait before moving to Israel, the Promised Land. Each edition bore the motto: "In the desert. In the wilderness. We are waiting. In the desert. In the wilderness. Travelling through. We will not turn back. There is only one goal: Eretz Israel."[26]

The best known newspaper of the Yiddish-language post-war press was the *Landsberger Lager-Cajtung*, which was read far beyond Landsberg, a town in south-east Bavaria, and sometimes reached a circulation of 15,000. Since in the first years after liberation it was impossible to find typewriters with Hebrew script in Germany, almost all Jewish camp newspapers originally appeared using the Roman alphabet—a rarity in the Jewish press. The newspaper *Ibergang* bore the English-language header JEWISH NEWSPAPER, and below it the notice "Organ fun der Federacje fun Jidn fun Pojln in der amerik.

The Landsberger Lager-Cajtung *was published in Yiddish, but in Latin script, because there were no typewriters with Hebrew script left in Germany.*

Zone" (Newspaper of the Federation of Jews from Poland in the American Zone).

The first Jewish theatre after the war, directed by Jacob Biber, was also produced in Föhrenwald. There were lively evenings made up of short comedy sketches, but also full-length plays that helped the community process the suffering they had endured in the concentration camps. Others imagined a radiant future in Palestine. The twenty-strong theatre company also staged the dramatic adaptation of Sholem Aleichem's *Tevye the Dairyman*, the tragicomic story of the village of Boyberik (based on the Ukrainian village of Boyarka). *Tevye the Dairyman* had first appeared on the map of world literature as a sequence of stories published up until 1916, and was adapted in the 1960s for the stage musical *Fiddler on the Roof*, in which the village was renamed Anatevka.

But most importantly, in the camp people were making love. Föhrenwald soon caused amazement by having the highest birth rate of all Jewish communities in the world. The camp also served as a central assembly point for Jewish orphans who had been brought to Germany by former partisans or adopted by sympathetic refugees. Föhrenwald was filled with the sound of children. By as early as November 1945, 27 teachers were giving classes at number 3 Michigan Strasse. The primary school with its academic curriculum was soon joined by a vocational school where pupils could be trained to become plumbers, tailors, carpenters, electricians, hairdressers or watchmakers.[27]

Turnover in Föhrenwald was very high. While many of the residents managed to emigrate to America or Palestine (or later to the state of Israel, founded in 1948), more and more newcomers were constantly arriving in the camp because others were being closed. In the end Föhrenwald was the last place left for Jewish DPs to live. When the camp was placed under German administration in 1951 there were still 2,751 DPs living between Ohio and New Jersey Streets. Henceforth it was called a "government camp for homeless foreigners," a term which the federal government greatly promoted because it obfuscated who was originally responsible for the homelessness in the first place.

When the last residents left the camp in 1957 they included both the long-term residents and people who had returned from Israel and other countries and who hadn't managed to find their feet in their new homeland. Not every emigration story was a successful one. Some of those who had failed to settle in new lands returned to Germany and the camp. These unfortunates were treated with a degree of contempt. As a "Special Report from Germany" had it:

One of the most embarrassing experiences for the Jewish visitor to Germany is that of Jews returning from Israel. [. . .] Just as they did in the time after the collapse of the Third Reich, they are sitting back in a camp and being maintained by Jewish welfare organisations. It doesn't take a great deal of imagination to guess that all kinds of dubious characters who were constantly falling foul of the law had arranged to meet up in Föhrenwald.[28]

The Upper Bavarian Föhrenwald Camp for Jewish Displaced Persons. The 15 streets had names like Kentucky, Wisconsin, New York and Missouri. The last inhabitants left the camp in 1957.

One of these "dubious characters" was called Yossel. He had emigrated to Palestine in 1946 but returned to Föhrenwald in 1952. He explained his actions to an American army rabbi as follows:

You'll think that I am crazy. But from the time I was 21 until now, the past fourteen years I have spent my life in camps. I was sent from one concentration camp to another. Then, after liberation, I lived in a Displaced Person's Camp. When I finally arrived in Israel, I was sent to a British detention camp. After a year there, I volunteered for the Israeli Army. Oh, I did quite well. I fought in the Negev and in the mountains of Galilee. Then, in 1951, I was permitted to take off my uniform and to try to become what I always wanted to be, a normal human being. By then, I was 33 years old. Too old to learn anything and too young to retire. I had jobs and could not keep them. I got a room of my own, but I felt lonely in it.[29]

The barracks and Föhrenwald camp were the only places where Yossel had ever felt at home. Even though he had been released from the camp, it had shaped him. He considered himself a camp lifer, and that had made him unfit for a life in freedom, had made him yearn for Föhrenwald, for a sheltered life dependent on the mercy of foreign administrators.

"Hardcore DPs" was the term given by the military administration to those who were unwilling to return home—about 150,000 of them, from all nations—and were still living in camps after 1951, in spite of countless repatriation and access programmes. Among these, however, the Jewish DPs were the least of their worries. Most Jews had wanted to leave Germany as soon as possible. They had, as much as they could, assumed responsibility for their own emigration; possessing a strong cultural identity, they could expect solidarity with Jewish communities around the world and a potentially bright future in Israel.

Many Poles were significantly more reluctant to return home. Although most Polish DPs had been repatriated in the first year after the war, by the end of 1946 300,000 or so still remained, persistently refusing to leave the camps.[30] Their chief reason was fear of the communist regime in their homeland, since rumours had circulated of deportations to the Soviet Union. The Polish government sent recruiters to the camps to arouse patriotic feelings, along with returnees who gave glowing accounts of their return to Poland. The aid organisation UNRRA promised to finance food supplies for the first 60 days in Poland for those who returned. Banners were hung in the camps exhorting people to return home. Each time a transport set off for Poland it was celebrated as a kind of gala event with music, flags and speeches.

But all the pressure and enticements came to nothing. The hardcore remainers clung to life in the camps, partly out of fear of communism, partly out of apathy. Where lethargy was involved, the originally caring strategy of the British and the Americans had unintended consequences; theirs had been a policy of sheltering the DPs from the German civilians lest they be exposed to racism, which could, in their view, have come to a head at any time given the potential for conflict over housing, work and food supplies. Over the years this "protective welfare care" turned into isolation and disenfranchisement, and the camp had become a substitute home for its inmates, from which they could not be removed without force.[31]

Yet many of the Russian prisoners of war and forced labourers did have a good reason to fear a return to their homeland, because the Soviets initially placed their imprisoned compatriots under a collective suspicion of collaboration. Many were accused of cowardice before the enemy and desertion. As such, they were treated harshly, interrogated and often deported to labour camps. In fact, there had been cases of Russian deserters; Cossack troops and the Vlasov Army, some of whom had been recruited from Russian POWs from 1944 onwards, had fought side by side with the Germans. But their example did not justify the general suspicion under which the millions of Russian DPs found themselves.

The Yalta agreement obligated the Western Allies to return Russian prisoners of war and forced labourers without exception. Anyone who refused would be sent home by force. Since the Soviet Union had paid for its victory with unimaginable levels of human sacrifice—between 16 and 20 Red Army soldiers for every fallen Western Allied soldier—it was obvious why the Russians should want to have all of their 8 million DPs back. However, many of them so violently resisted being returned that the British or American soldiers had to force them into the trucks with truncheons and rifle butts. Some Allied soldiers refused to execute these orders.

While many Russian prisoners of war cheered on their journey back to Russia, delighted to be going home at last, there were also those who were less enthusiastic, not all of them necessarily collaborators. In Dachau in January 1946 GIs used tear gas to clear two barracks of Russian DPs. When they stormed in they witnessed a gruesome scene of mass suicide. One American services newspaper wrote, quoting soldiers who were at the scene:

The GIs quickly cut down most of those who had hanged themselves from the rafters. Those still conscious were screaming in Russian, pointing first at the guns of the guards, then at themselves, begging us to shoot.[32]

The expellees and the Germans' shocking encounter with themselves

In June 1945 Ruth Andreas-Friedrich and a friend cycled into the countryside east of Berlin. After a few hours they saw a sign pointing towards the autobahn:

We climb over an embankment and stop as if frozen. Merciful heaven. Have we wandered into a migration of the people? An endless procession of misery is rolling away in front of us from East to West. Women and men, old and young, hurled together at random, as fate drove them together. Some from Posen [Poznan], others from East Prussia. These from Silesia, those from Pomerania. They're carrying their belongings on their backs. To anywhere, wherever their feet carry them. A child totters by. A pitiful little boy. "It huuuurts," he sobs to himself. He balances miserably on his bare heels and stretches his bleeding soles at a sharp angle into the air. "Bread dough, fresh from the oven," a woman behind him chants. She has said it a thousand times before, on her way through this foreign land. She says it again and again. In the same tone, with the same despair. "Bread dough, fresh from the oven . . ." Two cooking-pots rock on her back. They ring out the rhythm of her feet like bells. [. . .] That's someone dying, I think, and look in horror at the rickety handcart that a man is dragging behind him. It's a child's handcart, short, low and narrow. Into it they have stuffed two cushions, a bundle of straw and a quilt. Lying on the quilt is an old woman. White-haired, in her village Sunday best. Hands folded over her chest, she gazes solemnly up into the sky. Blue shadows darken around her nose. The cart jolts. Her head swings back and forth. Another ten or twelve breaths and her husband will be pulling a corpse.[33]

Shocked, the observer wonders: "What's going to come of this? Where are they being sent to, these ten million?" Her companion shrugs: "Where to? Anywhere! To the kingdom of heaven, if possible. Unless somebody can find a master-builder to add another storey to Germany."[34]

In fact, five years after the war, West Germany had almost 10 per cent more inhabitants than it had before the fighting broke out, yet a quarter of the country's housing had been destroyed. Twelve million expellees had set off for the west, most of them women, children and old people who had been mercilessly forced to leave their homes. This was a cruel retribution for the much more vicious extermination campaign that German troops had waged on Hitler's orders against the civilian population in the east.

By the end, 16.5 per cent of the population of West Germany would emigrate from the lost eastern territories; in East Germany it was as many as a quarter of the population. These newcomers were as diverse as any other group of Germans, counting among them Nazis and anti-Nazis, former dignitaries and opportunists, the once well-to-do and the lifelong poor. If a single fate could be taken as emblematic of that vast army of migrants, then it might be that of 16-year-old Ursula Wullenkordt, from Markthausen in East Prussia.[35]

Her mother ran a cattle farm on her own and her father was somewhere at the front in January 1945 when they received the order from the mayor to flee. They left the farm with its cows and pigs behind and, with their horse-drawn wagon, which they had laden with the barest necessities, they joined a chaotic trek of refugees while the noise of fighting from the approaching front could still be heard. After witnessing hideous instances of murder at the hands of marauding soldiers, mother and daughter were separated by a bombing raid in Pillau. Four months after setting off from her home village, Ursula reached the Hel Peninsula near Danzig, and on 8 May she took a boat with other refugees to the Danish island of Bornholm. From there a group of disarmed German soldiers brought her on a fishing vessel to Eckernförde, in northern Germany, where the British military commanders found her accommodation in the village of Güby. For now, the 16-year-old was safe, but still not in the clear. The widow Harms, with whom she stayed, lodged refugees in the haybarn under dirty straw, even though half of her house stood empty. Other villagers who were hosting refugees assigned them rooms, but not before they put the furniture in the attic and unscrewed the lightbulbs from the lamps, in case the "Polacks" used up the electricity. When the occupying British soldiers noticed that their orders to accommodate the refugees in a humane fashion were coming to nothing, they lined up the villagers in the church square and threatened them with the confiscation of their houses. After this, Ursula and eight other refugees were put in a room at the village blacksmith's house. The family missed no opportunity to let her know they wished her in hell. "Not nearly enough refugee boats went down," they hissed to the young girl. Fortunately, the close-knit information network maintained by the deportees over long distances paid off and Ursula's scattered family managed to come together again. In July 1945 Ursula's father arrived on crutches, and her mother was traced to an internment camp in Denmark in the autumn of 1946.

Since the Wullenkordts were skilled farmers, they managed to take on a run-down farm, which they leased in 1955, and got it up and running again. But now the cost of the rent soared to unattainable heights and they were forced to leave. The family took the nearest bankrupt farm under its wing and, once again, slowly revived it, until the rent rose here as well. Repeating this formula they revived one derelict farm after another, moving from "Hardissen to Roth, then to Ransbach-Baumbach, after that to the Rhine island of Königsklinger Aue, to Birkenfeld on the border with Saarland, to Neunkirchen near St. Wendel and finally to Reidenhausen in the Palatinate"—an odyssey of renovation that took them through the whole of West Germany and enriched many people, if not necessarily themselves.[36] In 1967 Ursula married a man who also came from East Prussia, and who was willing to share in this itinerant lifestyle. The final stage of her long journey came after reunification in 1992 and her husband's retirement, when the family returned to their old home. Today, the Wullenkordts' farm no longer exists, but nearby, in present-day Slavsk in the Kaliningrad Oblast in Russia, which was known as Heinrichs-walde until 1946, the family rents the land of an arable farm which it soon successfully expanded.

The post-war story of Ursula Wullenkordt, or Ursula Trautmann, as she became after her marriage, is typical of the fates of many deportees, not only in its successes but also in its endless struggles. Her ultimately unsuccessful attempts to put down long-term roots in new regions is similar to those of other expellees, although very few made their way so resolutely back to their old home.

The smug impression that the Federal Republic of Germany gave of itself in the 1960s, when it talked proudly about its "integration miracle," has been corrected by research carried out over the last few years. The attitude of many Germans towards their expelled compa-triots was no less hard-hearted than their behaviour towards the foreign DPs. The deportees were frequently reviled as a "gypsy pack" by many Germans, blond and blue-eyed though they might have been. They had adopted many of the tastes of their Hungarian or Romanian neighbours, such as a liking for paprika and garlic, and this was not well received by the West Germans. Some well-intentioned residents countered this hostility by evoking shared national roots—for example, Theo Breider from Münster, who, as director of the local tourist office, had been given the task of looking after the refu-gees. He tried to do so with, among other things, a poem in the regional dialect, which was intended to bring the locals closer to accepting the idea of national solidarity: *"Laot rin! Et ßind Menscken van uessem Blaut . . ."*

> Let them in! They are folk of our blood
> who have lost their homes and everything,
> they are German people, they are our children,
> their husbands were our soldiers.
> Open up your homes, open up your doors![37]

It was in vain. The *Zuzügler* (incomers or immigrants), as the author-ities called them at the time, encountered a wall of rejection.[38] They were given permission to stay in crowded cities for no longer than two days because of the immigration bans that had been imposed. Many communities excluded them entirely. In Bremen, where 50 per cent of housing had been destroyed and 50,000 people had been left homeless in a single night of bombing, there were posters that read: WE CAN'T TAKE ANY MORE PEOPLE! A STOP TO IMMIGRATION!

The Allies set up immigration commissions that sent most of the 12 million deportees to the countryside. Entire village communities that had stayed more or less intact throughout the long trek and wanted to remain together in their new country were deliberately separated by the commissions, in order to encourage integration. Because of tensions between locals and incomers the Allies anticipated violence and uprisings. Some locals, whether in Bavaria or Schleswig-Holstein, resisted the billeting so vehemently that the deportees had to be accompanied to their assigned accommodation by guards carrying machine guns.

The local farmers steeled themselves against the newcomers' distress with an obstinacy which far outstripped even that of their oxen. In 1946 the writer Walter Kolbenhoff reported from a village in Upper Bavaria:

> These farmers have never been stuck in air-raid shelters when the bombs rained down and the lives of their loved ones were extinguished. They have never trekked, shivering and hungry, along foreign country roads. While the others greeted as a gift each new day that life granted them, they sat in their farms making money. But that fate has not made them humble. It is as if none of it had happened and it had nothing to do with them.[39]

According to Kolbenhoff's account, one house owner even murdered a refugee and his three children because he didn't want to have foreigners living under his roof. Afterward he claimed they had moved on.

The "integration miracle" had to be performed with the help of the police. Local council staff, protected by German and Allied military police, passed through the villages and small towns, systematically seeking out "parlours" that were used only on special occasions, or empty maids' rooms. Undignified scenes played out when the farmers themselves were allowed to determine who they were prepared to take in from the incoming group of refugees. It was like a slave market. They chose the strongest among the men and the most beautiful among the women and scornfully rejected the weak. Some farmers saw the deportees as fair replacement for their lost forced labourers and reacted furiously to the suggestion that a decent wage should henceforth be paid to the "Polacks."

Even the terrible condition in which the refugees arrived was used against them. In 1946, when the repatriation transports (organised with a great deal of harassment and bullying by the Poles and the Czechs) arrived, and the deportees climbed out in a pitiful state, the locals talked about "40-kilo gypsies." The resistance to the expellees reached astonishingly absurd heights; one particularly duplicitous argument against accepting them lay in the claim that the expellees were more attached to the Nazis than the West German population, and therefore constituted a serious danger to the young democracy. As Prussians, the deportees were accused of being born militarists and yes-men, and allegedly particularly responsible for *Hitlerei* (Hitlerism). The farm-owner Hans Oheim from North Germany wrote disdainfully in 1947:

> You need not imagine that the spirit of Prussia has died. No, it lives on in all the people who have come to us from the East, and under whose alien rule we must now go on living after the state parliament elections.[40]

Unusually for farming communities, the SPD (Social Democratic Party of Germany) had won those elections—thanks to refugee votes, as the farmer correctly assumed.

The Danish minority in southern Schleswig raged particularly noisily against the new arrivals—for one simple reason. The presence of the expellees ensured that the proportion of Danes within the overall population became even smaller. The Danish journalist Tage Mortensen called them "Hitler's guests," and invented a character to exemplify what was flowing into the beautiful north, one "Frau Schiddrigkeit" from East Prussia:

> Frau Schiddrigkeit's hair changes between black and dark brown, her eyes are greenish, her cheekbones wide and her fingers strong and thick like those of the Polish girls who used to work on the turnip harvest on the southern islands of Denmark. [. . .] The Southern Schleswigs call the East Prussian mass of refugees a mulatto race. "Mongrels," mixed stock. Margaretha Schiddrigkeit is, judging by her appearance, a typical "mongrel," the descendant of many races and many nations.[41]

Racism lived on and was now turned cheerfully inwards. There was much talk at this time of "German tribes," and fears that their intermingling threatened the innate regional characteristics of local ethnic groups, whether they be Upper Bavarian, Frankish, Palatinate, Thuringian, Mecklenburger or Schleswigs. After the collapse of the country, the idea of a *Volksgemeinschaft*, of the homogeneity and superiority of one ethnic German community, had lost its sheen, but the arrogance had not declined in the slightest. The *Volk*, a term that had been heavily used in Nazi political propaganda to describe the entirety of the German people, was disavowed, and it was now the regions that suddenly revived their unique identities. Many people saw the internal German migration as a kind of multicultural attack on themselves. Tribalism blossomed and people distinguished themselves with customs, practices, faith rituals and dialects that set them apart from their neighbours, let alone from German Bohemians, Banat Swabians, Silesians, Pomeranians and Bessarabian Germans—all of whom were dismissed as "Polacks."[42]

The locals viewed even tiny differences in the religious practice of the incomers with great suspicion, as exhibited in their behaviour at feast days. Whether traditional Catholic May devotions were to be held in the open or in church, how a maypole was to be erected and who could sit in which seats at Mass in church—all of this created friction with the refugees, often leading to mass brawls. And if a difference in religious observances led to disputes between the Catholic

Bavarians and Sudeten Germans, each as Catholic as the other, the conflicts between Protestants and Catholics were considerably more violent. The Frankish priest of the parish of Bürglein complained in 1946, "It is unacceptable that the denomination [Catholicism] which is currently a guest in our Protestant Franconia should surreptitiously attempt to invade the buildings and affairs of our church."[43]

In this by now genuinely cramped space, the jostling German regional cultures clashed dramatically. After the war local mentalities differed much more than they do today. When swarms of pleasure-loving Catholic Sudeten Germans suddenly appeared in the pietistic regions of Württemberg, it was a real culture shock for the more strait-laced and devout locals. Corpus Christi processions were taken as a provocation and violently suppressed, and children were called into their homes when the "foreigners" passed through the village. The same was true in Hesse:

> The openness of the refugees was interpreted as garrulousness, the display of emotions as a lack of self-control, good manners as servility. So, for example, a local farmer's wife would go into hiding if visited by an old woman who tended to express her gratitude with a kiss of the hand.[44]

Rage was vented against the supposed slovenliness of the refugees, then against their superiority. Differences that look tiny today were enough to mark a substantial otherness between the tribes. Well-worn racist vocabulary was used again and again. The regional director of the Bavarian Farmers' Association, Dr. Jakob Fischbacher, described in a much-noted speech that it was unnatural for the son of a Bavarian farmer to marry a North German blonde. He demanded that the local farmers drive the incoming Prussians back to the east, "or ideally to Siberia."[45]

The hatred of immigrants that inspired such demagogues was rooted in the fact that the migration did actually result in the indisputable erosion of local traditions. Regional peculiarities, established over hundreds of years, were under threat. The vulnerability of these customs had already become apparent to those concerned custodians of what it meant to come from Bavaria, Swabia or Schleswig-Holstein, during the first wave of immigration that had come even before that of the deportees. During the war, masses of bombed-out and evacuated city-dwellers had flowed into the countryside and had often been billeted by the authorities with the same diktat they later applied to the deportees. The urbanites had shocked some villagers with their liberal ways, but they had also made an impression on others. The 5 million city-dwellers who had been distributed around the German regions, including many pleasure-loving young women who wanted to go partying even in the villages, had upset "traditional values." It didn't help that priests raged down from their pulpits against loose morals and condemned the painted fingernails and "shameless" clothing of the city people. In fact, the city-dwellers so turned the villagers'

Refugees from Poland on the trek to Berlin and farther west. The railroad tracks helped them to find their bearings.

heads that there was a wave of romantic intrigues, illegitimate children and divorces.

But love also helped to integrate the expellees. It was a particularly effective engine of modernisation. Young men and women ignored ethnic animosities to come together. But it was a while before the detainees stopped chiefly marrying into their own tribes, and a Bohemian German, for instance, was accepted by the parents of a Frankish bride. Even weddings between Protestants and Catholics, officially called "mixed marriages," were held with increasing frequency in spite of the bitter resistance among clerics. The Catholic partner in such marriages was usually excommunicated if the Protestant one did not change their faith. Often the excommunications were announced publicly during Mass along with terms of abuse. Some believers, torn between romantic love and loyalty to the Church, remained excluded from the community for the rest of their lives.

Part of the reason for the bitterness of these conflicts was the fact that the refugees were genuinely changing Germany. Before the war in West Germany there had been a population density of 160 people per square kilometre, now it was 200. In the cities this didn't make much of a difference, and in Berlin and Hamburg the proportion of deportees among the total population was just 6 and 7 per cent respectively. But in the state of Mecklenburg-Vorpommern in the north-east it was 45 per cent, in north-western Schleswig-Holstein 33 per cent, and even in the much bigger Bavaria it was 21 per cent. The immigration of outsiders gnawed away persistently at the inhabitants' certainty that the local way of life was the only authentic one. The sociologist Elisabeth Pfeil summed up the phenomenon as early as 1948 in the title of her book *The Refugee: Figure of a Changing Time*. The appearance of refugees, she wrote, "stirs up a world, and what happens happens not only to those who have fled and been deported, but also to the others whose house they entered and to whom they communicated their unease. The German people today can hardly ignore what has happened to them as a result of this great migration."[46]

In May 1948, when writing for the *Süddeutsche Zeitung,* the journalist Ursula von Kardorff visited a village that had formerly been home to 1,600 inhabitants, but had since had to take in not only 200 evacuees but also 800 Sudeten Germans. She wrote:

> From the sociological point of view a village today is as multi-layered as only the city was in the past. People who lived in Prague, Berlin, Budapest, Vienna, Bucharest and Riga are now, some willingly, some because they are forced to, getting to know both the good and bad sides of rural life. Marginal characters—and there are few others in this now cramped space—have found refuge here, be they deported gentry, painters, laid-off engineers, Hungarian officers, former diplomats, Baltic barons and those returning home whose return is blocked by the barbed wire that marks off the Allied zones, in short, "Prussia" beyond the River Main. The most curious-seeming are the intellectuals, who come and go like migrating birds, who turn on the water-pump at night to brew black coffee for themselves, who sleep for a long time in the morning and in the evening hold frivolous parties—in short, silly people who no longer want to be taken seriously.[47]

Altogether they brought huge changes to parts of the country that had remained unchanged even during the war.

Associations of expellees from various countries and cultures were organised in an attempt to keep their traditions and memories alive. Because of the often revanchist tones of their association officials, for a long time the expellees from the eastern territories were numbered among the most reactionary groups in the Federal Republic. They played a great part, in fact, in encouraging far-right unrest until well into the 1970s. Nationalist feelings were traditionally very pronounced among them, since they often came from ethnically mixed regions where their status as Germans had previously brought them all kinds of privileges and caused all kinds of conflict. In post-war Germany, on the other hand, when the nation no longer considered regional differences to be of great consequence, they stubbornly raised the nationalist banner. The older among them in particular later felt they had been abandoned for a second time, when more and more Germans were accepting of the new borders with Poland and

Czechoslovakia. They reacted with slanderous campaigns, particularly against Willy Brandt, the first Social Democratic post-war chancellor, who sought good relations with West Germany's eastern neighbours, identifying him as public enemy number one. Still, in 1950 the Federation of Expellees (*Bund der Heimatvertriebenen*) had undertaken in its charter "in memory of the unending suffering that the last decade in particular has inflicted upon people, to renounce revenge and retaliation." It also undertook to collaborate on the "creation of a united Europe in which the peoples can live without fear or coercion."

At the same time, in the ranks of the expellee associations there were a number of fanatics who could not accept the loss of the eastern territories and their former homes. The following letter, written in 1957 from Sudeten German Ernst Frank, who was now living in Frankfurt am Main, to Czech police officer Karel Sedlacek was not an isolated case. Without a word of salutation, Frank informed the Czech policeman:

> I am still the owner of the house and you are only the temporary administrator of my property. I am coming home again. Look after my house and garden. I or my family will come back and take it from you![48]

There is a paradox to this: however backward-looking many expellees might have been, in post-war society they acted as agents of modernisation. They helped to contribute to the creation of that cultural and social mix by which the young republic set such store. In their new and generally unloved home they helped to foment a process of deprovincialisation that reshaped the traditionally change-averse farming regions. The expellees stirred up the countryside, levelled regional differences and, in a first impulse towards cultural relaxation, ensured that the Germans could, decades later, unite around an abstract national identity based on constitutional patriotism. So, for example, in many regions—anticipating the later effects of television—they were responsible for the disappearance of dialect. The children of expellees, ashamed of their dialect of origin, instead spoke in as perfect a form of standard German as possible when at school, and the local children soon followed suit.

For regional cultures the expellees were what the notorious Eternit façade (a washable fibre and concrete material widely used in the 1950s to mask the frontages of rural buildings) was to village architecture. Just as local architectural traditions disappeared behind the grey uniformity of Eternit façades, standard doors and plastic windows, the less tangible qualities of the regional cultures were reduced to a single social-climbing middle-class society whose most dynamic members were comprised of expellees. They had, after all, been forced to shake off their old bonds and came to a new country like pioneers—subdued ones, admittedly, and with reactionary trappings, but pioneers none the less.

These German expellees from the eastern territories quickly ceased to be a burden and instead became a blessing to the German economy. They were usually quicker to adapt to new circumstances than residents of longer standing. Along with their possessions and their homes they had also lost many illusions, and were more flexible and ambitious in their attitudes. Two thirds of the previously self-employed incomers changed jobs after resettlement. Almost 90 per cent of the former farmers among them had to look for different lines of work, forming an army of potential workers who were ready to get to work without asking any questions. The swift upturn after the economic reform in 1948 would not have been possible without the hard-working contribution of the German expellees. Liberated from all the traditions of their old homes, most of them concentrated on nothing but the construction of a new life through labour. Many expellees were also educated to a high level and held qualifications, consequently they became the foundation of mid-sized industry that grew up in the underdeveloped rural regions of Bavaria and Baden-Württemberg.[49]

In spite of all the successful instances of integration it was not until 1966 that the last big barracks camps for deportees could be disbanded. Millions of people had originally been housed in Nissen huts, often with 20 people in a single room for years. They had lived in the converted concentration camp at Dachau, its subcamp at

Allach and other former sites of horror but under considerably more pleasant conditions than those experienced by the previous inmates. Many expellees did not shed the stigma of the camps for a long time, because even the simple, neat and tidy estates of small houses that were built on the edges of cities for the expellees were for a long time known locally as "camps," to make their otherness quite clear. These housing estates were marked by a curious combination of fragmentation and uniformity. It was as if a diverse collection of mavericks had discovered, through architecture, a neat and orderly way of living together in close quarters. Although their travails eventually reached a favourable conclusion, there was still something of the camp that clung to these estates, and even today it's hard to shake the feeling that, in the cynical homeliness with which these uniform houses are pressed so tightly together, the trauma of violence which the century of expulsions perpetrated against its people is still visible.

Often the neighbours of the new districts gave the estates nicknames like Little Korea, New Poland, Mau-Mau or Little Moscow, making it clear where they would ideally have wished to banish the residents who lived there. Mau-Mau was a term used to refer to immigrant estates, even though more bombed-out former residents of Hamburg or Mannheim lived there than actual expellees from the east.[50]

Today it is hard to imagine the depth of the discord among the Germans. The Allied military authorities, particularly the British, often warned of a threatening civil war. The Jesuit priest Johannes Leppich, a Silesian by birth, who was known as "God's machine gun" because of his polemical sermons, prophesied, "A revolution will come, of bunkers and barracks, if help does not come soon." The historian Friedrich Prinz summed up the situation:

> A contented look back at the successful integration of the expellees sometimes distorts our understanding of how close we were to social catastrophe; it was entirely possible that the expellees could have become Germany's "Palestinian problem."[51]

Catastrophe was initially averted by the Allies, who treated the German expellees from the eastern territories almost exactly as they treated the non-German DPs, even though they were initially careful to keep them from organising and being politically active. However, with the formation of the Federal Republic of Germany (West Germany) and the German Democratic Republic (East Germany), from 1949 on, the Germans had to figure out for themselves how to ensure justice between locals and expellees.

The expulsion of the Germans was a huge programme of expropriation by which the nations that had been invaded and looted by Germany paid themselves back for the war crimes that they had suffered. This was done in violation of international law and, in practice, often under odious circumstances. Even so, it was difficult not to see the fragmentation of Germany as a just punishment. Many German expellees wondered why they had to bear this penance alone, since they had not, after all, been solely responsible for the war. All responsible politicians were open to the abstract notion that the burden of responsibility needed to be distributed more fairly, but opinions were divided as to the extent to which this was possible, and how it might be accomplished in concrete terms.

The regime in the Soviet-occupied zone had an easier time, where it was able to adopt a more interventionist approach. More than a third of the real estate confiscated from the autumn of 1945 onwards was distributed to expellees, and over 40 per cent of the new farms created as a result of land reform went to the new arrivals from the east. This meant, however, that they could no longer refer to themselves as expellees. The socialist regime initially called them "new citizens" or "settlers." From 1949 they were unwilling to use those terms in order to avoid the suggestion of criticism of either the Soviet Union or the fraternal Eastern Bloc states. Fearing that the German expellees might drive a wedge between East Germany and its new allies, the socialist state did its best to treat locals and expellees equally. It worked relatively well, though the expellees were obliged to deny their history, and had no place within the official historiography of

the GDR. Any attempts they made to organise politically or culturally were immediately suppressed. Not all expellees accepted this,
and 400,000, including many who refused to undergo this loss of
identity, continued to move into the Western zones until the end of
1949, thus speeding the integration of the remainder in the GDR.

Meanwhile in West Germany a tortured discussion had begun
about compensation for war losses. A law concerning the distribution
of responsibility for war reparations—the Equalisation of Burdens
Act—came into effect in September 1952. Erich Ollenhauer, the then-
chair of the SPD, the West German Social Democratic Party, which
was at the time in opposition to the ruling Conservative Christian
Democratic Union (CDU), summed up the significance of the Equalisation of Burdens Law: "This is not a social law like a hundred others,
in which achievements and obligations are weighed up against one
another with painstaking precision. It is the law of the liquidation of
our inner war debt towards millions of our own compatriots."

To pay the "inner war debt," the debt owed by Germany to German citizens, everyone who had only suffered slight damage as a
result of the war was asked to compensate those who had lost the
most. Put simply, many people had to pay up to half of what they
owned so that those who had nothing could survive. In individual
terms the gigantic redistribution looked like this: the law determined
that owners of land, houses and other assets had to hand over the
value of 50 per cent of the property that they had owned as of the
deadline of 21 June 1948. The sum could be paid in quarterly instalments over 30 years. The beneficiaries were the "war damaged":
people who had been bombed out of their homes, the war wounded
and expellees. They were to be compensated for the loss of their
land and business assets, household goods and savings, but not for
cash and jewellery. There was also a social component to this whereby
those who had lost large fortunes received a smaller percentage compensation than those who had lost small sums. In order to calculate
the claims of the expellees and the burden of those obliged to pay,
so-called equalisation offices were set up, which would over the coming decades process 8.3 million applications from expellees alone.

Dull though it might sound, the law was a miracle of political negotiating strategy. The disputes over this spectacular redistribution operation were fought out with such obstinate ferocity that in the end hardly any ordinary citizens recognised what an admirable decision had finally been made and put into effect. Instead, after years of disputation in which no one could bear to hear the phrase "burden of equalisation" any longer, everyone was dissatisfied. Those unaffected by the war felt that they were being expected to pay too much, while the expellees saw the payments as a drop in the ocean. Because nobody was happy with the law, the ramifications of the process lay hidden for a long time, but it was as a result of this law that the deeply divided Germans were brought together—albeit without really noticing. And so it was, bickering on a level divorced from big words and ideologies, that the Germans came to democracy. The general querulousness that accompanied the lasting dispute about the equalisation of burdens was a sign that things were getting back to normal. The fact that the Germans fought out their "inner war debts" in this stubborn, sober and entirely undramatic way—and in the end united on a perfectly balanced compromise which took 25,000 officials and employees decades to put into effect—might not really have made anybody happy, but from today's vantage point it is clear what a fortunate path was struck. A struggle over the distribution of funds which had begun as an unabashed culture war between locals and incomers had been turned in a fair and pragmatic way into a parliamentary negotiation. The foundation stone was laid for what would later, in Germany, be called civil society.

Within a few years the national identity of the Germans had been profoundly transformed. What had been warmly celebrated under National Socialism as a racially unified *Volksgemeinschaft* was transformed in the post-war years into an enforced association of unloved ethnic groups. This in turn, during the boom years, turned into an unsentimental compromise-based society in which everyone felt only tolerably well treated. A new nationalism could hardly be built on this hotly disputed foundation—not a bad starting point for the young democracy.

On the road

In the first years after the war no one could have anticipated that things would reach this happy conclusion. On the contrary, for a long time streets, waiting rooms, emergency hostels and ruined apartments acted as home to many displaced Germans, and no one knew how long this situation would last. "The wind their home, the rain their roof" was the title that the author Wolfgang Weyrauch gave to his story in *Ulenspiegel* in 1946, in which he painted a portrait of several couples living in the street "happy, but in misery, miserable, but in happiness." While most homeless people wanted to establish a new life as quickly as possible, for others moving around became a normal way of living. Criminologists at the time identified a new type of vagrant capitalising on people's rootlessness. This included any number of confidence tricksters, who changed their identities according to the state of their fortunes. There were swarms of fake doctors, fake aristocrats and marriage impostors. Swindling was able to boom because everywhere there were people who seemed to have come out of nowhere. There were no friends, no social circles, no agencies to verify their old identities. Along with the homes that they had been expelled from, they also lost their CVs and drew up new ones. Bigamists were a special case. They included refugees and expellees who, for simplicity's sake, simply covered up an earlier marriage, but they also included people who preferred to maintain two homes at once, using one as a backup. They couldn't get enough shelter. With the trauma of being uprooted still so fresh, the family home became an obsession. Advertising in the 1950s would soon take the "cosy four walls" and extol them to a ridiculous degree—no wonder country roads lingered in many people's memories as a place of nightmare. In his novel *Off Limits* Hans Habe described life on the road:

> Like an over-full stomach, the P.O.W. camps had thrown up their surfeit. And they looked, too, like something vomited up. The indignity of defeat was the defeat of dignity: in rags and tatters the beaten Army

was hobbling back into its vanquished country. They had always been on the roads, these men—on the roads of France and Poland, Russia and Belgium. They had advanced together, but they were retreating singly. During their journey the road had borne them, now they were bearing the road.[52]

The long march became a common trope. Not only to have travelled "as far as one's feet would carry," as a famous television serial from 1959 had it, but to have made it all the way home was to many a source of lifelong pride. In Edgar Reitz's eleven-part film series *Heimat—eine deutsche Chronik* (*Heimat—A German Chronicle*), Anton Simon, who had walked all the way home from a Russian POW camp, 5,000 kilometres from Novosibirsk to Schabbach in the Hunsrück, has his boots cast in gold. Anton, who becomes wealthy after the war as a manufacturer of optical devices, puts the golden boots on a plinth in the foyer of his company as an admonition and a remembrance, a self-celebration and a demand for respect. The people of Schabbach were supposed to be able to count on people like Anton.

With tales of the long journey home, the German defeat was reinterpreted as a personal victory. Lucky souls like Anton had already earned the success of their new lives before they had even begun. For others the wandering seemed never to end. Wolfgang Borchert's play *Draussen vor der Tür* (*The Man Outside*), which had its first performance in November 1947, is about an unsuccessful homecoming. The home of the returning soldier Beckmann no longer exists and his wife has found someone else—a fate that he shared with many others. "And their home is then outside the door. Their Germany is outside, in the rain at night, on the road."

In 1945, already terminally ill, and after marching over 600 kilometres to his hometown of Hamburg, the 24-year-old Borchert wrote a companion piece to *The Man Outside*, a fervent evocation of the city:

Hamburg! It's more than a heap of stones, roofs, windows, carpets, beds, streets, bridges and streetlights. It is more than factory chimneys and honking car horns [. . .] Oh, it is infinitely much more than that. It

is our will to be. Not to be anywhere and anyhow, but here and only
here between Alster stream and Elbe brook—and only to be as we are,
we in Hamburg.[53]

The text continues for a long time in a similar vein; after the Eastern
Front, military prison and his flight home, Borchert was literally
clawing his way back into his city, into the "indispensable, inevitable
infinities of the comfortless streets." In hammering alliterations, he
sang of his hometown, imagining it completely untouched by bombs,
filled with the puttering of ship engines and the sound of sirens,
whereas in 1945 the harbour was in fact oppressively silent, shipping
languished and the quay facilities had been destroyed. "And when we
stand in the evening on the rocking pontoons—in the grey days—
then we say: Elbe! And we mean: Life! We mean: Me and you. We say,
roar, sigh: Elbe—and mean: World!"[54]

Wolfgang Borchert's prose poem "Hamburg" was the higher literary equivalent to the *Heimat* film—a celebration of the home village,
town or region—that would enjoy a vogue some decades later. By
then Borchert would be long dead. A day before the premiere of his
play *The Man Outside* he died at the age of 26 from liver failure,
thought to have resulted from the hardship of military service.

The "Song of the Cripple" by Erich Fried, written in 1945, is also
about the consequences of the war and the road. It picks up a widespread motif of the post-war period: the "limping man," the
"wounded veteran," who would be a regular part of street life for a
long time to come.

> We marched past death
> and left it behind us
> because death too loses its breath
> in the headlong alleys.
> We move into your homes on our crutches;
> nothing can threaten us now . . .
> So today let us be merry,
> for yesterday we were dead!"[55]

The idea of a weary death too exhausted to drag everyone along with it precisely captures the mood of those who remained engaged in the work of reconstruction. "Today let us be merry"—that is the sentiment that was taken up in cabarets. Erich Kästner wrote the "Marching Song 1945," sung by a "woman in men's trousers and an old coat, with a rucksack and a battered suitcase," for the Schaubude, a cabaret in Munich, which was one of the first established after the war. The backdrop showed a lonely country road and a bullet-riddled tank. The actress Ursula Herking, well known in Germany at the time from almost 60 films, carried the suitcase and sang to a dirgelike piano accompaniment:

> For the last thirty weeks
> I have wandered through forest and field.
> And my shirt is so full of holes
> that you would hardly believe it.
> I wore shoes without soles,
> and my rucksack is my wardrobe.
> The Poles have my furniture,
> the Dresdner Bank my money.
> Without home or family,
> dull boots and all the rest—
> yes, that was the famous
> Decline of the West.
>
> . . . .
>
> A thousand years have passed
> along with his moustachioed majesty [Hitler].
> And now we're supposed to start all over!
> Forward march, or it will be too late.
> Left, two, three, four,
> left, two, three—
> because our heads, because our heads
> are still solidly on our necks.[56]

The song had an incredible effect. Ursula Herking reported in her memoirs:

When I had sung the last note of the marching song, people leapt
from their seats, hugged each other, shouted, some wept, a barely
believable "Redemption" had taken place. It was only partly down to
me, it was just the right song, phrased right, performed right, at the
right time.[57]

The road exerted its pull and its magical power on the audience.
Without that omnipresence of displacement, of being removed from
home, it is hard to imagine the rapture with which the listeners
responded then, because reading these lines today they fall flat. But
witnesses testify that the spectators did indeed leap from their seats,
and if we listen to the sound recording, which has survived, it
becomes quite clear just how much Ursula Herking and Erich Kästner had captured the spirit of the times.[58] In that rather droning
Sprechgesang, spoken singing, that is typical of cabaret, Herking introduced a tone that alternated between arrogance and despair, rising at
the end to a slightly crazed growl. She damped down all the character's anxieties in such a way that they emerged all the more clearly.
As a result she captured the ambivalence of the time precisely. No
optimism without bitterness, no lament without gratitude: "In the
windows that lay in darkness light twinkles once more. Not in all
houses. Really, not in all . . ."

For others, "at home in the street" meant "at home beside the
tracks." Much travelling was done by freight train, even though regular passenger trains were travelling again too, albeit often without
windowpanes, meaning that when it rained, seats and floors were
flooded. Because of the irregular rail traffic, traveller numbers backed
up in railway stations, and the waiting rooms and tunnels were full of
stranded people whose journeys had been halted indefinitely. Anyone
who could afford it preferred to stay in a hotel, if they could find one,
but that had its risks, too; often trains would leave in the morning
even though they were scheduled to set off hours later, and so people
liked to stay close.

In November 1947 a report was published in *Ruf* magazine about a
night in Hanover station:

A wave of warm, thick air hits me as I go down the steps to platform 3. Among sacks, cardboard boxes, suitcases, apple peelings, scraps of paper and empty cigarette cartons hundreds of people sit and lie along the damp, shiny walls. Only a narrow path in the middle of the tunnel is left free. After some searching I manage to find a place for my suitcase in this jumble of bodies and luggage.

It wasn't theatres that reflected our post-war everyday life, the author went on, it was night-life in a Hanover station tunnel.[59] The director Gustav Fröhlich had filmed in the very same tunnel to obtain as authentic an atmosphere as possible for his film *Wege im Zwielicht* (*Paths in Twilight*), which led the same journalist to remark: "One man's misery is another man's film."

Train journey, 1948. Often there was only room on the roof and between the carriages. The journey from Hamburg to Munich often took a week.

In fact, railway stations were far more likely to appear in newspaper reports than in film scenes. The waiting room became a favourite motif of journalists' social critiques. Nowhere else did the newly revived Germany rub shoulders so closely with the one still mired in chaos, the settled with the homeless, the safe with the traumatised. Munich immigration commissioner Willi Irlbeck inspected the waiting room at Munich Central Station and recorded the conditions there in a report to his superiors. They provoked the shocked administrator into a burst of descriptive brio that would have put Émile Zola to shame:

> The hall is filled with haze, the space pervaded with penetrating odours. Young people who have already passed through every stage of moral depravity; girls who know about the reciprocity of supply and demand; deal-makers and opportunistic thieves for whom law and justice are empty words; released prisoners of war whose longing to see their home again had given way to an unconquerable revulsion; mothers for whose children waiting rooms and railway compartments have become a playground, boxes and cases a crib; human wrecks whose bruised bodies are their sole possessions, half-asleep, brooding, dirty and hopeless.[60]

Anyone who had to travel was setting off on a journey of incalculable duration. In summer 1947 the *Neue Illustrierte* commissioned its photographer to take the night train from Hamburg to Munich. He didn't reach Munich until eight days later. His only usable shots were from the first two days; after that the wear and tear was too much for his camera. The trains that did run were packed, but many were either cancelled or had to stop in the middle of the countryside because the tracks had been destroyed. Even the dangerous seats located on the buffers between the carriages, which passengers straddled precariously, were over-booked. "Not an uncomfortable seat," Ursula von Kardorff thought, "the only nuisance was the sparks from the locomotive, which burned holes in my raincoat."[61] Some travellers stood outside on the footboards, holding on to the door handles.

When the train stopped at stations along the way only a minority of the passengers were able to board. Some bold people risked climbing through windows into the compartments, where they were subjected to torrents of abuse. The front page of the *Neue Illustrierte* showed the actress Ilse Werner being lifted out of a carriage window with the help of fellow passengers, it being impossible to pass down the corridor and exit the train in the usual way.

Despite high levels of stress among the population, in 1947 some Germans were already travelling again for fun or relaxation. Of the 10,000 holiday homes on the island of Sylt, 6,000 were crammed with refugees, while the rest waited for holidaymakers as they had done in the past. On arrival, luggage was searched for black-market goods, but landlords assured their guests that the police had adopted a lax attitude and would tolerate a certain amount of extra income being made on the side.

The carefree holiday mood was rather overshadowed by the omnipresent misery of the refugees, but that didn't diminish the determination of many Germans to enjoy a first post-war holiday. Because of rationing, all hotel visitors had to supply the raw ingredients for their dinners, which were delivered to the hotel kitchen along with a piece of paper listing the name and room number and special instructions for their preparation. Holiday guests also brought with them their own ingredients for breakfast, as they did not want to settle for the cup of coffee, single slice of bread and five grams of fat that hotels were allowed to serve in return for food coupons. One newspaper report from Sylt showed a breakfast table groaning with tins of preserves. The astonished reader saw Nescafé, corned beef, beans in tomato sauce, honey and jam, all in great abundance. The paper anticipated any envy with the caption: "Such breakfast tables are by no means rare on Sylt, and need not belong to profiteers, but might also be those of care package recipients who have saved them up for their holidays. There are people who are delighted to see such a table nearby, and say 'Soon we might all have that again,' and there are people who will be annoyed about it for the rest of their holiday. Such people should not go to Sylt."[62]

IV

Dancing Frenzy

There is a tendency to imagine the post-war years in Germany as having been deadly serious. The dominant image and, to an even greater extent, the after-image of the time is one of anxious and despairing faces. That would seem quite reasonable given the prevailing misery and uncertainty. And yet it was also a time of laughing, dancing, flirting and lovemaking. This levity rarely appears in films and literary treatments, and the more recent they are the rarer it is, because it doesn't typically align with the seriousness of their plots. Frivolity did strike contemporaries themselves as inappropriate, but they went on partying anyway, many of them more extravagantly than ever before, and certainly with fewer inhibitions than they would show during the more prosperous years of the 1950s, when people were more inclined to guard their wealth within the privacy of their own four walls.

After the horrors of the bombing raids and the uncertainties of the first days of occupation, the joy of survival erupted with great force. The deprivations of everyday life among the ruins did not diminish the widespread energy—quite the contrary: the feeling of having escaped disaster (for some), and the unpredictable, entirely unregulated future led to a heightened intensity of life. Many people lived only for the moment, and if the moment was a good one, they wanted to drain it to the lees. There were outbreaks of exuberant delight in life, a devotion to pleasure that sometimes appeared almost maniacal. Threats to life were still everywhere, so they wanted to relish life to the full. A dancing frenzy broke out, people kicked up their heels wherever they could, and venues echoed with peals of uncontained laughter that many found irksome.

One Munich resident recalled:

> For months I went dancing every night, although of course there was no alcohol and nothing to eat. There was just a sour-tasting drink called Molke. Me and all the other dance-frenzy throng would rarely enjoy ourselves as much or be as cheerful as we were during those days, despite the absence of dinner and alcohol.[1]

And as in Munich, so in Berlin. Eighteen-year-old secretary Brigitte Eicke, for example, a pleasure-loving girl who practically devoured books, was forever going to the cinema or, even better, dancing. The fall of the Reich's capital did not strip her of her passions. She first stepped inside a cinema again seventeen days after the surrender; it had only opened two days previously. In the evening she recorded in her diary:

> I picked Gitti up at three and we went off to the Babylon with Anne-marie Reimer, Rita Uckert and Edith Sturmowski. It was really nice and we teased each other something rotten. The film was a load of tosh. *The Children of Captain Grand*, a Russian film, was all in Russian, and you couldn't really follow it.

Where dancing was concerned, Brigitte would need to be patient for a few more weeks. First of all, as a former member of the League of German Girls, who had become Party members as part of the programme called "The People Give the Führer its Children as a Birthday Present," Brigitte had to do penal labour clearing away rubble. But after the occupying Soviet forces declared all young people to have been seduced by the Nazis and granted them amnesty, they reinvented themselves as members of the anti-fascist youth committee and Brigitte was free to move from one dance floor to the next.

She first went out on the town on 8 July, to the Café Willa, on her own this time. The evening was a bit disappointing because of the lack of men, who were either still deployed in the field or sitting behind barbed wire: "There still aren't nearly enough men, it's mostly just girls dancing together." She also had to be home early because she had been assigned guard duty at the front door from 11 o'clock until 1:30. At this time apartment blocks on Prenzlauer Berg always placed two residents on guard at night in changing shifts, so that they could sound the alarm in the event of attacks by criminal gangs or drunken soldiers. From that day forward Brigitte Eicke would regularly go dancing, often several times a week.

Next, with her friends Kuzi and Lotti, she visited the Lucas, a bar with a dance floor: "Someone asked me up, they were playing a Csardas [a traditional Hungarian folk dance] [. . .] and I'd never danced to anything like that before. He led me wonderfully well." Over the next few weeks Brigitte Eicke and her clique moved from one reopened dance hall to the next. The entrances to the venues were cleared of rubble and provisionally repaired, sometimes with only the ground floor still standing, but that wasn't detrimental to their jaunty swing-dancing. They also went to the Prater, to the Casaleon in Neukölln, to the Neue Welt, to the Café Wien on Kurfürstendamm, from there to the Café Corso and finally to the Wiener Grienzing—but at this last venue three persistent GIs ruined the girls' evening: "Going into West Berlin is a waste of time," Brigitte wrote, summing up that evening. "It just costs lots of money and you get nothing out of it." You were better off going to the Plaza roof garden at the badly damaged Küstrin Station, Eicke observed, even though there was a man shortage there too. "Almost all the men were very young, and lots of them, but all shorter than average." Again and again the diarist wrote of her longing for "her soldiers" to come back from imprisonment or the unknown: "If only one of my boys were here, so that I didn't always have to pay; but first and foremost, of course, for them just to be here."

On a visit to Café Tabasco, Brigitte Eicke and a friend fell victim to "shills," young men employed by the managers to improve the mood of their predominantly female customers in order to get them to spend money. Two wild young men invited them to dance as soon as they entered the bar, and then encouraged the spellbound girls to order unwise quantities of cocktails and vegetable soup. But rather than keeping them company, as soon as the girls had ordered they pounced on the next new arrivals and, to Eicke's fury, began the whole charade all over again.

On they went to the Palais des Centrums, to the Casino, the International, the Café Standard and the Kajüte. In the course of the summer of 1945, the 18-year-old visited a total of 13 different establishments, which today we would call clubs—a number that would be considered substantial even in the party metropolis of present-day Berlin. And there were many more clubs that the curious young woman could have explored: the Piccadilly Bar, the Robin Hood, the Roxy, the Royal Club, the Grotta Azzurra, the Monte Carlo, to name just a few of the places in the sidestreets of the Kurfürstendamm.[2]

In the films of the German post-war period, it's almost exclusively the so-called racketeers—small-time hoodlums and black-market traders—who do the partying. With greedy, grease-glistening faces like those captured in Georg Grosz's caricatures of the Weimar Republic, they bite into fat cutlets, gulp down smuggled wine and snuffle at heaving bosoms. Dancing and partying were depicted as the obscene pleasures of unscrupulous money-grubbers, which was automatically censured in light of the general misery. The reality was completely different. The have-nots partied too. Just not all of them.

There were all manner of desperate people for whom partying was definitely a thing of the past: those who had lost their children while fleeing and were relentlessly in search of them; sick people who, for want of proper medical help, faded for months between life and death; the traumatised who had lost the will to live; and, finally, people for whom, after the end of the war, every laughing face looked like a mocking grimace. They sat there apathetically for a while and silently left the cheerful hubbub when things got too mad. But it would be a mistake to automatically see them as occupying the moral high ground, and the dancers as inured and blind to injustice and misery. If people felt that fun was inappropriate, it was seldom because of the guilt that the Germans had brought upon themselves.

Scene from the Hot Club, Munich, 1951. Wolfgang Borchert wrote in 1947, "Our whooping and our music are a dance above the abyss that gapes at us. And that music is jazz. Because our hearts and our brains have the same rhythm of hot and cold: agitated, crazed and hectic, uninhibited."

Usually it was their own misery that soured their mood; thoughts of their husbands in prison or grief for fallen relatives.

Anyone who could dance danced. The young student Maria von Eynern found an explanation for her suddenly explosive lust for life—which surprised even her—in the collapse of her old world:

> There are a lot of things involved—above all the authentic personal freedom that our ruined surroundings grant us, and which is distributed almost wastefully, in a fascinating way. We are unimaginably sociable. And in the end we are responsible for ourselves—for every joy, and indeed for every misstep in the jungle of confusion that trips up our beloved self.

The shock of collapse was followed by a sense of personal responsibility and a deep feeling of personal freedom. The student embraced a bafflement to which she gave a radically positive twist: "We," she wrote, as if speaking for a whole generation, "are creating around us an atmosphere of constant readiness to encounter the peculiarities of existence and deal with them. Freedom waves to us in every direction." There were, for example, no longer any conventions on clothing, "because nobody at all has anything 'conventional' any more—truly here is the freedom of the dispossessed and the intellectuals."

This new zest for life was not a privilege of the educated classes. The "unimaginable sociability" that Maria von Eynern was surprised to find in herself encompassed great swathes of society. While some people barricaded themselves away in the bastions of their bitterness, others immersed themselves in new acquaintances, friendships and love affairs. Migration and evacuation did not lead only to hostility, but also to attraction and curiosity. The fact of families being torn apart created misery and distress in some cases, but in others a liberation from oppressive relationships. The boundaries between rich and poor were also blurred; the experience of potentially losing everything overnight and the omnipresence of death took differences that had previously been fundamental and consigned them to the margins. This could also be conveyed as the "freedom of the dispossessed and the intellectuals" that Maria von Eynern wrote about in her diaries.[3]

Wolfgang Borchert, the writer and playwright who entered collective memory as the "Man of Sorrows" of post-war German literature, also experienced the odd combination of death's proximity and a delight in life. A zest for life in the midst of scenes of despair was often denigrated out of hand as a destructive greed for life. Some people felt that it was not appropriate to celebrate and dance so close to death, while others wanted to dance even more wildly in the presence of death and sorrow. In Borchert's writings this lust for life finds full expression. In his 1947 essay "This Is Our Manifesto" he describes the music of his generation, first as "sentimental soldiers' bawling," now luckily behind them, followed by jazz, which, along with swing and boogie-woogie, was played in Hamburg dance halls:

Now our song is jazz. Agitated, hectic jazz is our music. And the hot, crazed, lunatic song through which the drum rushes along, catty and scratching. And sometimes once again the old sentimental soldiers' bawling, with which they drowned out adversity and rejected their mothers. [. . .] Our whooping and our music are a dance above the abyss that gapes at us. And that music is jazz. Because our hearts and our brains have the same rhythm of hot and cold: agitated, crazed and hectic, uninhibited. And our girls have the same hot pulse in hands and hips. And their laughter is hoarse and brittle and clarinet-hard. And their hair that crackles like phosphorus. That burns. And their hearts beating in syncopation, wistfully wild. Sentimental. That is what our girls are like: like jazz. And the nights too, the girl-jingling nights: like jazz: hot and hectic. Agitated.[4]

The rhythm of the text itself is pure jazz. It is a pulsating paean to existence. It is a quiet yell in which the war still echoes, although already sublimated by the clarinet. The war is still present everywhere, even in the women's hair, which shimmers like phosphorus. Borchert's writing captured very precisely, not least in its intertwining of sensitivity and coarseness, the atmosphere in the dance halls in which the young men who had survived whirled "their girls" around. There were also, here and there, glorified early incarnations of rock 'n' roll. In the 1951 film *Sündige Grenze* (*Illegal Border*) by Robert A. Stemmle, for example, we see an Aachen youth gang dancing to boogie-woogie numbers with acrobatic dance moves of a kind that would be typical of rock 'n' roll only a number of years later.

And it wasn't just the cities that danced; in the country, too, there was dancing in inns and at fairgrounds in the open air. Larger events had to be authorised by the occupying forces, and anyone who set one up without a permit would have to pay a small fine. A weak beer was served, which many thought tasted "fake," because often schnapps was added to it. In contrast, the partygoers in the German wine regions seldom experienced a shortage of intoxicants. So much dancing was done that council officials repeatedly intervened to forbid events for which the military administration had already given permission. They took great care to ensure that young people under 18 did not have access to the parties. It must have felt strange to them, that only a few months previously they had been old enough to be sent to their death with the Volkssturm (the people's militia established during the last few months of the war), but were now not adult enough for a glass of wine.

Occasions for partying were often tied to Church festivals, which were celebrated with a renewed enthusiasm immediately after the end of the war. In late May and early June Catholic Corpus Christi processions celebrating the consecrated host could once again take place unhindered. The procession path would be richly decorated, with flowers that needed only to be plucked—and there were plenty of vases too; you only had to collect the brass artillery casings from the fields, polish them till they shone, and lo and behold, you had the loveliest containers for flowers.

One characteristic misunderstanding between the occupiers and Germans occurred at the St. Martin's Day procession in Koblenz on 11 November 1945, at which children traditionally dress up to commemorate the death of St. Martin of Tours, a popular saint in Germany's Catholic south. On this occasion, countless children with torches had gathered with, at their head, Saint Martin on his horse. One observer recalled the event:

> Suddenly the procession came to a halt. A French soldier standing guard at the Augusta Grammar School—still requisitioned as a barracks at the time—clearly feared that a protest demonstration was assembling. He stopped the procession and relieved Saint Martin, at the head of the group, of his sabre. When the soldier saw how many people were pouring out from behind the Rathaus arches, he fired a number of warning shots in the air and retreated. But the children would not be deterred. They raised their voices and marched on, their bright eyes fixed on the torches they carried in front of them. On Clemensstrasse jeeps full of French soldiers drove towards us. But they let us continue on our way and accompanied us to Clemensplatz. In front of their eyes we lit the Saint Martin's Day fire, and as the deacon spoke to the children they drove away.[5]

"My poor shattered Mainz"

In some regions of Germany the annual Carnival is called "the fifth season." Especially along the Rhine and in some areas of southern Germany the "days of madness," celebrated with great exuberance, are of great importance for people. Carnival, also known as Fastnacht, was not celebrated during the war, and a lot of Germans wanted to observe the tradition again once the conflict was over. Carnival has many historical roots; it is, like Roman Saturnalia, a ritual exception to the run of normal life, in which it becomes possible to run riot. With its disrespectful speeches and tolerated lewdness it became an outlet for people who were otherwise pious and disciplined. There is a strong Christian background to Carnival, and it is particularly widespread in Catholic areas. Its conclusion on Ash Wednesday marks the start of Lent in preparation for the Easter celebrations.

In cities along the Rhine the local carnival associations, led by powerful dignitaries, prepare the Rosenmontag (Rose Monday) procession. Caricatured scenes are pulled through the city on floats, focusing on political grievances. These processions, like the whole of Carnival, are a strange mixture of exuberance and dogged club mania, political criticism and sedately bourgeois self-promotion. Wanting to celebrate it under the conditions of Allied occupation seemed like a perverse venture, not least because of the political speeches traditionally delivered under the protection of "fools' licence."

When it came to distributing the necessary permissions for processions, the different occupying nations behaved in unpredictable ways. What one officer prohibited, another would allow without question. While in 1947 the British banned the traditional Rosenmontag procession in Cologne—the highlight of the German carnival held two days before Ash Wednesday, the beginning of Lent—the French practically commanded the people of Mainz to resume their famous carnival tradition, which had not been officially celebrated since the start of the attack on the Soviet Union in 1941. That, at least, is the account given by Karl Moerlé, one of the grandees of the Mainz carnival. In

October 1945 the city's French commander ordered Moerlé and two other men from the senior ranks of the carnival organising committee to come to his quarters. The three citizens—Seppel Glückert, Heinrich Hilsenbeck and Moerlé—appeared before the Frenchman as they had been bidden, punctually, but with a feeling of unease. Only in the rarest of cases did summonses of this kind bode well. They were all the more startled, therefore, when the commander informed them that they were to begin straight away on preparations for the following year's carnival.

The befuddled organisers were uncomfortable with the idea. What one military leader was happy with might not find favour with the next. Moerlé objected that in view of the bleak condition of the city he found it hard to imagine a carnival procession. The French commander refused to accept that argument; the greater the adversity, he insisted, the more necessary the carnival. In the interpretation of one historian of the carnival body, the commander "saw the civic celebration as a form of coping." He thought that the carnival, precisely in view of the bleak situation, would provide an outlet for the nervous energy running through the streets of Mainz, and would give the citizens a much-needed lift in the face of their adversity.[6] If the ageing dignitaries of the club whose purpose was to organise the carnival failed in this task, the military government would turn instead to event organisers from the local catering services and "commission professional entertainment forces."[7]

However, behind the French commander's urging that the revelries should proceed without delay, there may also have lurked a strategy of "deprussianisation," which the French vigorously pursued, hoping that a reinforcement of local cultural traditions in south-west Germany might help to diminish Prussian—and thus, in the eyes of the Allies—militaristic influence.[8]

As it was, in February 1946 Karl Moerlé and Seppel Glückert did not manage to put on a proper Rosenmontag procession, nor was it organised correctly. Traditionally the carnival should be planned by a requisite eleven-strong committee (the "Elferrat," or "Council

The people of Cologne started celebrating carnival again as early as 1946. Three years later the first "official" Rosenmontag procession was held under the motto "Mer sin widder do un dun wat mer künne" (We're back and we're doing what we can).

of Eleven") and managed by designated "Royal Highnonsenses" (citizens who acted as the prince and princess of Mainz for the duration of carnival). Carnival meetings would traditionally parody the government, with a strict hierarchy and ceremonial rules, and the carnival itself was an opportunity to mock authority and humorously comment on current events. But a carnival structured around parody and humour was harder to pull off immediately after the war and under the circumstances of occupation. Despite the challenges, the Mainzers managed to stage some elements of a traditional carnival, with witty speeches and a shyly sung carnival anthem. Seppel Glückert, who had been one of the few semi-courageous carnival orators during the Nazi era, when carnival was co-opted by the Party, reminded the "fools" (as carnival participants are known) of their failures as citizens, in a satirical verse typical of the local carnival style:

> For seven years, say it quite openly
> We have been robbed again
> and our city with its alleyways
> made to bleed from a thousand wounds.
>
> And before the war—do you want to know?
> We had to beat our breasts
> those of us who could not find
> the courage to free ourselves from servitude.
>
> We called "heil heil!" ceaselessly
> and let me add one other thing:
> many of our brothers and sisters
> that eternal "Heil" of former times
> whether spoken or sung
> never sounded in their hearts.[9]

Carnival verses such as the above were partly self-accusation and partly self-exculpation, and thus by the standards of the time involve quite a considerable confession of guilt. In St. Ingbert in the western Saarland region, at the carnival meeting of the Frohsinn Male Voice Choir Association, they sang: "We were all of us in the Party! My dad was in the Party! My mum was in the Party! My sister was in the Party!" and so on, all the way through all the family members.[10]

In the neighbouring occupied zone 180 kilometres to the north, the British didn't need to prompt the people of Cologne to party. In the extremely depopulated city, in which at the end of the war only 40,000 residents were left out of 770,000, a small carnival procession had been established as early as 1946, and moved through the ghostly ruins of the devastated city.

Over mountains of rubble, on paths through detritus and piles of stones, paths that had once been proud streets, whole groups of children in shabby but original costumes with home-made musical instruments made their way to the ring roads, some of which had been shovelled clear, and assembled themselves into a procession. Faces painted and arm in arm they passed singing through the streets. [. . .] By the time they reached Rudolfplatz, the procession had grown into a crowd of considerable size and of all ages, with many of the adults joining in.[11]

In the chronicles of the association (documents carefully written year by year by the organisers of Cologne's carnival), the organisation of the procession is described as "spontaneous"—although it may not be as spontaneous as all that, given the number of formal demands that carnival organisers require of an orderly procession. A Rosenmontag procession that not everyone takes part in was not in their eyes a procession at all. But the people of Cologne flowed through the city without the usual presence of the president of the association, the *Dreigestirn* ("the three stars" or "triumvirate" represented by the costumed trio of Prince, Peasant and Virgin emblematic of the Cologne carnival) and the so-called Elferrat, or Council of Eleven (the carnival planning committee) and enjoyed relaxed celebrations in makeshift costumes a year later, even when the city council banned "organised parades."

The prohibition was enacted on interesting grounds: "The seriousness of the times hangs over the carnival. So that the character of a popular celebration may be preserved for better days in the future, and in order to avoid any commercial exploitation, the arrangement of organised processions, public masked balls and fancy-dress parties is not permitted for the year 1947." The reference to "commercial exploitation" concerned the close relations between the associations and obscure drinking venues such as the "Concert-Café-Restaurant Atlantic," which were unacceptable to the city's officials because of the feasting and devil-may-care behaviour which they celebrated. The Atlantic was seedy but otherwise undamaged, and its upper floors were always packed to the rafters. The ground-floor restaurant, though, with its flower arrangements, maitre d', sommelier and trainee waiters, was already pretending to be Monte Carlo. It was plain that all this could not have been in line with food rationing. The Atlantic and "other stinking holes like the Pingpong and the Femina"—in the words of Bernhard Günther, an MP with the ruling conservative Christian Democratic Union (CDU)—came up time and again in Cologne City Council debates, since they were a home to black-market dealers and criminals. It was also here that the carnival associations met up again immediately after the end of the war, issuing invitations to "Gentlemen's Meetings" and "Cologne Soirées" at which, in return for a corkage charge, guests could bring black-market "knolly brandy," a home-distilled moonshine made from sugar-beets. Undaunted, the

"Laugh amidst your tears, and you will be their master!" was the slogan of the post-war carnival. "I'll build you up again quickly. You weren't to blame"—that was what they sang to the ruined cities. Montage from the Neue Illustrierte, *1948.*

Funkenmariechen—the carnival cheerleaders—did their high kicks and later strutted along the fire-scorched ruins through the razed and depopulated city to the sounds of the Florentine March.

The busy carnival official Thomas Liessem described the Rosenmontag procession in 1948, the first to be officially organised after the war, as the return of Cologne's identity:

> Before me I no longer saw the four flag-bearers and the police band in their heralds' uniforms. I saw only people wildly rejoicing, although with tears in their eyes. They waved at us from the burned-out empty window frames of the ruins and repeatedly used their handkerchiefs to dry their moist eyes. In the window of a crudely repaired house I saw a couple: the wife wore a cowl hat and a suit from the last century. She waved and wept her heart out as her husband leaned, arms folded, on the window-sill, sobbing uninterruptedly.[12]

Sentimentality has always been a part of the joy of carnival; in the first three post-war years it degenerated into lachrymosity. This was particularly applicable to Mainz, where the carnival motto from the end of the First World War had been dragged out again, "Laugh amidst your tears, and you will be their master!" The famous popular singer Ernst Neger updated the sentimental children's song "Heal, heal, little gosling" with a contemporary verse in which he addressed his ruined city like a crying child that is not to blame for its skinned knee.

> If I were the Lord God today,
> Then there's one thing I would do;
> I would take in my spreading arms
> My poor shattered Mainz.
> And stroke it gently and kindly
> And say, "Just be patient.
> I'll build you up again quickly.
> You weren't to blame.
> I'll make you beautiful again,
> You can't, you must not perish."

The triumph of laughter over tears was the sentiment of the Mainz carnival in 1950, and both tears and wine flowed in ample quantities. That year in Aachen the prize for "dispelling all hated seriousness," the avowed purpose of carnival, was awarded once again. The recipient was a British military attorney with Cologne's lower court, one Mr. James A. Dugdale from Burnley. The reason was pure gratitude: the Englishman had allowed an imprisoned smuggler to leave prison for the three mad days of carnival.

In Cologne the distiller and drinks importer Thomas Liessem presided incognito over the 1948 carnival committee. He had occupied the role of president of the Cologne "Prince's Guard"—the group in charge of the carnival procession—during the Nazi years.[13] Cologne's denazification office refused him a leading position in the carnival on the grounds that he had been an early joiner of the Nazi Party, and also forbade him to speak in public. To get round this rule, the committee put Commander Franz Oberliesen in charge of the Prince's Guard, while Liessem took care of the financial side of things behind the scenes.[14]

Under the motto "Don't complain, join in," the Cologne carnival under the Third Reich had become a spectacle of conformism. And so it remained when Thomas Liessem officially retook the reins in the early 1950s and the carnival became a conventional platform where leading dignitaries presented themselves. However, the Nazis had undermined one particular carnival tradition. They had decreed that the part of the Virgin in the *Dreigestirn* (a triumvirate of three figures, the Prince, the Peasant and the Virgin, who become the honorary "rulers" of Cologne during the festival) was no longer to be played by a man, as custom decreed. The idea of the Virgin being male reeked of transvestism and decadence to them. After the end of the war Cologne's Virgin was once again permitted to be bearded— but that was the only detail in which carnival once again depicted a world turned upside down; in all other respects it developed into a respectable parade of dignitaries, portraying a musty parallel state.[15]

"We're back and we're doing what we can," was the muted motto of the 1949 Cologne Rosenmontag procession. The carnival prince of that season (the figure leading the procession), the beer and wine distributor Theo Röhrig, drew up a list of what was required:

> The splendid prince's costume needed to be acquired, and the clothing for his adjutants, two pages and manservant who stood at his personal disposal. Three hundred princely medals had to be ordered, of first-class quality in bronze and enamel. Two passenger vehicles in the Cologne colours of red and white painted with the princely coat of arms, for him and his immediate entourage, were required, and also a bus for the guards. Also three drivers, one make-up artist, one dresser etc. [. . .] In addition there were the costs for committee meetings. [. . .] And then the items to be thrown from the prince's car: ten hundredweight of bonbons, also pralines, chocolate and several thousand bouquets. [. . .] Summa summarum: the price of a small villa.[16]

Despite the seemingly extravagant list, one member of the Rote Funken ("Red Sparks") carnival team later recalled a very pitiful parade at which Prince Theo had cut a poor figure. But perhaps his recollection took on a grim emphasis in order to reduce the disparity between the joyful procession and the depressing ruined landscape through which it crept, dragon-like, past posters showing an emaciated German prisoner of war behind barbed wire with the caption "Hundreds of thousands of your brothers are still living like this! And you—you're celebrating carnival?"

The occupying powers did not prohibit the satirical political commentaries that are an essential part of carnival. The 1949 Cologne procession, almost two kilometres in length, included a float entitled "Demont-Asch" (a pun on *Demontage*," or "dismantling") on the theme of the destruction of German industry. It included a papier-mâché figure of John Bull (representing England) using a carpenter's plane to smooth the naked backside of a *Michel* figure—the German equivalent of John Bull. This national personification of Germans often appeared in his nightgown and nightcap and alluded to a simple-minded, easy-going nature. Again and again the "Trizonesia song"

The carnival associations dared to make political statements again. On the float of the Lyskircher Junge in 1949 we see John Bull (personifying the UK) taking a plane to the backside of a figure representing Germany, while Uncle Sam (representing the US) holds him down—the "Demont-Asch."

was sung, the new carnival anthem of the inhabitants of the "Trizone." This had originated in April 1949, when the French zone of occupation joined the already existing Anglo-American "Bizone." A short time later, in September 1949, with the establishment of the Bundestag, this would turn into the Federal Republic:

> We are the natives of Trizonesia,
> Hei-di-tschimmela-tschimmela-tschimmela-tschimmela-bumm!
> We have lasses of fiery wild nature,
> Hei-di-tschimmela-tschimmela-tschimmela-tschimmela-bumm!
> We may not be cannibals
> but we're expert kissers.
> We are the natives of Trizonesia,
> Hei-di-tschimmela-tschimmela-tschimmela-tschimmela-bumm!

In terms that were already offensive at the time, the song's lyrics flirted with the idea that the occupied Germans were in some way as oppressed as indigenous people in colonised countries. German racists, of all people, now referred to themselves as "natives." Only for fun, they would claim, since the song would assert that Germany was in fact a nation of poets and thinkers, reminding the occupiers rather coarsely in the two last verses:

> But, foreign man, just so you know,
> a Trizonesian has a sense of humour,
> he has culture, and he also has spirit,
> so that no one pulls the wool over his eyes.

> Even Goethe comes from Trizonesia.
> Beethoven's cradle is well known.
> No, there is no such thing in Chinesia
> so we are proud of our land . . .

The Cologne baker Karl Berbuer, known as "the crazy bread roll," had written the song to the tune of a well-known march. In December 1948 the ditty was captured on disc, and became one of the five best-selling records of the years immediately after the war. The London *Times* wrote about the Trizonesia anthem as performed by the "crazy bread roll" under the headline THE GERMANS ARE GETTING CHEEKY AGAIN! The ditty was so widely known that it was sometimes played for want of a national anthem at the first international sporting events in which Germans participated, once even in the presence of Konrad Adenauer, Germany's first post-war chancellor. He reported in April 1950 at a press conference:

I think it was the previous year, there was a sporting event against Belgium in the stadium in Cologne. There were some uniformed members of the Belgian military present. Eventually the national anthems were played. When the German national anthem was due to be played the band, which plainly had a very efficient and quick-witted conductor, struck up the fine carnival song "I Am a Native of Trizonesia." [. . .] Many Belgian soldiers rose to their feet and saluted because they thought it was the national anthem.[17]

Because of such stories about the use of a frivolous carnival song as a national anthem, Adenauer managed to see to it that the third stanza of the German anthem the *Deutschlandlied*, his personal choice, was adopted remarkably quickly without much discussion as the national anthem of the Federal Republic in 1952.[18]

We need to devote particular consideration to the rambunctious carnival activity of the post-war years, positioned as it was within an intellectual space defined in many ways by seriousness and excessive drama. Contemporaries tripped over themselves to dress up the intellectual situation of the time in maximalist phrases that placed German suffering over that of Germany's victims. In the words of poet Ernst Wiechert's much-parodied "Rede an die deutsche Jugend 1945" ("Address to the Youth of Germany 1945"):

Here we stand in front of an abandoned house and see the eternal stars sparkling above the rubble of the earth [. . .]. More alone than any people was ever alone on this Earth. More reviled than any people was ever reviled. And we lean our brows against the broken walls, and our lips whisper humanity's old question: What are we to do?[19]

According to the Russian cultural historian Mikhail Bakhtin, the purpose of the laughter of carnival, dating back to the origin of such celebrations in the Renaissance, was to "upend the world orders." It was, he argued, the laughter of a people trying to put into perspective the world history it was heir to, and hence it was a laughter of fear as well as regret:

The ambivalent laughter of carnival in which death and rebirth, negation and affirmation, mockery and triumph are inseparably fused, is a universal, utopian and philosophical laughter.[20]

Not all Germans could understand the appeal of carnival, certainly not the Protestants from the far north of the country. In 1947 the reporters of Hamburg's *Der Spiegel* wrote about the madness that had broken out upon the shores of the Rhine. Their colleagues from the *Rheinischer Merkur* had tried to explain to readers the catharsis of carnival in these terms: "Carnival requires of the human being a transformation, an active involvement and devotion. In it the evil, the heathen in humanity finds expression. In a sense people are de-demonised for the whole year." That didn't work, *Der Spiegel* was pleased to conclude its report: "On Ash Wednesday the de-demonised citizens of Cologne sought in vain for their pickled herring"—a reference to the fish feast with which the Cologne carnival traditionally concluded.[21]

The Berlin journalist and author Arnold Bauer, accustomed to excess from his party-mad hometown, attended Munich's carnival in 1949 for the *Neue Zeitung* and described it as the ultimate purgatory. He saw the tiled swimming pool of a hotel, converted into a dance floor, as a "dance pit" in which the bodies of the poor souls writhed as the "temperature of civilised barbarianism rose to a boiling point." In the city's Haus der Kunst art museum, old and new divinities of the silver screen sat "posed like statues, as if on sacrificial altars." Deranged fauns and abdicated Caesars slipped among them as "onlookers of D-mark prosperity, draining the last dregs of the champagne glass." Among the costumed revellers the journalist spotted "hermaphrodites" and even the occasional "exotic with the charm of the subtropical regions." Arnold Bauer viewed the scene, in spite of his displeasure, as a sign of people coming together:

A slowly healing society needs, as a corresponding contrast, Bohème. The social world is only healthy when it can also tolerate parasites. Champagne at the Grand Hotel, the dregs in the red-light district. That is what the moral law decrees. The social decline of this country initially dragged everyone down with it. Everyone was one of the outlaws of the world. The reformation that is now beginning will force the renegade back into isolation. [. . .] Babylon is gone—long live Schwabylon!![22]

This last pun makes reference to Munich's bohemian Schwabing district.

Carnival became a popular metaphor for the Janus-headed nature of post-war Germany. The defeated society was shifting slowly into one based on merrymaking. The figurative painting of those years abounded in masked figures, sad clowns, melancholy dancers and weeping and crying faces.

The Rosenmontag tradition was restricted to the south and west of the country where Catholicism predominated, while in the Protestant north and east substitute parties, similarly excessive, were celebrated quite independent of the Church calendar. In Berlin, artists had organised the first "fantasists' ball" around the Gerd Rosen Gallery in 1946, at which, for want of suitable materials, the crudest imaginable costumes were worn, and licentious behaviour was positively encouraged. The decorations on the walls were fantastical, as one might have expected from respected contemporary artists like Heinz Trökes, a painter and friend of Kandinsky's, the Surrealist painter Mac Zimmermann and the painter and sculptor Hans Uhlmann. Heart and soul of the party was the troubled hellraiser Werner Heldt, who in 1949, together with a coterie of actors, writers and painters, founded the whimsically named artists' cabaret and jazz club "Badewanne" (Bathtub) in the basement of the Femina Bar in Charlottenburg, where grotesque Dadaist-inspired performances were staged.[23]

These post-war parties weren't so much dancing on a sinking ship as on one that had already capsized. The partygoers were amazed that they were still alive, and consequently prone to giddiness. The first real German post-war hit, "Drei Geschichten" (Three Stories), recorded by Evelyn Künnecke in 1946, was a nonsense song about, among other things, a knight fishing from high on a cliff but never catching anything. "But why? But why?" Künnecke sang with affectionate bemusement, and resolved the matter thus: "The reel didn't reach the sea." A lament in its form, silly in its subject matter, the ditty revealed the emergence of a quirky sense of humour.

The bafflingly good mood that many Germans found themselves

Bouncing in Bavaria. German and American musicians rubbed shoulders in the US Army jazz clubs. The main thing was that it had to swing.

in reminded the historian Friedrich Prinz of the traditional funeral feasts enjoyed by some societies.

> After Mars the God of War had cleared the field [poverty and misery still prevailed] but people still partook in that mood that suddenly spreads at big funerals in farming communities. As soon as the corpse is in the ground, the mourners, coming back from the cemetery, turn towards the funeral feast in the inn and merriment spreads at first hesitantly, then ever more emphatically, a feeling of joy at not yet having been stripped of the "sweet habit of existence."[24]

No feast could have done justice to this particular funeral; if a balance had been struck between the sheer quantity of mourning required and the funeral feast then the nation would have been trapped forever in a hysterical bacchanalia. But since for complex reasons surrounding the nation's guilt the majority of Germans had been denied the opportunity to mourn, as Margarete and Alexander Mitscherlich saw it in their great study *The Inability to Mourn*, the feast was manifested as a mood of often disconcerting licentiousness, which was certainly not without significance. The funeral feast is a universal anthropological phenomenon. It is one of the few rituals common to almost all cultures, albeit in different forms and intensities. Sad yet merry get-togethers are seen as a ritual both of grief and its repression; for many people they are an indispensable way of coping with death, in which the juxtaposition of contradictory feelings is ritualised.

While dancing went on in the ruins, death was omnipresent and anonymous. Some places still literally smelled of corpses—places where the war was fading particularly slowly. The businessman and art collector Max Leon Flemming had experienced this in his villa in Berlin's Tiergarten district, in one of the most heavily damaged areas of the city. Everything around him had been bombed to pieces and further flattened during the final battle; the neighbouring villas had once overflowed with pretty ornaments, which now lay in the rubble of their upper storeys. After the global economic crisis of 1929, Flemming, who had been phenomenally wealthy, had lived there "from wall to mouth," as one museum director put it, living off the gradual sale of his large art collection. He had become a respected member of the Berlin art scene, and after the war, along with Gerd Rosen, he co-founded the Rosen Gallery, which became the leading Berlin gallery of post-war modern art.

On 7 September 1946 Max Leon Flemming invited his many friends and acquaintances to a "Dance Overlooking the Ruins." Everyone received an invitation hand-painted in watercolours, on which, beneath a sketched ruined landscape of their surroundings, a typed message bade them to "dance into the greyish Sunday morning." The place: "4 Margaretenstrasse, third and fourth floor, in the middle of the Green Hell of the Pompeian-Berlin ruins," in the only house in the Tiergarten district "whose upper storeys have been preserved specially for this pious purpose." Costumes were optional: "Ladies little, gentlemen more." He asked his guests to bring alcohol if possible, and also to bring rationed bread and potatoes, the potatoes plainly boiled for preference. Having announced that the guests would be served "tomatoes from his own ruined garden," he added in a postscript: "And here is one more post-war request: please bring a glass and a fork." The events of the evening went unrecorded, but the party—once the guests had picked their way through the rubble—was no doubt a roaring success.

V

Love Amidst the Rubble

Homecoming of the burned-out men

One word that universally captures the idea of longing is "homecoming." In the post-war period, however, it lost much of its magic. To our present-day ears "homecoming" sounds like a brief, one-off process. But coming home from war and imprisonment was a long and often inconclusive undertaking. People spoke of *Heimkehrer* (literally: homecomers) as if coming home were a state of being, a profession or even a disability. Coming home was an endless process: one had come home and yet one had not. Even years after their return, some men were termed *Heimkehrer* as a way of excusing their strange behaviour.

Hundreds of thousands of German mothers and grandmothers talked about how their husbands, after many years, had suddenly turned up at the front door, holding discharge papers as if to identify themselves.[1] Or how a scruffy man in a soldier's coat had been loitering in the street outside the house. How he had kept staring up at her window, and how it had only gradually dawned on her that the man downstairs must be her husband. Or how someone down in the courtyard had approached her son so persistently that she had wanted to throw him out, and how her son had finally stood up and said: "Look, it's Dad."

Many had longed for the moment of return. In the nation's living rooms photographs stood in for the men while they were at the front.

Children were encouraged to look at them over and over again, so that the father could lodge at least in their imaginations. There he stood on the shelf in the best room as if on an altar, almost always in his uniform, with daughters on either side, looking seriously from under the huge brim of his military cap. He was somewhere in Russia or Egypt; back home the presumed spot where the picture was taken was looked up on a map and pointed out to the children. Far away from everyday life, he became the promise of a better life that would come once the war was over. The husband's return would mean an end to loneliness, to the constant stress involved in bringing up children alone under extreme conditions, and keeping them safe through air raids and scarcity. Every scrap of news from the front was precious, however bad. Dying men called out their wives' names to their comrades and they, amidst the panic of battle, struggled to keep those names in their heads so that they could later pass the message on. The women who came to railway stations clutching their husbands' photographs and studied the stream of returning men remained in the collective memory, even decades later. And many a soldier will have pulled from his pocket, for the umpteenth time, the crumpled picture of his wife, at least to keep fresh the memory of her face among the overwhelming sensations of the war.

And then all of a sudden he was standing at the door, barely recognisable, scruffy, emaciated and hobbling. A stranger, an invalid. The shock of the sight of him was described countless times, particularly when he came back from Russian prison camps. Eyes stared out of dark hollows from which all delight in life seemed to have vanished. The shaven skulls and sunken cheeks intensified the impression of one half-dead. Most children stoutly refused to sit on the knee of a ghost.

There were disappointments on the soldiers' part too. "I barely recognised my wife," one returnee later said. "I'd been away for ten years. There were admittedly some similarities with the wife I'd left behind, but the years of hardship had aged her. She was no longer the young, respectable girl that I had dreamed of so often. She was scrawny and grey and looked miserable."[2]

Usually though it was the other way around. Post-war German women often looked startlingly good, even as a *Trümmerfrau* in action. As long as the simplest cosmetic products were available, the need to "look one's best" remained intact, even under the harshest conditions. Returning men on the other hand generally had a neglected appearance. But appearances were easily dealt with. Harder to overcome was the inner devastation that was clear to all soon after their arrival.

The typical *Heimkehrer* was bad-tempered and ungrateful. He lay around sick on the couch, if there was one, and even though his family members had looked forward to seeing him again for so long, he made their lives hell. He was in pain, of course, but every day he let his family know just how much pain he was in. Very few of the men had expected to find their country, which had been bombed and occupied, so transformed on their return. Above all, it was now a country run by women, and as a result their wives had changed too. Rather than being pleased that their wives had managed without them, it made them feel uneasy. One man who had been deployed first with the German auxiliary naval force and then, having been seriously wounded in the Volkssturm national militia, frankly explained how he no longer got on with his wife:

> It took me a long time to understand that she had learned to say "I" while I had been away. She would always say, "*I* have," "*I* am." And I would always say, "I'm sorry, *we* have" and "*we* want." We only learned to interact with one another very slowly. We barely knew each other. We worked out how much time we had spent together in the seven years that we had known each other. It came to a total of 231 days.

During the war years women had learned that a city could be run without men. They had driven trams, cranes and bulldozers, cut screw-threads and rolled metal plates, they had taken over parts of public administration and the management of companies, although it was forced labourers rather than the women themselves who did the hardest work. They had learned to repair bicycles, attach gutters and replace electric wires. They had debunked all the arcane mysteries with which men in the pre-war era had performed their privileged jobs. And they had become used to making the most important decisions by themselves. They had arranged with the evacuation authorities to lodge their children near certain relatives, they had intervened in school problems and distributed household tasks fairly among the children. They had cut Hitler Youth squad leaders down to size and done their best to drive from their sons' heads any fancy ideas they might have had of being members of a master race. They had exerted authority and demonstrated toughness, but in many cases they had also turned their children into partners with whom they could discuss survival strategies, even if the children were really far too young for such responsibility.

Without fathers, many families had transformed themselves into a conspiratorial gang whose members relied on one another more than ever before. And those arrangements persisted during the prevailing chaos after the end of the war. The women profited from the mobility and resourcefulness of their children, and the children from their mothers' far-sightedness. With a little luck their talents dovetailed perfectly. The children looted and stole, the mothers fenced stolen goods, parlayed scarcity, haggled and exchanged. Many children were smarter at dealing with the black market than their mothers were, and sending them on thieving expeditions seemed less dangerous. The children's homes were so overcrowded that there was no need to fear arrest for that very reason. Children were unbeatable at running away through the rubble. They could usually evade the competition of the real criminals and were not taken seriously by either the police or the occupying soldiers.

In this ethical grey area, where in the past many rules had been broken for reasons of naked survival, mothers still tried to provide their children with a moral compass that kept a sense of goodness awake in them. This was a mammoth task which the mothers, seen from the distance of the present day, performed with distinction. No one at the time could have predicted that this generation of children would later, statistically speaking, become excessively ambitious, social-climbing, law-abiding young adults (unlike the future rebels of the 1960s and '70s, who were still in nappies in 1945). It is one of the most astonishing achievements to which wartime and post-war mothers can lay claim.

When the husbands came back home, they quite naturally assumed that would mean taking up their old positions as "head of the household" once again. But that position was not relinquished without a fight, particularly since most men no longer seemed fit for the role. They often reasserted themselves at home by the worst means available: accusations and bitterness. They couldn't suppress the feeling of being superfluous—and the better-off their family appeared to be, the more superfluous they felt. And yet on the other hand, if the family was in a state of financial hardship, there was little the returning husband could do to ease matters. For the time being he lived off his family. Out of shame, many of these men demeaned their wives' achievements. As a result, many returnees came across chiefly as curmudgeonly complainers: "Not a single kind word ever issued from his mouth. All he ever did was growl and curse. I tried to overlook some things that were really insensitive. In fact I never really got him back emotionally."[3]

Shortly after her husband's return, one woman dared to splash out on a roast for the first time in years to celebrate the joyous event. She proudly laid the table, but the children were extremely clumsy in their handling of the meat.

And my husband got very annoyed. [. . .] He thought I hadn't brought them up well and shouted at me and the children. During the blockade everything had been powdered, so the children didn't know how to eat with a knife and fork. They only knew how to use spoons, because there was nothing to cut.[4]

The homecomers' relationship with their children was the most difficult of all. Most returnees had hardly seen their children, and in some cases returned to meet them for the first time. They found it difficult to connect with their offspring and were jealous of their conspiratorial and playful relationships with their mothers. They thought their children were spoilt and often tried to whip them into shape with regimens of punishment and bullying drills that they remembered from the army. For a bad mark at school it was twenty-five sit-ups. Some former sailors performed the "Lucie Flagge" drill: on command the child had to change into their pyjamas within two minutes and fold the clothing they had taken off on a chair. Many mothers advised their husbands to try love, and to slowly build up their relationships with their children. But it was no good. The alienation between fathers and children, particularly with sons, often assumed dramatic forms. Children who had grown older than their years in the post-war months, hoarding and trading on the black market, couldn't see why they should suddenly submit to a sickly, useless tyrant, and the world war was followed by small-scale family wars. Women, unable to obtain divorces, which were quite difficult because of the state of the laws at the time, wore themselves out mediating, compromising and establishing fragile peace treaties.

Many marriages with *Heimkehrer* husbands collapsed because each partner felt nothing but disdain for what the other had endured. It wasn't just women who felt a lack of recognition, the men did too. Many soldiers only really grasped that they had lost the war when they returned to their families. It wasn't the sight of the male victors striding through the occupied country that brought home the defeat, all it took was the wife's—often imagined—pitying look at the sorry figure of the returning husband for them to feel humiliated. They also felt doubly responsible for the family's poverty; first through helping to start the war, and second by losing it. As protector of the family, this feeling of failure on a personal level usually weighed heavier than their guilt for Nazi crimes.

Doctors at the time identified the mental illnesses of those returning from the war as a complex of symptoms called "dystrophia," based on deprivations of one kind or another. Extreme collective experiences of hunger over long periods of time had profoundly changed not only the body but the psyche as well. In 1953 *Der Spiegel* reviewed a book on the subject by the psychotherapist Kurt Gauger and quoted:

All concepts and possibilities of customs and morality, ethics and law, cleanliness and corruption, comradeship and betrayal, even religiosity and bestiality, revolve around a terrible, animal re-evaluation of the subject of food.

Hunger led to an introverted egoism that then became a habit. Those suffering from dystrophia were not capable, even later, of thinking of anything other than themselves.[5]

The shame of defeat was in no way diminished by the fact that many wives made it quite clear to their husbands that they thought their soldiering skills left much to be desired. One woman who was 35 at the end of the war told the historians Sibylle Meyer and Eva Schulze how her husband had been taken prisoner with a whole troop of older soldiers and deported to Russia, even though they'd had many chances to overwhelm their guards:

> The Russians ordered the troops to go with them to Küstrin. They promised them that they would be released according to the regulations once they got there. The Russians understood the Germans very well, and knew that Germans needed discharge papers. And the old soldiers fell for it. It was a very odd story. And when they got to Küstrin they were told they had to travel on to Posen. So on they all trotted to Posen. They could have overpowered their guards easily, since there weren't very many of them. They dutifully trotted along to Posen! Then in Posen the squaddies were loaded on to wagons and carted all the way to Russia.[6]

In these lines we can sense a hint of almost pleasurable contempt combined with a loving pity for the husband. The feeling of having been collectively abandoned by their husbands was expressed time and again: "You just had to go and play your war games!"

In the first issue of the women's magazine *Constanze*, which published in March 1948, the writer and marriage counsellor Walther von Hollander described a wife's disenchantment. The wives had discovered that there were few heroes in the army, and in fact only a

Hildegard Knef behind the camera. "German men lost the war," she said, "now they want to win it again in the bedroom."

"dull-witted mass that was anything but heroic, a herd intimidated by sheepdogs which, at the shepherds' whistles, were trained to drive the sheep and keep them together." Many of the women, on the other hand, had found themselves having to act "more bravely, independently and death-defyingly" than this herd of men, "without the women having been honoured, cared for, given preferential treatment and decorated with medals."

Once this was acknowledged, the men's reputation plummeted in women's eyes. The journalist Marta Hillers wrote in her diary late in April 1945:

Deep down we women are experiencing a kind of collective disappointment. The Nazi world—ruled by men, glorifying the strong man—is beginning to crumble, and with it the myth of "Man." In earlier wars men could claim that the honour of killing and being killed for the fatherland was theirs and theirs alone. Today we women, too, have a share. That has transformed us, emboldened us. Among the many defeats at the end of this war is the defeat of the male sex.[7]

Many marriages were in any case not very durable, because they had been forged hastily during short leaves from the front. Couples had married to ensure that a beloved had a widow's pension, or to get a soldier a few days' break from battle. These relationships carried within them the memory of the Nazi regime's heyday, in which everything seemed to be getting better and wide sections of the population were able to enjoy luxuries they had never known before, as long as they were "Aryan." These were the marriages formed during a surge in prosperity, spurred on by pride in early victories and the primitive arrogance that resulted. Those grandiose fantasies still echoed as man and wife now sat facing one another in their new squalor. The demise of these romances, which had begun in an intoxicating rush and with the promises defiantly made against all the risks of war, was much more precipitous than the typical cooling associated with bourgeois marriages.

There were magazines that encouraged divorce, and those that vehemently urged that the couples give each other another chance. In December 1945, the author Manfred Hausmann published a letter "To a returnee" in the famous American-sponsored *Neue Zeitung* newspaper. He held that it was not only the lows of the war, but interestingly also the highs that were responsible for the fact that it was so hard for returning soldiers to find peace with their wives at home.

The war hauled you away overnight. It threw you into the most foreign countries. You saw the south, the easy charm of life in Greece, the bright colours of the Balkans, the great expanse of the Black Sea. You saw the boundless steppes of Russia, the mighty rivers, the frightening forests, the monstrous wastes. That in itself was a great deal. It had a stirring and shattering effect on your soul. But the rest of it was even greater. You had to fight, to burn, to destroy and to kill. You heard cries and saw faces that you will never forget. Now you know both the self-sacrifice of which mankind is capable, and the terrible depths of depravity to which he can plunge. You know destruction in all its forms. You have stared death in its empty eyes time and again. You have experienced how insignificant and lost a man can feel as he stumbles through the world's darkness. You have eradicated human lives, and strengthened your own a hundredfold by taking it to the edge. You have been more of a master than you ever were before or ever will be again. And time and again you have been driven harder than any slave. What you have been through, both the very high and the very low, obedience and coercion, risk and loss, triumph and despair, brotherhood and isolation, heaven and hell, that will never leave you. As one so changed, so deeply changed, you have returned home and turned up in front of your wife.[8]

Primeval man in the midst of terrible destruction, the hunter with his heightened senses, the unparalleled master, the figure of this brave warrior—these figures were hard to reconcile with the pitiful wraith in the unheated kitchen that was reported by a consensus of women. And yet that image must have tormented many returnees. After the war it took a deluge of realistic novels about returning soldiers for people to say farewell to the heroic image of the warrior and come to terms with the bleak reality of burn-outs. How were they to talk about this transformation to their wives, who now had to work on building sites because the proud warrior could no longer feed his family?

Hausmann had fewer sympathetic things to say regarding women's wartime experiences. The heroic rhetoric didn't really apply in this context, particularly since Hausmann imagined a wife as someone whose entire existence revolved around her absent husband and his possessions:

Do you think it was easy for her to assume responsibility for the upbringing of the children and the sole administration of your possessions? If you compare her experiences with yours, and don't forget that you are a man and she's a woman, then you can't help admitting that her sufferings are no less great than yours.

Particularly telling is the fact that Hausmann plays down the issue of property relations, since the chief topic of this newspaper article was the possibility of divorce. If after the war the couple still had possessions, then the wife had only been responsible for their "administration." In the event that the couple were not reconciled, Hausmann was anticipating the result in a spirit of male solidarity.

In happier cases the marital warfare ended in a long-lasting cease-fire. Couples learned to come to terms with each other, they adapted and made compromises. These laboriously consolidated marriages were usually sober affairs. Later the children couldn't imagine how they had been conceived in the first place, their parents' marriage having been so passionless. Often the bedrooms were the most inhospitable rooms in the apartment: unheated, the bed surrounded by armoires with suitcases dumped on top of them, sadly lit by a single ceiling light, they gave a clear statement of what their inhabitants thought of love.

Constanze strolls through the world

German women's magazines such as *Die Frau*, *Lilith*, *Regenbogen* or *Constanze* give us a special insight into the post-war period. They contained everything from everyday and practical ideas on how one could make oneself look nice to articles contemplating what would become of the vanquished country. In terms of circulation figures, *Constanze* was the flagship. From 1948 until 1969, when it was closed down and replaced by its rejuvenated successor *Brigitte*, it developed into one of the most successful women's illustrated magazines in the Federal Republic. The first issue was published in March 1948 and was edited by Hans Huffzky, who had previously been editor of the Nazi magazine *Die junge Dame*. From that magazine's editorial team he brought along Ruth Andreas-Friedrich, who would later become famous for her wartime diaries. Huffzky had a very acute sense of the psychological uncertainties of the time, and above all for what women thought and wanted to read. In the very first edition, in an essay entitled "Hats off to our women!" he confessed to his own "crisis of manhood":

> Ladies, hasn't something struck you yet about us men? Haven't you noticed that we're no longer the good old pre-war version? We have lost our former qualities. We no longer hold the old "positions" that we once did (in Bavaria, for example, 64 per cent of officials and 46 per cent of clerks were dismissed as a result of the denazification law). We no longer carry machine-guns, and can't tell you heroic tales anymore either. We wear our last ties and our next-to-last socks. And the 200 marks—at the very most—that we put on the table at the end of the month are no longer worth so much as a pound of butter. Our kisses on your patient foreheads no longer have the same melting fire. We don't bring boxes of sweets home anymore, and instead—if you aren't looking—we steal the last piece of sugar from your cupboard (later we say: It must have been one of the children!).

It was a powerful piece of self-reproach, expressed with great control and with a keen sense for the important details. Lest anyone imagine that *Constanze* was telling women what they wanted to hear, Huffzky added that men, too, felt that there was now "something rotten in the state of man." And he followed this with a sentence that hit home powerfully: "Each of us carries his own whiner around within him. Buried deep within his conscience, which makes it even worse."

Having expressed this cosy contrition, the editor-in-chief turned to the economic reality of his readers:

> Do you know Frau Müller, dear reader? She's the one whose husband is a clerk and earns 180 marks a month. Everyone knows how far that will go when it comes to feeding a family. More important than those 180 marks that Herr Müller brings home at the end of every month is the lunch that Frau Müller puts on the table every day. Her husband

has no idea that this is a unique piece of magic and requires a thousand little household tips and pointers. It's not only food. It is also the washing that needs to be kept in order. This Frau Müller is duplicated in millions of copies. She is the most German of women. We men see her, when it occurs to us, doing her daily work: cooking, washing, sewing, gardening, scrubbing, queueing, swapping, hammering, nailing, chopping wood, darning, mending, bringing up children, feeding rabbits, knitting the milkman a jumper . . . while we, in some office or other, far from the empty pots at home, are earning 180 marks at some meaningless occupation. If we should take our hats off to anyone, we men, then it's not to kings and emperors, not to priests and presidents, not to political leaders and company directors—we should doff them, as one man, to our wives.[9]

Doff your hats as one man! You don't smooth the jagged edges of the German man quite as quickly as that. And Huffzky doesn't stop there; another, more radical, argument is making itself apparent in the essay. While housework is emphatically highlighted and men's work dismissed as "meaningless" toil "in some office or other," the suspicion arises that what is being delineated here is an imbalance in the labour market. And sure enough, the idea that women might wield the levers of power "side-by-side with men" was a suggestion that Huffzky made in one of his most audacious statements: "I am so bold as to claim that they are well on the way to being leaders who, arm-in-arm with their husbands, or what is still usefully left of him, will one day be able to forge the destiny of our country." The idea was not in fact all that bold, as we know today. And yet for the time, the radicalism with which men are programmatically cut down to size in this first edition of *Constanze* is astonishing. In issues that followed, *Constanze* repeatedly showcased women who worked as the heads of companies and political and administrative departments.

Aside from that, of course, there were adverts for swimwear, and spring and autumn fashions, often remarkably well presented: on the left would be a page entitled "Constanze gets dressed" with suits, blouses and coats, and on the right "Constanze gets undressed" with taffeta petticoats and combinations. Under the heading "Constanze strolls through the world" there were articles about women wrestlers, cute lion cubs, obscure accidents and quadruplets. One piece asked the question "How manly is the American man?" Divorce tips were provided frequently, and readers were encouraged to be independent, for example to ride motorcycles. There were matter-of-fact reports about "taxi girls" who could be hired as conversation partners in bars. The occasional handsome man did appear in *Constanze*, but the magazine devoted much more space to women's faces, promoting an ideal based on both pride and a zest for life. And time and again—particularly in the

Female counterculture, 1947. It was a shock for many German parents when their daughter set off on the long journey west, "dressed in the style of an American teenager."

articles of the novelist and advice columnist Walther von Hollander—men were presented as burned-out losers who, with their penchant for aggression, had led the world into the worst disaster of all time.

It was a fundamental female conviction that the lost war had been a male invention, even though women had in no way lagged behind men in their enthusiasm for Hitler. In the pious women's magazine *Der Regenbogen*, published in Munich, which included traditional pictures of saints, images of gardens and dainty depictions of mothers rather than the racy, hedonistic representations of women that appeared in *Constanze*, men were seen as the chief cause of war. "The

The front page of the Neue Illustrierte *from 1948 confirms women's independence. They couldn't afford to stay at home. But they didn't feel like it anyway.*

world of men, which we allowed to become self-aggrandising, has suffered a shipwreck: the ruins are visible enough," Elfriede Alscher wrote in issue no. 8 in 1946. Women were, on the other hand, as long as they remained true to themselves, inclined towards peace: "Just as the woman who brings life into the world must always hate life-destroying war, she can never, if she is to remain true to her inner- most feelings, agree with a dictatorship."

In their life-giving role as mothers, women were presented as the polar opposite to men, who were governed by their death drives. This image combined the arguments of women's rights advocates with the idolisation of housework, as proposed by Hans Huffzky in *Con-stanze*. At the time, housework was viewed by many women as the foundation of a new political confidence. The Stuttgart politician Anna Haag, a member of the constituent regional assembly of Württemburg-Baden in 1946, evoked housework as the core of social life. "Our household must inevitably interest us above all else. This is not a matter of frills and furbelows, but of the life and death of our loved ones: about hunger and cold!" she exclaimed in a speech to a women's assembly of the Social Democratic Party in Karlsruhe in 1946. She also demanded more political representation of women, with her ideal being two thirds women, one third men.

> As this is about nothing less than the nature of our life on earth, about living and food, work and income, school and child-rearing, women and jobs, [. . .] war and peace, henceforth we women will have to bring to political activities the seriousness that they deserve![10]

The reality was a long way from Haag's suggested ratio. In 1949 in Bavaria just 8 per cent of women were active in public institutions, including church community organisations, and in the 1950s only 1 per cent of women in Bavaria were members of a political party.[11] They were better represented in the "cross-party women's commit- tees" founded in the four occupied zones immediately after the end of the war. These were supposed to support the military administra- tions by easing the worst grievances suffered by society. Mocked as "potato politics," some women's committees developed into powerful political associations, which enjoyed their greatest victory when the lawyer Elisabeth Selbert—one of only four women out of a total of 65 members of the Parliamentary Council—was able to introduce a controversial passage into the constitution of the soon-to-be-founded Federal Republic: "Men and women have equal rights."[12] These exceptions aside, however, traditional politics for a long time remained a man's domain. True to their often-cited life-affirming sensibility, women turned to the practical things of life, and chief among these, alongside food, was sex. It was a no less effective way of doing politics.

"Greedy for life, thirsty for love"

Women's independence, enforced by the anarchy of a country in collapse and men's failure, led to a boost in sexual activity. As in the late 1920s, when a new class of young female office workers adopted a "brazen" tone that had not been seen before, the post-war period was similarly energised by women who no longer wanted to be told what to do, and spoke for themselves all the more clearly. "I don't just want to be charming, I need to earn money," announces a young school-leaver in the 1948 film *Morgen ist alles besser* (*Everything Will Be Better in the Morning*), addressing an elderly gentleman who is smarmily heaping her with compliments. All the film's sympathies are with the girl; that fresh tone was precisely what more forward-looking circles in post-war society were keen to hear more of.

We hear over and over again that in 1945 Germany was a land of women. It's true, but in a shocking way it also isn't. The wave of rapes in the first few weeks after the arrival of the Red Army had confronted women with raw masculine aggression. There were also repeated attacks by soldiers in the western occupied zones. Vagrant criminals, veterans who had lost their homes, freed forced labourers with a lot of rage in their bellies, and various men with all kinds of mental disorders made everyday life for women a life-threatening experience. But that didn't mean that women were defeated—they continued to venture out in ever greater numbers. It wasn't just that they couldn't afford to stay anxiously in the home; they didn't want to anyway. The organisation of food supplies involved legwork that is unimaginable today, and black market expeditions led them far across town. And it wasn't just supplies; gathering news about relatives, friends and former workmates was also vital for survival. Women exchanged tips, kept networks active, and had to generally stay on the ball, and because there were no telephones, they walked, all across the cities and from village to village.

When they weren't hurrying briskly back and forth, they were often simply going for a walk. A surprising number of shots from newsreels and amateur documentaries show women strolling, some in groups, most of them alone. By the summer of 1945 cafes had already opened on the Kurfürstendamm. Those who could afford it—and there were many of them—sat in the sun and were served refreshments. Others just strolled about. The British Pathé newsreels mocked the "fashion" of the Berlin women on the Kurfürstendamm, showing their thick woollen socks paired with fashionably short dresses. One young woman appeared on screen in flat, homemade shoes that she had decorated with paper flowers—which might be considered quite modish today.

As dangerous as the times may have been, the desire for adventure continued unabated. The "incredible intensification of the sense of life by the permanent proximity of death" that Margret Boveri had described in her diary also found sexual expression. Many women yearned to at last experience something once more. The occasional ecstatic spirit of optimism in the first months after the war, mixed with the agitations of anxiety and loneliness, led to a sexual hunger which could sometimes assume bizarre features. Quite perplexing to today's ears is the 1946 pop song "S.O.S. Ich suche dringend Liebe" ("SOS, I'm Urgently in Search of Love"), in which the 22-year-old actress and dancer Ingrid Lutz sang of the sexual famine of those days. "Stop, stop, stop," she barks at her audience, and it sounds like the aggressive call of a guard hunting down a fugitive in the fog. "Hello, where do you think you're going?" she snaps. "What's your plan?" It sounded cold and brusque, and was sung with unabashed vulgarity: "SOS—I urgently need to kiss, SOS—I need to know today." The song was as remote as possible from the kittenish ideal widely thought to have defined the years that followed, in Germany as elsewhere.

The erotic emergency call that Lutz was making to her listeners existed in the context of the ever-present themes of a shortage of men, a coarsening of morals and profligacy. This musical parody of desire gives us an idea of the genuine enthusiasm with which some women went on the offensive. The Pan Am pilot Jack O. Bennett, who would later fly the first plane in the Berlin Airlift, recalled in his memoirs, *40,000 Hours in the Sky*, how in December 1945, when strolling along the Kurfürstendamm, "an elegantly dressed society lady" spoke to him and asked if he didn't want to accompany her for the evening. "I don't want money or food from you," she said. "I'm cold and I need a warm body."[13]

It was only after the spring of 1945 that many German men understood the extent to which they had lost the war. Fraternisation on the merry-go-round, 1946.

It could be that Captain Bennett was exaggerating in a spirit of vanity, but the awareness, still vivid in people's minds, that this night might be their last, led many people to be much more direct with each other than they would have been before the war. The widespread nature of this sexual audacity is confirmed by the fact that the Berlin Central Health Administration, concerned about the rise in venereal diseases, commissioned the director Peter Pewas to make a film warning of the dangers of sexual profligacy. Entitled *Strassenbekanntschaft* (*Street Acquaintances*), the film was released in 1948. Pewas turned the story about a girl named Erika into a cinematic work of art that demonstrated the helplessness of the post-war generation, "greedy for life, thirsty for love."[14]

1949 saw the publication of a collection of short stories entitled *A Thousand Grams*, which achieved a certain degree of fame because among other things it contained a manifesto for what became known as *Kahlschlagliteratur*, literally translated as "clear-cutting literature," also known as *Trümmerliteratur*, or "rubble literature." It dealt in stripped-back language with the plight of those returning from the war. Among the stories in *A Thousand Grams* was "Fidelity" by Alfred Andersch, which deals with a young woman's sexual desire. Her husband is in prison, so every day after lunch she lies down naked on the bed and torments herself with desire.

> These legs, she thought, someone needs to touch them. And somebody should stroke my belly. [. . .] It's all the easiest thing in the world. I'm twenty-seven years old and an unsatisfied woman. I need to take what I need without any kind of fuss. I know how to do that. The man with the flowers should be here soon. I'll dress myself prettily and invite him in for tea. And if he's shy I'll tell him in cold blood what I want.[15]

The story is called "Fidelity" because the woman goes on to imagine how terrible she will feel, troubled by her bad conscience once her most urgent desire has been satisfied. The literary merit of the text lies not in the woman's heroic renunciation of the postman or the man with the flowers, but the matter-of-fact way in which her desire is described—quite unadorned, in line with the principles of *Kahlschlagliteratur*, direct and laconic.

★

Around this time many temporary flat-shares came into being. Acquaintances were crammed together and friends moved into apartments that had formerly housed two but now had to hold six. This close proximity also brought, apart from a great deal of awkwardness, a constant exchange of ideas, comfort and love. A couple on the ground floor might split up and criss-cross into new relationships with a couple upstairs, for example.[16] A high turnover of partners meant new challenges, but also new attractions.

The flat-share—which the student movement of the 1960s and 1970s imagined they invented—was something that the collapse of Germany had produced all by itself decades before. *Constanze* was in the forefront once again; the magazine publicised the idea of the flat-share with photographic essays in which one could tell by the relaxed postures of the obviously attractive young people how exciting things were ("Loosen up, gentlemen!"). An article in 1948 entitled "Those Four from the Sixth Floor" introduced four artists—two men and two women—who lived and worked together.

> Here we see four young people at work, carving out their new life. Four who don't let things get them down. They are among the brave ones who have been tossed about but not broken by the storm. They are people you can find everywhere—oh yes, what a blessing—everywhere, among the workers and artists and seamen and professors and craftsmen and doctors.[17]

In *Film ohne Titel* (*Film Without a Title*), a wonderfully tender film about the end of the war and its aftermath by Rudolf Jugert, released in 1948, three women and a man live together in a bomb-damaged villa in Berlin: an art dealer and his sister, his ex-girlfriend and a rural housemaid, the farmer's daughter, Christine, played by Hildegard Knef. For large sections the film is dominated by a confident feminine tone provided by the elegant ex, while the sister, a former Nazi, tends towards the morose. There is a nonchalance with which the maid is accepted as the new girlfriend. This is followed by bombs, evacuation, and flight into the countryside—the film depicts a "romantic satire" where chaos knocks away social encrustations. It is saccharine and acerbic at the same time—and precisely because of that mixture it was a great success, aware as it was of the intellectual and emotional opportunities that lay in the exigencies of forced displacement.

Shelter and love—these themes were everywhere. In the 1950 film *Des Lebens Überfluss* (*Abundance of Life*) by Wolfgang Liebeneiner, often described as the "last rubble film," a hard-pressed couple rent out their half-ruined attic twice over, to two students, Karin and Werner. Each wishes that the authorities would evict the other, but for the time being they are forced to come to terms with living together in a very cramped space. Resoluteness, wit, a fighting spirit and confidence—Karin embodies all of these. In the end the pair are living openly together under the holes in the roof, in a much freer manner than we would commonly associate with this supposedly conservative period. Not everyone liked it. The couple were "worryingly unintellectual for students," *Die Zeit* observed.

There were also many women's flat-shares. In the industrial city of Duisburg 75 single working women set themselves up in a modern block of very small apartments. The 76th bell on the door belonged to the caretaker. It wasn't a bleak barracks for singles, nor was it a convent, but rather a "women's house" erected with social housing funds which created both a sense of community and the greatest possible degree of independence. There was only one condition: anyone who got married had to leave.

A surplus of women—being in the minority assures men of their supremacy

The sexual activity of women in post-war Germany was spurred on by a phenomenon that was on everyone's lips: the surplus of women. There were quite simply a lot of women and very few men. And many of those men were in a pitiful state, as they hobbled around on crutches, groaning and spitting blood. Of course, handsome men like the popular actors Hans Söhnker and Dieter Borsche didn't only exist on screen, but for each of these good-looking men there were dozens of women who fawned all over them. In a newsreel from 1945 we see a mature and apparently affluent couple strolling beside the rubble of the Berlin boulevard Unter den Linden. Again and again young women accost the elderly gentleman, and his wife has great difficulty shooing them away. Presumably the scene was staged, but it illustrated a phenomenon that was powerfully troubling people's minds.

More than 5 million German soldiers had fallen in the war. In addition to that there were 6.5 million men who were still in Western prisoner of war camps at the end of September 1945 and over 2 million prisoners were starving in Soviet camps. Even in 1950 there were 1,362 women for every 1,000 men.[18] The discrepancy was much greater among the younger age groups: of those born between 1920 and 1925 at least two fifths of young men didn't come back from the war. The imbalance in numbers between the sexes was particularly noticeable in the cities. At any rate, the much-circulated rumour that there were six women for every man in Berlin was not far from the truth.

"Six women to every man, six women to every man"—this suggestive, repeated line ran through the soundtrack of the rubble-film (Trümmerfilm) *Berliner Ballade* (*The Berliner*) which premiered in 1948, sometimes as a promise to men and sometimes as a fearful warning to women.[19] In the film the actor Gert Fröbe plays Otto, an emaciated returnee from the war who wanders like a wide-eyed ghost through the ruined city. In the devastated desert of Berlin's central Mitte district, he eventually manages to find his house. Although damaged, it is still standing, but "Frau Holle's Love Central" has been set up in his apartment, giving him a brutal introduction to the new morality. Otto flees again and wanders through Berlin, but is tormented by the surreal vision of six voluptuous young women romping around his scrawny figure. "Surplus of women, surplus of women!" are the words that ring out off-screen. At one point Otto wanders through a Berlin park full of loving couples, sitting under trees and on tree stumps. One couple sits in the luxury of an American jeep, chatting furiously past one another—the girl planning her marriage in German while the young GI talks in English about his father's meat-packing factory in Detroit. They don't understand each other, but they soliloquise away to their hearts' content. "A thousand hearts seek love, but many are so alone," the soundtrack whispers as the *Heimkehrer* wanders through the park. "A thousand hearts remain alone, and the search never ends." But not even the siren call of "I have an old air-raid shelter bed, where you can dream so sweetly" can lure the anxious Everyman between a woman's sheets.

In 1949 the magazine *Constanze* published a racist, scornful poem, "Very Sad Ballad of the Far Too Many Women," mocking the idea that the excess of women in Germany might somehow give a Black man a better chance of finding romance. When it came to inter-racial relationships, *Constanze* wanted to make its own views defiantly clear to its audience of white female readers.

As independent as they might have been, many single women yearned for the equanimity that a relationship could bring amidst chaos. However, one did not have to be very good at maths to work out that for statistical reasons not all of them were going to find that happiness. And for anybody who didn't feel like doing the sums, the newspapers provided this service and supplied the gloomy prospects free of charge. On 8 April 1951 the south-western *Rhein-Neckar-Zeitung* predicted that "half a million women between the ages of twenty-five and forty would have no chance of marriage, and would therefore in most cases have to go on working for years, if not decades."[20]

It wasn't just about love, it was also about subsistence, and working for a living didn't strike all women as the most attractive of futures, particularly since their prospects on the labour market soon deteriorated once more with the return of the menfolk. As a result the surplus of women became a hard-fought issue on the job market. Here, too, women competed against women. Single women were played off against married ones. If a woman was "taken care of at home" and still wanted to earn money, she was depicted as an insatiable money-grabbing "double-earner" who wanted to take work away from single women in need of employment. A state-sponsored campaign was launched against those accused of enriching themselves disproportionately. The *Kölnische Rundschau* newspaper of 5 May 1952 wrote, "We have a worrying surplus of women. Since not all of them can marry, they need to look for a job. Can it possibly be acceptable for married women who are already provided for to take jobs away from unmarried women?" In many German states female officials who were married to male colleagues were dismissed from their posts, ostensibly for the good of the children and a "thriving family atmosphere," but really because they were comfortably off.

The women's solidarity that had survived so many trials in times of deprivation faded away. With the first modest signs of affluence and more solid relationships with men, suspicion among women grew. Gone were the days when they had gone to dance halls and shared the few available men on the floor. Above all, single young war widows were suspected of wanting to steal other women's husbands. The daughter of one soldier's widow recalled:

> It was hard for me to see my mother being shunned by the "intact" families. "We war widows," she wrote later in her memoirs, "weren't invited by couples. We were complete outsiders. Single women were more or less ostracised." [. . .] The undamaged parted company from the damaged, the bereft were cast aside and the gulf between those who had got back on their feet and those who suffered long-term harm remained unbridgeable. My mother only developed friendships with other war widows.[21]

The atmosphere hardened as life began to return to normal. Freshly established families moved into their newly built apartments and set about further securing a regular life. Anyone who was alone was threatened with remaining so forever.

After the end of the war the divorce rate doubled compared to its pre-war level and peaked in 1948.[22] Meanwhile the search for new partners had intensified. The wave of divorces was followed by an unprecedented surge in marriages, which led in 1950 "to the marriage market being almost entirely depleted."[23] Almost 100 per cent of the men born between 1922 and 1926 got married. In parallel to this, women's chances on the labour market fell and men installed themselves once more as "heads of the household."

The surplus of women had eaten away at many women's confidence, while conversely men enjoyed the advantages of their greatly reduced numbers. Their self-reliance, greatly diminished by the dominant status that they found their wives enjoying upon their return, was suddenly restored. In line with the prevalent masculine ideal of the day, the old-school "lady's man" returned, successfully "corralling" women and using elaborate seduction techniques to ensnare the more recalcitrant. It's no coincidence that the term *frech*, meaning cheeky or brazen, was suddenly applied to the more desirable women just as it had been in the past. The "brazen behaviour" of such an independent woman was considered particularly sexy, since it implied that she could be "improved" with a little training.

A visit to the cinema at the time provided a ringside seat for the war between the sexes. Actresses such as Inge Egger, Barbara Rütting, Erica Balqué and Hildegard Knef were strong female characters—and were easily a match for the Uma Thurmans of the present day. In the 1952 film *Alraune* (Mandrake, or Mandragore in English) by Arthur Maria Rabenalt, the title character, played by Hildegard Knef, drives no fewer than four lovers to their deaths. In the film she is amorality personified: she is wicked, but she can't help herself. The way she provocatively throws cherries at a workman as he washes himself at a fountain beneath her window, or poses alluringly with a riding crop before sitting disconsolately on the edge of a fountain to mourn yet another lover is quite remarkable. And at the end of the film she doesn't settle for the safe harbour of a happy, loving relationship with a solvent gentleman, but instead takes her unbroken loneliness with her into the darkness.

Again and again the combative aspect of the erotic side of life came to the fore. Arrogance and aggression lurked behind the mask of every suave and elegant man. In May 1951 the men's magazine *Er* published an article entitled "The Military School of Love" in which the author recommended going on the attack. "Nothing delights a woman more than a skilful assault that means she never has to improve her deliberately clumsy attempts at self-defence." He goes on: "Ambush without presumption, force without brutality, is a matter of nuance. Diplomats say of a man who has instinctively grasped all details correctly: he has the upper hand." Use force, yes, but not brutality—and never apologise! Today that sounds like an instruction to make oneself as repellent as possible. Still, at the end of the article, the author admits that in the case of true love all "arts of war" are as nothing: "We need not show courage before the women we love."

The battle of the sexes also found expression in the form of competition over who suffered the greater deprivation, men or women? In Wolfgang Liebeneiner's film *Liebe 47* (*Love '47*), a free adaptation of Wolfgang Borchert's play *The Man Outside*, a man and a woman meet by chance on the banks of the Elbe. They do not know one another, but they are both weary of life. The fog looms, bombed-out factories line the quays, dead fish float in the river. "Pretty dirty," the woman says. "Unpleasant idea, killing yourself here." "Do you want me to move away a little?" the man asks. "Oh, no, stay where you are," she replies. "You're not disturbing anybody." Then it dawns on him: in the war you were never alone when you died. "What do you know about being alone?" the woman snaps at him. "You men left us alone! While you were charging around in the Urals, the bombs were raining down on our heads." Unlike the play on which it is based, the film concludes on a conciliatory note: the competition for the greatest misery is set aside unresolved, everyone has gone their own way through hell. In the end we see them together as a couple, with the opportunity for a new home. The landlady even gives them an egg she has been hoarding.

It was always a matter of eggs, of bread, of a roof over one's head.

"I feed my husband!" was a proud *Constanze* headline above an article about professional women helping their husbands through life. "I literally chose mine from the street," one relates. "He was just swimming about. He looked completely helpless." That gave the magazine's readers a boost. He was five years her junior, "practically a child." A tolerance for men "just swimming about" was the alternative to holding out for a strong man. *Constanze* repeatedly recommended choosing a man from among the 1.5 million war-disabled. It was a good idea "not to look for the man as an Adonis, but rather as a future companion." There was much discussion of the experience of seeing a leg-stump for the first time.

The nurturing qualities of women were a definite plus in the war between the sexes. In the lead article of the June 1946 issue of the Munich journal *Ende und Anfang (End and Beginning)*, a "newspaper of the young generation," one Dr. Laros wrote about the "eternal mission of women at this time." Now that "animalistic behaviour has exploded everywhere, with chilling egoism and violence," it was women's fateful task to sort things out again:

> From their essential and primal power of love, they must give men a new kind of understanding and grant them a spiritual home in which they can be themselves once more and, after years of destruction, be given a new reason to engage in positive work again.

In conclusion Dr. Laros issued a warning: "Woe to you, if you refuse to hear and to understand. The fate of our people is, more than it has been for a long time, in your hands."

Fair game in the East

The Allied victors, who had finally forced Hitler's troops to their knees after six murderous years, had engaged in nightmarish male violence. The experiences varied according to the zone of occupation. In the east, hostilities were followed by an unparalleled wave of

rapes. Over the last fifty years, these horrific rapes have been documented in such graphic detail that we can perhaps spare ourselves
from repeating them here.[24] Estimates of the incidence of rape are
extremely rough, and vary by the hundreds of thousands. As many as
up to 2 million women were raped, often repeatedly. The rapes were
accompanied by brutal displays of torture and murder.

The diaries and letters of the women of Berlin from those days are
filled with appalling descriptions of terrible crimes. Hardly a night
passed without men wildly knocking at doors, breaking in, beating
and raping the occupants. Margret Boveri summed up:

> I must say: waiting for bombs and shells at night took much less of a
> toll on the nerves than waiting for unknown men to break in. I am
> much less afraid of exploding metal than I am of explosive human
> beings. I got through two nights with sleeping tablets and didn't hear
> anything and only learned what had happened the following morning:
> Frau Hartmann in the house on the other side of the courtyard was
> raped four times; Fräulein They, whom I don't know, and who was
> 200% Nazi—couldn't have happened to a nicer person—once.[25]

Probably the most impressive testimony concerning the "business of
raping," as she calls it, is found in the diary of the journalist Marta Hillers, which became an international bestseller after it was republished
in 2003 under the title *A Woman in Berlin*. It was originally published
anonymously in 1959, and even today the author of the book is still
given as "Anonyma" on the title page, though her identity was revealed
with the book's republication, amidst a heated debate in the German
newspaper features pages about whether she should have been named
at all.[26] It took Hillers only two weeks to familiarise herself, as she
writes, with the whole "catalogue" of different types of rapist. She
experienced the brutal type, who took pleasure in his own ugliness,
gleefully letting the spittle drip from his foul-smelling mouth between
her parted jaws. She experienced the comparatively gentle types, who
helped her to her feet afterwards and patted her comfortingly on
the shoulders. And the communicative types who made themselves

comfortable in between and wanted to play cards with her. Luckily she did not experience at first hand the completely brutalised individuals who smashed women's teeth in with their rifle-butts.

Marta Hillers was a well-travelled woman. She had worked in Moscow and studied at the Sorbonne. The fact that she spoke reasonably good Russian made it easier for her to gain a protector among the Russians, "a wolf who would keep the wolves from my body, an officer, as senior as possible, commander, general, whatever I can get." The strategy worked, and Marta Hillers caught from among the officers a major with "stars" for herself. "I'm very proud I actually managed to tame one of the wolves—most likely the strongest in the pack—to keep away the others."[27] The major had a gentle side, and didn't make too many demands upon her. She was mostly disturbed by the sleepless nights that his bad knees gave her. They drew some warmth from the circumstances, and when the major was ordered home again after only a few days, she felt sadness at his departure:

> I feel a little sad, a little empty. I think about his leather gloves, which I saw for the first time today. He was holding them elegantly in his left hand. They dropped on the floor once and he hurried to pick them up, but I could see that they didn't match—one had seams on the back, while the other didn't. The major was embarrassed and looked away. In that second I liked him very much.[28]

The Russians had lost 27 million people in the Second World War. Hitler had launched a war of destruction against the civilian population and demanded that the Wehrmacht "disregard the concept of comradeship between soldiers."[29] His senior commanders had vigorously enforced this directive. The soldiers of the Soviet Army had been through terrible experiences: many of them had fought for four years without a day's leave, had gone past scenes of scorched earth, the devastated villages of their homeland and fields filled with corpses. Bewildered, they had pressed on into a conquered Germany, a country obviously much wealthier and more highly developed than their own. "I took revenge, and would take revenge again," said a Red Army soldier named Gofman, whose wife and children had been murdered in a massacre near Krasno Polje. "I have seen fields scattered with dead Germans, but that isn't enough. Many of them should die for each murdered child!"[30]

It occurred to some Germans that the vengefulness of the Russian soldiers was no different from the violence that the Wehrmacht, the SS and the police battalions had visited on Russia. One woman, who had been badly mistreated by the Russians, was magnanimous enough to admit: "I have suffered a great deal. But if I consider the matter reasonably, I say to myself, it was all probably just a terrible payback for what our men did in Russia."[31] "I brood and brood," Ruth Andreas-Friedrich noted in her diary. "I love the Russians, but I find their regime sinister." The other members of her circle of friends, all of whom had resisted the Nazis, "struggled with the same problem. They want to like the Russians and they can't. [. . .] They hate them and they are afraid."[32] At the same time there were some Red Army commanders who were ashamed of their marauding troops. Many soldiers were summarily executed as punishment. But attempts to impose sanctions succeeded only gradually. In Berlin, for a time, the Red Army issued German women with inkpots, instructing them to mark the men who assaulted them so that they could be punished by their superiors. But what woman would dare to further incite these already uninhibited men by taking such action?

Marta Hillers' diary ends at the end of June with the return from the war of her fiancé, Gerd—a terrible disappointment. Like others, this *Heimkehrer* could not bear the new confidence that was apparent in women. One evening when the couple were sitting with neighbours, the women in the group told stories "about our experiences over the past few weeks, then he really got angry. Gerd: 'You've all turned into a bunch of shameless bitches, every one of you in the building. Don't you realise? [. . .] It's horrible being around you. You've lost all sense of measure.'"[33] This defeated man perceived his fiancée's rape as a shameful dishonour not only to her, but also to him. What was on his mind first and foremost was his own reputation. Repelled, he pushed her away, rather than giving her comfort and warmth. Icy, emotional coldness ended many loving relationships. It was a constantly recurring theme in the literature of those years. The double injustice done to women by men's attitudes was rarely acknowledged. The effort that a man had to make in order to "forgive" his entirely guiltless wife was held to be overwhelming.[34]

If couples remained together, they tacitly obliged one another to remain silent. The restorative openness with which the women of Berlin spoke of "forced intercourse," as it was officially known, did not last for long, as the silence demanded by men like Gerd took hold again and the outrages that the women had endured were sealed away under cover of silence. Now it was shame that was collectivised. For the women in question it was a second injustice. If one of them made her experiences public, as Anonyma had done, she was vilified as "shameless."

When *A Woman in Berlin* was first published in 1959, the Berlin *Tagesspiegel* wrote:

> Over almost 300 pages it is very painful to read through the eyes "of a woman in Berlin." Not only because the subject is so gruesome—much, much more painful is the tenor with which the subject is addressed [. . .] The repellent way, for example, in which comparisons are made, the callous astonishment when someone else isn't allowed to talk about it, the condescending remarks about German men [. . .]. Most women, almost all of them, in fact, would not be capable of writing such a salacious book about the most terrible experiences of their lives.[35]

When the new edition of the diary was brought out by the author Hans Magnus Enzensberger in his "Andere Bibliothek" series, 44 years later, the author's sometimes sarcastic, entirely unsentimental tone sounded quite different to readers' ears. In 2003 the book was hurriedly reprinted. It was only after two generations had passed that many Germans were willing to face up to what had clearly been the most sensitive point of their defeat: the fate of women. And for a moment the "Wilmersdorf widows," those old Berlin ladies, living on their own, proud and often rather odd, were looked at with tender eyes.

Veronika Dankeschön in the West

Germans can now speak more openly about the fate of women after the war, but mention is hardly—if ever—made of the different mentalities in East and West Germany. Until the uprising of the citizens of the GDR in 1989 and the subsequent reunification of the country, the effects of the war diverged in many respects between East and West, with the most tangible distinction dating from the very end of the war. The sexual encounters that the Germans had with the invaders in East and West could hardly be more dissimilar. Even allowing for assaults by some occupying soldiers in the West, the overall image of the Western Allies is much more friendly, even attractive. The disparity is surprisingly seldom discussed, even when explanations are sought for the distinctly greater suspicion of foreigners in the East. While trivial explanations such as the early weaning of babies in socialist nurseries are put forward, the mass rapes are surprisingly rarely mentioned. Is it not much more plausible that the traumatic encounter with the invaders made people in the East much more withdrawn than in the West? The state-ordered silence that followed only deepened the effects on the collective mind. Though these events are more than seven decades in the past, mistrust is habit-forming and often passed on to the next generation.

In the West, too, a tangled mass of myths and imaginings surrounds the issue of rape in the war's immediate aftermath, and makes it hard to establish a realistic picture. The Cold War, sexual politics and wildly flourishing fantasies came together to form a jumble of contradictory feelings. In his book *A Nazi Childhood*, the gay American author Winfried Weiss, who grew up in Germany and moved to the United States, where he taught literature until his death, describes how as an eight-year-old, he found some rubbish left by foreign soldiers on the banks of the Isar, including used condoms. He knew enough about sex to be certain that they must have been used in intercourse with prostitutes. The boy loved and admired the GIs, which even abuse by one soldier couldn't tarnish. So he lifted the rubber admiringly into the air, stared at the "soapy-white substance" from which, in his childish perception, the much-admired supermen were made: "the white sheath contained the disreputable, dark, and beautiful essence of the Americans."[36] It would be hard to think of a more curious account of the overwhelming impression that the Americans made on many Germans than this one.

Not everyone succumbed to such a bizarre state of ecstasy over the "speed, precision and powerful bodies"[37] of the invading Western troops, though they were often given a surprisingly friendly reception, despite everything the Nazi propaganda machine had done to stir up fear about Western Allied troops among the Germans. No sooner had the last German snipers been finished off than the sound of rifle-fire was replaced by the rumble of tanks, and women and children appeared in the streets, often waving in greeting. Part of this was sheer gratitude at not having been liberated by the Russians.

The invading American, British and French troops did commit war crimes, and the French North African soldiers are said to have an especially poor record in that respect.[38] It is quite possible, however, that the reason this group of alleged perpetrators remained so stubbornly in the memory was simple racism, with the accusers somehow considering this behaviour to be typical of Moroccans. Severe caution is therefore best advised with regard to the appraisals of the time. In Stuttgart alone 1,389 women reported being raped after the arrival of French troops.[39] The highest incidence of looting and rapes was reported in Baden and Bavaria. In Bavaria, isolated farmhouses in particular were plundered by American soldiers and the women raped. Murder and manslaughter occurred too, and to some extent these were even tolerated as part of day-to-day life.

No population group was free of criminal energy and violent cravings. Gangs of German youths, released forced labourers and concentration camp inmates, German expellees from the eastern territories, and, of course, occupying troops, were all responsible for acts of murder and arson. It would be quite wrong to simply equate the amount of violence against women carried out by the Red Army with that perpetrated by the Western Allies.[40] There is plenty of testimony, even from the SS (who would have been unlikely to lie in this regard), that British and American soldiers at least behaved with relative propriety. In March 1945 one SS-Obersturmbannführer reported what he had been told by the residents of a town in the far west of Germany, after it had been temporarily reconquered by the Wehrmacht: "The Americans made a genuine effort to establish a good relationship with the population by giving them tins of food, chocolate and cigarettes." The townspeople had "the best opinion" of the Americans, and the women emphasised how well they had treated them, while their own troops simply "threw them into the street." In the end the Obersturmbannführer was forced to admit that the residents perceived the enemy as being morally superior:

> After the liberation of Geislautern from German troops, with the withdrawal of the Americans it was noted by German sources that the apartments in which the Americans had stayed had been left undamaged and nothing had been stolen. It was generally claimed that they had behaved better than our German troops.[41]

Some places, however, were less fortunate than Geislautern. They included those where German soldiers had put up fanatical resistance and GIs had lost their lives in pointless symbolic skirmishes. After facing gunfire from snipers in villages that had long since been taken, the GIs often vented their fury on the women. Some reports suggest that American soldiers responded particularly aggressively towards the German civilian population after being confronted by the conditions in the death camps they had discovered and liberated.

The American military leadership had ordered their soldiers to maintain a strict but deliberately unfriendly relationship towards the Germans. In their occupation directives, they portrayed German civilians as sly, malign and dangerous, as brutes who needed to be subjected to a hard and persistent re-education process before it was possible to deal with them. Unlike the Soviets, who, in line with their theory of fascism, officially thought of the German people as victims of a Nazi power elite, the Americans had always stressed civilian mass sympathy for and participation in the Nazi regime. For Americans, most Germans were fanatical Nazis and incorrigible criminals. They expected that they would still be dealing with fascist resistance operations and attacks by the Werewolf guerrilla group for a long time after the invasion.

In view of this, the military leadership had prepared their soldiers for a ruthless subjugation of the enemy and, in April 1944, forbidden any kind of fraternisation. No handshakes, no exchange of words, not the slightest approach of any kind was permitted. As they rolled in, the GIs were all the more surprised by the friendly reception they were given by pretty women and admiring youths, and they couldn't get enough of the grateful reactions prompted by the cigarettes and chocolate that they handed out of the jeeps in spite of the prohibition.

With the Americans, an unfamiliar army entered the country. The locals admired everything about them as they passed: their relaxed sitting postures, the confident laughter, their casual way of smoking. "The GIs' shoulders were as wide as wardrobes, their tight buttocks as narrow as cigarette boxes," as Hildegard Knef put it in her memoirs.[42] They were described as bursting with health, as unusually life-affirming and, we read repeatedly in numerous eyewitness reports, as being as "naïve as children." The emphasis on the childlike behaviour of the American soldiers may have had its origin in the fear that preceded their invasion. Every bit of clowning that the Americans indulged in was acknowledged with relief; particular gratitude was reserved for the "good-natured smiles" of the Black GIs. Nazi propaganda had been particularly keen to sow alarm about the Black soldiers of the American and French armies, leading many Germans to expect them to be terrifying and ruthless, so they were pleasantly surprised by the reality. Not only that, but the Black GIs, particularly those from the American South, were happy that there was no racial segregation in post-war Germany. The military discipline that had become a second skin for German soldiers was alien to the Americans. The ease with which the victors sat enthroned in their cars made them look like affable gods in the eyes of many women.

The sight of the victors rolling in made a lasting impression on the smaller boys, while the older boys were often just as shocked as their fathers by the attraction that the new arrivals exerted on many of the women. The men admired more than anything the motor vehicles of the Americans, which, according to a legend that rapidly circulated, were the primary cause of the German defeat; but they too noticed a certain civility in the behaviour of the uniformed victors. They were astonished to observe that subordinates could hand their superiors a document without rising from their chairs, and that it was possible to win a war without constantly clicking one's heels.

Above all, though, it was the lack of formality in the soldiers' attitudes that made the greatest impression. The American way of sprawling, their ability to make themselves comfortable anywhere, and to feel at home even when abroad, was found by some to be off-putting and by others charming. Equally, some women thought the offhandedness of the Americans disagreeable, seeing it as the arrogance of the occupier, while others were irresistibly attracted.[43] If

German women and American soldiers in a Berlin bar, 1945.

men could be so relaxed on enemy territory, how else might they express this relaxed masculinity?

Some memoirs reported how women quite literally "stood in line" at the quickly erected American barracks to offer their services in return for a few slices of salami, some chewing gum or cigarettes. That is a flippant exaggeration—approaching US soldiers involved risks and humiliation—but it is true that the GIs didn't have to make very much effort to make contact with German women. They just needed a bit of courage to get over the prohibition on fraternisation and to ignore the warnings of venereal diseases that were posted everywhere. The German women were soon universally known as "Veronika Dankeschön" (Veronica Thank-you), a play on the abbreviation VD for venereal disease. Given the lack of appropriate medication, this was a widespread scourge. In spite of all the risks, however, Germans and Americans flirted like mad. In the summer of 1945, no sooner had the Americans moved into their sector in Berlin, assigned to them by the Yalta Agreement,[44] than the beach at Wannsee was densely populated with couples who had arrived in uniforms and floral dresses and now lay in the sun in their swimming costumes, sub-machine guns next to picnic blankets.

In West Germany, whole columns of waiting girls were reported lining the streets leading to the barracks. There were even said to be caves in the woods near the soldiers' accommodation where young women camped in order to be closer to the GIs. American military police and German civil police regularly carried out raids to arrest the women and forcibly examine them for venereal diseases. As they did so the women were shouted at, roughly manhandled and sometimes abused.

Aside from these violent checks there were also gentler forms of guidance. In the town hall of Berlin-Zehlendorf in February 1947, 600 applicants were vetted as acceptable consorts for American soldiers, and examined by a committee of German teachers, doctors and administrative officials. Once these women were in possession of a "social pass," they were granted access to American clubs. The final approved list was forwarded to the Americans, who reserved the right to make the final decision.[45]

Until very recently it was generally accepted that material hardship was the sole reason that German women became "Fräuleins" (the German word simply means "miss," but it became a universal nickname), or *Amiliebchen*—Yank-lovers—as people liked to call them at the time. Doubtless there was terrible deprivation, which meant that many women could not be particularly choosy in their survival strategies. There are also numerous documented instances of women and young girls being sent to the barracks by their relatives, some of whom were real traffickers, fathers forcing their daughters into prostitution yet hounding them at the next opportunity as whores and traitors to the nation. But hardship and compulsion were not the only motives that inspired female interest in American soldiers. Active pursuit of them was also fired by curiosity about a different and, it was evident, a freer way of life. The film scholar Annette Brauerhoch sees the behaviour of the Fräuleins as an "unorganised and undocumented form of counter-culture." Her study "Fräuleins and GIs," published in 2006, is one of the few attempts to see love of the Americans as active desire and, among other things, a "protest against the German past."[46]

There was also a cultural or subcultural element to the search for a GI. Young women wanted to break free from the German way of life, from their often constricting and musty environments. But for a long time most German historians refused to contemplate the notion that there might have been a desire for the unknown, and that this was part of the attraction of GIs. The idea that active desire might have been involved struck them, and still strikes some of them, as entirely implausible. Only "unadulterated necessity" is allowed as a motive for collaboration, as if some Germans continue to see fraternisation as a kind of treason.

When it comes to German women in the post-war period, historiography suddenly turns into a minefield of statistics. It swarms with figures and tables about the country's economic situation, about occupations and work for political parties and community associations. There is little reflection on the joys of life. This restriction to the material aspect of relations with the Allies makes women into

The poster DON'T GAMBLE WITH VD *warns against venereal disease. The German "Fräuleins" were known as Veronika Dankeschön, Veronica Thank-you, as a play on the commonplace abbreviation VD.*

simply passive objects of poverty. In retrospect many Germans struggled to give credit to the women, who, as lovers of GIs, pioneered German-American friendship. In fact, however, they were in the vanguard on the long journey westwards, trailblazers of the liberalisation of the Federal Republic. Their unpolitical, purely personal actions blind us to the importance of the spiritual demobilisation of the Germans. As bleak and run-down as the dance halls that were set up around the barracks in villages might have been, it was Veronika Dankeschön who drew the sharpest line under the past, wholeheartedly, and often lovingly as well.

The fantasies prompted by occupation love-affairs gripped the public imagination. In Hans Habe's novel *Off Limits* a Jewish US major falls for the wife of a senior Nazi, a girl he was in love with at school before he went into exile in America; a Texan officer with S&M inclinations becomes obsessed with the wife of a concentration camp commandant; a young aristocratic woman takes up a job as a domestic servant for a US general—but woe betide them both if his wife flies in. One of the trashiest texts on the subject is an article from the gentlemen's magazine *Er* from 1950. It concerns a male version of the occupying forces sweetheart, a Vinzenz Dankeschön, so to speak, who is taken on as a diversion by an American female soldier. In the two-page story entitled "I've Got a Black Girlfriend" the journalist and author Hans Pflug-Franken spares no racist clichés. He refers to her, for example, as a "wild beast": "I actually hate her because she's like an animal that I have to love, whose language I don't understand. Perhaps I'm just an animal to her too, because she brings me nuts in big bags and feeds them to me." He takes the nuts, and he takes the affection, even though he isn't entirely comfortable with the sex. This unfamiliar woman frightens the man from Nuremberg; at the moment of orgasm he yearns for a wife who would lie there passively in the way that he's used to: "I need a woman who folds her arms under her head and stays still for as long as I want her to. But you bend too much; you take me more than I take you, you vampire." Masculine anxieties and blatant racism could not have been trumpeted more accurately.

Germany's survival, soberly viewed, in fact depended on the many women who worked in the service of the US Army. They did so as interpreters, cleaning women or shop assistants in the Post Exchange shops, which sold goods from home exclusively to members of the army. Even these working conditions created the possibility of numerous contacts, often leading to affairs of the heart—how many in all is anyone's guess. By 1949, at any rate, there had been 1,400 marriages between "Fräuleins" and GIs. That doesn't sound like a huge number, but how many flirtations, how many attempted relationships does it take to produce a figure of 1,400 marriages in the end? If we bear in mind how many administrative roadblocks were in place to prevent such marriages, it must have been a considerable number.

Twenty-four-year-old Daniel Militello from Brooklyn was the first American soldier to marry a German woman after the end of the war, after battling against a whole phalanx of prohibitions and obstacles.

As a member of the "Hell on Wheels" division he should really have been taking out snipers and resistance fighters.[47] Instead he met 16-year-old Katharina Trost. They fell in love and Militello, who had by now been sent east with his unit, kept trying to come up with ways to have himself sent back to Katharina in Bad Nauheim. When she became pregnant in 1945, Militello asked the American authorities for a marriage permit, but in vain. In November he had to go back to the United States, and in February he was discharged from the army. Militello signed up as a crewman on the freighter *Thomas H. Barry* and when, on his arrival in Bremerhaven, he was refused shore leave, he jumped ship and made his way south to Bad Nauheim, where he and his girlfriend initially hid at Katharina's grandmother's house. The couple were finally married in June 1946, but when Daniel Militello went to the American consulate to organise a passage for his son and wife, he was arrested and, a month later, forced to travel alone to the US leaving his new family behind in Germany. In the meantime his case was taken up by several American newspapers, which sided with the enamoured soldier. Finally, a New York congressman saw to it that Katharina Militello received her visa and was granted permission to fly to the US in November 1946, the first German war bride. By 1988 an estimated 170,000 soldiers' German brides would follow in this way.[48]

As married women the partners of GIs suffered no less from the disdain that these relationships elicited from the German public. Discrimination extended from sidelong glances to physical attacks. "It took five years for them to defeat us, but they can get you in five minutes" was the standard accusation. Some soldiers' brides were beaten up, or else had their heads shaved according to the international model of dealing with collaborators. Rumours even circulated of secret killings.[49]

Even in the absence of verbal abuse and physical slaps, there was an embarrassed silence. The intellectuals of the generation of 1968, who otherwise were determined to track down any sign of a continuity of fascist ideas, ignored the defamation of the GI brides, even though the subject could easily have been aligned with their anti-authoritarian critiques.[50] Many of these women were dissidents at the level of personal relationships, and proudly strolled down the streets with their uniformed American lovers, boldly returning disapproving gazes. It was not until 1979 that Rainer Werner Fassbinder made a film to commemorate the "disloyal" post-war German woman. While materialism is a central theme in *Die Ehe der Maria Braun* (*The Marriage of Maria Braun*), the dignity emanated by Hanna Schygulla in the title role testifies to an appropriate regard for the importance of the liberated woman as a force for social change. One recurring motif in the film, incidentally, is the American cigarette, mythically charged as both black-market currency and as bait. At the start of the film Maria is given a cigarette by her African-American boyfriend, and at the end, in the middle of the economic miracle, she blows her house up with one after forgetting she's turned the gas tap on.

It was, tellingly, the women's magazines that railed most vehemently against the condemnation of the "Fräuleins." In the article "Veronika Dankeschön: women and girls—the accusations against them and who they really meet," the magazine *Die Frau—ihr Kleid, ihre Arbeit, ihre Freiheit* (*Woman—Her Clothes, Her Work, Her Freedom*) objected to the idea that Veronika was primarily interested in cigarettes. In fact, women who had been cheated by the war of so many dances, boat trips, concerts and love affairs wanted to "live at last." And if here and there a materialistic perspective came into play, then it should also be admitted that in former times, too, love affairs and marriages were not always guided solely by love. Then comes the slur directed against the pious reading public—referring to a traditional practice in local and particularly rural newspapers, the magazine wrote: "Wasn't the desire to 'marry into a butcher's shop,' so often seen in personal ads, even more questionable than giving oneself out of pure hunger and bitter hardship? It didn't mean selling oneself for just a fleeting moment, but for a whole lifetime, in return for economic security." A whole life in return for a butcher's shop!

Here *Die Frau* is addressing the commingling of affection and calculation that many thought had been vanquished in modern society. Post-war privations brought material calculation in the selection of partners visibly back into play, often to a regressive degree. More interesting than the question of whether a relationship was entered into out of necessity or out of pure love was the difficult grey area in between, where both played a role. Marta Hillers provides a brutal example of this in her diary. Her cold-blooded attempt to find a pack-leader to protect her from the advances of the crude and primitive wolves is a primal scene from the world of partner selection. She herself is surprised by her feelings of gratitude at having found a certain shelter in the midst of anarchy, a feeling that leads in turn to actual affection. This was a time of wolves; the author embraces an animal legacy that lives on in her relationship behaviour and ensures her survival.

In June 1947 the magazine *Ja*, which saw itself as an intellectual sounding board for the younger generation, published a lead article under the heading "Dealing with the Allies," which argued for a "more open relationship" between the vanquished and the occupiers. The relationship was to be defined less by military compulsion than by a shared humanity that was the very opposite of Hitlerism. The author finds a model for the relaxed relations between occupiers and Germans in Veronika Dankeschön:

> Such a connection probably exists among the countless girls and women who have found their way into the arms of the others. It is the most human connection imaginable. We know, with no illusions, that many longings which went unsatisfied in the war years—full kitchens, loved ones getting through the war safe and sound—are more highly valued than humanity's greatest virtues. Also it will be self-evident that a lavish lunch and a secret food parcel is what determines many of these new relationships with the Allies right now.

In a mixture of contorted and unorthodox ideas that was typical of the time, the author of the article sees the love of an occupying soldier as being the erotic counterpart of the Marshall Plan (through which America supplied aid to Western Europe). Only those who are "unable to take this natural route to the Allies [. . .] for want of opportunity or talent or other qualities" could see the matter otherwise, and would, with their envy and suspicion, endanger the "general global understanding." An emphatically clear-eyed vision and the bold embrace of a new world go hand in hand here in a manifesto of generally accepted opportunism.

A closer look at the statistics of the time reveals the indissoluble kinship between love and calculation. "Advantage-oriented partner selection" is seen quite clearly in the countryside, where for generations traditional marriages of convenience between farmers had been a way of securing one's livelihood. The ten million expellees who arrived in this well-entrenched milieu of the villages of Bavaria and North Germany tried to make the best of the situation. If the radius of partner selection in these rural areas had previously been strictly limited to the locals, they were now joined by half of Silesia and Pomerania. And the result? There was a lot of flirting and lovemaking, but only very rarely did a young farmer take one of the new female arrivals as his wife. In the end the important thing was to marry one of the local farmers' daughters along with her copious dowry. The reverse was true of the male expellees. They did well on the rural marriage market, because they brought additional labour force into the house—not to mention that the father of the bride had an economical wedding because she was marrying an expellee of modest means. The expellees were fully aware of their situation: in defiance of any kind of tribal loyalty they preferred to marry into a local North German farming family, rather than bind themselves to one of the many penniless women who had fled along with them. The female expellees were, very demonstrably in statistical terms, the absolute lowest in the marriage market. This calculation in inter-German courtship, while it might have been rather distasteful from a romantic point of view, didn't bother the public in the slightest, who were more upset about women fraternising with the members of a victorious occupying power, which was seen as corrupt and a betrayal.

In the period of post-war hardship the love-life of Germans had become so de-romanticised that the most romantic film of the year caused an uproar. Even today people mistakenly believe that it was a brief scene of nudity that made the 1951 Hildegard Knef film *Die Sünderin* (*The Sinner*) the biggest scandal in German cinematic history. The Church was particularly enraged by the film's connection between intense religiosity and prostitution. Above all, though, people were outraged by the unconditional love that the main character, Marina, feels for her bohemian painter lover—mortally ill and losing his sight—whose life she takes, and for whom she takes her own life at the end of the film. The film was held to be a sin against the pure rationality of the economic miracle. What was more, Marina loved a man who had none of the smooth charm of the leading men who were beginning to reappear in German cinema. He was a derelict, and he remained so, one of those people who "were just swimming about." Voluntary decline coupled with wild passion was so contrary to the mores of the time that post-war society tore itself apart over the issue.[51]

VI

Robbing, Rationing, Black-market Trading—Lessons for the Market Economy

Most Germans made their acquaintance with hunger only after the war. Until then they had lived reasonably well by plundering the occupied territories. In many cities the municipal food offices had accumulated so many supplies that the inhabitants had got through the long period of the bombing raids without ever going hungry. As the war reached its end, however, what remained of this makeshift infrastructure collapsed almost completely. Given the disruptions to supply routes it seems miraculous that most Germans, if they survived at all, made it through the unusually warm summer of 1945 with a relatively full stomach. It was only afterwards that the food situation deteriorated and turned into the terrible disaster that was the "hunger winter of 1946–47."

The fact that this did not begin immediately after the end of the war testifies to a phenomenal ability to deal with crises on the part of the victors and the vanquished, both of whom were operating on unfamiliar terrain. If many bakers hadn't just carried on baking in the worst of the immediate post-war chaos, and if traders hadn't looked for new and improvised delivery routes, often in handcarts and without commissions, the hardship, particularly in the cities, would have been even worse than it already was. The frequently interrupted supply of food was temporarily sustained by the resolute actions of a few heroic individuals. The director of the Munich Food Office, for example, personally set off travelling around the surrounding area after he discovered early in May that Munich bakers only had enough flour for another five days. On his procurement trip he took along the chair of the Bavarian milling association, who knew the mill owners and was able to persuade them to deliver provisions.[1] Arduous though they were—even getting hold of lorries and petrol was a gruelling matter—these supply routes continued to operate surprisingly well. But most people had expected the opposite, complete collapse, and so even during the final battles there were hysterical scenes in some places as people stockpiled.

The first redistributions—citizens learn how to loot

"Early in the morning, at dawn, the looting started," the young secretary Brigitte Eicke wrote in her diary on 2 May 1945. With her Aunt Walli and many others from the surrounding area, Brigitte had moved into the courthouse in Berlin-Friedrichshain. This was on the Goebbels estate, a housing project built by Joseph Goebbels, the Nazi propaganda minister, in the mid-1930s, that had been hastily abandoned by its residents, particularly those who were noteworthy Party members.

> We had to clamber over corpses. The body of an old woman lay there, she was on fire. They dragged out everything you can think of from the courthouse basement, and I met Helga Debaux's sister, Vera, and we held hands and went down there too. It was so smoky that we nearly suffocated. It was all dark in there, you kept stepping on soft things as if stepping on corpses. The men broke down one door after another and it was all there, cigarettes, wine, schnapps, cream, playing cards, clothes, boots. In my haste I was able to grab a few jars of face cream rather than boots or something.

After searching the courthouse they went off to explore the abandoned apartments, until a few women had the obvious idea of breaking into the quartermaster's store:

After a lot of fighting and scrambling I was able to get hold of a bolt of coffee-coloured crepe silk, braces and all kinds of haberdashery. Then I went into the fur storage on the ground floor and found myself a lovely fur coat. Suddenly there was a sound of whistling and shooting and somebody said the Russians were here, and I thought, that's it, we're all done for. There were some soldiers standing by the exit and we had to put down the greatcoats we were carrying, and I was so scared that I just threw everything away. Thank God I managed to get out of there and make it home. Everyone was acting as if they'd gone mad and looting like hyenas, they were quite reckless, they lashed out at each other, not like humans at all.[2]

The extreme uncertainty of what the next few days and weeks would bring sparked a wave of pillage. People grabbed everything they could get hold of, and immediately found that their compatriots were tearing their treasures from their hands. People were seized by an intoxicating greed that made them grab things that they didn't even know what to do with. The main thing was that it didn't fall into anybody else's hands. There are many stories of goods that people had fought over simply being thrown away on the way home, as soon as the looters had come to their senses.

The *Süddeutsche Zeitung* reported that items worth millions had been looted in Munich during the days of the power vacuum. The ground was ankle-high with spilled sugar, and stolen cheeses were rolled home to people's houses. "The greed had become insatiable," the newspaper reported.[3] According to the article the wine casks in the Arzberger Keller were smashed open, and several women, presumably drunk, drowned in the wine that rose knee-deep in the cellar.

In all zones the Allies tried to restore calm as quickly as possible. To ease the tension, the Allied military administration opened up for the taking the food stores it had confiscated. Acting mayors were located and issued with instructions. Accustomed as they were to obedience, they surprised the military authorities with their brisk willingness to cooperate. Even so, most of them were replaced after only a few days. Allied investigative teams quickly got the hang of locating the former top executives from the Weimar Republic who had been fired by the Nazi state and appointed them to official positions. The Soviet-occupied zone was at first highly pragmatic about its selection of new administrators. When the communist Walter Ulbricht returned from exile in Moscow along with a group of other German Communist Party functionaries, they were given the task of getting public life going again and bringing local government under control. At the same time Ulbricht kept a very close eye on the mood of the population, and felt that he couldn't move too quickly. He imagined the reorganisation of the top level of Berlin's city administration as follows:

> We can't have any Communists as mayors, or at least only in the districts of Wedding and Friedrichshain. In working-class districts the mayors should as a rule be Social Democrats. In bourgeois districts—Zehlendorf, Wilmersdorf, Charlottenburg etc.—we need to put a middle-class man at the top, a member of the Centre, the Democrats or the German People's Party. Best of all if he has a doctorate; but he must also be an anti-fascist, and a man that we can work with.[4]

In many cities there were also Anti-fascist Action Committees, which arose out of the remnants of the resistance and the labour movements. Their offers of help, however, were often rejected if they started looking too much like an alternative form of local government in the eyes of the existing administration.

On the instructions of the Allies, new mayors had to ensure that members of the civil service, already seriously depleted by the war, returned to their workplaces to uphold what was left of any kind of order. Only later would they be subjected to political vetting, which frequently ended, in the American and Soviet zones, with dismissal on the grounds of previous Nazi Party membership. The French and the British were more lenient with their denazification, as their concerns lay predominantly with the efficiency of the administrative apparatus.

For all their differences, the offices in the various occupied zones had one thing in common: even though they were frequently distrusted by their new masters, who suspected that there were large numbers of Nazis in their midst, the officials and clerks who had remained at their desks performed their tasks unhesitatingly. The traditional ideal of the unpolitical German servant of the state helped them to follow the instructions of the Allied administration just as compliantly as they had served the Nazi state.

In Wiesbaden the mayor, Georg Krücke, who had been forced out of office in 1933, was returned to his post and given a three-page "letter of instruction" by the Americans which required him to implement all edicts by the military government with regard to a) maintaining law and order, b) eradicating National Socialism, Nazi bureaucracy, its accomplices and all military tendencies, and c) putting a stop to any discriminatory treatment on the grounds of race, religion and political conviction.[5]

Georg Krücke started at the easy end and concentrated on point (a). He summoned together his heads of department and tried to inform them as to what most urgently needed to be done. The most pressing matters were making the streets provisionally safe to access, clearing the fields of ammunition, inventorying supplies, inspecting meat and distributing it to the population, arresting illegal butchers, collecting wood from the nearby forests and coordinating the confiscation of property. The last of these measures were intended to ease hunger and alleviate the housing shortage. Accommodation was to be found for refugees and those who had been bombed out of their homes. Abandoned apartments were confiscated and furniture was transferred to "fellow-citizens harmed by air-raids," although they were formally designated only as "loans."[6] In some cities "members and supporters of the National Socialist system" were obliged to hand over clothes and household goods. In the city of Göttingen "production targets" were set and minutely quantified: in terms of men's clothing 1,790 coats, trousers, underpants and jackets were to be delivered, as well as 8,055 balaclavas; for ladies, 895 coats, 1,074 bras, 537 girdles and 890 pullovers.

The logic of food ration cards

The unstinting labour demonstrated by such a precise bra-and-pants-counting administration also made it possible to continue the rationing system of clothes, food and fuels almost seamlessly. The population had become used to rationing since the beginning of the war in 1939. However, the daily calorific value authorised by the Allies to the defeated people was lowered: in the British and American zones only 1,550 calories were permitted, which represented just 65 per cent of what doctors at the time considered necessary for the nutrition of the average adult.

The food ration card is one of the best known and most notorious objects of the post-war period, even if many Germans today have forgotten precisely how the management of the shortage economy actually worked. Food rationing was an intervention in the free market, which had already been attempted in Germany during the First World War; the French and the British had also used the same system for a time. Every inhabitant received one card per month, printed with stamps for a certain amount of bread, meat, fat, sugar, potatoes and "foodstuffs." When shopping, the customer handed over the appropriate stamp and paid the officially established price, as published on posters. Without these stamps you got nothing. Money on its own wasn't enough; you always had to have both.

The shopkeeper glued the stamps received from customers onto collection sheets, which then had to be presented to the wholesaler; only then would he receive new merchandise in the same quantity. It would be misleading to describe the shopkeepers as traders, because as officially controlled distributors they had no freedom to trade. If a shopkeeper gave the wholesaler stamps that didn't add up to the quantity of food he had previously received, he had to provide a plausible explanation for the discrepancy, otherwise he would be suspected of selling the goods on the black market and trading freely.

In legal terms, one didn't buy goods, one "drew one's ration." The concept of the ration was omnipresent, and in the cabarets of the post-war era jokes were made about "ration people" or the "ration-ised" character. The stereotype of "Otto Normalverbraucher" ("Otto the average consumer"), the equivalent of Joe Bloggs or "the man on the Clapham omnibus," also stems from this period. He is the person entitled to his 1,550 calories, the one who was never really sated and was able to watch himself in the mirror slowly shrinking into his clothes. Gert Fröbe played a version of this figure in the 1948 film *Berliner Ballade* (*The Berliner*). At that time he was a skeletal fig-ure who had nothing in common with the stout hulk who would play the greedy billionaire Goldfinger 16 years later in the third James Bond film.

The Germans had mixed feelings about food stamps. The wealth-ier among them, in particular, saw the restriction of their freedom to consume as an impertinence, and objected to finding that their money was no use to them. However much money they put down on the counter, legally they still couldn't have any more sausage and bread than their poor neighbour. Of course they were aware of the reason for this application of the nanny state: rationing was intended to prevent the affluent from buying up the market and leaving noth-ing for the less well-off. Hunger was to be distributed equally to all and kept within survivable bounds. That, at least, was the theory.

In practice, state control created a black market in a huge variety of forms, which only caused the differences between rich and poor to appear all the more starkly. Most traders had stockpiled goods from before the introduction of rationing, which they sold without stamps but at grotesquely inflated prices. Both buyers and sellers put them-selves on the wrong side of the law by violating the "consumer regulation penal ordinance" and a number of other laws. The penal-ties increased over the course of the food crisis from six months' imprisonment in 1945 to almost three years in 1947. In Saxony, profes-sional black-marketeers faced the death penalty as "food-supply saboteurs."[7] Following the logic of the rationing laws, anyone who had more than their permitted quantities and hence more than the bare necessity to eat was acting illegally, regardless of how they had got hold of it. This reversal of the burden of proof was explicitly endorsed in the first volume of the series of books, published in 1947, *Recht für Jeden* (*Law for All*): "If the individual acquires more than the quantity assigned and distributed to him, this is only possible on an unauthorised basis, on the black market."

The possession of food stamps made each individual an accredited member of a huge collective of food consumers who received, practically to the spoonful, exactly the same amount—a situation that infantilised the population and made them entirely dependent on the rationing offices. "Precious little rosewood coupons, numbers N4 and N5!"[8] the *Rheinische Zeitung* newspaper cheered when a special consignment of coffee appeared on food stamps for Christmas 1946.

Since stamps were issued once again almost immediately after the end of the war, it gave people the impression that there was still an authority taking care of them. As "life-justification cards"[9] they gave their owners a kind of certainty that even after total defeat they could still hold in their hands a "right-to-live card." Their disappointment was all the greater when it turned out that the cards by no means guaranteed that holders would actually receive the amount of foodstuffs, fat and sugar indicated on them. The quantities available fell far short of the authorised 1,550 calories per person. During the worst phases of the first three years after the war sometimes only 800 calories were issued. It was only then that it dawned on most Germans that the quantities indicated on the cards were, according to the fair-distribution logic of the rationing system, maximum values. In the downward direction, on the other hand, there were no limits—a misunderstanding which led to many Germans immediately feeling like the victims of an enormous fraud. On the "household identification card for skimmed fresh milk" it says: "A full ration allotment is not guaranteed; the milk distributor must issue equally the quantities available to him." In 1946 the *Süddeutsche Zeitung* published a photograph showing the actual available daily ration of the average consumer spread out on a table: half a tea-spoon of sugar, a piece of fat the size of a fingernail, a cheese portion the size of half a match, an eraser-sized piece of meat, a drop of milk and, admittedly, two potatoes.

Things got even worse in the winter of 1946–47, one of the coldest of the century. As well as the food shortage there was a lack of fuel, which was, of course, also rationed. The British military government had foreseen the disaster, and as early as the autumn of 1946 made forests available for anyone to cut. But very few people, city-dwellers least of all, were able to make anything of this offer, since they had no access to vehicles or tools. The last wooden beams had already been dragged from the ruins of the city—dangerous work in which many people were injured—when an extremely harsh winter descended upon the north of the country. In Kiel, on the north coast, people risked crossing the frozen inlets to the ships destroyed by enemy fire, which still loomed from the water and were now trapped in the ice. It was a reckless and usually vain venture, not least because the wrecks had already been plundered long ago. Trees lining the streets and in parks were cut down, although with disappointing results since the wood was too wet to burn properly.

Newspapers published tips on how to protect oneself against the cold: rub your nose and ears with your fingers and scrub your hands with a rough brush—and don't be afraid to creep under the bedcovers together! Instead of food recipes there were "tips on how to run the kitchen." It was under this heading that the magazine *Frauenwelt* (*Women's World*) issued advice, in a cautiously hypothetical tone:

> If jam is to be distributed, then I advise stretching it out by a factor of two to three. Mix it with unsugared fruit pulp, bottled in the summer, or, if there is none, grated carrots or grated pumpkin. A portion of grated beetroot can also be used without harming the flavour.[10]

In some cities, particularly in the British zone, there were strikes and demonstrations. A rumour circulated that the Allies were not only dismantling factories but also sending eggs, potatoes and meat out of the country. The British hurried to make it clear on posters that this was a "global food crisis," and the Germans were not the only ones who were going hungry. In Britain, too, they pointed out, food rations had been cut, and other countries, particularly India, were on the brink of famine. They explained in flyers that in the winter half of the bread and flour consumed by the Germans had been sent in from abroad. The nutritional needs of the British occupying forces were supplied almost entirely by food brought in from Britain.

It is telling that the British also thought the following explanation was necessary: "98 per cent of foodstuffs for displaced persons are now being imported, even though the German population bears responsibility for the feeding of these severely affected people." This explanation was aimed at the widespread assumption that displaced persons were living on the fat of the land in their camps. The "preferential treatment" of the former forced labourers and ex–concentration camp inmates had been a perennial complaint since the capitulation. Many Germans had reacted with envy and rage at the idea that the liberated prisoners were receiving special treatment in shops; they had been issued special food cards with higher rations, which was fair and medically recommended after the malnourishment to which they had been exposed for years. Nonetheless, some Germans were resentful: "All that was left for the German population was what foreigners did not lay claim to," one "impotent" contemporary wrote from the town of Lauterbach in Hesse.[11]

The Allies were now blamed for everything. By accepting the country's unconditional capitulation, the Allies had in the eyes of many Germans made themselves responsible for the state of food supplies. As grateful as people were for every bar of Cadbury's chocolate handed out from the trucks, and for all the gifts of Maxwell House coffee, they still reacted with fury when supplies ran out. "They're trying to starve us"—the accusation was always ready at hand. Even before the introduction of the Marshall Plan (officially called the European Recovery Plan, or ERP) in 1948, the Western Allies were already trying to ease the emergency. In August 1946 the first parcels sent to Europe by 22 American humanitarian organisations arrived in Germany. A total of 100 million "CARE Packages"—named after the private aid organisation CARE (Cooperative for American Remittances to Europe)—were distributed. Of the 12.5 billion dollars of economic and food aid covered by the Marshall Plan, Germany received about 10 per cent. By

March 1947 it was clear that the Cold War was coming, requiring both sides to be willing to treat the defeated population with greater care and attentiveness than they had originally planned to do. As tensions rose between the Western Allies and the Soviets, both sides increased their efforts to provide state support to the German people. The more urgently the Germans were needed as dependable allies, the more the desire for retaliation and compensation faded into the background. Demands for reparations became quieter and the dismantling of industrial facilities was reversed.

It was, however, a long time before the Germans came to understand that there might be a benefit to the border between capitalism and communism that now ran across the whole of their occupied country. It was only with the advent of the CARE Packages (which later became the stuff of legend), providing more and more people with moments of happiness, and certainly by the time of the gigantic food supply of the Berlin Airlift (which continued for over ten months beginning in 1948), that the grumbling fell silent and made way for lasting gratitude in the Western zones. In the Soviet zone, too, without the growing hostility between East and West it would have taken considerably longer for the Russians to declare their zone a "brotherland" (the official term used to describe the GDR) and grant it a comparatively high standard of living in Eastern Bloc terms. In this respect, the Cold War was a stroke of luck for Germany, in spite of the division of the country, the many hardships for the families who had been torn apart and the loss of any sense of united nationhood.

First, though, towards the end of 1946, people in East and West Germany once again had to deal with the fear of imminent death. It was unclear to many whether and how they would be able to survive the coming winter. Luckily they had acquired some survival skills beyond queuing outside empty shops. Accustomed on the one hand to the infantilising spoon-feeding of rationing, they had also very resourcefully developed private initiatives. They explored new avenues of self-help, monetised their possessions and sold off their gold. They engaged in projects that would be fashionably known today as "guerrilla gardening," "repair cafes" or "clothes circles," and added a grassroots economy to the official top-down version. Rather than staying in their workplaces, factory workers and mechanics joined forces to form small groups who travelled around the country offering repair work to farmers, in return for sausages, meat and vegetables. People also engaged in black-market trading, embezzlement and smuggling. The same population which, according to the logic of distribution, consisted of an army of ration recipients, was at the same time a people who looked after their own backs and put their own mettle to the test every day.

A nation of petty thieves—private initiative and criminality

The end of the war had redefined the terms rich and poor. Now a person could be considered rich if they had a tiny garden plot. Some people dragged soil all the way up to bombed-out rooms on the third floor and tried to plant a kind of raised garden bed between the remaining walls. Anyone who had been allocated a piece of "digging land" by the Finance Office could live off the preserved results of their labour through the winter. "In present-day Germany class differ-ences have almost disappeared," Chancellor Konrad Adenauer wrote to the industrialist Paul Silverberg in December 1946. "There is only one difference, which is whether or not you can cater for your own needs."[12] In many parks green spaces had been turned into vegetable gardens, most impressively in Berlin's magnificent Tiergarten park, which was now stripped of its trees, but where people performed unregulated farm work among the grand fallen marble statues. Some families had simply staked their own claims, and had to stand guard over their land day and night once the first vegetables began to appear.

The best off were the farmers in the German countryside. They were strangers to hunger. And rather than struggling into the ruined cities with their harvest, they could just wait for the city-dwellers to come to them. The city folk would show up with silver cutlery, pre-cious porcelain and cameras and go home again with half a sack of potatoes. But all kinds of paupers turned up as well, and lots of children and young people who were out of silver and still came to do their "shopping." Every day between 30 and 40 people would come to a farmhouse to beg, swap or buy. Of course they hated the farmers for the poor deals that they usually got, and which they had to agree to through gritted teeth. It was even said that some farmers had decorated their stables with carpets.

Food officials tried to discourage farmers from involvement in the black market by imposing legal checks. Stables and barns were searched, hidden harvests were confiscated and farmers acting in contravention of the regulations were arrested. There were also constant appeals to rural pride and a sense of responsibility for the nation as a whole: "Show the world and show the city folk that what is left of Germany is a society in need, in which those in distress are not abandoned."[13]

The actual mood among the urban population was reflected in a Social Democratic flyer that read:

Between three and five million food producers and food distributors sit there like maggots in bacon. Untouched by any misery, eating their fill and storing away precious goods. The time has come, the day is approaching when the starving will smash the windows of the sated and set fire to the farmsteads! Let them have no complaints; it is their own fault![14]

The more the hatred of the farmers grew, the fewer the scruples of the city-dwellers when it came to simply pilfering their harvests. Whole columns of cyclists took to the countryside to stockpile goods, their bicycles offering them better protection from attacks and allowing them to make off more easily in the event of a police roadblock. From Cologne on its own, about 10,000 people set off every day to lug food from the countryside back to the city. In the evening they could be seen carrying their gains home in suitcases, bags and rucksacks.

City administrations had to admit that the population could no longer be fed without this kind of "self-help." The collapse of organised infrastructure was compensated for by this ant-like form of transportation. Cologne's deputy mayor, Rolf Kattanek, said he was delighted by every hundredweight of potatoes that came into the city, quietly adding "legally or otherwise."[15] So it was that stockpilers carrying up to 30 pounds of goods from the surrounding foothills to Cologne went unpunished until May 1947.

Hoarding was not without its perils. The survival of the fittest was the rule in a time beset with criminality, and many people became victims of ambushes. Trains into the countryside were worryingly overcrowded, and became even more crammed in the evening when people brought back their bags of plunder, the load literally spilling

Urban gardening: growing vegetables by a tram stop in the middle of Dresden. There is much in the economy of 1945 that is reminiscent of the alternative economies of today, like this allotment, clothing exchanges and repair circles.

out of the doors. A lot of stockpilers stood on the footplates in the open doors; with one hand they firmly clutched the handle, while with the other they held the sack that they had thrown over their shoulder. Others balanced with their luggage on the buffers. One particularly perfidious kind of thief exploited this. Where the damage to the rails was such that the trains had to travel at a snail's pace, they lay in wait and then, with long grappling hooks, they nabbed the sacks and relieved the helpless passengers of the turnips they had taken such trouble to get hold of.

"Now everyone was fighting everyone else." It's a phrase that we read time and again in eyewitness statements from the period. "After the war we really got to know our fellow men," many Germans said. They spoke of the period as a "time of wolves," of the *Homo homini lupus* in his natural state," of the threatening collapse of any sense of law or justice. But was that true? Had morality really been abandoned?

"You need to have experienced it," the journalist Margret Boveri wrote in her diary early in May 1945 when she took part in the looting of a pharmaceutical warehouse.

> People climbed through the doors and windows, pulled goods from the shelves, threw what they didn't want to the floor, trampled each other down, "like wild animals," as an Austrian beside me put it. Of course glucose, which was all I was interested in, was long gone, but I grabbed a few things: throat lozenges, cough syrup, toilet paper. All the soap products were gone too, of course. So I came back under a cloud and shared what I had with Frau Mitusch.[16]

Reckless theft and affectionate sharing went hand in hand. Grabbing and giving; social breakdown and solidarity in a single breath. Morality didn't just dissolve, it adapted; standards were shifted but not completely abandoned. Margret Boveri later added:

> For a long time, in a state of confusion over who owned what, it seemed obvious to us to take what was available and to give where things were needed. The rage of those who later returned and dis-

covered that we had emptied all their jam jars, used their dining room chairs for firewood and gone on stealing lightbulbs from public places for ages struck us as more or less ridiculous.[17]

There was a lot of explaining to be done to children in particular when they saw their mothers stealing or were themselves sent out on thieving expeditions, as was commonplace in many fatherless families. Hopping coal or freight trains was an exercise that turned whole neighbourhoods, or just whoever happened to be in the street at the time, into gangs. The little ones threw the coal down and the grownups gathered it up in a flash. In February 1948 the *Rheinische Zeitung* reported on events at Cologne's Opera House, where a lot of trucks passed by carrying briquettes and had to stop at the pedestrian crossing.

> In a mad rush a pack of children pounced upon it, and with lightning speed as much of the load was thrown down as could be grabbed in ten seconds. Among the waiting people briquettes rained down into the gutter and in a high arc onto the pavement.

Most skilful of all was a nine-year-old girl who had previously gone to ballet, as she later told the reporter. Now she was perched on a mountain of briquettes on a lorry that was too high for the boys. "'Chuck me down something. I haven't got anything yet,' an old granny in a felt hood complained, holding out her bag." The coal theft escalated to involve uncoupling whole wagons. Once the train had set off again the wagons could be cleared at leisure. Occasionally signals on open stretches of track were set to stop by coal thieves, and the coal unloaded in a flash.[18]

Church authorities helped to ease any pangs of conscience that there might have been. In his famous New Year's Eve sermon, in the middle of the "starvation winter," Cologne's Cardinal Josef Frings put the seventh commandment, "Thou shalt not steal," into perspective. "We live in times when, under conditions of great hardship, individuals are allowed to take what he needs to maintain his life and health, if he cannot come by it in any other way, either through work or by asking." This pastoral homily made great waves, and the authorities protested. Frings went on to seek mitigating formulations, but it was too late: henceforth people called organised theft *"Fringsing."* "I *Fringsed* the coal," people said. Later Cardinal Frings himself was caught *Fringsing*; when Cologne churches were subjected to a systematic search by the British, huge amounts of illegally stored coal were found.

One had to take risks. In Berlin a hairdresser, who had been stranded while fleeing from the East into the city, broke into the abandoned shop of a colleague who had disappeared—whether he had died or fled, who knows. Now, every day in the shop he cut and curled hair, to the delight of his customers, who gratefully rewarded this welcome example of private initiative. In Munich someone had heard that the GIs were very keen on cuckoo clocks, with which they delighted their wives back in Illinois or St. Louis. He drove across the country, talking the farmers he encountered out of their cuckoo clocks, and sold them outside the barracks. An invalid on crutches who bore a startling resemblance to Hitler had taken up position outside the American travel agency in Munich. He stood by posters advertising Paris, London or the Riviera and had himself photographed in return for a donation. "You had to be vigilant to feed three children," one citizen of Dresden was recorded as saying.[19] "Be on the Qui vive" was a common phrase, meaning that you needed to be quick and well-informed, grabbing every opportunity by the scruff of the neck. Bystanders who witnessed "organising" and *"Fringsing"* felt not morally superior, but simply stupid. "We weren't clever enough," "I wasn't up to it," "my father wasn't good at stealing, but he was an excellent organiser"—these were typical comments from the time of the great *Fringsing*.[20] It was no longer a matter of being fair or unfair, only whether one was fit enough for the grey economy or not.

The sense of guilt was particularly insipid when it came to the illicit sale of coffee. In the villages on the Belgian border smuggling became a mass undertaking which was extremely profitable in the British zone because of high import duties. Police countermeasures

Organisational talent: one person forces the train to stop, the rest collect the coal.

became so severe that people soon talked about the "coffee front," and 31 smugglers and two customs men lost their lives in the conflict. Since customs officers were reluctant to fire at children, they were used in great numbers. Hundreds of children and young people ran over the border, their pockets full of coffee, and wiggled their way through the customs officers' legs. If the border guards did manage to grab a child from the swarm, they had to let them go again in the evening because the juvenile detention centres were already crowded with more serious offenders. Inspired by Italian neo-realism, the 1951 film *Sündige Grenze (Illegal Border)*, directed by Robert A. Stemmle, was an impressive cinematic tribute to the child smugglers of Aachen, who called themselves *Rabatzer* (rumpus-makers). Stemmle recruited 500 children and young adults, half of them from Berlin, to film in the original locations on the German-Belgian border. The scene when this crowd of scruffy children enter the railway embankments, pursued by customs officers and policemen, force their way under moving trains and fall on the border like locusts is one of the most gripping in post-war cinema—not least because it emphasised the permeability of the boundary between good and bad.

As was consistent with Cardinal Frings's sermon, the Aachen rabble-rousers had the sympathy of the Church, and on a number of occasions, it voiced its opposition to the use of firearms at the border. The smugglers expressed their thanks in their own way. St. Hubertus's Church in Nideggen in the Eifel mountains, right on the "coffee front," was severely damaged in the notorious Battle of Hürtgen Forest of November 1944. After a call for donations for reconstruction, smugglers threw so much money into the plate that the church was very soon able to welcome the faithful to Mass in all its former glory, and was known henceforth as St. Mocha.

In its 1947 New Year's edition, the Berlin magazine *Ja* drew up a rap sheet for the average middle-class family of three under the headline WE ARE CRIMINAL.[21] This family, "which might not have lived well, but it did live," had, in order to maintain its modest standard, to infringe many rules and laws that were clearly set forth in the article: stealing a wooden beam from a ruin, buying gentlemen's shoes from US Army stores on the black market, allowing ten glass windowpanes to disappear from the workplace, false statements for a ration coupon for underwear, and so on. All these crimes were part of the everyday survival routines of the magazine's readership. The offences added up to a total sentence of 12 years and 7 months for the family members had they been caught. The article concluded with the words "and we are what was once known as a decent family."

"Anyone who wasn't freezing stole," the novelist and future Nobel laureate Heinrich Böll observed laconically. "Everyone could rightly have been accused of theft."[22] Legal experts put it no less succinctly. As the *Recht für Jeden* (*Law for All*) series of books put it: "Everyone should be satisfied with the foodstuffs assigned to them and the amount of necessary commodities due to them."[23] They should have been, but they weren't. And couldn't be. "The phenomenon of crime in Germany," the criminologist Hans von Hentig wrote in 1947, "has reached a level and forms unparalleled in the history of western civilisation."[24] For Hentig, the general breakdown of laws and norms seemed to introduce a new phase in the collapse of civilisation. He was not shocked by the large number of capital crimes. However horrific the rise in cases of murder, robbery and manslaughter—in 1946, 311 murders were recorded in Berlin alone—Hentig was much more alarmed by the number of minor offences. Like his colleague Karl S. Bader he talked of a "deprofessionalisation of criminality," and its migration to the everyday conduct of the wider public.

The editor-in-chief of *Die Zeit*, Ernst Samhaber, established in his lead article in the edition of 18 July 1946 that the "law of the jungle" prevailed. He believed that "in Germany we are living in two worlds." In one world people tried to manage with only their ration cards, while in the other black-market dealings and dodgy business ruled.

> We can clearly distinguish amongst people from these two worlds. We just need to take a tram or a train in a German city. Then we see the gaunt, hollow-cheeked faces from the world of cash values. These are the unfortunates who have had to get by for months on a thousand calories, figures of inner depletion and famine. Next to them sits the man of material values, from the world of exchange—we don't need to go so far as to say the "Black Market"—round, blossoming, complacent. Anyone who lights a cigarette in the tram today belongs to this world beyond legal regulation. Today the underworld is forcing its way into the light. Even worse is the fact that it exerts a dangerous kind of attraction on what remains of the middle-class world. The spirit of lawlessness is on the prowl, eating its way through the increasingly narrow wall that separates chaos and order.

There may always have been two worlds, Samhaber recognised, but previously the lawless had sought the protection of darkness. Overall the illegitimate economy was threatening to devour the legitimate one. There was less and less to be had by lawful means.

Dabbling in lawlessness had its charms to which even the upper bourgeoisie had long been receptive. *Fringsing* could be mischievous fun. Even such a serious, morally right-thinking person as Ruth Andreas-Friedrich, the daughter of a privy councillor, divorced wife of a factory manager and a revered resistance fighter, discovered in herself a pleasure in "organising" that went far beyond the sober acquisition of life's necessities. "Trophy-hunters"—that was what she called herself and her friends, who proudly showed each other the goods that they had managed to get hold of. From the Russians she borrowed the word *Zapp-zarapp* that they used for their rampant confiscation of bicycles or suitcases. "*Zapp-zarapp*," the Russians said when they took some poor soul's suitcase away, and it sounded almost soothing. *Zapp-zarapp* was what Andreas-Friedrich said now as well. Described in this way, stealing "shed much of its derogatory tone." She noted in her diary:

> There is still a lot of Zapp-zarapp in Berlin. Only a few people so far have found their way back to lawful bourgeois behaviour. No doubt it is easier to leap out of the law than it is to find one's way back to it. [. . .] We don't plan to remain trophy-hunters. And yet it's hard for us. Much harder than we ever imagined.[25]

But did one really "leap" out of the law? Were there really two worlds in Germany, as the editor of *Die Zeit* imagined, clearly distinguishable as legal and illegal? Or had the morality of survival completely abandoned this *either-or*, accepting instead a *both-as-well-as*, an *it-depends* and a *more-or-less*? Furthermore, against the background of what the Germans had done in the war, was that not a completely grotesque question?

If we leave for a moment the broader picture of everyday German post-war life and focus from the distance of history on the debate concerning the criminality of the average citizen, it can hardly help but appear absurd. In the eyes of the world "the Germans" had long ago turned themselves into perpetrators of war crimes and genocide. They had bidden farewell to civilisation and left the circle of nations in which human rights applied. The degree to which they had repudiated themselves as a nation was apparent only to those Germans who

had emigrated. Within the country, it was not clear even to opponents of the Nazis, those who had been ashamed of the regime, just
how far they had fallen in the eyes of the world. Neither the murder
of millions of Jews nor the crimes of the Wehrmacht had deprived
the majority of Germans of the sense that order and respectability
were particularly at home in Germany. So they were all the more horrified at the extent to which criminality became standard in a time of
hardship.

A collective perception could hardly be more distorted. While
observers abroad once again saw the collapse as a chance for the reso-
cialisation of the Germans, the Germans themselves now felt for the
first time that they were sliding into criminality. It was only after the
war that the Germans saw themselves becoming perpetrators—
because they were stealing coal and potatoes. The fact that in
Germany alone half a million Jewish fellow-citizens had been stripped
of their possessions and driven from their homes, and in the end
165,000 German Jews had been murdered, was never so much as mentioned in any of the reflections on the possible reasons for the decline
of a sense of the law. The idea that the decline of civilisation, which
they now feared, had begun long before the end of the war was
entirely alien to them at that moment.

Life simply went on. The conscience that had failed so terribly
ticked on as if nothing had happened. Hunger dictated the next
steps and fear of socially uprooted, disorientated fellow men re-
framed people's morals. *Zapp-zarapp*, organised theft, trophy-hunting,
Fringsing—that was the vocabulary of relativisation and self-exculpation.
Fine distinctions were made between different kinds of stealing, designed to differentiate between protecting one's own property and
life and expropriating the property of others. A piece of coal was, once
it had been personally claimed by someone, more protected by the
collective sense of justice than when it merely lay on the freight train
as the possession of some abstract institution. The person who took
coal from a railway wagon was *Fringsing*; anyone who removed it from
a private coal cellar was stealing. Post-war Germans liked to use

animal imagery for their activities: the person who removed potatoes from a field was "hamstering" (stockpiling), while the person who stole them from the hoarding "hamsters" was a "hyena." And wandering back and forth between them was the "wolf," whose sociability one could never be quite sure of, since the "lone wolf" had just as frightening a reputation as the whole pack.

Most elements of the social value system had disappeared with the country's defeat, but "respectability," apparently of an apolitical nature, had remained as a social guideline. "Respectability did not exclude resourcefulness and cunning," the editor Kurt Kusenberg wrote in 1952 in the *Neue Zeitung*, in his almost elegiac look back at the school of hardship after the end of the war.

> In this semi-outlaw life there was an honour among thieves that was perhaps more moral than the cast-iron consciences of many upstanding people today. [. . .] The task was not to starve, but also not to lose one's morale. A mother stole a bag of sugar for her daughter. On the other hand, a host shared with his guest the last tiny scrap of fat, with no concern of what he would eat the following day. Doing good was harder than it is today, but much more rewarding. Every gift meant reaching into one's own substance [. . .] The spirit of St. Martin of Tours, giving half of his cloak to a beggar man, was out and about.[26]

In hard times property rights were not abolished, they were redefined. Anything that could not be attributed to a concrete individual had, in the popular sense of justice, passed into a vague kind of universal ownership, and was regarded as available for the taking. Even a nameplate on a door only protected an apartment under certain conditions. A tenant's lengthy absence eroded property rights to furniture and household goods, and they became common property. The owner might have fallen in the war, after all. For many, taking up residence in his home was perfectly legitimate, a kind of unofficial billeting that was accepted as a kind of informal aid. The state had

broken down to such an extent that anyone could consider themselves as its proxy.

There was also a feeling of a "higher injustice." The war had
robbed some people of everything, while completely sparing others.
If skill and hard work had hitherto been seen to correlate in some
way to success and property, that connection had now literally been
blown apart. What someone was left with and what they had lost in
the war was equally arbitrary, unearned and undeserved. The arbi-
trariness of war's vicissitudes inevitably altered attitudes towards
ownership. In the eyes of many, possession was "a chance result, justified by nothing and in need of change."[27]

Without a doubt, such shifts in the perception of legality also acted
as a threadbare cover for criminal motives. Double standards were
not in short supply. "Death to the black-marketeers!" the people
chanted at the hunger demonstrations in the Ruhr area—the same
people who traded on the black market on a small scale themselves.
But we cannot simply talk in terms of universal amorality. If they
assumed that they were witnessing the start of a conflagration that
would soon get out of control, the criminologists of the first post-
war years had seriously underestimated the adaptability, survival
skills and morals of ordinary people. In fact the opposite proved to be
the case: after the end of the years of hardship, the black-market generation developed into one of the most law-abiding in history. Seldom
could a population have, on balance, given the police so little work as
that of the two German states in the 1950s and they would also be
liberally mocked for their eager conformity.

We may conclude from this that the "time of misery" was in fact
the very school of morality that Kurt Kusenberg had pointed out.
The lessons it taught were fundamental and ruthless. Its method consisted of relativism and its goal was an education in scepticism. The
labyrinth of moral ambiguity was a challenge to many. The monetary value of Iron Crosses, for example, fluctuated throughout this
period—how annoyed people were to think that they had tossed their
Nazi insignia in the lake, or melted them down with the arrival of the
Allies. They should have hidden them, they later thought, not

destroyed them! Because the military decoration that in May 1945 had brought on furious attacks from occupying soldiers by November was now a much sought-after piece of memorabilia. In fact, the victors would swap whole cartons of cigarettes for all kinds of Nazi souvenirs. The moment when, for example, a bust of Hitler was bought by a GI in grateful exchange for three bars of chocolate was, for many Germans, a key event in the history of denazification, more effective than any lecture or Chancellor's speech.

The ration cards were a life lesson in themselves. The printed quantity was relative, like everything in life: 50 grams was 50 grams minus the quantity that wasn't available. Also relative was the price that was held to be "fair" on the black market at any given time. "One gradually becomes used to the fact that for one part of the population small change begins with a thousand-mark note, for others with a five-pfennig piece," Ruth Andreas-Friedrich wrote in her diary in January 1946.[28]

We might imagine that so much relativity must have been unbearable to the Germans, of all people. But there are two sides to any lesson, one that is painfully exacting, and one that is exhilaratingly liberating. A lot of younger people in particular changed worlds daily; they moved in social spheres shaped by completely different sets of values. Whether they were dealing with their families, with black markets or with occupying soldiers, they always acted according to differently coded systems. That could be exciting and profitable. For the ironic intellect of the author Hans Magnus Enzensberger, for example, a particularly mercurial and prominent intellectual of the Federal Republic, experiences on the black market were actually character building. Late in 1945 Enzensberger, who was 16 at the time, served successfully as an interpreter in the Bavarian town of Kaufbeuren, first to the Americans and, when they moved on, to the British. "What incredible power for a young person," Jörg Lau wrote in his Enzensberger biography:

Now he is not only morally in the right compared to his discredited adults, who were at first all suspected of having been involved. He also knows more about the new masters, because he can communicate with them and picks up a lot of things that remain hidden to everyone else. The sixteen-year-old is the medium without which nothing works on either side.[29]

For Enzensberger what worked above all was business; he swapped Nazi souvenirs for American cigarettes, and these in turn for more Nazi badges, ceremonial daggers, uniforms and even weapons. He got richer and richer in the process. There were times when he was storing 40,000 cigarettes in his parents' house. At a price of ten marks each, or 400,000 Reichsmark in all (£10,000 at the time), this was the equivalent of approximately £440,000 today—untold wealth for a sixteen-year-old.[30]

The trade in these symbols from two worlds, Lucky Strikes for Golden Party Badges, sharpened the senses and presence of mind of a boy who, 11 years later, would achieve sudden fame with his volume of poems *Verteidigung der Wölfe* (*Defence of the Wolves*).[31] In it, Enzensberger launched his violent lyrical attack against the lambs, the little people who shy away from any responsibility, "averse to learning, leaving the thinking up to the wolves." Young Enzensberger, on the other hand, balanced himself proudly in short trousers on the raw edge of history. It was an experience that would last him a lifetime. Jörg Lau writes about the pleasure Enzensberger derived from a society in ruins.

Even without school we can now learn a great deal about politics and society: we learn for example that a country without a proper government can be a very pleasant thing. On the black market, you learn that capitalism always gives a chance to the resourceful. You learn that a society is something that can organise itself without central orders and guidance. In conditions of scarcity you learn a lot about people's real needs. You learn that people can be flexible, and that solemn convictions may not be as unshakeable as they seem. [. . .] In a word: in spite of hardship it is a wonderful time if you're young and curious—a brief summer of anarchy.[32]

The black market as a school of citizenship

Anyone who can't get what they need from their regular shop will eventually do their shopping elsewhere. Any market restriction automatically creates its own black market. The Germans had had enough time in the First and Second World Wars to get used to it. They were already quite crafty by the time the black market changed completely in terms of quality and size after the capitulation. While most Germans had initially traded only with one another—for example, soldiers on leave from the front selling off goods they had picked up in France or Holland—new players, such as occupying soldiers and displaced persons, now joined, turning the market into a thrilling source of foreign exoticism. The fact that these same traders were people who only yesterday the Germans had been shooting at or treating like slaves only made the market all the stranger—and all the more attractive. The foreigners extended the range of products on offer with desirable goods that people would have sold their own grandmothers to get hold of: Hershey bars and Bommel chocolate; graham crackers, Oreos and Cracker Jacks; Butterfingers, Snickers, Mars Bars; Jack Daniel's and Old Fitzgerald Whiskey; and a detergent called Ivory Snow.

These products came from the warehouses of the refugee aid organisation UNRRA (United Nations Relief and Rehabilitation Association) and the US Army Post Exchange stores. People went to the black market as the vanquished, but also as trading partners. They too had something to offer. Sometimes they just wanted to have a look at the chequered bazaar where there were all kinds of new things to experience and learn about. It was an absurd situation: the war's winners and losers, its victims and perpetrators, met illegally to strike a deal, to find a win-win situation. However, the structure of the exchange was extremely asymmetrical. Some had goods from all over the world that had suddenly acquired an exorbitant value because of rationing: butter, margarine, flour, chocolate, oranges, brandy, oil, petrol, paraffin and thread. Others offered leftover luxuries: watches, jewellery, cameras, silver cutlery, items which had formerly been expensive, but when one's stomach rumbled they suddenly seemed worthless compared to a sandwich. Anyone who, in a moment of great hunger, swapped a Leica camera for two dried sausages could say they had got a good deal. But as soon as they had eaten their fill, the swap looked like an ill-disguised theft to which they had fallen victim. The black market was for many a harsh place, where they gave away whole family inheritances for things that, in the past, they had never paid the slightest attention to.

While some satisfied their hunger through black-market trading and became poorer and poorer, others wallowed in money like the Disney character Scrooge McDuck. American soldiers multiplied their wages ten times over by selling on foodstuffs that had been imported specially for them. They did so by the shipload, on a huge scale, via a finely detailed distribution system from the harbours to the barracks, involving all ranks of the military. The British, French and Russians all followed the same method, but on a much smaller scale.

The German black-marketeers were just as organised as the Americans. On the markets, one could find illicit industrially produced and handmade goods that wholesalers and producers had withheld from the legitimate, regular market. In March 1948, for example, the police in Braunschweig found 28,000 tins of meat hidden in the walls of a wholesaler. In Hamburg 31,000 litres of wine, 148 tonnes of fruit and 15 tonnes of coffee were impounded, a tiny portion of what was touted every day.[33] In Berlin alone there were sixty black-market outlets, from the best-known, Alexanderplatz, to smaller markets in local neighbourhoods. The rationing offices estimated that at least a third, sometimes even half, of the goods in circulation in Berlin were being traded illegally—that proportion makes it clear how unavoidable it was for Germans to make these morally suspect purchases.

In the markets one was moving among hardened criminals who did not flinch from committing any kind of felony. These could include the large-scale forgery of ration cards or their theft from the issuing offices. The cards were then sold by the bundle on the black market. People liked to give them as birthday presents—an early form of today's gift cards. But for such a loving gesture one had to deal with the shady characters who ran the markets. Smartly dressed, although somewhat at odds with the occasion and their surroundings, always with a cigarette in the corner of their mouths, their shoes polished and their hats either cheekily tipped back or pulled forwards over their faces, chic from top to toe, they strolled around, presenting themselves as collection points for goods of all kinds.

Anyone entering the black market would find themselves dealing with these people, and it was extremely important to judge them correctly. It was a fast-track lesson in understanding people, defined by a "culture of suspicion."[34] One had to be able to gauge one's fellow man very precisely, seeking their faces for signs of trustworthiness or treachery. In that way one tried to track down the remnants of respectability and fairness without which no trading system can survive for any length of time. Only on the black market was the seller subjected to more minute scrutiny than the goods themselves.

It was not simple to gain access to the market. Black markets didn't have regular stalls, aside from a few exceptions, such as Munich's famous Mühlstrasse, where a whole series of shoddy-looking huts and sheds ran along the street, a pitiful sight even though a huge treasure trove of goods was stacked up inside. Black markets usually consisted of individuals who would walk up and down hissing the names of their wares at potential customers, or else stood clustered in little groups. You had to summon a certain amount of courage if you were to go over and mingle. Some black-marketeers looked strikingly glammed-up, particularly the women, who wore the jewellery they wanted to swap. They used their bodies as displays, which spared them having to approach strangers of their own accord. What lingers in the collective memory are the long coats of the traders, with whole rows of watches, jewellery, medals and so on fastened to their inside linings. When offering for sale, the traders would open their coats with a gesture like the obscene motion of a flasher.

Black market by the Gedächtniskirche in Berlin. In the black market, Siegfried Lenz recognised "scenes of an audacious if muddled poetry," and a "dapper surrealism."

The black market required a proximity that was disagreeable to many participants, and which they had to overcome. Approaching traders made people feel embarrassed or uncomfortable. The traders sometimes stood so closely together that they formed a conspiratorial circle, a "crow-like intimacy" from which buyers felt excluded.[35] One first had to literally force one's way in and join the cramped and whispering huddle, which was at its tightest at the moment when the goods were being examined, fingered and sniffed at. People were, legitimately, suspicious, because the wares on offer were often fake or spoiled. Margarine was adulterated with engine grease, bags of potatoes were often mixed with stones, inedible wood oil was sold as cooking oil, and sometimes "schnapps" came from the anatomical display jars looted from medical and scientific institutes, in which organs, foetuses and all kinds of animals had been preserved. And there was nowhere one could go to complain. Perhaps it was as a delayed reaction to these experiences that the Federal Republic later became the first country in Europe to introduce an institution for comparative product investigation: the Stiftung Warentest (Goods Testing Foundation).[36]

Gradually barter was replaced by a form of financial exchange; it was more practical to repeat human history's development towards monetary transactions on the black market. The difference being that traditional currency was replaced by cigarettes: as trading in dollars between soldiers and civilians was forbidden, and trade in Reichsmarks had become too unsafe with the constant looming prospect of currency reform, cigarettes took the place of banknotes. The cigarette became the cowry shell of the post-war era. Its exchange rate might have fluctuated, but it remained one of the more dependable certainties of those years. It was ideal as a currency: it was small, it was easily transported, stacked and counted. It came in packs the way banknotes came in bundles. By its very nature, it had an ephemerality even greater than that of money: people's whole earthly possessions went up in smoke in the form of bartered cigarettes. They glowed and burned, they were everywhere and yet they were always in short supply. Their new status as currency took the already considerable allure of cigarettes to new and dizzying heights.

The cigarette was a medium of victory and defeat. German men scrambling in the dust for a few cigarette butts flicked away by occupying soldiers is one of the most vividly described post-war scenes. The image filled many with contempt, others with bitterness. So this was what the master race had come to. They enviously watched the casual smoking of the Allies. Young Germans clumsily copied their gestures. Special attention was paid to the moment of throwing the cigarette on the ground and stamping it out. No occupying soldier held the stub long enough for it to almost burn his fingers. They tossed away the cigarette butts with a heedlessness that simply couldn't be copied. The German lads from the black market never quite managed that, but they did try to act, when smoking, as if they had enough cigarettes in the cellar to do them till the end of time which, as in Enzensberger's case, was sometimes so.[37]

Since cigarettes served as currency, the smoker was like a person burning banknotes. More than ever, smoking became a celebration of the moment, with which one triumphed over thoughts of the future. Women, too, wanted to have access to that feeling. The old right-wing saying "German women don't smoke" was now once and for all a thing of the past. For now, the matter was a practical one; cigarettes were valued by the authorities for their capacity to suppress hunger. That was one reason why tobacco was promoted in Germany with official backing. In the Soviet-occupied zone, the area of land set aside for tobacco cultivation increased by a factor of 60 within a single post-war year. The plan was to kill two birds with one stone: weaken the black market and assuage hunger.

Dodgy as the traders might have been, smoking remained important as a ritual of communication. Offering a cigarette that peeped out of the pack, the circling of the lighter, the moment of a certain shared contemplation for the duration of the first few drags—these were all social acts that were all the more important in the suspicious atmosphere of the market in that they contributed to mutual assessment and the establishment of trust. In this way Lucky Strikes and Machorkas performed valuable services in making connections between people in the dubious social mix of the black market.

In an atmosphere of mistrust and curiosity, the black market was a vital learning experience for the Germans, offering a radically different trading experience and providing a fundamental corrective to the *Volk* community fetishised by the Nazis. It was a lesson that remained in the memory for many years. Its lack of defined rules, which "rewarded the cunning and punished the weak," created an economic terrain "in which people had apparently once more become wolves towards their fellows," as the historian Malte Zierenberg writes.[38] The widespread wariness so characteristic of the 1950s found a powerful source here. That narrow-minded, stuffy atmosphere that lingered around the black market was the smell of mistrust. Even the appetite for cleanliness, tidiness and order in 1950s Germany, which appeared strange to the next generation, had an origin in the chaotic conditions of the illegal markets. Where some saw restrictions, others saw opportunities: "In the sea of rationed hunger it appeared [. . .] as a last bastion of freedom, private initiative and survival."[39] The author Siegfried Lenz devoted melancholy memories to the market, first broadcast on the radio and successfully published in book form in 1964 under the title *Lehmann's Stories or So Fine Was My Market*. With ironic sentimentality the narrator looked back, from the boredom he now felt about the economic miracle, at the shortage economy that he saw as having stimulated his finest talents and brought people together in "shady familiarity."[40] "Never was the creative impulse greater than it was in those days." The market offered "scenes of daring if twisted poetry" and a "curious surrealism," as for example when a lady with a rather faded elegance approached, carrying on her back a twelve-point stag's antler which she was taking home as a present for her husband.

The black market only thrived because of the existence of its opposite pole, the rationing system. On the one hand the wild interplay of raw market forces, on the other rationed per-capita distribution. People were caught between two different systems, always experiencing both at the same time: the state *dirigisme* of the shortage economy and the anarchic freedom of the unbridled market. Two conflicting logics of distribution, both of which had severe shortcomings. This daily exercise in practical sociology, with all the exertions that it entailed, explains the unshakable faith that West Germans would later bring to the system of the "social market economy," which, from 1948, became the patent remedy for the emerging Federal Republic. The very phrase sounded like a magical formula, because it reconciled both sides: the caring state ensuring that everybody got something and a free market system that was demand-led and placed the consumer at its centre.

The few black-market years ensured that the social market economy became an article of faith for generations. Its "father," Ludwig

Erhard, the Federal Republic's first Minister of Economic Affairs and its second Chancellor after Konrad Adenauer, became a symbol of the growth years. Erhard had a massive head resting on a stout body; a side parting of his hair that began directly above the ear; and a cunning and intelligence hidden behind a huge mountain of cordiality. His most striking feature: he smoked cigars. Ludwig Erhard brought to an end the age of cigarettes as a currency, in both real and symbolic terms. At last the cigarette could shed its multiple coded meanings. Erhard's cigar, a fat Dannemann, would become the trademark of the new age. People no longer hastily dragged on their stubs as if there were no tomorrow. From now on they puffed away happily.

VII

The Economic Miracle and the Fear of Immorality

Currency reform, the second Zero Hour

On the night of 17 June 1948 20-year-old British private Chris Howland was the last member of staff left in the Hamburg studio of the BFN (British Forces Network). The head of the music department and the most popular DJ in the whole of Northern Germany—revered not least by the German audience for the large amount of pop music in his programmes and the casual tone of his presentation—was just bidding goodnight to his listeners with the number "Throwing Stones at the Sun" by Benny Goodman, when two British military policemen appeared. DJ Howland was uneasy; the appearance of the policemen in their red uniform caps seldom boded well.[1] But they just pressed an envelope into his hand and told him to read out the contents at 6:30 the next morning when he started the day again with the early show *Wakey-Wakey*. "Will do," Howland said, took the envelope and made as if to set off for home. But that was not to be. The military policemen forced him to put the sealed envelope on the table and wait with them until the birds were tweeting, the sun was rising over the bruised city and it was time once more for *Wakey-Wakey*.

When morning came, Chris Howland opened the envelope as he had been ordered to do and read:

The first law of the reform of the German currency promulgated by the Military Governments of Great Britain, the United States, and

France will go into effect on June 20. The old German currency is hereby invalidated. The new currency will be the Deutsche Mark, which will be divided into 100 Deutsche pfennigs. The old money, the Reichsmark, the Rentenmark and Mark notes issued in Germany by the Allied Military authorities, will become invalid on June 21.

The Germans had been waiting for months for this moment. There had been a lot of talk about a currency devaluation. No one trusted the Reichsmark anymore and everyone who still had enough swapped them for tangible goods. Apart from the millions who were starving, there were any number of Germans who had more Reichsmarks than they could spend, and who led a life of officially illegal luxury purchased at astronomic prices. Doubts about the Reichsmark meant that traders had held back more and more goods, hoarding for the day when there would be a stable currency with better prices in the future. In the early summer of 1948 the shops were very nearly empty, because rumours about the coming D-Day were constantly spreading.

Now the time had come. Throughout the day listeners to BFN would learn more about the procedure. Everyone would receive an allowance of 40 Deutschemarks, which they could collect on Sunday 20 July at the ration card issuing offices in exchange for 60 Reichsmarks. A month later they would receive an additional 20 D-Marks, in exchange for the same number of Reichsmarks. Any Reichsmarks beyond the first 60 would be practically worthless: 1,000 Reichsmarks would have a value of 65 D-Mark.

In this way about 93 per cent of the old Reichsmark supply was destroyed without replacement. Savers were left with only 6.5 per cent of their assets. Resistance against this "historically unique expropriation" remained modest.[2] According to a report in *Der Spiegel* only black-market traders demonstrated against the reform, whose effects they had instinctively predicted with great precision. A day before the target date "about forty black-marketeers held a demonstration outside Cologne Central Station with white baseball caps, Camel cigarettes, a bottle of schnapps and a big placard that read RETRAINING FOR BLACK-MARKET TRADERS. Then on Sunday afternoon they stood grimly by Cologne's Porta Nigra and the Eigelstein Gate and flogged American cigarettes for 60 D-pfennigs, German Boscos for 30. There was barely any uptake for this unusual Sunday trading."[3]

Currency reform was at the heart of a whole series of measures with which the Americans wanted to help the German economy back on its feet. Under the Marshall Plan, these policies were designed to give economic support not just to Germany but to the whole of Europe, and also to diminish the influence of the Soviet Union and the risk of communist uprisings. These massive financial efforts were triggered by the withdrawal, in March 1947, of an exhausted United Kingdom from the Greek civil war, in which a communist guerrilla force was fighting against a conservative government that was supported by the British. The American president, Harry S. Truman, reacted to the British withdrawal with a rousing speech in Congress on 12 March 1947, in which he pledged henceforth to help every nation willing to defend the values of freedom against the terror of a minority supported by Russia. The so-called Truman Doctrine painted the future as a competition between two ways of life—democratic capitalism versus totalitarian communism—and thus, less than two years after the end of the war, repositioned power among the victorious Allies and the losers. The Cold War was declared. Russia and the Western Allies became adversaries, who wanted to turn the losers of yesterday into the partners of tomorrow. A few ex-Nazis already saw themselves transitioning into a new war against Russia, side by side with the Americans.

A short time later the American secretary of state, George C. Marshall, offered the European states extensive credits in order, as he put it, to "restore the confidence of the European people in the economic future of their own countries and of Europe as a whole." In exchange, "The manufacturer and the farmer throughout wide areas must be able and willing to exchange their product for currencies, the continuing value of which is not open to question." This was the European Recovery Program, which came to be better known as the Marshall Plan. The United Kingdom received 3.2 billion dollars, France 2.7 billion, Italy 1.5 billion, West Germany 1.4 billion—the latter was the only one required to repay the funds, in order to preserve some sense of proportion between victory and defeat. The foundations were laid for the Organisation for European Economic Co-operation (OEEC); from 1947 it included West Germany, which was represented by the Military Governors. Just two years after the end of the war, foundations for the future European Economic Union were in place; West Germany, under the careful guidance of its American probationers, would become a future member of the union, in spite of the destruction of the war, as it still possessed all the facilities required for a powerful industrial state.

The division of Germany was thus already in the cards, even before currency reform established a demarcation line between East and West as a currency border. Once this had occurred, the Soviets matched the move three days later and undertook a currency reform of their own: up to 70 Reichsmarks per person were exchanged for new East German marks to the same value; only savings up to a level of 100 marks were recognised. But the Eastern zone did not yet really have a new currency. The old notes simply had pre-printed coupons stuck over them—a method that won them the nickname *Tapetengeld*—wallpaper money. According to the orders of the Soviets, this was to apply to the whole of Berlin. But the Western Allies decided to introduce their D-Mark in their Berlin zones, too. This first instance of open conflict between the four powers in Berlin's city council, which had until now met together in East Berlin, led to a final split that would result in the political and economic division of the city.

From 24 June 1948 the Soviets tried to starve West Berlin by blocking access routes to the three Western zones. The British and the Americans responded to the blockade with the Berlin Airlift. In an immense effort, over the following 15 months more than 2 million tonnes of food, coal and other vital goods were flown into the city, which was otherwise cut off from all supply routes. Huge cargo planes landed in West Berlin's airports every two to three minutes. Even the Wannsee lake was utilised. Because airport capacity was inadequate, the British deployed ten of their enormous Sunderland flying boats, which were launched from Hamburg harbour and landed on Berlin's biggest swimming lake. Until September 1949 the sky over Berlin was filled with the roar of the so-called *Rosinenbomber* (raisin bombers), whose tireless operation the West Berliners remembered with wistful gratitude for the rest of their lives. The noise of the planes was music to their ears, and helped get them through the winter cold and the ever-present pangs of hunger. With the airlift the victorious Western powers assumed the role of protector. The Reich capital, long the target of international hatred, had within a few years turned into a stoutly defended "frontline city of the free world"—a rapid development that caught many thoughtful observers off guard, and short-circuited what would later be called *Geschichtsarbeitung*— coming to terms with history.

In terms of planning customs reforms for the Western zones, the Americans assumed the leading role in the trio of the Western Allies. Even the new Deutschmark had been printed in the United States. The notes were shipped to Bremerhaven in 12,000 wooden crates quite sensibly stamped with the word "Doorknobs" by way of disguise, and from there, under conditions of the strictest secrecy, they were distributed around the country. On 20 June a total of 500 tonnes of banknotes with a face value of 5.8 billion Deutschmarks were available in the ration card issuing offices and at town halls.[4] Lieutenant Edward A. Tenenbaum, the 27-year-old who had been put in charge of Operation Bird Dog, later boasted, not without justification, that he had commanded the greatest logistical achievement of the American military since the Normandy D-Day landings.

Almost at the last moment it had occurred to the Americans that it might be a good idea to give the Germans the feeling that they too had a say in the matter. On 20 April 1948 they invited 25 German financial experts, under strict conditions of secrecy, to the former Luftwaffe airbase at Rothwesen near Kessel. Admittedly there was not much left to discuss, the sole purpose of the meeting was to deprive the Germans of the argument that they had not been consulted. They did, however, get to write the information sheets to be distributed to the German population.

Of course, American commitment to the process was not entirely disinterested. Unwilling to go on feeding West Germany indefinitely, the Americans were seeking ways of stimulating the economy and recognised that a crucial obstacle lay in the weakness of the Reichs-mark. "I can't afford to work" was a phrase heard often in the post-war years. The black market continued to advance, and the barter econ-omy, "organising" and illicit deals ate up more than half of the country's labour force. Many people had only taken on their jobs to have secure housing and food ration cards, before swapping them for something more lucrative. It was only the necessity of obtaining the new currency that finally led to the revival of the regular economy. The willingness to pursue regular employment increased just as rap-idly as the willingness of the traders to sell their goods "normally" rather than illicitly. Farmers now also had a reason to sell their har-vests on the public market. This created the widespread perception that shops filled up with goods overnight, and was therefore quite correctly spoken of in terms of a miracle. So powerful were the effects of the reforms that they have sometimes been described as the "Big Bang" that led to the foundation of the Federal Republic a year later.[5] Contemporaries felt that the currency reform had a much more drastic effect than the passing of the Basic Law of the German Constitution enacted by the Parliamentary Council on 8 May 1949 in Bonn, which established the terms of West German democracy.[6] No event of the post-war era is so vivid in West German memory as the currency reform, which was staged as an opera on a massive scale— and all without a director. The recollections of the writer Hans Werner Richter, who experienced two miracles on the first day of the new currency, demonstrate the sense of being overwhelmed that was typical of the time:

On the way we passed by a small shop in which we had previously paid with ration cards, an essentially miserable cornershop, and it was here that the miracle of currency reform, the actual miracle, began. The shop appeared completely changed. It was practically bursting with goods. The displays were decorated with every imaginable kind of vegetable: rhubarb, cauliflower, white cabbage, spinach, everything that we had been deprived of for so long. [. . .] We went into the shop and now another miracle happened. If before the service had been not exactly unfriendly but often sulky, now we were welcomed with great politeness. We had gone overnight from being ration-card-buyers and supplicants to being customers.[7]

Not even the pride that was felt at having the right to free elections could compete with the satisfaction at once again enjoying the status of "customer." Going shopping normally also represents a moment of freedom that can only be considered trivial by someone whose right to shop has never been compromised. Certainly, the rationing of all foodstuffs did not end with the currency reform, and many people suffered under a wave of price increases, but the sudden presence of a "world of commodities" at least gave them a clear vision of the future. Things were noticeably improving, and anyone who was not yet profiting from the upturn felt confident that they would soon be able to do so. The rage that inspired the last general strike of the post-war years, called on 12 November 1948 in response to profiteering, was fed by the hope that there might soon be more to distribute than mere scarcity. When, on 1 January 1950, only sugar was still rationed, one Cologne newspaper crowed:

We're breathing out. [. . .] Many disagreeable points of contact between the population and public offices, burdensome even to the administration itself, are on the way out. We can eat what we want once more, the shopkeeper no longer needs to collect our stamps and worry about his shrinking income. Those days are behind us. All in all it was 160 months—4,600 bitter days! There is butter again—and we are talking about sugar again.[8]

The period of limited consumption that the cheerful author is calculating here, with a slight degree of imprecision, goes back beyond the end of the war to 1939, with the start of the rationing economy. It is a radically consumerist view that ignores the interval of the capitulation as if, sugar aside, the war was only now really coming to an end. Currency reform was the articulation of that feeling. It represented the mythical launch of the economic miracle. In June 1948 the long-missed goods that had been held back suddenly reappeared in great quantities from hidden kitchen gardens. In theory, anyone could now order a Volkswagen, at a cost of 5,300 DM and with a delivery time of only eight days.

It was quite a happy summer, although the material situation for most of the population was only improving very slowly. The aphorism "half of economics is psychology" is thought, appropriately enough, to go back to the Federal Republic's second post-war Chancellor, Ludwig Erhard. Rarely was it more fittingly applied than to currency reform. The cities were still in ruins, housing in a wretched state, cars unaffordable, fabrics coarse and expensive, but the dusty grey of existence was now bathed in a new and warmer light. No sooner had the currency replacement occurred than the normally rather serious *DND im Bild*, the "illustrated magazine for politics, the economy and culture" published in the French zone, showed on its front page a full-page beauty in a bikini, lolling comfortably on a pool float with a happy smile on her face. The young woman was an allegory for the newly founded Federal Republic. The abbreviation of the magazine's title, DND, standing for "Die neue Demokratie" (the new democracy), was echoed in the picture caption as "Diese Nette Dame" (this nice lady).[9] DND, the picture suggested, was actually a seductive, half-naked, powerful siren designed to lead the population out of its post-war misery.

The fact that the shelves could fill again so quickly demonstrated the genuine promise of the economy and industry, which had been much less severely damaged than was commonly assumed. More than three-quarters of industrial capacity had been preserved. The Nazi militarised economy had modernised and greatly expanded machinery in its factories, and as a result industrial productivity after the war was only slightly below the level of 1938. The expellees who came into the country from the eastern territories provided a huge pool of well-trained, highly motivated workers, willing to get to work once the conditions were in place for industrial activity to become viable again. For both of these reasons, the breathtaking economic upturn that would begin after 1950 was not as miraculous as talk of the economic miracle might suggest.

Still, the psychological effect of the currency reform was like a thunderous starting shot. Currency reform seemed to set the clocks of history back to zero for a second time, only three years after the Germans had acknowledged the need to start over from the beginning at the end of the war.[10] Hardly anyone could escape the magic of this carefully stage-managed beginning. There was also an egalitarian element to the mass-psychological success of this restart. By giving all citizens the same sum of 60 DM, currency reform had radically

Mood-making. Along with currency reform, the French-licensed DND ("Die neue Demokratie") introduces a new form of state on its front page: "Diese Nette Dame"— "This Nice Lady."

devalued savings, and sent everyone back to "Go," like a game of Monopoly. It produced the magic trick of equality of opportunity that remains a part of the founding myth of the Federal Republic.[11] No material object can speak so eloquently to this as the Volkswagen, even though (or precisely because) it was a pet project of Adolf Hitler.

Wolfsburg, the human plantation

The Beetle was adorned with a wolf. Until the 1960s, every Volkswagen had a wolf walking on its bonnet. Or more precisely, as it was described in the statutes of the city of Wolfsburg, "a golden, blue-tongued, backward-looking wolf [. . .] walking rightwards on the crenelated wall of a twin-towered silver castle." It looked appropriately traditional but had in fact been designed in 1947 by the art teacher and heraldic expert Gustav Völker. The reality was that nothing about Wolfsburg was old, not even the name. There has only been a place called Wolfsburg since the end of the war, or more precisely since 25 May 1945. Before then it was called "Stadt des KdF-Wagens bei Fallersleben," City of the Kraft-durch-Freude (Strength through Joy) Car at Fallersleben, and in 1945 not even its inhabitants believed that it was a city. Everyone in Wolfsburg was a transplant, it was said. The town took its name from the nearby castle of Wolfsburg, whose surrounding lands and farms had for centuries been the source of its owners' wealth. The Renaissance castle still stands east of the factory today, outside the town's boundaries as designated at the time. The lord of the manor, Günther Graf von der Schulenburg, sold the castle before it was expropriated in 1938, and with the proceeds built himself a substitute residence in Tangeln, 40 kilometres farther to the north, which remains the most recently built castle in Germany to this day.

In 1950 reporters from *Der Spiegel* came to Wolfsburg and discovered a "misbegotten human plantation," the "Gomorrah of the second Republic." In terms of appearance and atmosphere it was reminiscent of a gold prospectors' settlement in the Klondike. In the first years after the war few could have imagined that this work camp would become, ten years later, the symbol of the economic miracle, the epitome of the smooth-running mediocrity that would typify the young Federal Republic. The historian Christoph Stölzl would later write: "If a visitor to Germany between the 1960s and the 1980s had asked where he could experience the character of Germany in a single day, one would have had to send him to Wolfsburg."[12]

The history of Wolfsburg began in 1938. Adolf Hitler wanted an automobile that would be affordable to wide sections of the population. It was to cost less than 1,000 marks, be reliable and durable, and have an air-cooled engine. Hitler himself is said to have made an early sketch, which already suggested the characteristic rounded beetle shape. However, the established German automobile manufacturers balked at the specifications, thinking the price unrealistic. Hitler, on the other hand, thought them incapable of building a car for the people because they were fixated on luxury automobiles. He summarily commissioned the German Labour Front (DAF), the Nazi organisation of employers and employees, to build a factory and plan a city to go with it. The DAF's state-operated leisure organisation, "Kraft durch Freude" (Strength through Joy), found the ideal site near Fallersleben; it was accessible to transport because of its proximity to the Mittelland Canal, the Ruhr–Berlin railway line and the autobahn, and was completely undeveloped land right in the middle of Germany (as the German borders were drawn at the time). The central location was important, because Hitler's industrialists dreamed of a factory from which the car buyer could collect the car in person. The construction of a smart hotel was planned where the prospective buyer could stay while making that purchase of a lifetime, along with a modern showroom for customers where they could have the technical specifications of the car precisely explained, before driving it home on the brand-new autobahn.

Hitler wanted an affordable car like Henry Ford's Model T, but with a distinctly modern appearance. The fact that the German middle class was lagging behind its international counterparts in terms of car ownership didn't sit easily with Nazi propaganda concerning transport for all. When the foundation stone was laid for the factory on 26

May 1938, Hitler promised to build a car that would be attainable for 6 to 7 million people: "The motor car will cease to be an instrument of class division. It will become the people's vehicle." The state-sponsored KdF car would not compete with Mercedes: "Whoever can afford it will continue to buy the more expensive car. The broad masses cannot do so, and this car was made for them." The speech ended as protocol decreed with a lengthy homage to the Führer, repeated cries of "Heil," cheering and applause. "The people of Lower Saxony," as an emotional gauleiter (regional Nazi Party leader), Otto Telschow, bellowed into the microphone, "lay their heart, my Führer, at your feet."

Hitler's plans combined the most up-to-date technology with a hint of folksiness. The KdF-car city was eventually to have a population of 90,000, and it was to be a kind of garden city in the so-called *Heimatschutzstil* (protection of national heritage style), a mixture of modern and traditional architecture. Its idyllic, rustic style—which included traditional German features such as pointed roofs, balconies, dormer and transom windows and, most importantly, wooden shutters—was mandated for every house in Wolfsburg. The cosy rural aesthetic of the residential area was to contrast forcefully with the massive factory, which ran like a fortress for a total of 1.3 kilometres along the opposite shore of the Mittelland Canal. The front of the building was punctuated by a series of projecting towers, which stood out like the teeth of a widely spaced comb. Its forbidding character as a bastion was further reinforced by its grim clinker-brick façade. Even today, its monumental monotony and stubborn repetition of the defiant towers still define the face of the Volkswagen factory. The factory's power station, constructed in the same monumental style, has five chimneys that loom into the sky like anti-aircraft guns.

While the factory was erected at great speed, the quaint garden city remained a dream on paper. Hardly anything beyond a small but elegant housing estate, built on the Steimker Berg for the families of the leading engineers and technicians, was ever constructed. With the invasion of Poland and the start of the war, the motorcar for the masses became just as much of a hollow promise as the model city.

The consumers' dream of a people's car became an armaments factory, the model city a work camp. Only a few copies of the Volkswagen, designed by automotive engineer Ferdinand Porsche, had been built. Rather than the Beetle, it was the Kübelwagen, a military utility vehicle, with an open bodywork and bucket seats on a reinforced chassis, the clumsy answer to the American jeep, that came rolling off the factory floor. The propaganda bubble of the Kdf car burst, to the disappointment of many savers who had taken out expensive loans and already paid for their cars—336,000 people had been involved in the finance programme, but only 630 cars in all were delivered. There were no refunds, and when many tried to get their down payments back immediately after the war, they did so in vain.

Rather than the planned terraced houses with little vegetable gardens, up went monotonous rows of quickly assembled barracks with trampled earthen floors. Italian workers sent by Mussolini's Hitler-friendly regime moved into the so-called community camp. Nazi planners had to abandon their proudly declared programme to build a churchless town. Instead a bar was consecrated as a church. A big dance hall was also deemed necessary to make life in the cold north bearable to the Italians and keep their spirits up with entertainments, doubtless with a certain quotient of propaganda.

The neighbouring "Eastern Camp," by contrast, was unendurable. Here Polish and later Russian forced labourers were crammed in behind barbed wire. There was also an outpost of the Neuengamme concentration camp, as well as a few smaller camps inside the factory, which now concentrated on manufacturing munitions rather than motorcars. Some of the prisoners slept in big damp, stuffy, windowless basement rooms beneath the factory floors. They only came out to go to their workplaces. Several hundred Hungarian Jewish women and female Yugoslavian partisans lived in the locker rooms of Hall 1. They only ever saw daylight when they were moved to other buildings in the factory complex.

In 1943, 10,000 forced labourers were working in the City of the Kraft-durch-Freude Car. They comprised two thirds of the workforce. The camp was home to 2,500 Frenchmen, including several hundred volunteers from a Vichy government–sponsored youth organisation. On top of that there were 750 Dutchmen, of whom 205 were students who had been sentenced to forced labour for refusing to sign a declaration of loyalty to the Führer. The remaining Dutchmen had been forcibly recruited in "call-up operations." Like the French, they were housed in the barracks of the "community camp," since most of the original Italian residents had already been sent home. As was consistent with Nazi racial theory, the French and Dutch inmates received better treatment than the "Eastern workers"; they could move freely around the miserable estate, and received higher wages. On Sundays they walked about wearing smart suits, in curious contrast with the oppressive surroundings. The Dutch in particular tried to improve the atmosphere in the camp, organising shared events among groups of workers of various different origins, and acted as "intermediaries between the German management staff and the foreign workforce."[13] Unlike the concentration camp inmates in the factory, the Polish forced labourers were among those who were not kept locked up at all times. The regime had recognised that a minimum of freedom of movement had a morale-boosting effect on the labour force.

In order to maintain obedience among the "free" workers, drastic punishments were doled out for the slightest offences. Members of the factory security and the Gestapo patrolled the paths of the KdF town, the surrounding area and the works facilities. Anyone who attracted their attention ran the risk of being put in the work education camps, from which they emerged broken in body and spirit, if indeed they emerged at all. One in eight of the forced labourers there experienced the terror of those education camps at least once. Fear of the atrocities that went on in them, as well as the comparatively better conditions in the work camps compared to the concentration camps, may explain the surprising levels of compliance in the factory. Workers were also beaten while at work in the factory itself, and foremen would call in factory security to help. They preferred not to bring in the Gestapo because they tended to hand the workers back in such a terrible state that they were no longer fit to work.

Early in 1945, 9,000 foreigners and 7,000 Germans lived in what would later become Wolfsburg. On 10 April American troops passed through the area. They crossed the canal, leaving only a small unit in the factory grounds, because the commander was unaware of the significance of the works that they had captured in passing. Factory security and the SS had fled, and there was a menacing power vacuum in the KdF city. Some of the Eastern European forced labourers took their fury out on the factory facilities, and to some extent on the remaining Germans, but the Dutch and French workers stepped in and largely managed to calm them down.

The 1951 bestselling novel *Die Autostadt* by Horst Mönnich tells the story of VW as an exciting industrial adventure, depicting the disputes between the liberated forced labourers in a manner typical of the time. According to Mönnich, "thousands of Russians and Poles came together to storm the barracks and smash everything to bits":

> The Germans left behind in the city had no weapons. But they did have two fire engines. They drove these into the crowds to cause confusion. The red color of the vehicles had the effect of a matador's red cape on a bull. The crowds were filled with rage. But their resistance was broken.[14]

The scene is pure fantasy. There is no evidence for Mönnich's account of "foreign workers" taking up a position by the factory gates to grab German workers at random and beat them up. Forced labourers did take their revenge on those foremen and overseers who had mistreated them particularly savagely; this happened in many camps on the day of liberation and was observed and tolerated by the Allies. Nor is it unlikely that there were individual cases of riotous behaviour and such instances were reported in some places.[15] But Mönnich misconstrued the causes of the violence by downplaying the inhumanity of slavery and instead attributing the brutality to the ethnic character of the "Eastern workers," whom he consistently compares to animals. While he depicted the forced labourers as a nameless mob, he gave each British and American character an individual name.[16]

The Germans, the British and the Americans soon got on splendidly

in Mönnich's "Autostadt." In his version they talked shop about technical details and spoke respectfully about the wounds they had recently
inflicted on one another during the war. Mönnich even had a German
engineer repeat by heart Carl Sandburg's hymn to the industrial city of
Chicago, to demonstrate how spiritually close the Germans and the
Americans were—unlike the hordes from the East, from whom Wolfsburg now had to be liberated.[17]

Horst Mönnich had served in the Wehrmacht as a "war reporter"
and cabled home harrowing stories of the Allied armies' invasion of
the homeland. After the war he became a member of the important
post-war German writers' association Gruppe 47. The bigoted depiction of the foreign workers may in fact have contributed to the huge
success of the novel *Autostadt*, which had sold over 100,000 copies
by 1969. But the book's sales were primarily a result of the fervent
enthusiasm for technology, to which Mönnich gave free rein in his
hammering, factual staccato style. His heroes were inventors, engineers, foremen—a technical elite for whom a functioning engine was
more important than freedom and democracy. The book concludes:

> Men went, new men came. The right men kept coming at the right
> time. Who are these men? The answer is simple. They are men of
> imagination, devoted to the cause for good or ill, and they are passion-
> ate by nature. Their passion is the motor car. That's why it can be done.
> That's why it was possible.[18]

At the end of the war the right man at the right time was called
Ivan Hirst. In June 1945 Lower Saxony was assigned to the British
zone of occupation, and the Americans moved out. The British military authorities placed the administration of the factory under the
command of the 29-year-old engineer, Major Ivan Hirst, who had
run a British tank-repair workshop in Brussels during the war. He
was to see what could be salvaged from Wolfsburg. The ultra-modern
conveyor belts and large-scale stamping machines that the Germans
had already sensibly stored away to protect them from air raids would
serve equally well in Birmingham. But Hirst, with his passion for

Wolfsburg, "a misbegotten human plantation"—that was what Der Spiegel *called the city, which was just twelve years old in 1950.*

technology, was more interested in the factory itself, and even more in the rounded motor vehicles that could soon be rolling out of it once again. With great tact he managed to deter his superiors from dismantling the factory. Once his superiors had got over its comical appearance they were quite taken with the Beetle, and happy for it to be driven round under their auspices. But the threat of disassembly hung for a long time over Wolfsburg Motor Works, even after the factory had resumed its activity. The British Army ordered 10,000 of the highly reliable cars to restock their decimated fleet.

By 1948 the factory's production figures were nowhere near the desired goal. An under-motivated, transient workforce meant that production went into effect far more slowly than hoped. Many workers skipped their shifts so that they could look for food—a common problem prior to currency reform. There was also the fact that the

German managers at the Volkswagen factory had certain inhibitions about being as brazenly active on the black market, under the noses of their British bosses, as other companies—a real competitive disadvantage that led to bottlenecks in terms of deliveries of raw materials. Ivan Hirst tried to use the full power of his military rank to get hold of things that his buyers couldn't scrape together on the black market. In order to feed his workers, in 1947 he had the land around the factory reploughed and planted with grain. By late summer Wolfsburg Motor Works was surrounded right up to the factory gates with magnificent, golden-yellow fields of wheat.

In March 1946 Hirst was able to organise a first-anniversary party. He sat for photographers in a Beetle garlanded with fir-tree branches. Above it a banner proclaimed: "The 1000th Volkswagen built during March 1946 coming from Assembly Line [sic]." And so it continued for the next few months: on average 1,000 Beetles were produced each month for Allied needs, all painted in khaki colours. For German customers the car remained unaffordable, although the Deutsche Post received a limited contingent for the delivery of parcels and letters.

The British refused to accede to the wishes repeatedly expressed by the people of Wolfsburg for the community camp "to be cleansed of foreigners."[19] Instead, more and more Eastern Europeans came to Wolfsburg even after the end of the war. The Allies used the site as a camp for displaced persons from all over Germany who had to stay there until their repatriation had been resolved. At the same time attempts were made to bring back the "local" forced labourers—the ones who had stayed in Wolfsburg. The *Wolfsburger Nachrichten* newspaper wrote retrospectively on 29 January 1950:

> In 1945 and the spring of 1946 the big American articulated trucks were constantly driving to the Laagberg [camp], fetching DPs from Berlin. These people from all imaginable countries were collected right here and then transported back to their homelands. [. . .] A colourful mixture of people flowed together on the Laagberg, and the camp was actually nicknamed "The World in Miniature." At a time when the camp was at is busiest, there were more than forty nationalities in all.[20]

There was much coming-and-going in Wolfsburg. While many DPs departed the camps to finally return home, the barracks filled up again with German refugees and expellees coming from the opposite direction. Many stayed only temporarily, working briefly in the factory, and then continued their journeys westwards. The more output expanded, the more the camp city attracted scattered individuals from all over Germany. And the factory needed a workforce. In the period between 1945 and 1948 the number of new appointments and dismissals was three times as high as the overall number of employees. The British drafted German POWs to join the existing workers. There were also "Eastern workers" again. DPs who resisted repatriation and preferred to live in the camps on the provisions provided by the Allied refugee relief organisation were also temporarily placed under an obligation to work. It was a remarkable mixture of people that came together in Wolfsburg. Discharged and homeless soldiers, rootless young men eager for any kind of comfort after their experiences in the war, and former forced labourers who had no reason to go home—a camp of lonely, stranded people.

It is striking that one of the first bars to open in Wolfsburg was called Heimat, meaning "Homeland." Nothing was more unavailable here than "home." The wide concrete streets led through nothing to nowhere. They were the only part of the grand infrastructure of the huge planned Nazi model city that had actually been completed, and they served as a constant mockery to the inhabitants of the desolate urban landscape. Conversely, the few houses that had been built often lacked access roads: beaten paths led to scattered buildings whose locations made little sense. And the barracks that stretched precisely in rank and file revealed themselves, as one approached, to be places of chaos and neglect.

Potatoes, sugar beets and vegetables could be grown around them, and attempts were even made with tobacco. Rabbits, chickens, ducks and even pigs were kept, even though the latter were forbidden. Most of the barracks were run-down, however, and with each fresh exodus they looked worse. Many workers downed tools without notice from one day to the next, and when they moved out of the camp, they took with them any furniture that was still halfway usable. Consequently, any new employees had to sleep on the floor at first. "Wolfsburg is a product of Hitler's hubris," wrote the Berlin *Tagesspiegel* in 1950.

> It has the same features of National Socialist bankrupt assets as the nearby Salzgitter site [a steelworks near the Volkswagen factory]. Rudiments of a city [. . .], dumped without ceremony in a stretch of wasteland, impressive façades masking pitiful barracks quarters, grand motorways leading straight into cart tracks, a landscape that was not blessed with beauty even before, rootless people from all parts of Germany, a conglomerate of negative superlatives.[21]

This would have terrible consequences. In the local elections in Lower Saxony in 1948 Wolfsburg sank even lower. The far-right German Right Party (Deutsche Rechtspartei, DRP) won 15,000 of 24,000 votes and thus became the largest faction in the council—in the other boroughs in Lower Saxony the DRP rarely achieved over 10 per cent. A few months after this scandalous result, which went down in history as the "Wolfsburg shock," the result of the election was annulled and the people of Wolfsburg voted again. But things went wrong once again. The German Party (Deutsche Partei, DP), the successor to the DRP, which had been banned in the subsequent election, still won 48 per cent of the vote.

What was the source of this renewed outbreak of right-wing extremism? If it had been widespread throughout Germany it would have surely led the Allies to immediately forbid all preparations for the establishment of the Federal Republic. Reporters came flooding in from all zones of the country to visit the "Nazi" borough. "Wolfsburg is a colonised city, the extremists are victorious here, and because many of them are refugees from the East they can't be the Communists," *Der Spiegel* wrote after the election.[22] The reasons, however, were easily discernible: too many men, too many refugees, too many uprooted people, too many former soldiers, too many young people. It didn't occur to anyone at the time to call it an urban lab experiment: Wolfsburg was too dirty for that, both figuratively and literally. The city fell very quickly into disrepair: a half-formed place with only a ten-year history. The reports on the far right in Wolfsburg neglected to mention that there was no legacy of tradition to shield the residents against the extremism of loud-mouthed hotheads. No church, no family structures, no bourgeois heritage, no architectural identity to stabilise the ragtag population. There was not a single place in the city that could have restored the inhabitants' faith in the possibility of some kind of permanence. There was only the factory and its obscure workforce, "containing many questionable figures."

But if these barracks-dwellers looked out of the windows of their miserable dwellings and across the canal, they saw a factory that looked like the impenetrable walls of a mythical city with a bright future ahead of it. The Volkswagen factory looked as if it had been beamed in from a fantasy film—and it still looks like that today. It was a solid fortress, compared with the fragility of existence exemplified in the ramshackle barracks. The technological legacy of Nazism must have looked to the people of Wolfsburg like an inextinguishable beacon of hope.

The factory was all that Wolfsburg's inhabitants had, and they saw little reason not to be proud of it. The small but forceful core of medium- and low-ranking employees, who had remained in Wolfsburg despite all the instability, was largely forged by the imagination of the Nazi period and its labour organisation, the German Labour Front. The skilled workers, on the other hand, had an elitist view of their technical mission, and felt bound to the factory with all their soul. As a result the metalworkers' union IG Metall had little chance in Wolfsburg. Here there was a political truce between the workforce and company management. The works council of the Volkswagen factory saw "all the manual and white-collar workers as a closed, democratically run, performance-oriented community," which made common cause in fighting the battle for the future.[23] Trade union speeches about the interests of the workers fell on deaf ears here. When a Wolfsburg member of the Social Democratic SPD claimed that all the city's ills emanated from the Volkswagen factory, there was a furious backlash from the city's residents, who, in response, voted for the far right.

This social, psychological and political situation might well have exploded at some point in the 1950s had not a true leader appeared in the form of a new general director put in place by the British in 1948, who was able to transform the reactionary longings of the people of Wolfsburg after their humiliation. He was famously known as "King Nordhoff," but the title was an understatement. Heinrich Nordhoff called his labour force his "work colleagues," and they called him their "general." Nordhoff had run an Opel vehicle factory in Brandenburg during the war. He had been a "military business manager" and was therefore unacceptable to the Americans in a management role. To the British, however, who were more lax in this respect, he seemed exactly the right person to step in as Ivan Hirst's successor. Being the man in charge was part of Nordhoff's character. With his pointedly quiet voice and a self-image that was controlled down to the tiniest detail, he developed a leader's charisma that effectively introduced discipline into a chaotic rabble. It wasn't long before the labour force resembled a working army that joyfully took up their positions and worked like clockwork. By means of the most modern production methods, iron discipline and motivation through constantly growing profits, the "work colleagues" soon had Beetles rolling off the production line at a rate of 100,000 a year, a scale only imaginable in America. After a visit to Wolfsburg for a jointly written article in the *Frankfurter Hefte* in 1950, the sociologist Karl W. Böttcher and the journalist Rüdiger Proske wrote: "The hierarchy of the fully rationalised factory in many respects resembles the hierarchy of the Wehrmacht, and the working groups in the factory look like a battalion in the field."[24]

Germany in the 1950s is usually seen as embodying the triumph of personal consumption within the family circle. Here, however, there was an aspect of the economic revival that is often forgotten among the usual pictures of fridges, camping trips to Rimini and milk-bar flirtations; the disciplined formation of an industrial society operating at maximum output, a world of concrete, steel, coal and coke gas, in which people worked until they dropped.

Wolfsburg had become the epitome of a factory society. There was hardly a works that so perfectly illustrated the notorious Stamocap—state monopoly capitalism, as post-war Marxists called the system in which state and private capital had become indistinguishable. In 1949 the British had initially put the limited liability company in the trusteeship of the state of Lower Saxony. In 1960 the "VW act" was passed by the West German parliament, consolidating the privatisation by transforming the company into a joint-stock corporation in which the state and the Federal Republic each held 20 per cent of shares while the rest were privately owned. That did nothing to alter the impression that Volkswagen was an effectively state-owned part of Germany Inc. The company was the embodiment of the "technological veil" which, according to the social theorist Theodor W. Adorno, had been laid over

The general poses in front of his army of workers. Volkswagen boss Heinrich Nordhoff celebrates the manufacture of the millionth Beetle in 1955.

the market-shaped relations of labour and capital in the form of a dense intersection of industry, administration and politics.

King Nordhoff always tried to give the impression that the private economic structure of his company had been abolished, and "he was committed to the society of the Federal Republic as a whole."[25] And German society largely fell for it. "The factory belongs to nobody, and hence to the general public," *Motor-Rundschau* postulated in 1949.[26]

In fact it was exactly the other way round. Long after the end of the war the city was still in thrall to the factory, so the municipality could never assert itself against Volkswagen. For most inhabitants the city administration seemed to be a division of the Volkswagen company.

At first the city could not call a single square metre of its land its own, as everything belonged to the Volkswagen company. For a long time the city and the factory's directors argued about property rights. Without that legal security it was impossible to contemplate the construction of necessary infrastructure. A year after the currency reform hardly anything had been done to ease the housing situation. According to research by the British, "municipal inactivity" was the most important issue in the 1948 election results. It was not until 1955 that the city got hold of the 345 hectares of land for the "communal requirement" of streets and public squares, as well as another 1,900 hectares to "satisfy additional claims for basic infrastructure."[27] This radically altered the situation; the city was no longer constricted by private land ownership, and had complete control over the planned construction, which it undertook with great enthusiasm. With the best will in the world, the buildings that went up couldn't have been seen as anything but bleak. On the bulldozed plots of land, endless series of austere workers' houses appeared, curiously naked buildings that could never quite shake off the spirit of the camps, divided by broad tracks that fully bore out the name of *Autostadt*. A kind of town centre was just about discernible, but the buildings were a conglomeration of crimes against architecture.

And yet the people of Wolfsburg felt surprisingly at home in this functional wasteland. Urban sociologists came from all over the world to investigate what a city with no real centre, without tradition and without any kind of comfort did to its inhabitants. They didn't find anything very alarming. Wolfsburg even bored its critics. Unlike such places as the Ruhr it evaded critical attention. While the city and the factory together formed a prototype of the social market economy, and while the path that Wolfsburg, the "integration machine," had taken to create "a new type of industrial citizen"[28] out of a random assemblage of camp inmates, could stand as a symbol for the post-war history of the Federal Republic, the left-wing opposition took surprisingly little interest in King Nordhoff's massive empire. The reason may lie in the solid peace in labour relations that prevailed under his rule.[29] The opposition-Left intelligentsia shamefully averted their eyes from such a tame workforce. Heinrich Nordhoff, the London *Evening News* was surprised to note, was bathed "in the glow of an unearthly God raining blessings down over his people."[30]

In the course of his life, which would end in the politically iconic year of 1968, Heinrich Nordhoff was draped with medals like a Ruritanian ruler. He was awarded the Grand Cross of the Order of Merit of the Federal Republic with Star and Shoulder-Sash, the Commander Grand Cross First Class of the Swedish Order of Vasa and the "Friend of the Italian People" medal; he was made Comendador of the Brazilian National Order of the Southern Cross, Grand Officer of the Order of Merit of the Italian Republic and Commander of the Papal Gregorian Order; he was awarded numerous honorary doctorates and was a citizen of honour several times over—the quantity of his ennoblements was in inverse proportion to the modesty of his project. After his death his corpse was laid out in the white cloak of a Knight of the Holy Grail in the experimental hall of the research and development department at the VW complex. The VW employees queued for ten hours to say farewell to their general director.

Anyone strolling through Wolfsburg today will dismiss the idea that there was once little more here than a gigantic barracks camp and a monstrous factory as the sheerest lunacy. The city of Wolfsburg has become a temple to consumerism, although one that has at its heart preserved the early dreams of the people who founded it. Since the early sixties the unrelenting grimness has been softened by individual buildings of outstanding charm: Alvar Aalto's 1962 House of Culture, for example, or Hans Scharoun's 1973 Theatre Building. Since the millennium, however, Wolfsburg has reinvented itself as a social artwork devoted to the automotive lifestyle in a futuristic park and exhibition setting. The so-called lagoon landscape near the factory grounds, its gloomy monumentality alleviated by dramatic exterior lighting, with its many bridges, hills, curving paths and elegant pavilions, with "dancing water fountains" and a scent tunnel by the artist Olafur Eliasson, looks like a cheerful park in a carefree but totalitarian feel-good utopia. A playground of nature, culture and high-tech set against an aseptic industrial backdrop, behind which robots build perfect automobiles. In between there are architectural masterworks such as Zaha Hadid's Phaeno Science Centre, a cathedral of learning, or Gunter Henn's no less spectacular MobileLifeCampus. Untroubled by doubts about its future viability, consumerism is displayed here with an ardour entirely uncomplicated by ideas of ideological freedom.

Hitler's original "Strength Through Joy" idea of turning a visit to the factory into a full-blown experience for people who wanted to collect their cars directly has now become reality. You can stay in the Ritz-Carlton near the factory and in the morning watch your newly purchased car being plucked automatically from its parking shelf 40 metres up and delivered to you with an elegant, miraculous technical gesture. Visitors can sample the car museum, design displays, tracks for test drives, and sound and art installations. The fact that the visions conceived during the Nazi era have been realised 80 years on in a massively exaggerated form is impossible to ignore in the face of the overwhelming aesthetic idealisation of the act of buying a car— and might even seem a little inappropriate given the peaceable nature of the country where this has become a reality.

Startup—Beate Uhse discovers her business model while selling door-to-door

The revival of large enterprises such as Volkswagen in the West, or the Eisenhüttenstadt steel complex in the East, which experienced huge growth in the 1950s and 1960s, does not tell the whole story of the economic development of post-war Germany. The post-war chaos was the ideal setting for solo entrepreneurs. Independent businesses often began with small ideas and no means of production. Some people did their neighbours' ironing in the kitchen, while others marketed their own hard-heartedness. For fifty pfennigs they would slaughter rabbits for anyone who didn't have the stomach to do the job. One example of a career that arose out of nothing was that of a young pilot named Beate Uhse. She had grown up in East Prussia, the daughter of a liberal farmer and a doctor. Accustomed to independence from an early age, she went to various boarding schools because no formal education was available in her home village of Wargenau. For a year the 16-year-old went to England as an au pair to learn the language, and at the age of 18 she was awarded her pilot's license. A year later, after winning an international flying competition, she was given a position as a test pilot at the Friedrich Aircraft Works in Strausberg. Test piloting was a dream job for her, because it required equal amounts of aeronautical skill and technical know-how. As a Luftwaffe captain during the war she flew dive-bombers and fighter planes from various arms manufacturers to the airbases where they were needed.

When the Red Army overran Berlin, she flew from Tempelhof Airport with her 18-month-old son, Klaus, and his nanny, Hanna, in a small hijacked civilian plane to Flensburg and landed recklessly at a British military airport. Released after a few weeks as a prisoner of war, she and her son found lodgings at the school library in Braderup, a village in North Frisia, where they stayed for almost three years. There was barely any more flying to be done, so Beate Uhse earned her living in a variety of trades. She helped farmers in their fields in return for payment in kind, and traded in everything imaginable on the black market. She sold toys and buttons door-to-door. She offered her services as an interpreter of dreams in newspaper advertisements. But nothing really quite worked Then, on one of her many trips through the villages she had an idea. While selling buttons she chatted with many women, and what she learned from them in terms of their concerns especially about sex and sexual misbehaviour led her to write a guidebook on contraception. Her eight-page treatise, the size of a school exercise book, in which she set out the so-called calendar rhythm method, was called "Paper X."

The pragmatically minded former pilot sensed the powerful desire for sexual adventure after the end of the war. Many people who had fled or been exiled had, like herself, found themselves in new situations and were trying to form connections. The desire for mutual comfort, curiosity and novelty quickly brought people together

Beate Uhse, at the time still Beate Köstlin, received her flying licence in 1937 at the age of 18. Later she became a test pilot and ferried fighter planes to military airbases.

sexually—but that didn't mean that a child was welcome, particularly in this confusing new world. In the introduction to her book Beate wrote:

> If we procreated instinctively no married couple today would be able to guarantee their children a decent life worthy of a human being, or a suitable upbringing. So we have a social duty to make a sharp separation between the satisfaction of sexual urges and procreation.

Although she spoke of married couples, the sentiment was even more applicable to the many unmarried couples. In "Paper X" she explained the "results of medical research over the past few years," according to which "women are only fertile on a few days between two periods." No one knows exactly how ill-informed the Germans were after the end of the war, and it's possible that many of them still adhered to the prohibition on any kind of contraception decreed by Heinrich Himmler in January 1941. In "Paper X" Beate Uhse re-addressed the subject of contraception in the spirit of the new age: "More and more, all over the world demands are being made, under the term 'birth control,' as the Americans call it, for the systematic restriction of female fertility."

No sooner had she written her guidebook—which she didn't even check for spelling mistakes—Beate Uhse travelled to Flensburg where she had it printed by mimeograph. She also ordered up large quantities of advertising flyers, which she mailed out by finding the addresses of the residents of Husum, Heide and other cities in the region in electoral registers and telephone directories. She also cycled around for days delivering the advertisements by hand. She wanted two Reichsmark for every "Paper X," as well as 70 pfennigs for dispatch. That worked out at between a quarter and half a cigarette in black-market currency, a handsome price at the time.

It worked. "Paper X" was a great success. In the first year, 1947, as many as 32,000 women ordered the eight-page pamphlet.[31] Beate Uhse could hardly keep up with the demand for reprints. She registered her one-woman business properly with the British military authorities as "Betu Dispatches." The "Distribution Company for Marital Hygiene" formed the core of an erotic goods company which even today, 70 years later, is listed on the stock exchange as "Beate Uhse AG" and boasts 470 employees and an annual turnover of 128 million Euros.[32]

For decades Uhse maintained the principle of distributing her advertising unrequested across all households, even though this gave the legal authorities the opportunity to bring case after case against her. But Beate Uhse fell foul of the law for the first time, not because of violations of the moral code or corrupting the young, but for breach of price regulations. A ruling by the Flensburg Health Office established that asking two marks for a few pages that were worth three pfennigs at most amounted to daylight robbery, even though it found nothing objectionable in the content of "Paper X." The authorities—and there were several, including the "Central Office for the Control of Bogus Companies" in Hamburg—concluded that the contraceptive pamphlet was not worth its price because there was nothing new in the guidebook. Beate Uhse had probably "forgotten" to mention gynaecologists Kyusaku Ogino and Hermann Knauss, who first developed the calendar rhythm method of contraception.

Others didn't care much for such technicalities. They were more worked up about the book's "incitement to fornication." In 1949 a criminologist from Catholic Münster was the first to accuse Beate Uhse of endangering public morals. The relevant legal office in Flensburg, however, found that "Paper X" and the advertising sent out for it had "not insulted or endangered either modesty or public morals,"[33] although accusations were flying in from every corner of the country, except the Protestant north of Germany, which still adopted a pointedly liberal line. But when Beate Uhse expanded her distribution to include additional pamphlets and erotic aids of all kinds, a whole new wave of legal cases came sweeping towards her. Throughout the course of her professional life she had to endure a total of 700 trials, until the laws were relaxed at the end of the 1960s and there were no further grounds for prosecution.

Meanwhile Beate Uhse had remarried. In 1947 she took a short holiday on the island of Sylt, which she had financed by selling butter that she had brought from Braderup—on the black market, of course. She met Ernst-Walter Rotermund at the beach. They found they had a lot to learn from one another, because he distributed hair lotion by mail order, just as she did with her pamphlet. Rotermund, who was divorced and had two children, and Beate Uhse, widowed with one child, married in 1949. They moved in with Rotermund's aunt and uncle in the parsonage of St. Mary's in Flensburg, where Rotermund's uncle was a pastor. There were thousands of such patchwork families after the war. Rotermund enthusiastically threw himself into his wife's business, and along with two assistants, they packaged the orders, wrote out address labels and answered countless letters, all while working from St. Mary's Church. It was not until 1951 that they moved into new offices and warehouses, because the business was constantly growing, and the catalogue was now 16 pages long.

There was a huge appetite for her goods. In 1951, for the black-and-white front cover of the catalogue she used the face of a young woman looking with concern at the viewer. She wears a high-necked jumper, and only the woman's serious face looms from the black of the surroundings. There was not a hint of erotica, and the image would have been more suited to an existentialist treatise than a "specialist business for marital hygiene." But written along the bottom of the picture were words that suggested privacy and intimacy: "Is everything all right in your marriage?" If not, help was at hand; in the following pages, for example, there were "Hona-6-bonbons to overcome a temporary lack of interest."

Impotence was a serious problem in the post-war years. Many prisoners of war had come back so emaciated and ill that they didn't feel like doing anything at all, let alone having sex. In the November 1949 issue of the magazine *Frauenwelt* the GP Dr. Konrad Linck wrote:

> The returnee is seriously ill, whether he is thin or fat. This finding alone allows us to assess the returnee's marital situation. Years of poor nutrition have also led to an expiry of the function of his gonads, so that he is actually returning to the family not as a man but as the oldest son.

This condition is, of course, unclear both to the man and to his wife. It is likely to lead to tragic misunderstandings, to suspicion, jealousy and finally to a complete collapse of the marriage, even though both partners are fundamentally willing to maintain the marriage.[34]

But we might reasonably doubt whether Beate Uhse's bonbons alone would have solved the problem. Every third customer included with his order a letter in which he requested advice for sexual problems. In 1951 Beate Uhse employed her first regular member of staff, a medic who gave out information under the less than original pseudonym of Dr. Rath ("advice" in German), and who was also supposed to be researching new potency-enhancing remedies.[35]

To emphasise the beneficial nature of her products, Beate Uhse published letters of thanks in her catalogue:

Many thanks for sending your brochure which has helped me and my husband enormously and, with its clean style, freed us from dubious moral ideas. I will take the liberty of directing my group of acquaintances towards your valued company so that many people may avail themselves of your help.

Another customer wrote: "My oppressive marital problem was treated so sympathetically that I could not neglect to say thank you."[36]

"Marital hygiene"—Beate Uhse's public face was as aseptic as the phrase sounds. The "Countess Dönhoff of sexual liberation"[37] (referring to a journalist prominent in the anti-Hitler resistance) was the advocate of a kind of sexuality that was, as a matter of principle, free of secrets. She advocated nudity and so-called comradely marriage. Free love, on the other hand, masturbation or indeed homosexuality did not initially appear in Uhse's world. Her consulting service was devoted exclusively to heterosexual couples whose pleasure she wished to enhance—the wave of pornography that would later come to characterise her business, as represented by the notorious X-rated video booths in the street outside her shops, would not appear until the 1980s. However, Beate Uhse would be in the forefront of that business too, even though she was by that time of pensionable age. In the year 2000 she was ceremonially awarded the "Hot d'Or d'Honneur" in Cannes, the best-known film prize of the pornography industry.

But the Beate Uhse of the immediate post-war age stood for sexuality without obscenities; one of her catalogues showed an elderly bourgeois couple who looked as if they were taking an autumn stroll. Her slogan, "Bring Sunshine into your Nights," could apply to her whole programme. She particularly liked to be bathed in the dazzling light of science. One intellectual kindred spirit was the American zoologist and sexual researcher Alfred Charles Kinsey, whose research into sexuality also shaped the Germany of the 1950s. Kinsey had asked a large number of subjects, supposedly representing the average American, about their sexual activities, and made some astonishing discoveries. Practices that had hitherto been considered perverse and isolated occurrences were suddenly revealed as widespread and more or less commonplace. Kinsey was a proponent of enlightenment in the literal sense: changing things by bringing them to light. Beate Uhse was sympathetic to this method, since she saw herself not as a missionary but as an objective, unprejudiced observer who simply saw things clearly. Even before the two Kinsey Reports appeared on the German market she brought out a summary, correctly spotting their potential as bestsellers.

The task of the "virtuous guide through the erotic wonderland," as Beate became known,[38] was to discuss sexuality in such sterile language that it remained open to interpretation at a time when the predominant tone was one of respectability. She explained her sex toys with refined tact. She offered her ridged, nubby and serrated condoms as being a suitable way of "bringing women of a rather cool disposition, or those still slumbering, to particularly deep and powerful experiences of love."[39]

Beate Uhse was utterly unashamed of her trade. Rather than hiding herself away, she openly approached her customers with her advertising brochures, presenting herself as a capable, modern woman. With her short, boyish hairdo, her wiry, athletic appearance and puckish cheerfulness, her manner was "natural" and almost conspicuously unerotic—the wholesome face of the erotic retail trade. By putting herself, her name and her biography so confrontationally at the centre of her marketing, she stripped her business of everything secret and grubby, and put herself in the public eye as a serious and gifted engineer in a spanking clean workshop for sexual happiness. She left nothing to chance; her personality-based marketing was thought through from the start. She even marketed her marketing strategy. A good five decades after her first business activities she presented her marketing guidebook at the Frankfurt Book Fair, a kind of "Paper X" of self-marketing. Entitled *Sensually into the Market—A Guidebook for Difficult Markets*, in it she describes how she deliberately put herself at the centre as a wife and mother, as a pilot, an athlete and a hands-on businesswoman, to eradicate the slightest hint of incorrectness from her business image.

She was still targeted by concerned guardians of virtue, however. In 1951 she was found guilty of distributing immoral writings and objects. Her catalogue lacked the "discreet and reticent style" that the "advertising of such delicate things" required, the civil court in Flensburg found. Her goods were liable to "encourage fornication." One aggravating feature for the court was the fact that it was a woman advertising indecent objects, and one who came from a good home and had enjoyed an excellent upbringing.[40] An appeal was rejected by a judge who confirmed her "shamelessness," stating that her brochure catered to "lustfulness" and that she violated the law with an obtrusive stubbornness. The next appeals court did lift the ruling on the basis of procedural irregularities, but reiterated that the brochure "violated the healthy views of the population on sexual matters."

From then on one complaint followed another. The police and the courts brought a total of 2,000 cases against her, 700 of which resulted in legal proceedings. She won almost all of these cases thanks to her outstanding lawyers and personal skill. One notorious accusation levelled against her was mental harassment, based on the fact that her advertising was distributed indiscriminately and thus reached households that had no wish to be exposed to it, in one case including, of all places, a seminary for Catholic priests. She got out of that one by henceforth using a double envelope. On the outer envelope the sender's name remained anonymous as ever, while on the inner one it referred to possibly offensive content and advised recipients who might be disturbed by it to throw it away immediately. Anyone who did not do this was thus held fully responsible.

Beate Uhse cannily opened the world's first sex shop in 1961, the day before Christmas Eve—a clever move, relying on the idea that people might have better things to do than protest against a new self-service sex shop.

The name Beate Uhse remains well known in Germany, although new entrepreneurs, later waves of liberalisation and the internet mean the sex and intimacy business is wildly different today. Her advocacy for a more open-minded, relaxed attitude towards sexuality in the fifties and sixties made a lasting impression, and she was officially recognised for her work in the field of sexual liberation when she was awarded the German Cross of Merit in 1989. She died, highly regarded, in 2001.

Is Germany drowning in filth?
The fear of waywardness

The obstinacy of the battle waged against Beate Uhse, and indeed countless other representatives of "moral degeneration," has informed Germany's image of itself in the 1950s, and almost completely overshadowed the cheerful, free-spirited sides of the period in public memory. No sooner had the economy consolidated itself in 1948 than a new campaign was launched with hysterical fervour as the "battle against filth and trash." It was on everyone's lips, leading to the introduction in 1953 of a law against the distribution of writings liable to corrupt young people. A phalanx of moral guardians painted a jet-black picture of the future of Germany at the very moment when for most people it was beginning to brighten. Before currency reform, the "criminal inclinations" of a society dominated by hoarders, coal-thieves and black-market traders had underlain fears of a moral decline in Germany. When the economy turned around and criminality subsided, the moral condition of the younger generation became the focus of fears for the maintenance of order. They had to be protected from their newly won freedom.

Those of a nationalist and conservative tendency feared the spirit of the young republic. The liberal influence of the Allies, the new films and books, abstract art and cheerful, swinging, "exciting" music were a source of horror to them. They suspected—quite rightly—that these influences would fundamentally change German society. Comics were equated with "pictorial idiocy," "salacious illiteracy," the "glorification of violence" and "spiritual poisoning." They were an "invaders' literature" that was distributed in "girls' swag-bags," as one commentator colourfully put it, as "opium for children," a "people's plague" and a "cultural outrage."[41] When a 14-year-old hanged a five-year-old from a window frame because he "wanted to see how people hang," it was interpreted as a consequence of repeated consumption of comics.[42] Teachers regularly searched children's schoolbags for comic-book characters like Mickey Mouse, Akim, Sigùrd and Fix & Foxi. The comics were confiscated and, once there was enough trash in the "poison cabinet," publicly burned in the playground.

Apart from comics, "sexual squalor" haunted the first post-war years as a horrific bogeyman. Meanwhile the phenomenon of the wayward young generation could not be easily dismissed. The war had left 1.6 million children without one parent or fully orphaned, and some of them didn't even know their own names. Roaming young people drifted across the country alone or in gangs, robbing, rampaging and prostituting themselves. But many adults chose to see this sad anarchy not as the consequence of war or totalitarian brainwashing by the Nazi regime, instead identifying the invasion of "filth and trash" as the cause. The fault for the "contamination of youth" rested with the "modern world"—and, interestingly, the same arguments that had been levelled against the modern Weimar Republic were resurrected. From this perspective the gradual economic revival and the normalisation of living conditions were not seen as a turn for the better, but as part of the menacing situation that, back in 1933, had been the "crisis of the age."

In 1953 Hans Seidel, the chief business manager of the "Regional Organisation for Youth Protection in North Rhine Westphalia," defined the new "crisis of the age" in a manner typical of this culturally reactionary discourse, as:

> Marked from within by the historical process of the separation of modern people from values crucial for life, for which we employ terms such as materialism and nihilism. This separation, which also involves the loss of connections provided by nature, above all community, means both a division within essential cultural norms and their degeneracy. So love degenerates to erotica, professions to breadwinning, physical exercise to sport, music to entertainment. Modern technology leads to an overemphasis on the material and on a faster pace of life, creating both arrogance and fear. Civilising influences are also subject to these effects, as well as processes of industrialisation and urbanisation, and indeed the de-naturing of all of our living conditions.[43]

De-natured and degenerate, and separated from the natural benefits of the community—from that *völkisch* point of view—the access to Western culture encouraged by the Allies automatically became a danger to youth. For this reason, those employed officially by the young Federal Republic to ensure the protection of minors saw "40% of our young people as being habitually engaged in criminal activities, backward in terms of their health and particularly endangered."[44] Seidel's colleague Helma Engels, a psychologist, saw the great majority of young people as merely a collection of "pleasure-seeking, unbridled adolescents" completely trapped "in their obsession with the cinema, their terrifying unquestioning nature, their complete reliance on instinct, all the way to entirely irresponsible early sexual activity, without a sense of community, attached only to the present, tangible moment."[45]

This was a grotesque misappraisal of the situation. The publication in 1952 of a youth study carried out by the Shell Oil Company, which has continued to investigate the transformation of values among young people every four years until the present day, gave the all-clear. It presented a picture of an extraordinarily well-behaved generation that had been astonishingly adept in dealing with the traumas of the war and the years that followed. The study did not prevent the police and youth authorities from waging a campaign against young people who were considered "difficult to educate." Above all the spectre of "wayward girls" prompted levels of alarm in the authorities which, from the perspective of the present day, appear actually pathological.

Concealed beneath the fear of moral corruption was irritation with a younger generation that had often turned contemptuously away from the older one, but obviously without being able to stand on its own two feet or to express its disappointment in a non-destructive manner. In the eyes of the children, the older generation had fundamentally disavowed both the dictatorship and its downfall. The more fervently the young had believed in Hitler, the more betrayed they now felt. Seeing their parents as losers who had not been able to protect them against the loss of domestic security often threw the children entirely back on their own devices. In 1947 Alexander Mitscherlich wrote of a "generation gap."[46] He described the anarchic nihilism of many young people. He recognised in the "strangeness and wildness of their words, the twitchy aimlessness of their gestures," how "sceptical about the world" they had become, how infinitely disappointed by the "work of their fathers."[47] He was pained by the widespread "disrespect of the younger generation towards older people, and the order of life identified with them," although he empathised with them and basically applauded them. Less sympathetic members of the older generation, on the other hand, felt bitter about the estrangement of the younger generation. They were furious about the many young girls who sought the company of foreign soldiers, listened to their music, followed their foreign fashions and learned their language. Bundled in with the Americanisation of young people was the whole shame of defeat and the errors of their parents—who in their hysterical battle against the "wayward youth" sought an outlet for their own frustrations that were outwardly cultural and apolitical, but meant that one could remain a Nazi without openly presenting oneself as such. They waged a surrogate war against their own children, against Beate Uhse, against comics, against what they disparagingly referred to as "negro music" and jitterbugging—in short, against what they would call all kinds of "filth and rubbish." There were obvious echoes of the 1930s in the revived use of the terms "Hollywood trash" and "cultural Bolshevism" around this time to identify degenerate works.

Many young people were orphaned in every respect: literally and philosophically homeless, psychically traumatised and simply starving. In their desolation they staggered from one dubious benefactor to the next. Rather than understanding and charity, in many institutions all that awaited them were beatings, drills and mindless work. In notorious children's homes, the staff terrorised "fallen girls" whose sole crime was to have had underage sex. Among boys, on the other hand, crimes against property earned them the attribute "wayward," which led to character-breaking punishments. The labels given to the girls in their files as "moral imbeciles," "lacking in substance," "abnormally instinctual" and "untrainable" provides a sense of the brutal strategies for improvement and punishment that their minders came up with.[48]

While the sex drive of boys was accepted as God-given, educators saw the sexual activity of women as a witchlike threat to public peace.[49] Hence the most violent rage of the early anti-porn activists was directed at Hildegard Knef, who played the confident prostitute Marina who guides and protects her lover in the film *Die Sünderin* (*The Sinner*). And because she was a woman, the prosecutors came down much harder on Beate Uhse than they did on her male colleagues in the world of the sex industry.

The Catholic Church could, however, claim to have criticised sexual liberalisation even during the Nazi regime. The Church had been suspicious of the Third Reich's youth organisations from the outset. In their eyes both the Hitlerjugend and the Bund Deutscher Mädel (Hitler Youth and League of German Girls) encouraged sexual immorality in young people. Many parents had taken a dim view of the way that the state had deprived them of their role in their children's upbringing, and lured their offspring away from them with the promise of tempting adventures. Father Peter Petto, welfare spokesman for the Catholic Church, saw the Hitler Youth and *Flakhelfer* generation (teenagers recruited as anti-aircraft assistants) as being corrupted by the state. In a speech to teachers he explained in 1947:

> Many of them have passed through the school of disrespect, of arrogance, of mass drilling, of the falsification of conscience, of antireligious influence. They have been deadened by the barbaric habits of war and, by the deadly boredom and monotony of existence, made hungry for sensual pleasure. Their profound disappointment makes them feel in many ways like a lost battalion. They represent the large percentage of the restless wanderers.[50]

It is telling, however, that Father Petto—who showed himself to be empathetic and humane, and vociferously condemned the abuse in children's homes—should have placed a hunger for sexual pleasure on the same level as the spiritual deadening of war.

No matter from which direction concern about the "worship of sexual desire" came, the alarmism of the guardians of virtue was a threat to the tender shoots of post-war liberalism, severely enforcing prohibitions and stamping out any manifestations of life that struck them as disagreeable. After the passage of Article 131 of the Constitution in 1951, dealing with the reinstatement of those officials who had lost their posts after the end of the war because of edicts of the Allies, a whole cohort of incriminated former Nazis returned to official service. It has even been suggested that the Federal Criminal Police Office (Bundeskriminalamt—BKA) was only set up to battle against "trash" in order to provide an activity for former Nazi colleagues, who now needed to be reintegrated.[51] Right on the front line of the BKA's battle against "sexual pathological publications," for example, was the Criminal Counsellor Rudolf Thomsen. The former SS-Hauptsturmbannführer had previously served in Krakow in "gang identification and control," a term often used as a euphemism for the murder of civilians. Thomsen had been singled out for praise by his superiors for his work in Poland.[52] Five years later he fought just as resolutely against moral decay and attempted to coordinate the various offices and initiatives in the struggle against child delinquency.

Luckily, the social fabric of the young Federal Republic was significantly more resistant to such repression than the popular image of the musty 1950s would have Germans believe. Publishers, film distributors and authors fought legal battles against accusations from the right and sued their accusers. The press strongly resisted the "advancing authoritarian vision of the state," as *Die Zeit* called it in 1952.[53] The "anti-authoritarian temperament" is not in fact an invention of the protestors of 1968, and the term appeared as early as 1951 in *Der Spiegel*.[54] But the moral guardians were also aware of this social current. Just as the German economy got back on its feet, a regular culture war exploded around the freedom of words and images, and the boundary between morality and lasciviousness. Cologne's Cardinal Frings, who had already declared worldly laws to be of secondary importance over the hoarding issue, now issued another call for self-policing if the state would not agree to intervene:

> We want to form a massive phalanx, a mighty movement, and challenge the governments of the country and its regions not to rest until such things [referring to the film *The Sinner*] are impossible in future. If nothing else helps, we will rely on ourselves.[55]

Violent protests, stink-bomb attacks and brawls accompanied the premiere of *The Sinner* and led many Churchmen and moral fanatics to break the law themselves. But the state itself guaranteed artistic freedom. One policeman told a court that he had "never seen such a violent demonstrator as the minister Dr. Klinkhammer" from Düsseldorf, accused of intimidation, disorderly conduct and resisting arrest.[56]

VIII

The Re-educators

The Allies go to work on the German psyche

When the Allied armies crossed the borders into the German Reich, they brought with them elaborate plans for the administration of the occupied territories. They prepared in advance to reach accommodations both with POWs and the civilian population. And there were extensive plans for the greatest task that they faced after the physical victory: remoulding minds. How were the Germans to be cured of their arrogance? How to eradicate the racism with which they had been drip-fed for twelve years, and which no amount of lethal carpet-bombing had managed to destroy?

Allied troops had enlisted German emigrés to work in psychological warfare and secure the permanent capitulation of their compatriots. For the Soviets, for example, that meant the "Ulbricht Group," named after Walter Ulbricht, the future head of the Communist SED (the Socialist Unity Party of Germany, the ruling party of the GDR) and a KPD (German Communist Party) functionary who had fled Germany in the 1930s and emigrated to the USSR in 1941. This group fell under the auspices of the seventh division of the political central administration of the Red Army. Germans and Russians had been working closely together in this propaganda department since the beginning of the war. Among the Russians there were many who had developed an enthusiasm for Bach and Beethoven, Hölderlin and Schiller, and a great interest in the long history of Russo-German relations. Among the Germans there were journalists and authors who used their creative skills to write flyers and radio commentaries, such as the German Communist writers Erich Weinert, Willi Bredel (future president of the GDR's Academy of Arts), Alfred Kurella (active in the Socialist Unity Party) and Friedrich Wolf (later to be East Germany's first ambassador to Poland).

On 30 April 1945 the ten-man Ulbricht Group flew from Moscow to Minsk and on to Meseritz in Poland, from where they travelled on by truck, past bullet-ridden tanks and the bloated corpses of animals to Bruchmühle, east of Berlin, where furious machine-gun salvoes were still being exchanged. The Ulbricht Group's task was to identify politically reliable Germans who could be used to construct a new administration. They vetted defeated Germans as to the level of their trust in the goodwill of the Soviets, and also tried to persuade them to hand over active Nazis.

The Group was also to ensure the immediate establishment of an anti-fascist, democratic press. Five of the ten members of the group had gained experience as journalists with the German-language broadcaster in Moscow; these included Gustav Gundelach, Wolfgang Leonhard and Karl Maron, later deputy editor-in-chief of *Neues Deutschland* (the official newspaper of the Socialist Unity Party). Rudolf Herrnstadt, a Jewish former writer with the liberal *Berliner Tageblatt*, travelled from Moscow a week later with the task of establishing a daily newspaper by 21 May. His communist colleagues had originally wanted to leave him behind in Moscow because they believed that a Jew would encounter too much resentment in Berlin and might damage their cause. On 8 May Herrnstadt stumbled through the rubble of the Mossehaus in Berlin's newspaper district, amidst the corpses that still lay strewn on the ground, in search of a working printing press and typewriters. Along with Fritz Erpenbeck (the author of the Moscow-published novel *Kleines Mädchen im Großen Krieg* [*Little Girl in the Big War*]), he recruited trustworthy former colleagues—a challenging task in the ruined city. By way of reinforcements, he asked the Red Army to let him have the best editors from the *Wochenpost: Zeitung für deutsche Kriegsgefangene* (*German Newspaper for Prisoners of War*).

One potential colleague after the other got in touch, and once they had found a suitable headquarters in the form of Otto Meusel's print-works in Kreuzberg, they were ready to go by 22 May. The first issue of the *Berliner Zeitung* appeared in an edition of 100,000, with the famous headline BERLIN LEBT AUF!—Berlin comes back to life!

The American army also had Germans working for them to conduct psychological warfare. German emigrants, including many young Jews, but also German-speaking descendants of immigrants, had volunteered to put their abilities at the service of the anti-Hitler coalition. Most of them had been trained in Camp Ritchie in Maryland, a train-ing camp for US military intelligence, which outwardly resembled a golf club, idyllically situated on a lake at the foot of the Blue Ridge Mountains. At the camp, emigrants speaking over fifteen different lan-guages were trained to use psychological warfare on German soil.

Hans Habe in his tailor-made uniform. In 1945, as a major in the US Army, he founded 16 German newspapers, with the Neue Zeitung *as their flagship.*

They learned interrogation techniques, how to spy behind enemy lines, how to wear down the fighting spirit with disinformation or, even better, the truth. The Ritchie boys, as they were known, were a highly trained troop united not only by their hatred of the Nazis but also by their love of German culture. Among them were Americans who had studied German literature and thus mastered the language, including, notably, *Catcher in the Rye* author J. D. Salinger. The German Ritchie boys included the authors Klaus Mann, Hans Habe, Stefan Heym, Hanuš Burger and the future cabaret artist Georg Kreisler.

The most glittering among them was undoubtedly Hans Habe. The journalist, born in Budapest in 1911 as János Békessy, had been appointed editor-in-chief of the *Österreichische Abendzeitung* at the age of twenty, after doing some research for the *Wiener Sonn- und Montagspost* in Hitler's birthplace of Braunau and discovering that Hitler's real name would have been Adolf Schicklgruber had his father not changed his own birth name. He later worked for the well-known *Prager Tagblatt* as a correspondent at the League of Nations in Geneva. Habe, who said of himself, "I was unusually attractive, and I didn't lack qualities of the heart," was able to boast at the end of his life that he had married three of the wealthiest women in the world. He married six times in all. After a short first marriage to Margit Bloch he married Erika Levy, the daughter of a Viennese lightbulb manufacturer. She was unable to stay by his side for long; after Austria's *Anschluss* with Nazi Germany in 1938 Habe, the son of a converted Jew, was immediately stripped of his citizenship. He went to France, where he joined the French volunteer army. True to his frequently expressed decision to make his life even more exciting than his novels, he enlisted as a parachutist. Taken prisoner by the Germans, he managed a daring escape that was later turned into a novel by Erich Maria Remarque, *The Night in Lisbon*. From Lisbon he made the crossing to the United States where, almost as soon as he had met his next wealthy woman, the future United Food heiress Eleanor Close, he volunteered once more in the fight against Nazi Germany, this time with the US Army.

That was how Hans Habe came to Camp Ritchie. He landed with

the 5th Army at Salerno in southern Italy, an operation that cost many lives, in a uniform that he had had tailored according to his own specifications—a privilege normally granted only to generals, but Habe loved being smart, and had been awarded this concession after impressing his military superiors with his combination of courage and elegance. During the northward advance he was made director of the press department of the Psychological Warfare Division. Immediately after the capture of Luxembourg, in September 1944 he oversaw the popular broadcaster Radio Luxembourg and turned it into a brilliant propaganda arm directed at the enemy. Aachen, the first German city to be taken, fell late in October. From then on Habe would immediately establish a newspaper in each reasonably large city as soon as it was conquered, to win over both luminaries and ordinary people to the American side. His most important partner in this was fellow Ritchie Boy Hans Wallenberg, the son of the former editor-in-chief of the newspaper *B.Z. am Mittag*. Beginning with the *Kölnischer Kurier*, from April 1945 onwards 16 new newspapers began publishing just as soon as ceasefires had been declared in their cities. Publication happened thanks to a very sophisticated set of logistics. The 16 papers had a central editorial office under Habe's direction, based in the confiscated Hotel Bristol in Bad Nauheim, north of Frankfurt. Stories were ferried daily by plane or jeep to the local editorial offices, where they were combined with local reports and announcements from the regional military administration—a system that anticipated the present-day structure of German local newspapers under a trans-regional umbrella organisation.

In parallel with Habe's highly efficient establishment of his newspapers, the Allied administrations also awarded press licenses to German magazine and newspaper publishers who had not been connected to the Nazi Party. These papers included the *Frankfurter Rundschau*, the *Rhein-Neckar-Zeitung*, the *Süddeutsche Zeitung* and many smaller newspapers in the provinces. Later, weekly publications like *Die Zeit* and *Stern* also appeared. American supervisors' control over the so-called licensed press led to practically maternal feelings of responsibility and a bitter competition within the military administration. The licensing teams viewed Hans Habe's well-equipped, government-financed papers as a kind of unfair competition to their German-owned and -operated babies. One of the biggest areas of conflict lay in the permanent battle for scarce supplies of paper.

Rudolf Herrnstadt's publishing empire in far-off Berlin also expanded in the face of these difficulties. In addition to the *Berliner Zeitung*, he set up the *Neue Berliner Illustrierte*, a beautifully produced magazine that soon employed outstanding photographers and illustrators. This was followed by *Die Frau von heute* (*Today's Woman*), the youth magazine *Start* and *Demokratischer Aufbau* (*Democratic Reconstruction*). By 1947 1,700 people were working for the German publishing house Berliner Verlag.

Habe and Herrnstadt faced the same task: how to make Germans trust the newspapers of the occupying powers? The papers were read carefully, because conditions were at first so uncertain that people were eager for the smallest piece of information that might help them find their bearings. In these circumstances, it was not difficult to achieve large circulations. But how did one achieve the degree of affection among the readership that made a newspaper more than a mere bulletin of instructions about curfews and food rationing? This question developed into an awkward competition between the Allies for the favours of the Germans in their respective zones. The focus was not only on the press; the policy of denazification and re-education that the Allies had agreed upon was based on a balance between punishment and trust-building: eliminating the guilty and identifying the *Mitläufer* (literally meaning "fellow-travellers" or "tag-alongs," a term used to refer to people who had been significantly involved with the Nazi Party but were not charged with Nazi crimes—usually indicating that they indirectly or passively supported the regime) with the help of genuine opponents of the Nazis who had survived the regime. Without basic trust in the goodwill of the victors, lasting peace would have been impossible.

In theory, the Soviets had a comparatively easier time of it. Their philosophical conviction that history "inevitably" strove towards a classless society enabled them to believe in human goodness, even among Germans. In the second issue of the *Berliner Zeitung*, Herrnstadt presented a quote from comrade Stalin highlighted in its own box: "The experiences of history tell us that Hitlers come and go, but that the German people, the German state, remains." By interpreting fascism as a terrorist dictatorship over the working class, the Soviets created an ideological path to quick forgiveness. They might have considered the German masses guilty of not putting up enough resistance, but they were much less inclined to see the Germans as fundamentally evil in a way that many Americans, and some Britons, did.

While the Germans were much more fearful of the Soviets than they were of Americans or the British, when it came to their propaganda the Soviets were much more forgiving. From the first day, they offered the Germans the prospect of reconciliation. In the *Berliner Zeitung* Karl Maron of the Ulbricht Group, by now "First Deputy to the Mayor," wrote on 23 May 1945:

> The world has seen German men disproportionately involved in arson and destruction. May it now see us engaged in peaceful reconstruction and just atonement, so that we may once again walk with our heads held high, and Germany may once again occupy its place in the peaceful family of nations.

The Americans, on the other hand, couldn't see their way to offering the Germans the chance of rehabilitation so soon after the war. They had no communist theory of history that would have enabled them to view Germans as Hitler's victims. On the contrary, they saw the average German as a militaristic, authoritarian, hardhearted character for whom the Führer's state was the most representative form of government. At any rate they were far from ripe for democracy, and would continue to remain a huge danger to world peace. As a matter of principle, every German was to be seen as an enemy.

The practical consequences of this attitude were apparent in the prohibition on fraternisation, which the Western Allies had enacted just prior to their victory over Germany. They forbade their soldiers to have any contact with the civilian population beyond the barest necessities. The US Army G-3 handbook, published on 9 September 1944, called for the "avoidance of mingling with Germans upon terms of friendliness, familiarity or intimacy, whether individually or in groups, in official or unofficial dealings."[1] A memo on the theme of "The Conduct of American Military Personnel in Germany" put it this way:

> Without demonstrating vengefulness or spite, the behaviour of the Americans should express cool hostility and distaste. [. . .] It should be made clear to the Germans that they are responsible for the Second World War and will not be forgiven their terrible oppression of other peoples under German rule. [. . .] They will learn not only that Germany will be punished a second time for her aggression with a defeat, but also that she will have brought down upon herself the contempt and horror of those whose affection she would actually like to have.[2]

Handshakes were forbidden, along with the distribution of chocolate, shared visits to drinking establishments, shared partying and, of course, sexual relationships.

It is well known that the soldiers did not stick to these rules for long. They were surprised at how little most Germans corresponded to the image from the "Handbook for American Soldiers in Germany," and were even irritated by the assiduous servility that they came across everywhere. Still, for the first few months the prohibition on fraternisation ensured a certain reserve, particularly since there were constant reminders of it on posters, in brochures and in cinema advertisements.

The Soviet soldiers behaved quite differently. They created an extremely contradictory impression. As brutal as many of them appeared, particularly when drunk, they could also surprise with a boundless cordiality, often inviting Germans off the street to victory parties and spontaneous celebrations. Their impulsive warmth was as legendary as their volcanic violence. They loved dance music and classical concerts, theatre and acrobatics, and immediately after the guns finally fell silent they began a bacchanalian round of revelry.

They reopened huge numbers of theatres, concert halls and music halls that had been closed during the war. On 26 May 1945, only two weeks after the end of the war, the Berlin Philharmonic gave their first concert in the Titania-Palast after the musicians had cleared it of rubble with their bare hands. It was amazing enough that the concert should have taken place at all, as 35 members of the orchestra were dead or missing, many of the instruments were in storage and the rest had been confiscated by a Russian military band. On the conductor's podium in his black tails was Leo Borchard, the same Borchard with whom Ruth Andreas-Friedrich had, only a few weeks previously, clambered over the body of a white ox in a rear courtyard to hack a few pieces of meat from it with their blunt knives.

By mid-June 1945 music halls and cabarets had reopened on Russian instructions, along with 127 cinemas which were visited by between 80,000 and 100,000 people every day.[3] The Six Waldos, the Two Rodellis, the Three Kritons, the Comics' Cabaret, the Schall und Rauch Cabaret, the Expresskapelle—all of these circus and music-hall acts had their work cut out satisfying the Russian appetite for entertainment. The Russians didn't care about pleasing the Germans, but after the difficult years at the front they themselves wanted to savour to the full the products of the West's entertainment industry. "They made the German population participate in this joy, they mingled with the audience, as victors they had no fear of contact, and perhaps they also wanted to be liked," writes the cultural commentator Ina Merkel.[4]

The Russians devoted themselves to German high culture with equal enthusiasm. While the Americans remained stubbornly suspicious of the German classics, and wondered whether this highbrow posturing might not have more to do with German barbarism than appeared at first sight, the Russians uninhibitedly honoured the German cultural legacy. Luckily for them Weimar, the home of German classicism, lay in their occupied zone. As early as July 1945 Red Army soldiers, along with a large press presence, had removed the scaffolding built by Nazi gauleiter Fritz Sauckel around Weimar's monument to Goethe and Schiller to protect it from bomb damage. A month later the commander of the 8th Guards Army and head of the Thuringian Military Administration, General Vasily Chuikov, accompanied by a large entourage, paid a visit to the monuments and graves of the two Weimar classicists. After a long address by the general it was the turn of the bestselling author Nikolai Virta, who declared:

> Hitler's disciples wanted to constrain Goethe and Schiller, they wanted to conceal their most beautiful and light-filled ideas. [. . .] Today, as we open the graves of Goethe and Schiller, we are at the same time opening the prison in which their thoughts of the happiness of human beings, the friendship of nations and justice were locked away.

Nikolai Virta declared that National Socialism had been un-German, a theory that the defeated Germans happily agreed with and enthusiastically applauded.

On the American side, such an emphatic understanding of German high culture was shared only, if at all, by a smattering of emigrants and academics with an interest in German literature. Most of them had a sceptical attitude towards the cultural tradition of the Germans and questioned why the cultivated German professorial class had been among the worst of the Nazis.

Hans Habe, however, was a hard-line opponent of the prohibition on fraternisation. He believed that denazification could only be successful if the Allies mingled with the Germans and as a result were able to distinguish between good and bad Germans. Without contacts he couldn't run a newspaper, so his German and American colleagues needed to work closely together. Habe's magnum opus began publishing in Munich on 17 October 1945: the *Neue Zeitung*, a trans-regional paper under his overall editorship, published by the Information Control Division of the American military government. The paper was quite explicitly an "American newspaper for the German population" as it stated in its header, but at least half of it was devoted to writings of the German intelligentsia. From Theodor W. Adorno to Carl Zuckmayer, almost anyone with anything significant to say wrote for its pages: the playwright and novelist Max Frisch,

German psychoanalyist Alexander Mitscherlich, the novelists Hermann Hesse and Alfred Döblin, Thomas Mann and his son Heinrich Mann, also the critic Alfred Kerr, publisher Peter Suhrkamp, poet and journalist Oda Schaefer, poet and playwright Ilse Aichinger, novelist and short-story writer Luise Rinser, theatre critic Friedrich Luft, German writer and member of Gruppe 47 Reinhard Lettau, novelist Hermann Kesten, critic Walter Jens, poet and playwright Wolfgang Borchert, journalists Ruth Andreas-Friedrich and Ursula von Kardorff, author Günther Weisenborn. This is only a small selection that gives a sense of how wide the range of participants was. Hans Habe had brought in novelist Erich Kästner (who would go on to be nominated for the Nobel Prize in Literature four times) as head of the features section, with writer Alfred Andersch as his deputy. The Jewish German-American writer Stefan Heym was part of the American editorial staff, but there were other Germans such as the cabaret artist Werner Finck and the future game show host Robert Lembke. For Hildegard Hamm-Brücher, who would many years later, as an FDP politician and foreign office minister, become one of the most impressive politicians of the young republic, working on the *Neue Zeitung* as a young science editor was a lesson in democracy:

> This was a training in a new way of thinking, with new experiences every day. [. . .] We were also treated in an open and democratic way. After three years I had advanced to a position that others still trapped in the authoritarian mindset would only reach twenty years later.[5]

The *Neue Zeitung* was an impressive newspaper: large-format, elegantly designed, intelligently and provocatively written. Its pages actually contained disputes, which was a novelty for German readers since 1933. In one of the first editions, the philosopher Karl Jaspers, in his "Reply to Sigrid Undset," denied the collective guilt of the Germans.[6] Undset, a Norwegian author, had previously rejected the possibility of a re-education of the Germans, since their deeds "had been committed on the basis of German thought," which as a historical constant was defined by "presumption, arrogance and aggression."[7] She believed that re-education was impossible because it meant that children would have to break with their parents. Jaspers replied to the Nobel laureate's article, "Summarily condemning a people as a whole seems to me to run against the requirement of being human." He even considered the "self-education" of Germans to be a possibility. However, that required admitting to the millions of murders that had been committed, a ruthless examination of one's own co-responsibility involving a degree of mutual tolerance and adaptability, and an open discussion of the past. "The important thing is to regain our German life under the conditions of the truth. We must learn to talk to one another." That meant nothing less than a change of character that extended all the way into linguistic forms: "Dogmatic assertion, shouting at people, being defiantly outraged, the wounded honour that interrupts conversation at every opportunity—all of this must cease to exist."[8]

The *Neue Zeitung* was a forum for independent minds and a more pluralistic journal than anyone could have expected from an occupying power. Where else could one read both the cultural theorist Theodor W. Adorno and Chancellor Ludwig Erhard? Under the editorial control of Erich Kästner the features section, a third of the paper, considerably increased the lustre of the *Neue Zeitung*. Hans Habe, who contributed an editorial and many other articles to each issue, and ran the editorial office firmly but in a collegial fashion, basked in the glow of circulation figures as high as 2.5 million, along with a further 3 million orders that could not be fulfilled because of lack of paper.

Without friendly cooperation between the German and American editors, however, a paper like the *Neue Zeitung* would, in Habe's view, have been impossible. What was true on a smaller scale for the editorial office also applied to denazification as a whole, in that Habe wished for more harshness towards the guilty, but also more openness towards the "exonerated." The 20 or so American members of the editorial team who came in wearing crumpled, baggy uniforms—it was only Habe who wore a neatly tailored and meticulously ironed suit, like a dressage rider—got on well with their German colleagues. The relaxed and open atmosphere was viewed with suspicion, though, by the American military authorities. Habe soon came to be seen as intellectually unreliable, a "fraterniser" who had been thoroughly duped by the insolent Germans.

Habe also encountered reservations of a different kind. Some Germans chafed under the denazification process, particularly when it was practised by Germans who had American passports. Not many people knew that Habe was not German, but was in fact a Hungarian Jew. We might speculate endlessly about whether that knowledge would have made matters easier or more difficult for him. Habe himself was sure that the Germans would greatly prefer to be re-educated by foreigners than by their own kind. For the foreigners, it was all just part of a ritual.

While most denazification measures appear rather harmless in retrospect, the defeated Germans saw them as a humiliation. Above all the intelligentsia of the Third Reich—the teachers, professors, authors and journalists—felt that it was inappropriate for them to be treated with such suspicion. For example, every adult in the American zone had to fill in a form containing 131 questions that was used as the basis for dismissals from public service—a bureaucratic procedure that prompted much mockery. The questions were not always precisely put. Some betrayed a lack of knowledge of the various Nazi associations, but not only that, trust in the value of such simplistic empiricism, entirely alien to German thinking, struck them as both presumptuous and naive. "Were you in the German National Socialist Party? Did you ever hold one of the following posts in the German National Socialist Party: Reichsleiter? Gauleiter? Kreisleiter? Ortsgruppenleiter? [Reich leader, District leader, County leader, Local group leader] Did you leave the church? Were you in the Hitler Youth? Was your wife Jewish or half-Jewish? Was your wife ever in the NSDAP?" Many Germans were very unsettled by the idea of being seen in this way. The author Ernst von Salomon wrote a novel about this supposed impertinence, entitled *The Questionnaire*, which became one of the biggest bestsellers in post-war Germany after its publication in 1951. Using the questionnaire as the basis of the book, he develops a 600-page autobiography, proving that the complex life of a nationalist, conservative German intellectual could not, with the best will in the world, be captured by such a foolish set of questions.

★

In general, of course, all Germans were under Allied suspicion after the end of the war. Even the most self-righteous could see that. It was part of the logic of war. As far as the Nazi *Volk* community were concerned, however, Germans returning from exile had no business judging anybody, or indeed saying anything at all. Critical or educational interventions by German returnees were held by many Germans to be a particularly monstrous presumption. While Habe might have been well liked within the circle of his closest German colleagues, outside of his sheltered editorial office he encountered a loathing that depressed him. Germans closed ranks against the supposed arrogance of emigrants. This was more than the defiant grumbling of a horde of former Nazis with guilty consciences, and the attacks against Germans who returned under Allied protection were not reserved for private conversations. Post-war West Germany fostered a lively culture of debate and allowed the arguments between those who had stayed and those who had left to be played out in public. The argument about and with Thomas Mann became a notorious example of this. Since 1940 the 1929 Nobel laureate had regularly written radio speeches from his exile in California, which were broadcast to his compatriots by the BBC. In a total of 55 talks, most of them around eight minutes long, he had enlightened his listeners about the crimes of the Nazi regime, spoken of "moral madness" and described from his external perspective how the country was ostracising itself from the community of humanist-inclined nations.

Now, immediately after the end of the war, many Germans hoped for a moral boost from the celebrated author's return. Walter von Molo, former chairman of the poetry section of the Prussian Academy of Arts, who saw himself as a particularly outstanding representative of German culture, wrote an open letter to Thomas Mann, the acknowledged global man of literature, which was published in the *Hessische Post* on 4 August 1945 and reprinted in the *Münchner Zeitung*. In it he asked Mann to return to Germany, a country that was not, von Molo believed, a perpetrator, but above all a victim:

> Please come soon, look into the furrowed, sorrowful faces, see the unspeakable suffering in the eyes of the many who played no part in the glorification of our darker side, who were unable to leave their homes because so many millions of people here had nowhere else to go, here in what had slowly become a concentration camp, in which everyone was either inmate or guard.[9]

Even though this request was intended flatteringly, identifying Thomas Mann as the one person urgently needed in Germany, the writer felt that it was thoroughly insensitive. He had no wish to return to a Germany in which Nazi followers tearfully saw themselves as victims and acted as if they had all been living in a big concentration camp. So he replied with an article entitled "Why I Am Not Returning to Germany," published in the New York German-language newspaper *Aufbau* and passed on to the United States Office of War Information (OWI), which printed it in various German newspapers, including the *Augsburger Anzeiger*, from where it spread very quickly. Mann connected his refusal with a general attack on the authors who had chosen "internal emigration" (remaining at home but refusing to get involved with politics) and who believed that they could remain guiltless by escaping into unpolitical writing: "In my eyes books that were published in Germany between 1933 and 1945 are less than worthless and not worth picking up. They have a smell of blood and shame about them. They should all be pulped."

These authors were extremely put out. Thomas Mann had lumped them all together, the hypocritical and the upstanding, the agitators and the downhearted, and hurled them all in the bin. Even many of those involved in the Allies' re-education project were shocked, because Thomas Mann's contribution was not exactly helpful. And it was also inaccurate, if only because his books had continued to be published in Germany until he was denaturalised in 1936. Did they need to be pulped as well?

Those who had stayed at home argued back. Frank Thiess (author of the novel *Tsushima*, later published in English as *The Voyage of Forgotten Men*) explained in an article entitled "Internal Emigration," published in the *Münchner Zeitung* newspaper on 18 August 1945, that it was a sense of duty that had kept him from emigrating. It was comfortable to run away, and he, Thiess, had served literature by enduring the regime. He had known from the beginning that, if he was ever to survive "this terrible era," he would "gain so much for my intellectual and human development that I would emerge from it richer in knowledge and experience than if I had watched the German tragedy from the boxes and stalls of foreign lands."[10]

Thiess's opponents on the Allied side gave no ground. To describe the emigrés as comfortable spectators of the German tragedy who had left their compatriots in the lurch was an outrage to all those who had had to leave their homes under the most dire conditions, probably not voluntarily, and who had in all likelihood been robbed of their entire wealth. In the case of the highly successful Thomas Mann, exile had indeed been congenial, and Thiess's observation was an envious dig that further soured the atmosphere.

Despite the bitter arguments, there were at least open debates in Germany once more. This public spat, conducted via newspaper, went on sale in the form of a brochure in the summer of 1946. It provided a great deal of intellectual enjoyment for the public, because all the participants were highly skilled writers who knew how to express and entertain. Their extravagant verbal displays vied for the approbation of some kind of justice. They were dazzlingly gifted at flourishing their mutual disparagements, their rhetorical assertions and their wounded vanity like so many competing peacocks.

Conducting a debate of the kind that Karl Jaspers had demanded was also the most important concern of the *Neue Zeitung*. Hans Habe looked on with concern as many Germans formerly critical of Hitler's regime, and who should in fact have felt liberated, distanced themselves from the occupying powers and suddenly made common cause with former Nazis. In November 1945, under the headline SOLI-DARITY MISUNDERSTOOD, he addressed the phenomenon whereby many Germans who had stayed out of politics clearly believed, on the basis of a certain sense of honour, that they had to extend a hand of friendship to the defeated National Socialists: "Nothing is so seductive to the Germans as the possibility of the grand gesture, of a kind of medievally undigested chivalry."[11] But in Habe's view it was an abdication of responsibility to let the foreign victors have the final reckoning with the Nazi criminals all by themselves.

If even the impervious Hans Habe had struggled with the wall of hostility that he sometimes encountered, especially from educated circles, 300 kilometres northwest of Munich an even more depressing drama was being played out. In Baden-Baden, Alfred Döblin, the once celebrated author of the novel *Berlin Alexanderplatz*, who had been forced as a Jew to emigrate, had returned like Habe and Herrnstadt. In the autumn of 1945, on the request of the French, he moved into a re-education office in the confiscated Grand Hotel Stephanie. Döblin, by now 68, sat down at his desk there every morning in a smart French uniform and began his work on the reorganisation of a democratic intellectual life on behalf of the Paris Ministry of Information. What was required for this, in his view, was the establishment of a literary journal which he named *Das goldene Tor* (*The Golden Gate*). The front page showed a stylised version of the eponymous Golden Gate Bridge in San Francisco, which was already unusual for a French-financed literary magazine. Döblin set to work with gusto, revived old contacts, wrote letters and scripts for Südwestfunk Radio and edited manuscripts submitted by German writers for publication. But this was the sore point: he painstakingly picked through their writings and censored them where he saw fit. His former colleagues were furious and humiliated. Döblin was perplexed by their reactions. Why, after a war that had cost countless millions of lives, would an occupying power not presume to practise censorship for a transition period?

When he addressed a group of writers in the southern city of Freiburg and invited them to work on *Das goldene Tor*, he was met with hatred, muted at first and later quite open.

> I felt it was a difficult thing to be trying out, because these were dis-appointed, formerly arrogant Germans, and now we were supposed to be picking up where we left off. I remember how they listened to me, alien and mute, and my words froze in my mouth. It was hard to rouse these people. When nobody spoke, I had to ask them indi-vidually to express themselves, each in turn. I knew in advance that the answer would be no. Now it came out: they didn't want to col-laborate, meaning with the French. They wanted to continue along their own bleak nationalist path. For long stretches their speech was very agitated, and the audience spat with rage at what was being done to them.[12]

They thought he saw himself as somehow superior. And wasn't he?

In 1947 he risked a brief trip to his beloved Berlin. He was to deliver a lecture to an audience of old friends and readers in Charlot-tenburg Palace. Even on this occasion, he did not remove his French uniform. He wore it with both caution and defiance. He loved it. When Döblin entered the hall the audience initially began to applaud enthusiastically—the creator of the most famous Berlin novel had returned! "But then silence fell," the author Günther Weisenborn reported.

> The man who appeared at the door had the face of Döblin, but he was a French major in uniform. Hands were lowered in bafflement. Only a general politeness owed to a guest followed [. . .] and no one uttered the acclamation that should have greeted the Berlin writer. Nothing against French officers, we had met many of them, but was this really our Döblin? Of course there were Germans who worked for Ameri-can, Russian, British or French military agencies. But most of them had taken off the uniform or wore them only rarely. Whatever the reason, Döblin looked like a foreign guest, and he soon left.[13]

The man who had described Berlin as the "mother soil of all his ideas" was without a home.

Hardly a single audience member knew that Döblin's 25-year-old son, Wolfgang, whom Döblin and his wife had had to leave in France when they fled to America, had killed himself in just such a French uniform. Cut off from his French military unit, Wolfgang Döblin, a prodigiously gifted mathematician, had shot himself in a barn near the village of Housseras in the Vosges, shortly before German troops could take him prisoner.

The problem was widespread; 750 kilometres from Baden-Baden but just 20 kilometres from Charlottenburg Palace, where Döblin had given his reading, and yet in another world altogether, Rudolf Herrnstadt, the successful founder of the *Berliner Zeitung*, was also getting into difficulties. He, too, was rubbing people the wrong way. He was uneasy in his old homeland and struggled to find the right words. The problem wasn't the Russians, or the readers, it was his own fellow Party members. The journalist was annoyed by the formalistic language, the bureaucratic German, the sterile Party clichés from which reality had to be laboriously distilled. Above all, he suffered from the poor reputation of the Soviet Union in the occupied zone. Herrnstadt loved the Russians, he had spied for them in Nazi Germany and they had protected him after he was exposed. He had met his wife, Valentina, in Russia and survived the tyranny of Stalinist denunciations. He could never forgive his German colleagues for the malicious undertone with which they spoke under their breath about the Russians, while otherwise keeping their own heads down. Herrnstadt was convinced that only a sanctioned debate could lead to an improvement in relations between Germans and Russians and move the situation a little way towards the "friendship between nations" that was constantly boasted about in the propaganda. So in November 1948 he wrote a full-page essay, not in his own Western *Berliner Zeitung* but in *Neues Deutschland*, the party newspaper of the ruling Communist SED (Sozialistische Einheitspartei—Social Unity Party) in the GDR, entitled "About the 'Russians' and About Us." The text caused a sensation, because it was the first time that the barbaric behaviour of the Red Army in the Soviet zone during the flush of victory had been openly discussed. He didn't mention the rapes, but he did write of how the Red Army arrived:

> in clotted boots with the dirt of history still clinging to them, resolute, inflamed, alert and on edge, sometimes brutalised—yes, brutalised, because war brutalises people, who has the right to get worked up about that? If anyone does, then it's those who, like the Soviet Union, have spent decades doing their utmost to prevent it.[14]

There was talk of assaults, and especially the scene that had become a post-war metaphor, of having one's bicycle stolen, *Zapp-zarapp*, from under one's backside.

Rudolf Herrnstadt, editor-in-chief of the Berliner Zeitung *from May 1945 and later of* Neues Deutschland, *was sidelined after the uprising on 17 June 1953.*

Neues Deutschland was inundated by letters to the editor. A whole corridor was requisitioned to help cope with the baskets of letters, Herrnstadt's daughter Irina Liebmann later reported. He could afford to be as open as he was because his forthright statement was wrapped up in a resolute affirmation of the Soviet Union. It was practically glowing, insofar as that was possible given his circumlocutions. But it was also awash with risks, because right at the beginning of the piece Herrnstadt had expressed his reservation that in the SED, "the most progressive part of the working class," the attitude towards the Soviet Union was "inadequate, because [it was] timid, divided and still under the influence of Russia's adversary." This was a harsh criticism of the SED, accusing the party of not being loyal enough to the Soviet Union. Herrnstadt was so firmly on the side of the Soviets that Ulbricht even suspected him of spying on the SED Politburo on behalf of the Russians. He belonged to the minority of diehard communists in the GDR who were less attached to their own power machinery than they were to the historic mission of a classless society based on freedom and self-realisation. The contrast between communism's vision of history as a form of salvation and the petty formalism of his comrades was unendurable. His daughter remembered him suddenly coming to a stop when they went for a walk, and saying: "When one is doing everything, everything new for the first time in world history, and one hasn't learned how to do it and has no experience, do you not think that at first one will do everything, everything wrong?"[15]

Herrnstadt took the bull by the horns and allied himself directly with the workers. Over many pages in the *Berliner Zeitung* he reported on progress in the construction of the Stalinallee, a postwar flagship architectural project to rebuild a great boulevard in Stalin's honour. He celebrated the vigour of the workers and the commitment of the populace to this model construction project. Herrnstadt was delighted by the plan not only to build inexpensively, functionally and purposefully, but above all magnificently—in a palatial manner as beautiful and old-fashioned as he considered appropriate to the working class. The aesthetic of the Russians was closer to his idea of beauty than the functionalism of his German comrades. The Soviets had on several occasions prevented the destruction of Prussian architecture, which they viewed as a precious historical legacy, corresponding to their conservative taste. He attacked the bureaucratic machinery, upbraiding it for its "unserious behaviour, frittering away the interests of the workers, playing fast and loose with their good will." He opposed the "narrow-minded delight in issuing orders." He published the construction workers' demands for better terms and fairer wages.

> That atmosphere of openness and joyful advancement for all that arises out of the certainty that every useful initiative is being encouraged and that whoever is right invariably receives justice—does it prevail here? It does not yet prevail here. Not in the Party, not in the state.

Herrnstadt's fate was sealed when those same construction workers on the Stalinallee who had been celebrated in the *Berliner Zeitung* organised a demonstration on 16 June 1953, which would lead to the notorious 17 June uprising in which over a million East German citizens protested against poverty and Sovietisation, nearly bringing down the government. The uprising led to a few internal Party reassignments, followed by informal tribunals in the Politburo and finally by a meeting of all the staff at *Neues Deutschland*. Herrnstadt's daughter wrote:

> He was able to return to his editorial office, but only in order to be humiliated once again at very close range. All the people who had worked with him were sitting there. Fred Oelssner [a senior member of the East German Politburo] came in, the star witness of the conspiracy, and spoke for three hours about enemy activity, and then everyone else had to state their position. [. . .] Out with it, what have you observed about your boss, what has ever seemed bourgeois about him, or aggressive, or simply arrogant, unfair and mean? Then they were all doing it. They were tearing down what they felt were protective walls that had been built around Herrnstadt. Afterwards some people seemed to be ashamed of what happened, because of all those

that I was able to ask, no one admitted to being present. But this "open discussion" continued until three in the morning.[16]

The ruling party of the GDR had lost one of its greatest idealists.

In the West, the situation in Munich escalated, too. Hans Habe's American superiors were irritated by his high-handed approach towards the regulations, particularly his candid dealings with the Germans. They punctiliously counted to check whether the ratio of two to one set out in the regulations—two American writers to one German—was being adhered to. In fact at the *Neue Zeitung* the proportion was just about one to one. The general responsible for collecting the data had erroneously included the Americans John Steinbeck and Carl Sandburg on the list as Germans, because their names had a German ring to them. Habe made such thorough use of that embarrassing error that it saved him from any consequences. Of course, the revenge when it came would be all the more terrible.

Habe enjoyed arguments and verbal jousting, and would happily have cut the lead article to make space for readers' letters. On the letters page, headed "The Free Word," one reader even reported on a GI in a jeep who had knocked over a child and then simply sped away. The final straw came only when Habe's friend and deputy Hans Wallenberg published a lead article which assailed the Soviets over the lack of freedom in their zone. Public criticism of one of the four powers was taboo in 1946, since the Cold War had not yet openly broken out. When, half an hour before the paper was due to go to press, Habe refused to print a long speech by Winston Churchill in its entirety on the front page, the break was complete. Habe was said to have been infected by the Germans: "You have gone native" was the judgement, delivered in English. At the end of 1946 he cleared his desk and, having been honoured with the Bronze Star Medal and Oak Leaf Cluster for "heroic and meritorious achievement," he left the army.

This was followed by a salacious scandal that was soon played out in public: back in the US Hans Habe resumed his campaign on the marriage front. He divorced Eleanor Close and married the actress

Ali Ghito, whom he had known for several years. Shortly after the wedding he met Ghito's colleague Eloise Hardt and fell madly in love all over again. He married Eloise Hardt two years later, in 1948, in Mexico, immediately after divorcing wife number four in the same country. Ali Ghito refused to recognise the divorce, however, and planned her revenge—with some success. Back in Germany after 1950, Habe, who was writing several books at the same time, including one called *Our Love Affair with Germany*, experienced a public attack more damaging than anything that had come before. On 1 June 1952, *Stern*, the most successful illustrated magazine of the young Federal Republic, published an article under the headline GET THIS VILLAIN OUT OF GERMANY! Editor-in-chief Henri Nannen used the gossip and hearsay that Ali Ghito had served him up for a political and cultural reckoning of unbridled malevolence.

Ghito, christened Adelheid Schnabel-Fürbringer, wanted to sue her ex-husband for bigamy, but before she was able to do so she paid a visit to Henri Nannen with the relevant documentation. Nannen leapt into action. At last he saw an opportunity to scoop Habe, his competitor who, under a new editor, was delivering daily fireworks at the *Münchner Illustrierte*. Nannen hammered away triumphantly at his typewriter: "The most colourful shimmering soap bubble of political post-war life in Germany has burst." And he continued in similar style: "Hans Habe, alias János Békessy," "Galician immigrant" and "American propaganda major," had, "after many years of self-inflation, suddenly had the air let out of him." Luckily for Germany, Nannen wrote, it was nothing but "bilious spittle that dripped from that muzzle." He had tirelessly tried "to beslobber the reputation of anyone who had held the post of doorman at some point in the Third Reich." In short, Habe was "a latent political danger to Germany."[17]

Dripping spittle, a slobbering muzzle, disowned origins and a reference to the Jewish background of the "Galician immigrant" and "propaganda major," as well as the headline's demand that he be ejected from the country—one would need to read it twice to believe that this tirade was the work of a journalist who would soon become one of Germany's leading commentators.[18] Even by the standards of the 1950s, which were rich in heated verbal exchanges, it was a vicious attack.

Nannen's and Habe's pasts were mirror images of one another in a sense: trained art historian Nannen, a former contributor to the journal *Die Kunst im Dritten Reich* (*Art in the Third Reich*) had produced military propaganda for the Nazis during the war, as a war reporter with the Southern Star division of the SS-Standarte Kurt Eggers's propaganda formation. This unit had waged psychological warfare against the Americans in Italy, the very place where Habe had fought in 1944. Nannen's article was uncharacteristically brazen. He really wasn't a common-or-garden-variety right-wing extremist and anti-Semite for whom hatred had become a habit, but a pioneer of liberal journalism in West Germany. As an eighteen-year-old school student in Emden in northwest Germany, he had been in a relationship with the Jewish Cilly Windmüller, the same age as him and his "great love," as he would later repeatedly assert. Cilly's parents had died in a concentration camp, and he claimed that he had helped her with the complicated formalities required for her to emigrate to Palestine. Nannen would later travel to Israel several times to see her again (and indeed to fall in love with her daughter).

So why this mean-spirited article? There wasn't enough room in the ornamental fishpond of German journalism to let several fighting fish live in peace at the same time. The fact that Habe, the "most successful re-educator of the Germans" (as he called himself), had morality on his side, and also had about him the cosmopolitan elegance of the now-vanished Habsburg monarchy, and more than a hint of Hollywood good looks, must have got up the nose of the bull-headed Nannen, originally from East Frisia, a rural region not traditionally renowned for its suavity. Added to this there was also a collective coarsening of sensibilities; Nannen's short-tempered journalistic attack is consistent with the striking thoughtlessness with which anti-Semitic clichés were dragged out as if the Holocaust had never taken place.

The actress Hildegard Knef, however, who was friends with both Habe and Nannen, was furious. "You've done something unworthy of you," she told the editor of *Stern*.[19] Then, without telling either of them what she was doing, she invited them both to her apartment in Hamburg's Hotel Atlantic at the same time. Nannen arrived first. When Habe turned up Knef left the room, locked the door from the outside and told them she would only open it again when they had both had it out. Knef's plan actually worked. The two stags made their peace, drawing up a "small Atlantic pact," which was published in the *Münchner Abendzeitung*.[20] Later Hans Habe even wrote several times for *Stern*, but his novels, which Nannen was keen to get hold of, were instead published in instalments in *Quick* and the *Neue Illustrierte*.

Even *Der Spiegel* was not immune to outbreaks of hatred where Habe was concerned. When his autobiography appeared, bearing the typically self-centred title *Ich stelle mich* (*Turning Myself In*), the magazine devoted its lead story to it. The author of the article delightedly quoted the vainest boasts from the book and then for nine whole pages dismembered Habe for bragging about his adventurous life on the stage of the world's most illustrious battle zones, ballrooms and registry offices. The headline was typical of the *Spiegel* journalist's style: MISCARRIAGE OF A CHARACTER.[21]

Inhibitions were relaxed in Vienna, too. The *Bild-Telegraph* newspaper couldn't help smirking at Habe's autobiography in parodic shtetl-German: *"Ich bin nix gekommen, mich zu berühmen, ich bin gekommen, mir zu beknirschen"*—I come not to boast, but to repent.[22] This "Jewifying" (as Habe called it in his letter to the editor) was all the more misplaced in that even his most implacable enemies had to acknowledge the polished linguistic style he had at his disposal, since it had been a source of envy often enough.

Today, Hans Habe is nearly forgotten. But his influence as the leading newspaper journalist in the early post-war years cannot be overestimated. He gave his German employees and colleagues—and his readers—more than a breath of democracy and a taste for the value of an open-minded approach to controversial debates.

Returning emigrant Alfred Döblin's experience of re-education work took a much sadder turn. After years spent under the occupying regime, objectively his reputation as a "cultural commissar" didn't seem out of line and *The Golden Gate* survived much longer than most comparable journals. Döblin had successfully founded the Mainz Academy of Sciences and Literature, encouraged literary life in the French zone and done a great deal for the dissemination of French culture in Germany. When he left military service in 1948 at the age of almost 70, the French government awarded him a generous settlement of 7 million francs, which would have been roughly the equivalent of half a million dollars or 300,000 pounds today.[23] This recognition must have filled him with pride and gratitude; but it did not strengthen his sense of being at home in Germany again. Döblin saw himself as a failure, as completely misunderstood—"a foreign guest," as he had been perceived at the reading in Charlottenburg Palace.

Döblin's own literary successes remained modest. The radio commentaries, which switched between his typically grotesque humour and an unfamiliar lofty tone, did not find favour with the broadcaster. His great autobiographical account *Schicksalsreise* (*Destiny's Journey*), published in 1949, found so few readers that his publisher consoled him with the suggestion "It may be to do with the times that the people who used to read your books no longer understand them as they should."[24] In fact, it was a matter of perspective. After 12 years in exile the elderly author viewed his nation from the outside and saw it as a hive of pointless activity. Having had much time to brood and grieve, he described,

> . . . people here are running back and forth like ants on a pile of garbage, agitated and work-crazy among the ruins, and their honest concern is that they cannot immediately act for want of material, for want of instructions. [. . .] It will be much easier to rebuild their cities than to lead them to experience what they need to experience and understand how the war came about.[25]

The phrase "lead them to experience" reveals the refined perspective of the educator. Many people didn't want to be educated, not by him, a German, whether he had a French passport or not. When

Döblin stepped down as head of the department of literature at Mainz Academy, Friedrich Sieburg was his successor. Döblin saw it as a portent. Sieburg, the future features editor of the enormously influential *Frankfurter Allgemeine Zeitung,* might have been a well-read student of Romance languages and literature and a sharp-witted conservative thinker, but he had also been a consul and Nazi propagandist in Paris in the services of Hitler's foreign minister Joachim von Ribbentrop, and had been subject to a publication ban by the French until 1948. When the Wehrmacht invaded Paris in 1940, Döblin, who had found a new home there, had been forced to flee, first to New York, then to Los Angeles. And now Sieburg was driving him out of the Mainz Academy!

Döblin also found little support among the other returning emigrés. Most of them kept their distance, because as a Jew in exile he had found his way to a deeply felt Catholicism, which was seen as a betrayal in the eyes of many. So Döblin, always an ideologically unreliable individual, a gifted satirist who was not given to heroic statements, found himself caught in the crossfire of the big cultural guns. The Jewish German-American author and thinker Ludwig Marcuse wrote of Döblin in the New York journal *Aufbau* in 1953,

> He was surrounded by many flags and the most famous deserter of the time. Today he is Catholic, just as he was once a Jew, a Berliner and a near-Communist. He has worn out an unusually large number of uniforms because he was the least sedentary German of those decades.[26]

In the next sentence the philosopher Marcuse suggested Döblin for the Nobel Prize. By that time, however, Döblin had not been living in the Federal Republic for five months. On 28 April 1953 he formally contacted Theodor Heuss, the first president of the Federal Republic of Germany, for permission to leave and went into exile for a second time. "It was an instructive visit," he wrote to the president, "but in this country, where I and my parents were born, I am superfluous."[27]

By this point the 75-year-old author was already so weak that he

The author Alfred Döblin as "Cultural Colonel" in French uniform, 1946.

had to be carried on a stretcher by two porters to the station platform, where he waited on a wobbly chair beside his wife for the train
to pull in. When he died two and a half years later he was buried in
Housseras in the Vosges mountains near the Franco-German border,
beside his son, who had shot himself here when he was surrounded
by the Wehrmacht. One of the greatest writers that Germany ever
produced did not even want to be buried there. The body of Döblin's
wife, Erna, joined him three months later on the other side of their
fallen child. She had turned on the gas tap in their Paris apartment
and neglected to light the flame.

IX

The Cold War of Art and the Design of Democracy

A hunger for culture

From May 1945 a "hunger for culture" broke out in Germany, a phenomenon that became a core concept in the post-war era. This hunger was more easily sated than its physical counterpart. All of a sudden there was more than enough supply to meet the demand. Contemporaries found the speed with which the culture industry resumed its work after the end of the war to be profoundly inspirational, and produced many dramatic words about new beginnings. Hundreds of reports mention the tears that flowed at the first concerts after the war.[1] It must have been overwhelming. These people had survived the inferno and at least for the moment, when they once again listened to Beethoven in battered concert halls, observed the orchestra playing perfectly together and saw that the conductor was fully in control, they felt that they were still a civilised nation. In spite of everything. A miracle? A shabby trick? Audacious or fraudulent?

Goebbels had closed all the theatres on 1 September 1944, enlisting even cultural workers for the war effort. It had come to nothing, and now that everything lay in ruins people could allow themselves a visit to the theatre again. There was hardly anything to buy in the shops, so the theatre or the cinema were the places to offload accumulated Reichsmarks. As a result, a disproportionate amount was spent on culture. Between 1945 and 1948 theatre ticket sales ran at upwards of 80 per cent capacity—an astonishing figure.[2] It was only with the introduction of currency reform that West Germans lost their culture again. As food supplies grew the hunger for culture declined, not least because it became important to save the D-Marks that were in such short supply. With affluence came thrift—one of the paradoxes of economic behaviour. By 1948 the number of tickets sold had dropped by half, and the theatres had entered their first post-war crisis.

Immediately after the end of the war, however, 60 urban theatres opened again in the Western zones across Germany, half of them in temporary spaces. On the bill were old standards from the classical repertoire, but soon there were also contemporary works by playwrights such as Thornton Wilder, Eugene O'Neill, Jean-Paul Sartre and Maxim Gorky—depending on the zone of occupation. The smaller towns and villages didn't go without either. There were many repertory companies in the country, driving from place to place in old trucks with wood gas carburettor engines, performing Shakespeare, Strindberg and *Charley's Aunt*. Young bohemians took the villagers' breath away. The cities saw the beginning of the era of small private theatres with tiny stages on which the actors performed without scenery and with only a handful of props—ideal for existentialist dramas.

Cabarets appeared in backrooms in bars. Beethoven still rang out in concert halls, but soon so did the newly rehearsed sounds of Igor Stravinsky, Béla Bartók and Paul Hindemith, hesitantly followed by Arnold Schönberg. Audiences also had an appetite for grand opera again, however hard it was to cross the bombed-out city to attend a premiere. On 2 September 1945, Berlin saw the first *Fidelio* in the Deutsche Oper, and a week later the Staatsoper in the Admiral's Palace in Vienna opened with Gluck's *Orpheus and Eurydice.*

Shortly after the end of the war, though, the Berlin Philharmonic had to start looking for a new conductor again. On the evening of 23 August 1945, Leo Borchard, who had led the ensemble since May, and his girlfriend Ruth Andreas-Friedrich were invited to dinner by a British colonel after a concert. It was a wonderful evening in a villa in the Grunewald, "with very white sandwiches and very real meat," as the starving Ruth Andreas-Friedrich later wrote in her diary.[3] They drank a few whiskies, talked about Bach, Handel and Brahms and generally chatted. Curfew was declared for a quarter to eleven. "It doesn't matter, I'll bring you home," the British officer reassured them, and drove his guests across the city in his official car. There had been a gunfight between drunken Americans and Russians the previous evening, and now there was a certain nervousness in Berlin. But not in the British limousine where they animatedly continued their cheerful conversation. The two Germans were glad of the cordial tone of the occupying officer, and he was still excited about the concert. At the Bundesplatz in Berlin-Wilmersdorf, on the border between the British and American sectors, he missed a stop signal that an American sentry had given with his torch. Seconds later the car was riddled with bullets. Leo Borchard died instantly. He had been granted just 108 days of the peace that he and Ruth Andreas-Friedrich had so fervently yearned for as members of the "Onkel Emil" resistance group.

The Allies quickly covered up the incident—nothing had happened to the British driver, after all, and the Americans, in their pragmatic way, soon found a replacement for Leo Borchard. Only four days later, the American music officer John Bitter presented the Berlin Philharmonic with a new conductor: Sergiu Celibidache. On the following evening, 28 August 1945, he gave his first concert with the orchestra. One more corpse here or there didn't matter so much.

Most Germans preferred to satisfy their hunger for culture at the cinema. They were knowledgeable viewers and spoilt for choice, as the UFA (Universum Film AG, the German state film company in the 1930s and 1940s) studio had kept them well supplied with films whose ambition had been to compete with Hollywood. At the end of the war, much of UFA's production pipeline just carried right on after a short pause. The Allies winnowed out the worst propaganda films and let through a large number of unpolitical-looking films. There were also productions from America, Russia and France. *Gone with the Wind* made a particularly big impression: Carl Raddatz and Hannelore Schroth simply weren't a match for the monumental grandeur of Vivien Leigh and Clark Gable.

But the biggest favourite of German cinema-goers was Charlie Chaplin. He had already been celebrated as a superstar on his first visit to Germany in 1931. Now, after 12 years of censorship, his 1925 film *The Gold Rush* drew huge crowds. Audiences recognised themselves in the misfortune of the starving, shivering and beaten tramp. Chaplin's composure as he eats an old shoe, slicing it as delicately with his knife and fork as if he were eating a trout, drew laughter as audiences recognised that decorum remained important even when one was starving. Erich Kästner reported on the cinema in the *Neue Zeitung*:

> The young people seeing the film for the first time are laughing just as loudly and with as much pleasure as when *The Gold Rush* was new. And that delights us, the grey-haired Chaplin connoisseurs, wholeheartedly. We were secretly worried that National Socialism might have ruined young boys' and girls' taste for such things. Thank God it didn't succeed.[4]

Still, the German public had to wait another 12 years for Chaplin's brilliant parody of Hitler in *The Great Dictator*; after two test screenings in Berlin in 1946 American cultural officials decided that the Germans were not yet ready to laugh at Hitler. *The New York Times* reported from the Berlin screening: "The people have admired Hitler for a long time, and don't want to be told today that they were following a buffoon."[5] The theatre critic Friedrich Luft was in the audience, and found that he himself wasn't yet ready for Chaplin's Adolf: "The original joke came at too high a price for us to be able to smile at quite yet. So don't show us this film now. Maybe later. Very much later."[6]

In some cities the local military administrations had decided to force Germans to watch documentary films about the concentration camps. The procedure was well-intentioned, but relatively unsuccessful from an educational point of view. Many viewers simply looked away, or else spent the whole film staring firmly at the floor. Some who had seen the mountains of corpses on the screen vomited or collapsed in tears as they left.

Theatre and film director Hanuš Burger, one of the "Ritchie boys," originally Czech and later known as Hans Burger, had assembled footage from different concentration camps into a film that was to be shown in cinemas under the title *Die Todesmühlen* (*Death Mills*). The Office of War Information, however, was nervous about actually showing the 80-minute film because it was far too sophisticated and long-winded in its treatment of the structures of the camp system. It asked Billy Wilder, of all people—one of Hollywood's greatest comic geniuses, who had emigrated from Germany in 1933—to rework the film. Wilder, who had lost many family members in the camps, took a look at *Death Mills* and passed judgement on Hanuš Burger in these terms:

> You've stirred the rubbish around, with all due respect, but nobody's interested. And where the camps are concerned, after ten minutes I felt ill, and I'm used to a few things. I even spent the night in a home for alcoholics for *The Lost Weekend*. Your film will antagonise people. And, objectively speaking, as unlikeable as we might find the Germans, they are—I'm quoting the people from Washington verbatim—our allies of tomorrow. And we cannot afford to antagonise them.[7]

Under Billy Wilder's supervision, the film was cut to 22 minutes. In many places it ran for a week with no alternatives. During the first week of April 1946, in the 51 cinemas in the American sector in Berlin only *Death Mills* was shown and 74 per cent of seats remained empty. In Berlin fewer than 160,000 people saw the film. How they responded remains unknown.[8] At any rate, the re-education authorities had doubts about its success. Because the film addressed Germans collectively as guilty participants, it made it too easy for them to dismiss the matter as merely propaganda. Emphasis on collective guilt, they argued, ignored the examples of resistance among the Germans, and would lead Nazis and anti-Nazis to stand shoulder-to-shoulder against the Allies. Along with the theory of collective guilt, which had never been seriously adopted by the Allies, *Death Mills* dropped out of the re-education programme of the Psychological Warfare Commission in 1946.

The Americans planned the use of their cultural resources quite strategically. More than half of the films shown immediately after the end of the war were comedies. They hoped to achieve a greater pedagogical effect from Fred Astaire than from Humphrey Bogart, who would only become a cult figure in Germany twenty years later. They avoided war films completely. The Soviets, on the other hand, in the form of *Zoya* and *Rainbow*, screened two films that unsparingly showed the horrors of the Waffen-SS while also incorporating them into a gripping plot.[9] The fact that they also showed a comedy, *Jolly Fellows*, a particularly turbulent, wild and practically Dadaistic musical which won critical favour, was also unexpected, since Russian film-makers usually made rather solemn works documenting the "cultural achievements" of the Soviet Union.

In post-war Germany it was the visual arts that prompted the greatest excitement. As soon as the first exhibitions had opened, disagreements over artistic style escalated into a test of political attitudes. The question of whether or not one was supposed to "recognise something" in a painting divided not only people's opinions but also political camps, and soon enough East and West. The crucial issue of abstraction—whether a brightly coloured dot in a painting could assert itself in absolute terms and settle for being nothing but a brightly coloured dot, or whether it needed to point to something real outside of the painting—split the world in two. Art became a battlefield of the Cold War, with abstract art the creative beacon of the West and realism the aesthetic imperative of socialism. But before that final outcome was reached there would be heartbreak, careers would be destroyed, feuds endured and even secret agents called into play.

How abstract art decorated the
social market economy

The potency of politics in art had a history. In the "Degenerate Art" exhibition mounted by Joseph Goebbels and first shown in Munich in 1937, visitors were guided along a course of supposed abominations.

The works shown, by Emil Nolde, Paul Klee, Ernst Ludwig Kirchner, Franz Marc, August Macke, Willi Baumeister and many others had been confiscated from German museums and were shown, in the words of the exhibition guide, "to give an insight into the terrible closing chapter of cultural decline" that the Germans had been forced to suffer before the Führer had wrenched the wheel around at the last moment. The intention was to demonstrate the extent to which the ostensibly sick society of the Weimar Republic had deified the ugly and nurtured the abnormal. The mood among visitors was divided. There were the witless, who roundly mocked the paintings as if on command, but also the lovers of these suddenly prohibited paintings, who used this opportunity to see the works one final time. In photographs of the galleries we can see a surprisingly large number of thoughtful visitors, people who appear to be unsettled by the paintings, but who may also be wondering why they are being shown in this defamatory context.

Eight years later the works of the prohibited artists could finally be seen again, in the Schaezlerpalais museum in Augsburg, in the Stuttgart show "Extreme Painting," in Celle in "Liberated Art," in the Rosen Gallery in Berlin and in the exhibition "After 12 Years," also in Berlin. In most cases these exhibitions were a mixture of various different styles: late expressionism, melancholy figuration in the style of Karl Hofer, the surreal dream-worlds of an artist like Mac Zimmermann or the abstract pictorial symphonies of Ernst Wilhelm Nay. Every option was available. A very diverse group of creative artists full of post-war vigour came together at the Rosen Gallery in Berlin, which had opened, quite adventurously, on the Kurfürstendamm after the end of the war: Werner Heldt, Juro Kubicek, Jeanne Manne, Heinz Trökes and many others who painted in very different styles, but who were united by their desire to make good art. Style was of secondary importance, but the paintings had to be first-rate. As early as 1946 Heinz Trökes predicted the coming battles over which schools of art were "correct," when he said at an exhibition opening in Galerie Rosen:

Let us not fall from one intolerance into another. We will be able to paint without being inhibited in our most secret depths. But we need to have a damned clear head for that. The war finally swept away everything sentimental. How are we to paint what we want to paint? I don't want to dictate a programme for us artists to follow. That's a lazy trick. Let's go to work.[10]

For now, exhibition organisers and gallery owners wanted to provide a snapshot of the art that had been forbidden under the dictatorship but had been produced in secret nevertheless. The biggest survey came in 1946 with the "General German Art Exhibition" in devastated Dresden where 597 works by 250 artists were shown in the former Army Museum on Nordplatz. Here, more or less every artistic trend was shown (apart from propagandistic Nazi naturalism). The intention of this exhibition, mounted by Will Grohmann, later a spokesman for abstract modern art, was to rehabilitate the art that had been ridiculed by the state and give a comprehensive view of the various trends that were setting about shaping a pictorial language for the new age. That was the thing that really mattered. More than the other arts, the visual arts were seen as a telescope into the future: it was forever being said that it reflected the "energies of the time," that it pointed the "way into the future," or that it represented the "platform" from which the present would depart. Art served as a kind of pattern of tea leaves in which viewers hoped they could read clues to the coming destinies of German society.

In most of these exhibitions visitors were able to express their opinions on questionnaires that were left lying around the gallery. These were to act as a safety valve for strong reactions, but also to help produce a clear assessment of the populace's attitudes towards art after the years of dictatorship. The result disturbed the organisers: over 65 per cent of visitors criticised the Dresden exhibition because of the many modern works it contained. The more conventional the works, the better they were received. For foreign visitors the results were reversed: here the favourability rating for modern art reached 82 per cent.[11] On the German side, on the other hand, there was much mockery and laughter. Young people in particular were either unimpressed or furious. Some called again for eradication of the art and concentration camps for the artists. There was so much swearing at the Augsburg exhibition "Extreme Painting" that Erich Kästner wrote an article in which he worried about the "illiteracy of taste" among the "generation raised as young barbarians," and called for effective art education.[12]

That education was largely provided by the press. Many newspapers explained the trends in contemporary art to an unsettled public. As well as outright rejection, however, many Germans felt they had been cut off from international culture for 12 years and wanted to reconnect with it. While there was brusque dismissal from some quarters there was also a desire for knowledge and excitement about cultural matters which might appear unsophisticated from our contemporary perspective, accustomed as we are to an unquestioning attitude of "anything goes." "Must an artwork be natural?" the magazine *Die Frau* asked in 1947. It showed one of Picasso's cubist portraits of women and explained: "It is entirely customary to speak of the two faces of a woman. Everyone will take such a phrase figuratively. But if a painter actually incorporates such a figurative term into a painting, the layman is horrified."[13] In 1946, in *Der Standpunkt*, a highbrow magazine, the art historian Otto Stelzer explained expressionism. It did not need to be seen as the only viable artistic route, Stelzer wrote, but expressionism was certainly not, as National Socialism had claimed, degenerate. "What is in fact degenerate is something quite different: the public's attitude towards art."[14] He did not write that in a spirit of accusation or arrogance, but with a sense of grief and concern.

Members of the cultural scene were very concerned about the general public's taste and understanding of art. Their alarmed attention had to do with the significance that National Socialism had placed on aesthetic judgement. One important pillar of "dictatorship by consent"[15] had consisted of allowing the masses to think that their taste determined the aesthetic decor of the Third Reich. The idea promulgated in Nazi media that the people and the elite stood culturally side by side had been essential to the construction of the "people's state." This feeling that the "people" defined the terms of art was still palpably present in cultural circles after the end of the war. Art was not an extravagant adventure playground for investors, but a necessary arena in which sociopolitical conflicts could be played out and agendas set. The questionnaires were designed to sound out the actual state of mass taste, and determine how representative the dissenters were, those who vented their revulsion at the "lunatic rubbish" by cursing and swearing in the galleries. Might it be revealed through art that the majority of Germans still had profound sympathies for the defeated Nazi regime?

"The protestors were not inveterate Nazis," Hans Habe wrote in the *Neue Zeitung* in 1945:

> They make noise because they are allowed to make noise. For them, democracy consists in being able to give free expression to their feelings of pleasure and displeasure. It consists in respecting the achievements of others, or simply allowing other people to have their tastes and making an effort to understand what touches them. [. . .] They have yet to learn that in a democracy unpleasant ideas disappear as the result of a natural process of elimination, without decrees. But also without booing.[16]

Such a calming voice had to be imposed on the debate from outside. Most German defenders of modern art sounded almost as dogmatic as their attackers. At the opening of Berlin's Gerd Rosen Gallery on 9 August 1945, for example, the art historian Edwin Redslob declared that modern paintings provided the "light along the path that our people are bound to walk."[17] But not everybody saw things that way. Many of them still had antlers mounted above their lumpy sofas. In 1956, according to a survey by the Allensbach Institute for Public Opinion Polling, two thirds still preferred "real oil paintings of landscapes," followed by religious subjects. Prints of sad clowns also slowly came to occupy living-room walls, hesitantly followed by the blue horses (by Franz Marc) of classical modern art. Only 3 per cent of those questioned warmed to abstract art.[18]

Nonetheless, the art of the post-war period in the West was soon so steeped in the dabs, blurs and cross-hatchings of artists such as Heinz Trökes, Willi Baumeister or Emil Schumacher that it seems today as if there had been nothing else at all on the canvases of the time but their cheerful abstractions. Abstract art became the predominant cultural form of West Germany to such an extent that many opponents derided it as the new "state art." The figurative artist Karl Hofer, whose melancholy, unheroic realism had been just as reviled by the Nazis as the work of the abstract artists, found its dominant presence in the mass media highly depressing. "In their blind eagerness the hacks are losing all sense of proportion," he wrote bitterly in the Berlin *Tagesspiegel*: "Worryingly, this attitude comes close to that of the Nazi state with its Gauleiters and its SS." The expressionist Oskar Kokoschka also saw himself as being sidelined, and raged against the supposed masterminds behind the success of abstraction, the exhibition organiser Werner Haftmann and the art critic Will Grohmann: "In the immediate future the non-figurative party is planning another Reich Chamber of Culture [the Nazi government art agency] led by Herr Haftmann or Herr Grohmann rather than Dr. Goebbels."[19]

In fact, the media presence of their competitors must have filled the figurative painters with envy. Willi Baumeister, above all, was extremely photogenic. In 1947 he appeared on the front cover of *Der Spiegel*. Hands in his pockets, he stood with his feet wide apart, photographed from above, on a huge stage set that he had painted for a ballet performance by the Württemberger Staatstheater. His decorative hieroglyphs, creatures that look like they came from cave drawings, swiftly drawn pictograms and wing-like calligraphies seemed to float beneath his feet. The painter presented himself as a master of signs—he would confidently reply to his critics that he didn't paint creation, he himself was the creator. Two years after the honour of the front cover, for his sixtieth birthday *Der Spiegel* gave Baumeister a whole page to explain his art—in typical Baumeister lower-case letters. Even after periods he began new sentences in lower case. The magazine permitted this pretentious obstruction to the flow of reading and even framed the text in a decorative box. Chancellor Konrad Adenauer could only have dreamed of such a privilege.

Willi Baumeister was descended on his mother's side from five generations of decorative painters. He himself, before becoming an art student, had studied for the same profession. When he lost his professorship at the Frankfurt School of Applied Arts in 1933 and was prohibited from exhibiting he found a job, like a number of other avant-garde painters, in the Wuppertal paint factory owned by the connoisseur and businessman Kurt Herberts. Officially he was devel-

Willi Baumeister on the front page of Der Spiegel *in October 1947. His painting defined the look of the early Federal Republic.*

oping new camouflage paints and writing technical instructions, but at the same time he was making wall decorations. Baumeister went on painting in various studio spaces, without an audience. He worked on non-figurative compositions, which, in their bold colours and relaxed balance of radical forms, already contained everything that would make him famous after 1945. At the same time, he experimented with a sign-like, hieroglyphic-style formal language whose theoretical foundations he set out in the book *Das Unbekannte in der Kunst* (*The Unknown in Art*). The manuscript, completed in 1944, was published in 1947.

Because of his uninterrupted productivity in complete isolation, immediately after the war Baumeister was able to place a large number of works on the market. This made it easier for him to appoint himself the head of an artistic movement, which would soon define the self-image of the young Republic. This German abstract art was more harmonious and decorative than the abrasive, disturbing compositions that similarly minded artists were producing in other Western countries. For all the noisy expressions of rage that broke out occasionally, German modern art was crucially characterised by a desire for beauty, even decoration. Not everyone liked it, but it had the potential to be commercial. Critics who liked to see art history as an advancing struggle between brave heroes and cowardly hacks later rebuked the complacency of post-war German modern art. They objected to its decorative character, spoke in terms of a "tamed avant-garde," "expensive craft" and an apolitical search for harmony.[20] But when it came to winning over an initially sceptical public, the decorative quality of post-war art was a valuable asset.

Some of the works most frequently reproduced were from Baumeister's *Monturi Cycle*. These paintings are usually dominated by a floating black surface, a large, inorganic form that seems to linger on the canvas with a strange weightlessness. This black form, with its slightly monstrous appearance, has a certain unfinished quality, as if it can't quite decide whether it would rather be rounded or angular. It is slightly fringed here and there, losing elements that have split away, and which, along with other coloured shapes, surround the central form. These shapes, often described as "formal attachments," also seem to float. Gently attracted and repelled, all the elements are in delicate but entirely serene equilibrium.

Baumeister's paintings are reconciled to chaos. They consist of rootless objects that have found their way to a state of surprising harmony. Anyone who wished to could see them as an embodiment of the spirit of revival that inspired the young Federal Republic, and feel confident that they might themselves find a place in it. Dieter Honisch, Director of the Nationalgalerie in Berlin, later described the *Monturi Cycle* as if it were Ludwig Erhard's social market economy:

> In the constant give-and-take of all the parts that go to make up the painting, a community of solidarity comes about, which can be interpreted in terms of both form and content, in which each one plays its own little game not only at the expense but also to the benefit of the other.[21]

It was the pictorial language of an elite but it also established a tone. No serious office was shown in a publicity photograph without abstract paintings on the walls. It was chic art for chic people. At the Documenta art festival in Kassel, female visitors were seen wearing dresses in the same patterns as the paintings they were looking at. Now the art trade wanted to know precisely who was buying what art, and commissioned the newly established Allensbach Institute to conduct a survey. The result: Willi Baumeister and his contemporaries from the Tachiste avant-garde were bought by future-oriented sectors of the population, by industrialists, electrical engineers, business directors and managers. More nervous bank managers, professors and lawyers, on the other hand—the classic, cultivated bourgeoisie—preferred to buy a more moderate modern art, along the lines of expressionism and impressionism.[22] Soon it was part of the young Republic's identity that the tastes of the populace and the cultured minority were going separate ways again. Art emancipated itself from the approval of the people, and the people in turn from the need to recognise themselves in the outward character of the

Willi Baumeister: Monturi with Red and Blue, *1953. Anyone who wanted to could see in his paintings the upturn that was inspiring the Federal Republic, embodied in uprooted objects that had achieved a surprising harmony.*

Federal Republic. The fact that large sections of the population came to accept a state-sponsored artistic avant-garde, even if they couldn't make head or tail of it, was a positive sign of the development of democracy, because it meant a recognition of cultural diversity. For that reason the victory procession of abstract art in West Germany could also be seen as an indication of successful denazification.

The development of art in East Germany took a very different course. Here the impressive stylistic pluralism of the 1946 Dresden art exhibition came to quite a swift end. There was growing pressure on artists in the GDR to turn away from "modernist," "decadent" and "formalistic" styles. If they were to collaborate successfully on the project of creating a society worthy of humanity, the artists had to use forms that the people could recognise and understand. The doctrine of socialist realism was given a huge boost by an article published by the director of the cultural department of the Soviet military administration, Alexandr Lvovich Dymschitz, in the *Tägliche Rundschau*, the Soviet equivalent of the *Neue Zeitung*. The essay concerned the "formalist direction in German painting." Dymschitz, a literary expert and art historian, as well as a political officer in the Red Army, criticised the spiritual emptiness of modern art. It was nothing but the "philistine poeticization of suffering" and the "decadent aestheticizing of the repellent and disagreeable." One need only look at what had become of the wretched Picasso, he pointed out. This artist, once so promising, who had fought alongside the people as a partisan, had lost himself in a sick, unnatural painting that idolised misery.

Mentioning Gorky's socialist realist style as a model, Dymschitz instead demanded a painting whose goal lay in the "overcoming of suffering, the victory of mankind over the fear of life and the terror of death."[23] This critique of self-referential experiments was formulated in an entirely charming way, because it offered artists the possibility of working on the project of a better future, and thus reaping the gratitude of history, people, and party. The text made an impression because it revealed an extensive knowledge of the German art scene as a whole. Soon it was being discussed in training courses across the Soviet-occupied zone, and gradually hardened into the dogma of socialist realism.

The Cold War had found an artistic fault line. The more divided the Germans in West and East became, the easier it was for abstract art to establish its pre-eminence in the West. The insistence on figurative painting in the GDR made it easier for Western artists to present themselves as an aesthetic alternative and establish abstraction as the West's trademark artistic style. Seen as the art of freedom, it acquired a charisma that was effectively a political statement, and was all the more convincing in that it did not have to explicitly present itself as such. It represented a playful celebration of being, which embodied pure vital energy, and was played out freely on large canvases. And because of the excessive application of paint, which was trowelled, trickled and applied in thick encrusted layers, abstract painting represented an extravagance which in a sense appealed to a higher form of affluence and continued to shape the post-war era almost as a kind of inner compulsion.

The American propaganda strategists recognised very quickly that art could be very useful in the promotion of democracy. Like the Soviets, they grasped the importance of painting for post-war nation building, but unlike them they found it harder to guide art in a suitable direction. For them, abstract art was a good aesthetic programme for the denazification of the imagination, but even better than that, it was well suited to standing up to the Soviets and giving West Germany an aesthetic identity of its own. By means of abstract painting the Americans were able to make "Socialist Realism look even more stylised, more rigid and confined than it actually was," the American CIA agent Donald Jameson said.[24] The Americans put a huge amount of energy into encouraging abstract art. They organised grants for young painters, financed exhibitions and bought paintings in large quantities. At the same time, private initiatives and state sponsorship went hand in hand. Often high-ranking military officers bought art and recommended individual artists to the various funding bodies. Of great benefit to any artist, for example, was the acquaintance of the German-American Hilla von Rebay, director of the Guggenheim Foundation in New York. She had excellent knowledge of the German art scene and supplied artists and gallery owners with all kinds of financial support.

The first painter in Germany that von Rebay took under her wing was Juro Kubicek from the circle of Berlin *Fantasten* (Dreamers) associated with the Gerd Rosen Gallery. The artist, born in 1906 of German, Hungarian and Czech descent, had started out as a window-dresser at a Wertheim department store, and had worked as an advertising executive and exhibition designer before being sent to the Eastern Front in 1942. At the Rosen Gallery he exhibited planar abstract landscapes strongly influenced by French cubist artist Amédée Ozenfant. In December 1947, under the auspices of the Defense and State Departments, he took up an 18-month residency at the University of Louisville, Kentucky, where he taught young students general art studies. The actual purpose of the residency was to train the artist himself. And it worked. Although Kubicek experienced the limits of American tolerance when the puritanical Louisville Ladies' Club took vehement exception to his oil painting *Die grosse Schwarze*, he returned to Berlin as a committed devotee of the US in the summer of 1949. The influence of Jackson Pollock, whose action paintings he had encountered in New York, was unmistakable.

In the US Kubicek's painting had freed itself completely from any figurative models. Instead of continuing to break down nudes, landscapes or trees into vibrant abstractions, he now completely abandoned reference points in the real world. With endlessly trickling lines of paints he created galaxy-like textures that did what abstract art was expected to do at the time: they floated. Stencilled grids formed delicate, transparent forms that slid through the picture-spaces. The influence of Pollock was impossible to ignore, but not suffocating. Kubicek had managed to refute the theory that one could not learn from Pollock without in the end painting exactly the same way as he did.[25] Kubicek, like the whole of the West German Informel movement, remained concerned with decorative cosiness. While Pollock's colours gave a stronger sense of having been thrown onto the canvas, battered the retina more roughly and challenged accepted taste, Kubicek's harmoniously whirling lines achieved the feeling of cohesion of a world that might have been alien and incomprehensible, but was still ultimately well ordered.

Like the symbolic images of Willi Baumeister or Heinz Trökes, Kubicek's paintings conveyed an atmosphere of balance that exuded confidence. The Americans must have considered their investment in the painter as having paid off, because he was such an outstanding ambassador. After his return to Germany, he took over the Work and Art Studio in the newly founded Amerika Haus on Einemstrasse in Berlin. Here he gave free lessons in art, applied art, and fabric, furniture and jewellery design. This connection between art and craft proved to be quite successful. Kubicek's students managed to sell some designs to the by now booming decorative arts industry. In a long row of display cases looking out onto the street, the Amerika

Haus presented new pieces from the Work and Art Studio, which embodied the latest design ideas. In this way the work of Kubicek and his students could also teach and inform those passing by.

Kubicek's work is exemplary of the American re-education strategy. A clear line can be drawn from the genius of Jackson Pollock to the broad gestures of the Berlin students in the painting school of the Amerika Haus. It is no coincidence that it was Jackson Pollock who played such a guiding role. Pollock, with his huge and imposing drip paintings, which led him to be known as "Jack the Dripper," seemed to embody the best characteristics of America. He was, as the myth surrounding him would soon establish, a real cowboy, who had grown up in Wyoming, a child of the rugged pioneer spirit, so not a Europeanised product of the intellectual East Coast. His drip paintings looked like the remains of violent explosions, the results of a volcanic eruption whose after-effects could be felt even in the exhibition spaces of Venice, Munich or Kassel, where they impressed Europeans with the indomitable vitality of the United States. That was the view held, at any rate, by at least some American politicians involved in foreign policy, who soon took an active role in the world of international art exhibitions.

With abstract expressionism—of which Pollock was the most striking example—American art had liberated itself from the great shadow of Paris and become a leader in the international art scene. With the outsized amount of attention that artists like Jackson Pollock, Robert Motherwell, Mark Rothko and Barnett Newman attracted in Europe, America could easily fight back against its clichéd image as a nation without culture. The United States was now actively assuming a pioneering role. This led to a paradoxical situation: "If that's art, I'm a Hottentot," President Truman had said in the Museum of Modern Art in New York in 1947, confident of the thunderous applause this statement would receive from the majority of Americans. That didn't prevent his Cold War strategists from seeing that very same art as the best way of putting America effectively on the world stage. Certain that Congress would never authorise the funds required to export that art, the CIA turned abstract expressionism into a clandestine operation. So it was that artists who were mocked in the US Congress as heretical daubers were deployed by American foreign policy experts for aesthetic propaganda. Rothko, Pollock and Motherwell might have seen themselves as homeless radicals and lonely individualists at home, but abroad a concerted exhibition effort turned them into ideal representatives of America.

The task was delightfully paradoxical and the CIA was only too happy to take it on. Agent Thomas Braden ran, under the bland name "International Organizations Division," a department of the espionage agency that sought to wage the Cold War by means of art and culture. Operating according to the principle that "to encourage openness, we had to be secret"[26] he set about making the artistic avant-garde part of the competition between the two major powers for the favour of the rest of the world. Parts of the CIA turned into art dealers, sending the best works of American expressionism out on exhibition tours, to biennales, and on loan so frequently that at times the Museum of Modern Art in New York looked quite empty.

Tom Braden, Michael Josselson and many other CIA cultural agents worked within a close network of private and state-sponsored initiatives.[27] Only rarely was it later possible to discern precisely where the covert operations ended and the conventional diplomacy of the State Department began. The most effective cover organisation for the CIA in the cultural sector was the Congress for Cultural Freedom. Headed by journalist and anti-communist Melvin J. Lasky and Arthur Koestler, himself a former communist and author of the novel *Darkness at Noon*, this was a meeting of intellectuals from all over the world held at the Titania-Palast in Berlin between 26 and 30 June 1950 with a view to drawing up a manifesto in opposition to all kinds of totalitarianism. By now Soviet propaganda had successfully claimed the word "peace" for itself. All over the world "peace partisans" met below the symbol of a white dove to demand a ban on atomic weapons, which only the US had at the time. The international Congress for Cultural Freedom would emphatically counter this effective Soviet propaganda with their own emphatically revived concept: "Freedom."

The Congress was largely directed by former Communists who had renounced Stalinism, including US philosopher James Burnham, novelist Arthur Koestler, anti-fascist Italian writer Ignazio Silone, German journalist Richard Löwenthal, French-Austrian novelist Manès Sperber and Austrian author Franz Borkenau. But also involved were the British historian Hugh Trevor-Roper (author of *The Last Days of Hitler*) and the German historian Golo Mann (son of Thomas Mann), who had worked with the US secret broadcasting channel 1212 during the war and later with Hans Habe in Bad Nauheim, helping to set up the American press in Germany.

Among the many busy men at the Congress was the Russian composer Nicolas Nabokov, a cousin of the famous writer Vladimir Nabokov. Until his emigration in 1933 he had lived in Berlin and had returned to Germany in 1945 as a member of the Psychological Warfare Division of the US Army. Nabokov was a specialist in interrogation, and had played an important role in the relatively swift release from prison of the conductor Wilhelm Furtwängler. Later, between 1964 and 1967, Nabokov would run the Berliner Festspiele, a series of cultural events that had shown an exhibition of American art with works by Pollock, Motherwell, Rothko and others as early as 1960. And who was responsible for the graphic design for the Congress for Cultural Freedom? Juro Kubicek![28] For conspiracy theorists the postwar cultural commitment of the CIA is the gift that just keeps giving. The journalist Frances Stonor Saunders, who has researched this history more thoroughly than anyone else, even claims: "Whether they liked it or not, there were few writers, poets, artists, historians, scientists or critics in post-war Europe whose names were not in some way linked to this covert enterprise."

The CIA decided to use the congress as a surveillance network and turn it into a permanent institution. From its headquarters in Paris, and with branches in many countries, a small head office would help those European opinion-makers who were critical of capitalism to avoid falling under Soviet influence. Its specific targets were left-wing intellectuals who were resolutely opposed to Stalinism. These people would never have accepted money from the CIA voluntarily, so the subsidies had to be processed via cover organisations such as publishing houses and foundations. And even if they had been willing to take the money, open support would have compromised the artists and intellectuals to such an extent that they would have been useless for the purposes of the intelligence services. So many artists received CIA money without knowing it. For example, the novelist Heinrich Böll's secret contact was his publisher, Joseph Caspar Witsch of Kiepenheuer & Witsch, an enthusiastic representative of the Congress for Cultural Freedom in Cologne.[29]

Through this congress, the CIA financed a large number of highly respected intellectual magazines, such as the journal *Der Monat*, founded in 1948 by Melvin J. Lasky, which included contributions from Theodor W. Adorno, philosopher and essayist Hannah Arendt, American novelist Saul Bellow, the Hungarian-British writer Arthur Koestler and the German Thomas Mann. The intelligence agency also financed *Tempo presente* in Italy, founded by Ignazio Silone, and the French journal *Preuves*, run by Swiss journalist François Bondy. It paid for translations of George Orwell's *Animal Farm* and supported the film adaptation. And with countless participations in exhibitions it encouraged the spread of abstract art in Germany, whose victory parade was complete in the 1959 Documenta II art festival in Kassel, which was filled almost entirely with non-figurative art.

How the kidney table changed people's thinking

To explain the triumph of abstract art after the war there is one more factor, perhaps the most important one, that needs to be explored. Never again did the avant-garde in art and industry rub shoulders as closely as they did at this time. While many people spoke out against abstract art within the picture frame, they'd already let it into their apartments long before, in their curtain fabrics and soft furnishings.

Lyrical abstraction came into the sitting room via the back door, and even wardrobes, furniture upholstery and wallpaper soon came to resemble a cross section of the art market. Willi Baumeister and Juro Kubicek designed curtains for the Pausa textiles company, Fritz Winter tablecloths for the firm Göppinger Plastics, Heinz Trökes designed carpets, Hann Trier and Hans Hartung upholstery.

Some of the designs were difficult to produce because the artists didn't know much about fabric technology, for example ignoring the finer details of pattern repeat and the limited distance between a motif and its repetition. Instead, they designed "conveyor-belt pictures" that were barely practicable to print on lengths of cloth. Real textile designers like Margret Hildebrand or Thea Ernst were more successful in transferring the formal vocabulary of abstract painting

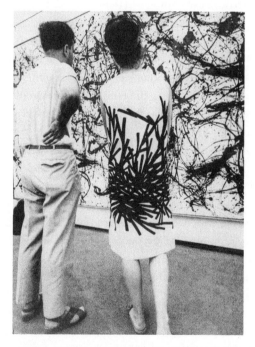

Visitors to Documenta II, 1959, in front of a painting by Jackson Pollock. Never before had art and design been so closely entwined.

to fabrics. The results didn't always look good in people's apartments, because the large-scale, intensely coloured patterns needed to keep a certain distance from one another, and to be surrounded by quiet surfaces. They were really only suited to the enormous rooms of a modern industrialist's villa, but that didn't stop many people from sticking up wildly patterned wallpapers in apartments which were far too small to accommodate them, leading to a claustrophobic feeling of chaos.

It was almost a blessing that people couldn't generally afford to undertake a complete redesign of their apartments in the new style. For now, avant-garde design entered people's homes in the form of small objects. The new design rage took off in the form of vases, planters, bowls and coffee tables. Everyday accessories turned into striking small-scale sculptures. Anything was possible, as long as it wasn't symmetrical; everything had to be curved, bellied, compressed and angled. There was a curve style and a bowl style, an egg style and a grid style. "Harnessed kinetic energies with unmistakeable elements of spatial tension" were on display everywhere.[30] Biomorphism triumphed: vases were now long-stemmed, blossom-shaped, slender as a swan's neck, organic. And the emblem of the whole era was the kidney-shaped table, which would horrify the younger generation.[31]

The ubiquitous "kidney table" would become the decorative symbol of denazified living. With spindly, splayed legs, it generally attracted the eye: looking at once asymmetrical, vulnerable and skittish, it embodied the opposite of the heavy oak style that it superseded. Shod with delicate little brass booties, girdled with a gold-coloured edging and often covered with Mediterranean mosaics, it looked like a parody of the stout traditional robust table. Solidity was out. Everything needed to be easily cleared up and put away. Floor lamps with flexible cones (*Tütenlampen*) fulfilled the requirements of adaptability; their three shades on moving articulated metal arms meant that lighting accents could be constantly changed. The ideal of this new lightness was also down in part to sheer necessity: in cramped temporary conditions, furnishings often had to be either rearranged or crammed together. There was no longer any room for the colossal, and what

Kidney table with a swivelling top and a record player and radio underneath. Its thin, splayed legs made a striking contrast with the massive oakwood Reich Chancellery style.

was needed instead was furniture that could be folded and stacked. That way four people could be accommodated in three rooms, with even the added possibility of an office in the bedroom:

> The desk is next to the sofa bed. Against the wall, covered over with a curtain, is a shelf for documents. The lady of the house sleeps in a folda-way bed, above which a shelf holding toiletries is permitted. This folding bed is to be separated off from the rest of the room by a curtain, so that the gentleman of the house can also receive his business clients here.[32]

Some amenities were imposed on the Germans by force. In the apartments confiscated by the occupying forces, many GIs had simply sawn off the legs of the tables so that they could put their feet up more comfortably. When the owners returned months later, after overcoming their initial horror they acknowledged how comfortable it was. It made the coffee table cosier. The sparseness of the emergency housing developed into a new ideal for living. People built cupboards out of fruit and beer crates, propped bedsteads on bricks and through vigorous sandpapering transformed battered furniture into a desirably raw state. An early variant of shabby chic came into being, for which many newspapers provided useful tips:

> Of course something also has to happen to the three-part mattress. My aunt, who was spared the bombing, promised me that I could rummage among her remaining belongings. It's even quite fun when different parts of the mattress are covered with different bits of fabric, and if there isn't enough to go round, if you need you can put something quite horrible underneath. Nobody can see it, after all.[33]

Both rich and poor adopted forms of easy living. The expensive, delicate shelves of the furniture company Knoll International did away with side supports entirely, giving them a weightless appearance. The same company manufactured desks with thin steel legs from which the drawers seemed to float. A world of plush and heavy oak furniture had gone up in smoke, and now people wanted to create an aesthetic with an unencumbered air, with slender banisters, boldly curved concrete, frail glass and curved walls. The colours were pastel, the lines delicate, the drawings dappled, the patterns fluid. One was best off walking through this world on crêpe soles, the brothel creepers introduced by British soldiers which became the cult shoes of the 1950s.

For the urban planning competition "Around the Zoo" in 1948, the architect Sergius Ruegenberg designed an airport in a tiny space right next to Berlin's Zoologischer Garten railway station, with a waiting room that looked like some sort of deranged and futuristic giant umbrella. The extravagant airport was never built, but the model was at least used for the film *Berliner Ballade* (*The Berliner*) by Robert A. Stemmle, the famous "rubble film" which looks back at the postwar misery from an imagined Berlin of 2048.

In search of a design for the new age the architect Sergius Ruegenberg designed this terminal for the urban architecture competition, "Around the Zoo."

Virtually weightless design was not all about eccentric taste, as people would later imagine, when it was frequently lumped together with such popular fads as pseudo-Italian pop music, kitschy snack bowls and overstated sunglasses. Designers were much more concerned with transforming a broader taste, with "defining and shaping the character of design in contemporary Germany," as the architect Wera Meyer-Waldeck somewhat grandiosely put it on the occasion of the exhibition "Neues Wohnen" (New Living) in 1949.[34] So the typical design of the 1950s set out to represent not only the whole of society, but a zeitgeist at odds with the predilection for massive oak furniture that was still dominant. The post-war generation relinquished the heavy, old-fashioned style only bit by bit, and the kidney-shaped table looked particularly incongruous if it had to challenge all the gloomy oaken monsters furnishing the rest of the apartment. In the imagination, however, these confused environments grew into the bright, generous, airy flat that their residents dreamed of. The kidney-shaped table was both a statement and a promise of the future: a building block towards a better world that would soon become affordable.

Twenty years on, 1950s chic struck many as meretricious and misplaced. Yet the weird furniture was a part of the mental healing of the Germans. Some people overcame the past through interior decoration. Anyone who sees reason as the only valid agency of denazification may think this impossible. But perhaps one can alter oneself a little by altering one's surroundings. Design determines consciousness, one might argue. There is much to suggest that part of the self-education of the Germans was performed through their senses of sight and touch. Be that as it may, redecoration was undertaken to such an extent that even today design lingers in the national memory as one of the most prominent remnants of the 1950s.

Every milk bar, however small, linked itself in its optimistic, pastel clarity with a lifestyle that was probably depicted most strikingly by Berlin's Kongresshalle, or "House of the World's Culture." Constructed in 1956–7 as part of the International Building Exhibition, the hall, with its asymmetrical shell-shaped roof, impressively contradicting the traditional solid architectural vocabulary of verticals and horizontals, became the most iconic building of the 1950s, and an emblem of the era. The Kongresshalle presented itself as the eloquent repository of a new form of civil society.[35] Large numbers of people were able to assemble there in rooms, which, in spite of their size, offered something almost resembling cosiness. Beneath the arched roof, and because of the open structure of the building, each individual visitor was granted space—quite at odds with Nazi architecture, which deliberately diminished individuals. The building conveyed a sense of self-determination that served to encourage free speech. Anyone who suffers from agoraphobia should give this public space a go.

Designed by the American architect Hugh Stubbins, the Kongresshalle was built intentionally close to the Soviet sector on the initiative of Eleanor Dulles, the US State Department's representative in Berlin. While the Cold War was a central concern, the location was also important because as a huge inner-city wasteland it embodied the devastating consequences of the Nazi dictatorship. In this desert landscape the Kongresshalle looked like a spaceship that had just landed from another galaxy.

It is hardly surprising that the first event to take place in the Kongresshalle after its opening was organised by the Congress for Cultural Freedom on the subject of "Music and the Visual Arts," under the direction of anti-communist Melvin J. Lasky, at which cultural theorist Theodor W. Adorno, art critic Will Grohmann, composer Boris Blacher and others talked about abstract art and atonal music. These topics, among countless others urged on by the Americans, would continue to accompany and shape the destinies of the Germans for a long time to come, just as the Soviets tried to do on their other side of the border. Shepherded and guided, symbolically accommodated respectively in an American or a Soviet aesthetic, and motivated by tireless interventions by the Allies, the Germans slipped into a way of life which later, in the West at least, made it very hard to grasp how such a peaceful people could have allowed the Nazis to flourish for 12 years and taken such terrible guilt upon their shoulders.

X

The Sound of Repression

Germany had been conquered one metre at a time. First, Aachen in the west in October 1944, then it was six months before the US Army crossed the Rhine and advanced the 500 kilometres or so to Magdeburg and Leipzig. In the east it took the Red Army three months to cover the 200-odd kilometres to Berlin after it had crossed the Oder-Neisse Line at the end of January 1945. At Seelow Heights on the Oder more than 120,000 German soldiers had faced them and fought bitterly—in vain.

The surprising thing was that after the battle was over, barely a shot was fired. Wherever the Allies had taken a stretch of land everything was suddenly peaceful. The invading soldiers couldn't understand it: these Germans, who had gone on fighting furiously long after the situation had been proven hopeless, were revealed as the tamest of lambs as soon as they had capitulated. The fanaticism seemed to fall from them like a second skin. No resistance, no rearguard action, no suicide units. There had been a few scattered snipers who fired at the Allied troops, but they were the exception. The Allies hadn't expected this. What had happened to these Germans? Years of bombing hadn't been able to demoralise them. In the last weeks of the war before retreating they had ruthlessly murdered hundreds of thousands of forced labourers and prisoners. It seemed only logical that they should continue raging with the same contempt for humanity, as long as the smallest opportunity still presented itself. The victors imagined the young adults in particular to be like abandoned wild beast cubs who could only be approached with pistols and iron bars, and who would have to be tamed as part of a long-drawn-out process.[1]

The Nazis themselves had prepared the ground for this. In October 1944 the Reichsführer SS Heinrich Himmler had seeded the idea that they would encounter resistance from the so-called *Werwolf* (Werewolf) guerrilla group. Two months before the end of the war Goebbels had decreed that every German was now to consider themselves a part of Operation Werewolf, and continue fighting to the point of self-annihilation. For the Werewolves, he declared that:

> Every Bolshevik, every Briton and every American on German soil is fair game. Wherever we have an opportunity to extinguish their lives we will do so with pleasure and without regard for our own life. Hatred is our commandment and revenge our battle cry. The Werewolf is judge and jury and decides over life and death.[2]

In fact hardly anything happened. The few Werewolf operations that took place were carried out by regular Wehrmacht and SS soldiers, and directed almost exclusively at war-weary Germans. The cruellest operation was the murder of 16 men and women in Penzberg, Upper Bavaria, on 28 April 1945 by "Upper Bavaria Werewolf," led by the author, cultural officer and SA brigade leader Hans Zöberlein. The victims had previously deposed the Nazi mayor and tried to hand the village over to the Americans without a struggle.

This terror against the German people was also responsible for the murder of the mayor of Aachen, Franz Oppenhoff, on 25 March 1945. Appointed to the position by the Americans, he was shot by an SS unit that had parachuted in behind enemy lines. After the capitulation, however, such revenge attacks stopped almost completely and there was no further sign of partisan actions. It seemed as if the fascism in the souls of the Germans had vanished into thin air. Instead of wild beasts, waving people stood by the side of the road and took chocolate from the hands of the occupiers. How was that possible? Surely the hatred that had made them sacrifice even schoolchildren in the final battle could not have been a fleeting spectre?

In November 1945 Stefan Heym, a US soldier of German-Jewish origin working in psychological warfare, dared to go to a football stadium in full American uniform, and to his own amazement nothing happened to him. It was the first official match after the war: Munich versus Nuremberg. Heym and two companions sat together in the front row, the only Americans in the stadium, visible to everyone and vulnerable to attack. Sergeant Heym wondered: "Would that have been possible, three German occupying soldiers at a sporting event among twenty thousand Yugoslavians or Belgians or Russians, all safe and in one piece?"[3]

Where had they gone, the proud master race, who would supposedly rather have died than endure any form of foreign rule? It wasn't just the occupiers who contemplated this question, many Germans did too. Most of them had dropped their loyalty to the Führer as if flicking a switch—and at the same time wiped clean, at least in their own minds, the whole of the past. How else would it have been possible for any German to ask, two years after the end of the war, the oblivious question "What makes us so unpopular around the world?," as the magazine *Der Standpunkt* did in January 1947—as if the war had never happened. The author herself provided what she called the "harsh answer." "Germany is the problem child of Europe, the whipping-boy of the world. It is as true in the family of the world's nations as it is in human families: there are favourite children. The role of the pet is played by Switzerland—and the *enfant terrible* is Germany. Chance? Fate? It cannot be explained in terms of nature, history or national development."[4]

It is difficult to comprehend how the author could have written such a thing. What had happened in the mind of a person that led her, so soon after the end of a brutal war that had caused 60 million deaths, to play down the aggressor as a "problem child" and a poor "whipping boy," is one of the great wonders of the human psyche. The author was not malicious, and certainly not naïve. In the rest of the article she talked about Hitler, of course, and quoted Thomas

Mann's speech about "Germany and the Germans," as well as Max Picard's book *Hitler in Our Selves*. She was well intentioned, but she wrote things that today seem unspeakable. Doubtless shaken to the core, she nevertheless chatted cheerfully on. The term "repression" was later applied to this handling of the immediate past. The word is imprecise, but not inappropriate. In the case of the article in *Standpunkt* we even witness the paradoxical process of repression coinciding with an attempt at enlightenment. The author clearly wants to address the question of the German calamity, but as she reflects on the reasons for it, she diminishes a world war to the level of a family feud.

With the war over, the reinterpretation business went to work just as busily as the people rebuilding the ruined cities. We tend to imagine repression as a silent process, and a lot has been said about silence after the war, about the muting of both weapons and words. In retrospect, the post-war Germans saw themselves as the strong but silent types, who had to deal with all that they had suffered without a word. The opposite was the case. There may have been a withholding of speech here and there, but by and large talking did not die out. On the contrary, particularly where their own affairs were concerned, many Germans were practically chatterboxes. The smallest occasions for a speech—the anniversary of a riding club, for example, or the reopening of a school—offered the opportunity to engage verbally with the historically unprecedented maelstrom in which the German people found themselves. One article about the particular challenges faced by those in the teaching profession began:

> The lurching unconsciousness into which the German people were plunged by the mendacious lunacy of the subhumanity that had risen to power was followed by the inevitable collapse, the most shocking physical and mental hardship that any people has been forced by fate to endure. The soul of no other people has ever been churned up deeper and more often and thus better prepared for the seed of the new spirit than that of the Germans.[5]

Superlatives that placed the suffering of the Germans high above the suffering of other nations sluiced through the German press, through brochures and tracts. And here we may talk about repression in an entirely literal sense: the authors wallowed so expansively in their own suffering that there was no room and no thought left for the true victims. Some were already positioning themselves as losers and turning their unique shame into a claim for leadership. In an article from 1947 pleading for the encouragement of shared values among European youth, the author wrote:

> Perhaps we Germans recognise the seriousness of the hour more keenly than other people because we have stood closer to the void, and there is less in our way to distract us from our knowledge of the harsh truth.[6]

One factor contributing to the subsequent impression of silence was the *Trümmerliteratur*—literally "rubble literature" but also referred to as "clear-cutting literature"—that would become emblematic of the post-war mindset. Read today, its language, stripped down to the basics, suspicious of ornament or ideological phrasing, might give us the impression that the whole of the post-war era was equally laconic. In fact, "clear-cutting literature" lived in aesthetic opposition to a loquaciousness that had regained the upper hand.

Without a doubt the Germans were deeply shaken. They wanted heating for their apartments, and they wanted meaning. Climbing through the ruins alongside robbers and coal thieves were all manner of diagnosticians of the age, trying to give a name to the calamity. What the Germans were going through was "not a collapse but a disruption," an unnamed feature writer wrote in *Die Zeit* in February 1946—probably the paper's future editor, the author and essayist Josef Müller-Marein.

> We know of an Oderbruch, a Netzebruch, a Warthebruch [areas of marshland]. Our forefathers built on them, opened them up to agriculture. And behold, where the danger of sinking was greatest,

strength and spirit found particularly fruitful ground. From the *Faust-ian* deed a more beautiful future grew."[7]

When assuming responsibility for the reconstruction of the occupied city of Aachen in November 1944, the architect Hans Schwippert set out some fundamental principles. The "most dangerous intellectual evil," he wrote, was "the German hereditary defect of a false separation between theory and practice." The "distortion of creativity" had led to the "degeneracy of labour." When it came to the "dirty and almost desolate reconstruction," his first task, as he saw it, was the re-establishment of the "dignity of labour." Then "human labour would return from exile," and would regain its homeland and its dignity.[8]

The collapse of the repressive state order generated an exuberant production of meaning among the Germans. Bread might have been in short supply, but there was no shortage of free-floating theories of salvation and a wild search began for the words that might establish intellectual order. Everywhere one saw people deep in conversation—that was how it seemed to Theodor W. Adorno, who reported on his startling experiences of intellectual life when he returned to Germany from his American exile. From the other side of the world he had been convinced that the Nazi regime had left behind nothing but barbarism. He had expected to find nothing but "stupidity, ignorance and cynical mistrust of anything intellectual." Instead he had encountered an "intellectual passion" that hadn't existed in the old Weimar Republic. "Intellectual forms, such as the tirelessly probing conversation that seemed to have become a thing of the past and had almost vanished from the world, are springing to life once more." Adorno insisted that this "rapt spiritualisation" was by no means limited to college students, but surprisingly widespread. "The seriousness with which new literary publications are privately discussed would barely have been imaginable twenty years ago."[9]

The philosopher and sociologist was not entirely at ease with this idyll, however. Adorno, recently returned from the world of the American entertainment industry, saw this general brooding in his homeland as a self-infatuated provincial complacency that struck him as somehow insubstantial. The pleasure of the "mind enjoying itself" reminded him of "happiness in the mazes of old-fashioned little towns," the "dangerous and ambiguous comfort of being hidden away amidst provincial matters [. . .] Often in all the excitement and animation I cannot dispel the impression of something shadowy, the mind playing with itself, the danger of sterility."[10]

Staying silent, talking, listlessly closing ranks

There was only one subject that the outpouring of speech within Germany persistently excluded, and that was the central one: the murder of the European Jews. Amidst all the exuberant torrent of words about beasts of war and fault lines, there was hardly so much as a word about the Holocaust. Discussion of the Jews was also out of bounds.

The inability to talk about the persecution of the Jews was felt keenly by an emigrant who, just like Adorno, had returned from the United States in 1949, albeit only for a six-month visit. She experienced it at first hand, as a denial of her own existence. The philosopher Hannah Arendt, who had been forced to leave Germany in 1933 as a Jew, was a director of the organisation Jewish Cultural Reconstruction,[11] and reported for various American agencies on the "aftereffects of Nazi rule."[12] Apart from the four-power city of Berlin, whose citizens, as she attested, "still thoroughly hated Hitler" and where she sensed a free-thinking atmosphere with hardly any animosity towards the victorious powers, she was horrified by the mental state of the rest of the country. The widespread indifference, the general lack of emotion and the obvious heartlessness were only the "most striking outward symptom of a deep-rooted, stubborn and sometimes brutal refusal to face up to what actually happened and come to terms with it." A shadow of deep mourning had settled over the whole of Europe, but not over Germany. Instead, a feverish, manic industriousness served to keep reality at bay. What the social psychologists Alexander and Margarete Mitscherlich would later describe as the "inability to mourn" turned the Germans into "living ghosts who can no longer be reached with the gaze of human eyes and the grief of human hearts."[13]

Taken as a judgement, this impression of Hannah Arendt was literally annihilating because it wrote the post-war Germans out of the list of healthy nations and assigned them instead to the realm of zombies. Alone among the busy corpses, one can imagine the horror felt by Hannah Arendt in Germany, particularly in Munich, the "capital of the movement."[14] She found no solace among the Germans she talked to, and described how their generous forthrightness always died the moment she revealed that she was a Jew:

> There generally followed a brief awkward pause; and after that came— not a personal question, such as "Where did you go after you left Germany?"; no sign of sympathy such as "What happened to your family"—but a deluge of stories about how Germans have suffered.[15]

Here the silence is once again hidden away in an energetic eloquence, a "deluge of stories." One can understand the bitterness with which Hannah Arendt received the inability of her German interlocutors to show an interest in the fate of her Jewish family, which by any decent human standards would have been the least that one might have expected. But we might wonder whether behind the wounding obduracy of her German acquaintances, rather than pure heartlessness, there might not have been a degree of shame. A shame which for a long time destroyed the normal reflexes of a conversation between Jews and non-Jewish Germans.

It may be that for the Germans that Hannah Arendt spoke to, the crimes committed against the Jews were no less than what they essentially remain: unspeakable. Would it then have been a more hopeful sign for the mental state of Germans if they had been able to talk immediately about the robbing and murder of the Jews with the same eloquence as they used in discussing their own suffering? Their voices failed them here, and silence genuinely reigned. A helpless, wounding silence.

"Burn your verses, say nakedly what you must," wrote the poet Wolfdietrich Schnurre. If, as Adorno famously stated, "to write poetry after Auschwitz is barbaric," then what of speech? Not many people were prepared to lay themselves bare. One was loquacious or one was silent. Very few found the appropriate words. The right words were a sheer impossibility.

The murder of the European Jews represents a crime whose monstrousness affected the subsequent life of every German and plunged them into the undertow of the unsayable as soon as they thought about it. This is why the majority of Germans did not immediately face up to their guilt. Germans kept their heads down, they grew tongue-tied, they chattered away unmoved, manically, as if they had been wound up. Adorno wrote to Thomas Mann from Frankfurt at the end of 1949:

> Apart from a few touchingly puppet-like rogues in the old style, I have not yet seen a Nazi, and by no means merely in the ironic sense that nobody wants to have been one, but in the much more uncanny sense that they believe they weren't; that they completely repress it. Indeed, one could even speculate that they were not Nazis in so far as the fascist dictatorship, in view of its empty and humanly alienated character, was never appropriated like a bourgeois system of social life, but always remained at once alien and tolerated, a malign opportunity and a hope, something beyond identification—and this makes it demonically easy today to entertain a good conscience precisely where the bad one lives.[16]

In the Declaration of Guilt issued by the Evangelical Church on 19 October 1945, the murder of the European Jews is not explicitly mentioned, despite individual pastors insisting that it should be. The same is true of the confession of guilt by the Catholic Bishops' Conference in August 1945 in Fulda. Here, too, the Jews were not named, any more than the Roma, the Sinti or homosexuals. They are only implied in a vague confession of "crimes against freedom and dignity," while actual mention of them is withheld:

> We regret it deeply. Many Germans, including some from our ranks, allowed themselves to be beguiled by the false doctrines of National Socialism, and remained indifferent to crimes against human freedom and human dignity. Many, though, were complicit in the crimes through their attitudes, and many became criminals themselves.

Individual bishops had to fight hard just for the inclusion of the phrase "some from our ranks."

Shame vied with comfort—and usually lost. In discussing the past many means of evasion were opened up to avoid responsibility. One of the most common of these lay in the conviction that people had fallen victim to National Socialism as if to an intoxicating drug. They had participated in the monstrosity by themselves becoming its victims. Nazism appeared to the post-war Germans as a drug that had turned them into willing tools. Hitler had "abused the German capacity for enthusiasm" was one popular phrase which made it possible for even the most devoted Hitler-worshippers to feel duped rather than guilty. The drug was given a number of names; often it was quite generically "evil," or even a "potentised evil that invaded our age on a massive scale never known before and never even guessed at."[17] With mythological fervour a demonic power was evoked, which had shattered the "varnish of civilisation" and released the "powers of destruction."

Such mythical interpretations emphasised an inevitability of fate that absolved the German people. Evil could have broken out anywhere, after all, not only in Germany. On the other hand, the constant evocation of demonic power alluded to the dimensions of the crimes that Germans had committed.

"Our gods had become devils" we read in many diaries. That in itself was an acknowledgement based on real experience, which provided subjective evidence that the writer in question had been a victim of Hitler. During the last phase of the war, in fact, the SS and the Gestapo had begun to exercise a regime of terror over the Germans, who were increasingly reluctant to fight. Under threat, young and old were enlisted into the Volkssturm, the last-ditch defence force formed around this time. In arbitrary drumhead court martials self-appointed judges condemned more enlightened people to death as deserters. From this point onwards Nazi rule was characterised by the impression of a senseless frenzy to the death on the part of heavily armed lunatics who had decided to drag everyone with them to their destruction—and in some respects that version of events prevails today. Compared to the long duration of the regime, however, emphasis on the final Gestapo reign of terror gives a distorted picture that helped to veil the mass acceptance of National Socialism. Most of the time Hitler had little need to resort to the coercion of his own people, since he was able to rely on the loyalty of the broad majority. It was not until the endgame that the cohort of leading Nazis melted down into a zealous hard core who wreaked terror on their own people and disgustedly rejected the majority of the population, who now recognised the remaining fanatical defenders of the system as torturers and devils. The tyrannical exercise of terror by the Nazi elite during the last few months of the war had been enough for the bulk of former Party supporters to see themselves as Hitler's victims.

Another way in which Germans sought to excuse themselves as victims consisted in holding the war itself generally responsible, since the morals of all involved had been dragged into the abyss by the criminal reasoning of war. The beast of war that had fallen upon "the little people on both sides" made the question of who had started it look like a trivial and self-opinionated matter. This clumsy reasoning was highly popular because it allowed for the possibility of holding out the hand of friendship to the military victors. In the magazine *Der Ruf*, originally written by German prisoners of war in American camps under US supervision, and which constituted the core of what would later be the writers' collective Gruppe 47, Alfred Andersch imagined himself in a future alliance of people who, even as enemies, "had been through shit"—and the essence of the matter could hardly be described more vividly.

In the ruined anthill of Europe, in the middle of the aimless swarm of millions, small communities are already forming to do new work: in defiance of all pessimistic predictions new centres of power and determination are forming. New ideas are spreading across Europe. [. . .] It seems to us—in spite of all the crimes committed by a minority—the bridge built between the Allied soldiers, the men of the European resistance and the German front soldiers, between the political concentration camp inmates and the former Hitler youth (who no longer are!) seems entirely possible.[18]

This was a problematic text in many respects, but what was most striking about it was that for his spiritual fraternisation project Andersch expressly refers to "political" camp inmates, not to those persecuted for their race.[19] It is part of the irony of the story that Andersch was right in his essay: five years after the end of the war that "bridge" was in fact built when the Federal Republic, along with Belgium, France, Italy, Luxembourg and the Netherlands, established the "European Community for Coal and Steel" and another five years later joined NATO, rearming itself under that treaty.

The image of the post-war years would not be complete without mentioning the many who were not proud of the "reckless devotion of their entire being," of which Andersch spoke, but who instead suffered a constant pang of conscience and wanted to begin the democratisation process deep within themselves. The writer Wolfdietrich Schnurre, for example, took guilt as his main subject. He felt guilty because as a soldier he had not rebelled but had instead unthinkingly obeyed. Three years after the war he still felt himself, deep inside, to be the hypocritical *Muschkote* (squaddie), with authoritarian traits:

I notice, when I talk to other people, how he [the "squaddie"] grovels and presses himself lasciviously against the wall, the scoundrel. I have lasting feelings of inferiority because of him. I am, for example, unable to recognise the person facing me as an equal. He is somehow a know-it-all and a superior, a corporal, colonel, officer or something of the sort. And the immortal squaddie in me tightens his buttocks before him and lets his hands fly to the seams of his trousers.[20]

The cloak of silence was not as impermeable as later generations imagined. Neither is it true that only the generation of 1968 attacked their parents and grandparents over the war crimes. Even formerly enthusiastic members of the Hitler Youth and the *Flakhelfer* (generally schoolchildren recruited as auxiliaries by the Luftwaffe) generation rebuked their parents for helping Hitler to power and keeping him there during the war. Many saw themselves as victims not only of Hitler, but also of their parents. In the magazine *Benjamin*, as part of a discussion on the question "Are our parents guilty?" in 1947, 28-year-old Achim von Beust, a founder member of the Christian Democratic Union in Hamburg, explained:

> The majority of our parents were not and are not democrats, and I see that as the fundamental evil. Hitler knew how to persuade the Germans that they were a privileged species within human society. Most of our parents went along with that madness, partly out of carelessness, but also out of a lack of conscience. Of course they influenced us, their children, and thus assumed a great burden of guilt.[21]

However, criticism of parents was not so much a combative issue as a melancholy one. Whether their misfortune had been caused by some demonic power, capitalism or their own greed, most Germans thought, "Wipe the slate clean!" and closed ranks with a reluctant shrug. "I'm busy enough looking after myself," "from now on I'm just thinking about myself and my family"—these and similar sayings represented the fundamentally dismissive attitude that they adopted towards others. The figure of the apathetic Everyman known as "Ohnemichel" now appeared as the self-referential riposte to the "one for all" of the Nazi *Volksgemeinschaft*. (The name is a play on the words *"ohne"* (without) and *"mich"* (me), combined with the older national personification of the "German" Michel.) The national community had now made way for a suspicious, weary form of solidarity among the Germans, stripped back to the bare minimum, in which their enormous contradictions could be hidden and buried. They had, after all, become well enough acquainted with this character during their daily deceptions on the black market, arguing over bread and coal, and fighting to keep a roof over their heads. The difference between Nazi Party members and opponents of the regime now paled quickly, to make way for the moral value that was most important in post-war thinking: whether one could remain even partly respectable amidst the general collapse, and maintain any kind of ethical standard in the struggle for survival.

While post-war Germans might have been exhausted, irritable and cured of any kind of nationalism, they agreed on one thing: they forgave each other their Nazi crimes. The fact that the Germans did not want to settle scores with one another was the second phenomenon that surprised the Allies. If they felt like victims, why did they not take revenge on their tormentors? The Allies had initially expected civil unrest, with a wave of violence as the opponents of the Nazis got even with their persecutors. Many of those who had been involved in the resistance were expecting the same thing. But the struggle for survival after the regime's collapse had "taken the wind out of their sails," as Ruth Andreas-Friedrich noted in her diary in October 1945:

> The block warden who bullied us, the concentration camp guard who abused us, the informer who had betrayed us to the Gestapo. Fate cheated us of our personal reckoning with them. Indeed, in February, March or April, in the weeks after the final battle when informing flourished and even the most mindless understood how shamefully Nazism had betrayed them, then people were ready for reckoning. For the three days between collapse and conquest—countless thousands of Germans would happily have put their enemies to the knife. To each his own personal tyrant. "An eye for an eye," we swore to ourselves in those days. "The first hour after the collapse belongs to the long knives!" Fate had other ideas. [. . .] Before St. Bartholomew's Eve could fall, yesterday's vampire had become today's companion in suffering. A companion in the resistance against shared misfortune.[22]

In her report on Germany Hannah Arendt also contemplated the idea of the missed uprising:

> The only conceivable alternative to the denazification program would have been a revolution—the outbreak of the German people's spontaneous wrath against all those they knew to be prominent members of the Nazi regime. Uncontrolled and bloody as such an uprising might have been, it certainly would have followed better standards of justice than a paper procedure. But the revolution did not come to pass, and not primarily because it was difficult to organize under the eyes of four foreign armies. It is only too likely that not a single soldier, German or foreign, would have been needed to shield the real culprits from the wrath of the people. This wrath does not exist today, and apparently it has never existed.[23]

So "private retribution" didn't take place—but the magnitude of state retribution was also insufficient. Between November 1945 and October 1946 24 "chief war criminals" were put on trial, including Hermann Göring, Alfred Jodl, Rudolf Hess, Robert Ley, Joachim von Ribbentrop, Hjalmar Schacht, Hans Frank and Baldur von Schirach. The Allies had each assembled committees to collect incriminating evidence; the American team alone consisted of 600 staff, and the trial dossiers filled 43 thick volumes. The significance of the trial for international law was enormous. Certain legal concepts were employed for the first time, such as "crimes against humanity" and "crimes against peace." Jan Philipp Reemtsma, founder of the Hamburg Institute for Social Research, later summed up what had happened: "The merit of the Nuremberg Trials is that it is now accepted that not *every* crime can be exculpated on the grounds that it is political, and we must for that reason call it a civilising intervention."[24]

International interest was accordingly great. Reporters from 20 countries travelled in, and 240 seats in the courtroom were reserved for reporters. These included such famous authors as John Dos Passos, Ernest Hemingway, John Steinbeck, Louis Aragon, Ilya Ehrenburg and Konstantin Fedin. Even Marlene Dietrich attended,

With the Nuremberg Trials the time of simultaneous interpreters had arrived—a world premiere. There were over 400 interpreters working in Nuremberg, but only a very few were able to do simultaneous interpretation.

although only as a spectator. Future chancellor Willy Brandt was there reporting for Norwegian newspapers, and Erika Mann, the daughter of the Nobel laureate, for the London *Evening Standard*. Their reports were received with great interest by readers, even though the hope of gaining a better understanding of the Germans was largely to be left unmet. Only in Germany, where the trial was conducted, was the reaction broadly one of indifference. Wilhelm Emanuel Süskind, reporter for the *Süddeutsche Zeitung*, and later editor-in-chief, complained:

> Already we inevitably have foreign observers saying of us that the attitude of the average German towards the Nuremberg Trial is quite markedly one of indifference, or at best of scepticism. Unfortunately,

that is true. [. . .] Neither can we easily contradict the second observation often made by our English and American critics: the Germans, they say, would really prefer it if the Allies held a short trial in Nuremberg—if they hanged about twenty people, to put it baldly. We are used to that, of course, from Hitler's time—but it is in fact a sad triumph for the spirit of a drumhead trial, the [Nazi] People's Court, that such a spirit continues to prevail.[25]

The psychological calculation among the mass of *Mitläufer* (Germans who had "passively" supported or followed the Nazi Party) was clear: with a quick trial followed by the death of the ringleaders the matter would be resolved quickly and painlessly for everyone else, and people would be able to continue undisturbed with their everyday tasks, which were taxing enough. Even the defendants followed this tactic, identifying themselves right at the start of the trial as the seduced victims of Hitler, Himmler and Goebbels, who had effectively escaped punishment through suicide.

Alfred Döblin had also hoped that the trial would have a cathartic effect on most Germans, provided, that is, that they followed it with attention and compassion. In order to make this possible, under the pseudonym Hans Fiedeler, he brought out a brochure entitled *Der Nürnberger Lehrprozess* (*The Nuremberg Learning Process*), printing an initial 200,000 copies, in which, for didactic reasons, he adopted the perspective of a German who, unlike him, had not spent the previous 12 years in exile. In this he described how the trials—this "world theatre" (a term used by several reporters)—was the "first manifestation of the world conscience," the "restoration of humanity to which we, too, belong."[26] Later Döblin suspected that readers bought the brochure only for the pictures of the defendants.[27]

By the end of the trials two of the perpetrators had died, and of the 22 remaining, three were finally acquitted, and seven sentenced to several years' imprisonment or life. Only 12 were given the death penalty. They were hanged on 15 October 1946, apart from Göring, who took a poison capsule a few hours before he was due to be executed. The corpses were taken to Munich and their ashes scattered in a

End of the Nuremberg Trials on 1 October 1946. In the print room of the Palace of Justice exhausted translators, secretaries and huge amounts of paper were left behind.

secret place now known to be the Conwentzbach stream, which flows into the Isar near the Ostfriedhof crematorium.

The past was by no means "dealt with." In subsequent trials, 185 further representatives of the Nazi elite were brought before the courts—concentration camp doctors, lawyers and leading industrialists—representing only a tiny proportion of the main guilty parties. A great number of lower-level National Socialists also faced military courts, as well as civil courts staffed by German civilians under Allied supervision. These civil courts, 545 in all, put over 900,000 people on trial and graded them according to different levels of involvement: major offenders, offenders, lesser offenders, followers and persons exonerated. In the end, only 25,000 National Socialists were found guilty, of whom 1,667 were major offenders.

As a final accounting that looks quite meagre. Still, in the American zone all the government officials who had joined the Nazi Party before 1937 had had to clear out their desks. While one in three of them had returned to their posts by 1950—and more would follow—at the beginning a certain degree of punishment was achieved across the board. In the end 3.7 million cases were opened, though only a quarter of them actually reached court. This meant that 3 million people were left in a state of anxious uncertainty about the possible outcome of their cases.[28]

In order to understand the way in which Germans soberly closed ranks during these years, we must direct our attention to one aspect of the civil court proceedings: the reversal of burden of proof. It was not up to the prosecution to provide evidence for the guilt of the accused. Instead the accused had to demonstrate their innocence. Acquittal for lack of evidence was theoretically excluded. The logical explanation for this was that a Party member had already made himself guilty through his membership of a criminal organisation. He now had to present reasons for his exoneration.

The large-scale defence process before the civil courts brought people together. Defendants went about asking non-incriminated acquaintances, respected non-Nazis or Nazi victims themselves for so-called *Persilscheine*—denazification certificates—testifying that while the defendants might have been Party members, in practice they had been on the right side. This might mean, for example, that they had helped an old Jewish woman across the street or made jokes about the regime. The future parliamentary deputy Eugen Gerstenmaier, who had been involved in the 20 July plot to assassinate Hitler, related that he had been greatly in demand as an issuer of *Persilscheine*:

> Because people said to themselves: he's just out of prison, and he was there on 20 July, that must make an impression on the Americans and also on their German representatives. At any rate there was no way of escaping questions about and requests for *Persilscheine*.[29]

These testimonies were later construed as mendacious attempts at whitewashing—the epitome of post-war German dishonesty and as symbols of a largely failed, cunningly circumvented denazification process. But the *Persilschein* business is not quite as simple as that. If a known former Nazi block warden had to rely on exonerating testimony from blameless or persecuted individuals, this would not be lost on the court. It was an unpleasant document to require. Those whose help was solicited would undoubtedly have felt a certain triumph, silent or otherwise, and there would have been limits as to what they were willing to testify.[30]

A miracle that it turned out so well

The collective agreement of most Germans to count themselves among Hitler's victims amounts to an intolerable insolence. Seen from the perspective of historical justice this kind of excuse—like the overwhelmingly lenient treatment of the perpetrators—is infuriating. For the establishment of democracy in West Germany, however, it was a necessary prerequisite because it formed the mental basis for a new beginning. The conviction that one had been Hitler's victim was the precondition for being able to shed all loyalty to the fallen regime without feeling dishonourable, cowardly or opportunistic. This was all the more welcome in that in both East and West people had to place themselves under the protection of their former enemy for a considerable time. Both constructed friendships—the Russo-German friendship of nations in the East and the one between the Federal Republic and the Western Allies—were able to function only thanks to this victim narrative, which reached its apex in the assertion that the Germans had in fact been "liberated" in 1945.

With the conviction that they had been tricked and exploited, the fiery ideological core within every Nazi was apparently completely extinguished, and they were able to place themselves at the service of democracy as unreservedly as if they had worked the miracle of inner denazification on their own through hard intellectual labour. The fate of victimhood that people volubly assigned to one another—known in sociology as "self-victimisation"—stripped most Germans of any obligation they might otherwise have felt to engage with the Nazi crimes committed in their name.

The "communicative silencing" of the past, as the philosopher Hermann Lübbe described the process in 1983 with an appropriate degree of paradox, made it possible for tens of millions of still devoted Nazis to integrate themselves into a society that had made a consensus out of anti-fascism, in terms of both its constitution and self-image. Lübbe's sober description of silencing as "the medium, necessary from the point of view of both politics and social psychology, of the transformation of our post-war population into the citizenship of the Federal Republic" has been both seen as a lasting justification of repression and denounced amidst keen protests.[31] By now, however, even historians who are driven by an indefatigable interest in a minutely detailed examination of Nazi crimes and the policy of their disavowal agree with the thesis "that the granting of political amnesty and the social reintegration of the army of 'Mitläufer' was both necessary and inevitable."[32]

In his inaugural speech as chancellor in the German Bundestag, Konrad Adenauer addressed the question of amnesty for "some mistakes and misdemeanours" which were the result of the "harsh tests and temptations" that "the war and the confusions of the post-war era" had led to:

> The government of the Federal Republic, in the belief that many have atoned for a guilt that was subjectively not heavy, is determined where acceptable to put the past behind us. On the other hand it is absolutely essential to draw the necessary lessons of the past in the face of all those who challenge the existence of our state.[33]

Adenauer, a courageous opponent of the Nazis, who was repeatedly harassed and arrested by the Third Reich, put his personal notion of amnesty into practice when he appointed the lawyer Hans Globke as head of the Chancellery. As one of the authors of the Nuremberg Racial Laws, Globke had been considerably involved in the ostracism and persecution of the Jews. His reappearance as a senior politician in the Federal Republic led in 1950 to a furious parliamentary debate, with claims that the state had perverted the course of justice. Adenauer responded to the enraged reaction to Globke's appointment to the Chancellery office: "One does not throw out dirty water while one does not have clean."

Adenauer's retention of Globke called the moral integrity of the young Federal Republic into doubt and threw many democrats into a state of fury and despair. Such cases repeatedly offered East Germany a welcome opportunity to associate the supposedly "essential identity" of the Federal Republic with the Nazi state. Egon Bahr, later an important politician in the easing of tensions within the fledgling Federal Republic, alongside Willy Brandt, but at the time a journalist for RIAS American Radio in West Berlin, reacted with horror to Globke's reinstatement, which was a prototype for the larger reintegration of many senior Nazis. The judiciary, the intelligence services, the medical professions and universities all swarmed with former regime loyalists, who resumed their old functions in the state and blithely continued to climb their career ladders. Later Bahr considerably revised his view of Adenauer:

> At a distance of decades my judgement has softened under the realisa-
> tion that the old Adenauer had a huge task to perform. He was faced
> with a state that had six million Nazi Party members, and expellees
> from the East among whom the proportion of Nazis was no smaller.
> He had to ensure that this explosive mixture did not detonate. That is
> statesmanship.[34]

Elsewhere Bahr continues: "I believe that the greatest accomplishment that Adenauer performed was to integrate the state, and Globke was an instrument or a sign or a signal of that."[35]

As the Globke debate shows, the silencing of crimes was not in fact total, as the familiar picture of the submissive 1950s might suggest. Younger historians have replaced the concept of repression, in the sense of giving concrete form to the "communicative silencing" described by the philosopher Hermann Lübbe, with the notion of tacit "sayability rules" which regulate the broad area between remembering and forgetting.[36]

We cannot, then, speak of repression in the deep psychological sense, because new scandals from the right wing kept disturbing the peace and making it clear that Nazism had not disappeared completely. In their own way, the far right kept the memory of Nazi crimes alive. On 25 November 1949 the Bundestag deputy Wolfgang Hedler, a member of the far-right "Deutsche Partei" (DP), which attracted many former Nazis, declared that "such a fuss was made about Hitler's barbaric treatment of the Jewish people. We might be divided on the issue of whether the use of gas to kill the Jews was the right one. There might have been other ways of getting rid of them." For this monstrous remark Hedler was indicted, but was subsequently acquitted for lack

American military government brochure about the system of Nazi Party membership. In the summer of 1945 the Nazi membership card files fell into the hands of the US Army: 10.7 million cards, one for each Party member. The news gave many Germans sleepless nights.

of evidence by three judges, all of whom were former Nazi Party members. To see to it that justice was done, upon entering the Bundestag, from which he had recently been excluded, he was beaten up by Social Democratic SPD deputies. He was thrown out of the party, but the Deutsche Partei, along with the conservative CDU, its Bavarian sister party the CSU and the liberal FDP, remained part of the Federal Republic's first governing coalition.

Such events raised fearful questions, both domestically and abroad, of the extent to which National Socialism was still at work in German society. The Germans remained a mysterious, unsettling people to the rest of the world. Admittedly the normative anti-Nazism of the Republic seemed to be no weaker than it is today; anyone who publicly resisted it could be sure of immediate ostracism. Anti-Semitic outbursts by "incorrigible" Nazis, which occurred repeatedly, were immediately silenced by an enlightened majority who at the same time only wished that the past could be consigned to oblivion. The desire to be done with the past was so widespread that immediately after its foundation the Bundestag sought one initiative after another to repeal the political purges of the Allies, including the "Federal Amnesty" of 1949, the recommendations for an end to denazification in 1950, the 1951 law on the reintegration of dismissed officials and the second Amnesty Act of 1954.

The most significant of these was the 1954 Amnesty, because it expressly referred to the so-called end-phase crimes, usually committed against deserters, those unwilling to fight and forced labourers. While crimes of homicide did not qualify for immunity, the spirit of the law was intended to draw a legal line under the past. The law required perpetrators to be able to prove that they were acting under orders. Some 400,000 people benefited from this law, most of them having been accused of fraud, robbery or theft. That did not, however, diminish the symbolic significance of the law exonerating most Nazi perpetrators. Seen from our contemporary point of view, with the Holocaust so clearly before our eyes, and with the memory of the crimes committed by a substantial core of German culture, the most startling and shocking aspect of this law is the matter-of-factness with which the police and the public supported war criminals, even those accused of serious crimes.[37]

People were not shy about demanding "compensation for the victims of denazification," or renaming war criminals as "war convicts." So the "collective shame" of which President Theodor Heuss had spoken in 1949 cannot have reached very far; it did not, for instance, extend to pension claims. Former Nazi officials ensured that they received unreduced pension claims from their work for the regime. Even members of the SS received the appropriate credit from the pensions agency in spite of their membership of what was deemed to be a criminal organisation. The fact that the Allies initially rejected these pension claims was taken as a grave insult by the former Nazi elite. The young Federal Republic bought their loyalty by correcting this supposed instance of "victors' justice." In retrospect, the verve with which the fight was waged for integration or even "compensation" of Nazi criminals, and the breadth of the consensus that this policy enjoyed, might make us doubt the capacity for democracy of the majority at the time. But their political representatives dismissed such objections. For them the call for amnesty was not a call for the continuity of Nazism, but for the crucial determination to start anew. According to the spirit of the age it was not important where someone came from, but only where they wanted to go, as many, including Hermann Lübbe, phrased it. But how could one know where one was going if one didn't know where one came from? Was every new beginning not destined for failure without an engagement—if only a legal one—with the past?

It could be—this would be the most charitable interpretation—that the loud calls for an amnesty for Nazi criminals were due to people's identification of their own shared guilt, the suspicion that those who had been arrested were behind bars as surrogates for the majority. As evidence for such a subliminal sense of shared responsibility we might cite the fact that the passing of Paragraph 131 in 1951, which governed the reintegration of dismissed Nazi officials, was not seen as a victory for Nazi ideas. Instead, the integration of "incriminated persons" was carried out under the tacit assumption that their Nazism had been extinguished just as thoroughly as that of the majority of society. Luckily this did not have to be put to the test. By the mercy of conformism and abetted by a healthy economy, the most stubborn elements of the old Nazi elite, although lastingly aggrieved by normative democratisation, could be safely contained.

At any rate, amnesty was demanded so vehemently by the majority that in most cases even the SPD, the party most obviously opposed to the Nazis, limited itself to a pragmatic silence. The relationship between denazification and democratisation was like that between a pair of feuding sisters; each would be unthinkable without the other, and yet they could not seem to agree with each other. If the majority of the people had had their way, there would have been no denazification worthy of the name. Yet without denazification, no stable democracy would have been imaginable, in which the will of the people was appropriately expressed. It was a paradoxical impasse, which would have been impossible to grow out of without resorting to repression.

Afterword

Happiness

How could a nation that perpetrated the Holocaust become a dependable democratic country? There is no all-encompassing formula for that. It's a sum of experiences that tells a story that can't be defined as a concept. Hardship played its part, and regret, and conflicts about the integration of the expellees, the black-market school, division into West and East, art and, not least, the help of the Allies, who went from being victors to confederates, to kindred spirits.

We may condemn post-war German society for its unwillingness to face the truth; but we are surely obliged to agree that it accomplished an extraordinary feat of repression, a process from which later generations profited to a substantial degree. That denazification should have occurred in spite of a widespread refusal to engage with the past, and that both German states were cleansed of Nazism in spite of the large-scale return of Nazi elites to their old posts, is a much greater wonder than the so-called economic miracle. Almost as unsettling as the scale on which Germany became a global nightmare is the somnambulistic certainty with which it went on to regain its respectability.

If Germany's recovery is a miracle, it is so precisely because it was so unspectacular. Alfred Döblin had dreamed of Germany becoming an "unassuming, civil, respectable reality," because he saw this as the polar opposite to the pompous, anti-bourgeois Nazi tyranny.[1] He could not have guessed that his dream, in the form of a middle-class society in the Federal Republic and the supposed idylls of the GDR, would become an often caricatured reality, the much-mocked paradise of mediocrity. The intention of this book has been to explain how the majority of Germans, for all their stubborn rejection of individual guilt, at the same time managed to rid themselves of the mentality that had made the Nazi regime possible. The radical shock of disillusionment played a central part in this, as great a part as the megalomania that went before it; but so did the attraction of more relaxed ways of living as embodied by the Allies, the bitter education of the black market, the struggles to integrate the expellees from the eastern territories, the spectacular arguments about abstract art, the pleasure in new design. These all encouraged a change of mentality, on the basis of which a democratic political discourse slowly came to flourish.

Another factor that helped to contribute to the positive outcome for the post-war recovery was the power of the economic upturn. This had enabled 12 million German expellees, 10 million demobilised soldiers and at least as many bombed-out residents to be housed somewhere, in provisional dwellings which it would have been premature to call homes. Whether the Federal Republic would have achieved its legendary political stability without the "economic miracle" is a question which—luckily—must remain pure speculation.

This good fortune is entirely undeserved. That the Germans in East and West had, within a few years, worked their way up to the economic summit of their respective global power blocs had nothing to do with historical justice. For decades there was no widespread engagement with the murder of millions; that only began with the Auschwitz trials that lasted from 1963 until 1968. "The optimistically conceived phrase that life goes on is in fact a measure of the damnation of the world. Life goes on because human conscience is lifeless," Hans Habe writes in his novel *Off Limits*, the "novel of occupied Germany" first published serially in *Die Revue* in 1955. Habe, the re-educator in the service of the Americans, had a sober sense of the priorities that the will to survival demanded of everyday life. He goes on:

Birth and death, pregnancy and sickness, poverty and toil, a room, warmth, copulation—even in the most glorious hours of mankind these remain the symbols of a life that goes on, of hope springing anew, and of rebellion withering.[2]

But the "rebellion" didn't wither; its death was feigned. Repression only ever plays a waiting game. The younger generation later assumed the task of "dealing with the past," and combined it with a historic victory over their parents, staging it, in its wildest phases, as a civil war. Nowhere else were the global wave of protests of 1968 as remorselessly and as personally directed against the parents' generation as in the Federal Republic. Having to experience their children as presumptuous, even frantic, accusers was one of the after-effects of the repression process in which the Germans had engaged after 1945. So in the late 1960s the wartime generation experienced the accusation of collective guilt all over again—this time from within the family. "Let's defy the Nazi generation" read one flyer from 1967:

Let's stop Nazi racial rabble-rousers, Jew-murderers, Slav-killers, socialist-slaughterers, all of yesterday's Nazi shit from spreading its stench over our generation. Let's catch up on what was missed in 1945. Let's drive out the Nazi plague. Let's do a proper denazification once and for all. [. . .] And in the process we will paralyse the whole apparatus of this rotten society.[3]

In practice little of actual consequence followed on from this expression of fury. Even the generation of 1968 had little interest in a detailed examination of the Nazi involvements of their parents' generation. They preferred to develop theories of fascism designed to identify capitalism as a preliminary stage of dictatorship, and to dramatise the reprisals they suffered as fascistic. Even the former black-market boy Hans Magnus Enzensberger dealt in the new currency of radical ideology, which turned into a grotesque exaggeration of conditions in the Federal Republic and ended up playing down National Socialism. He wrote in 1968:

The new fascism feeds on the stock of the economic miracle. [. . .] It can't risk mobilising the masses, it needs to keep them in check. It relies on the middle class, the ones who are integrated, the ones who cling on tightly. This new fascism is not just a portent, it became a reality a long time ago. It is an everyday, self-contained, internalised, masked and institutionally guaranteed form of fascism.[4]

It is only in the last two decades that we have started to have any conception of the extent to which "very ordinary Germans" backed National Socialism. The mass character of the regime has been demonstrated, and detailed research has provided us with a more sophisticated vision of the nature of individual guilt within that system, as set out most clearly in Götz Aly's book *Hitler's Beneficiaries*.

During that same period among the younger generations there has been a growing willingness to accept "the culture of remembrance," which has certain unsettling qualities. According to the website of the Federal Agency for Civic Education:

By the year 2005 the united Germany had risen, after the Second World War, to become in a way a victorious power. At the celebrations of the 60th anniversary of "D-Day" and hence, of the defeat of Hitler's "Third Reich," the German Chancellor Gerhard Schröder and his delegation no longer had to hide themselves. The successful German democracy was ennobled by the presence of government officials within the circle of the former Allies.[5]

Accordingly, in many statements by Germany's political representatives, there is a certain unspoken pride at the editing of the past, which complacently asserts a moral superiority over other nations who feel less need to deal with the dark sides of their history. Germany sees itself as a "world-export champion in the field of coming to terms with the past,"[6] though how stable and open to discussion German democracy really is has not yet been put to the test in a truly existential crisis. In 1946 the philosopher Karl Jaspers established a set of rules for discussion in the introduction to his lectures on the question of guilt. Jaspers was sure that the most effective cleansing of Germans must consist of a profound change in their attitude towards discussion: "Germany can only return to itself when we communicate with one another."[7] For Jaspers, the precondition for this was unsparing honesty. He knew that through excessive relativisation we can duck out of any kind of obligation, and therefore urgently demanded:

> Let us learn to talk to one another. That is, let us not merely repeat our opinion, but hear what the other person thinks. Let us not only assert, but reflect in context, listen for reasons, remain prepared to reach a new insight. Let us inwardly attempt to assume the position of the other. Yes, let us actually seek out that which contradicts us. Grasping what we hold in common within contradiction is more important than hastily fixing exclusive standpoints with which the conversation draws hopelessly to an end.[8]

Much is said these days about the threat of division in society. Perhaps Jaspers's lessons, intended for a fragmented, conflict-prone country, deserve to be learned by us all.

Acknowledgements

I should like to thank many authors who are listed in the bibliography, particularly Annette Brauerhoch, Ina Merkel, Benjamin Möckel, Stefan Mörchen, Leonie Treber and Malte Zierenberg. They have all cast a more or less distinctly anthropological view of post-war Germans, and to make them seem strange through intense observation. For stimuli, criticism, encouragement and tips I thank Birgit und Ulrich Jähner, Barbara Osterhoff, Hanna Schuler and Gunnar Schmidt.

I would like to thank Shaun Whiteside for his excellent translation of *Wolfszeit* into *Aftermath*. For their careful editing of the English translation, I thank my editors Suzanne Connelly at Ebury and Keith Goldsmith at Knopf.

Notes

I: Zero Hour?

1 Friedrich Luft, "Berlin vor einem Jahr," *Die Neue Zeitung*, 10 May 1946. • 2 The compromise of establishing 8 May at 23:01 hours as the official date for the end of the war did not quite hold, however: the US observes VE Day on 8 May, while in Russia the day of victory is celebrated on 9 May. In the GDR, too, the Liberation Day school holiday did not happen until 9 May. Other countries have dates of their own, such as the Netherlands, with *Befrijdingsdag* on 5 May and Denmark with *Befrielsen* on 4 May. • 3 Egon Jameson reported on Walter Eiling in the *Neue Zeitung* of 14 July 1949, under the headline SET THE LAST VICTIMS OF THE GESTAPO FREE AT LAST! • 4 As an example of this we might quote the comprehensive study by Uta Gerhardt, which considered the radical change of system from the Führer's dictatorship to parliamentary democracy, introduced by the complete handover of sovereignty to the Allies, as far-reaching enough to merit the name of Zero Hour in more than a figurative respect: "The temporal dynamic of the programme of measures contained a zero phase. It is apparent that *Zero Hour* was not only a metaphor. In fact, *Zero Hour* corresponded to the political model for whole social areas of life." Uta Gerhardt, *Soziologie der Stunde Null. Zur Gesellschaftskonzeption des amerikanischen Besatzungsregimes in Deutschland 1944–1945/46* (Frankfurt am Main, 2005), p.18. • 5 Ruth Andreas-Friedrich, *Der Schattenmann. Tagebuchaufzeichnungen 1938–1948* (Berlin, 2000), p.303. • 6 Anonymous, *A Woman in Berlin*, trans. Philip Boehm (London, 2011), pp.168–9. Original publication: Anonyma, *Eine Frau in Berlin. Tagebuchaufzeichnungen vom 20. April bis 22. Juni 1945* (Frankfurt am Main, 2003), p.158. • 7 Andreas-Friedrich, p. 66. • 8 Keith Lowe, *Savage Continent: Europe in the Aftermath of World War II* (London, 2012), p.16. The foregoing figures and the comparisons between casualty rates in Hamburg and the whole of Europe are also taken from this book. • 9 Wolfgang

Borchert, *Das Gesamtwerk* (Hamburg, 1959), p.59. • 10 Schelsky wrote: "This generation is in its social consciousness and its confidence more critical, sceptical, suspicious and more lacking in faith or at least illusions than all previous generations of young people, it is tolerant if one wishes to call the assumption and acceptance of one's own and other people's weakness as tolerance, it is without pathos, programmes or slogans. This intellectual sobriety paves the way for a kind of moral virtuousness unusual in the young. This generation is in private and in social relations more well adjusted, resourceful and certain of success than any youth before. It masters life in all the banality in which it presents itself to people, and is proud of it." Cf. Helmut Schelsky, *Die skeptische Generation. Eine Soziologie der deutschen Jugend* (Düsseldorf, Cologne, 1957), p.488. • 11 Anonymous, p.206.

II: In Ruins

1 Quoted from Klaus-Jörg Ruhl (ed.), *Deutschland 1945. Alltag zwischen Krieg und Frieden* (Neuwied, 1984), p.166. • 2 Quoted from Leonie Treber, *Mythos Trümmerfrauen. Von der Trümmerbeseitigung in der Kriegs- und Nachkriegszeit und der Entstehung eines deutschen Erinnerungsortes* (Essen, 2014), p.84. • 3 Cf. Jürgen Manthey, *Hans Fallada* (Reinbek bei Hamburg, 1963), p.145. • 4 Cf. Treber, p.82. • 5 Leonie Treber uses the examples of Freiburg, Nuremberg and Kiel to demonstrate the transfer of German prisoners of war to the municipal authorities. Ibid., p. 97. • 6 Barbara Felsmann, Annett Gröschner and Grischa Meyer (eds), *Backfisch im Bombenkrieg. Notizen in Steno* (Berlin, 2013), p.286. • 7 In the West too, however, there were also citizens' clear-up operations such as the famous Rama Dama in Buch, in which women also took part. Precise figures can be found in Leonie Treber's dissertation. • 8 Cf. Marita Krauss, "Trümmerfrauen. Visuelles Konstrukt und Realität" in Gerhard Paul (ed.), *Das Jahrhundert der Bilder. 1900–1949* (Göttingen, 2009). • 9 Quoted from Treber, p.218 • 10 Erich Kästner revisited his hometown of Dresden for the first time in September 1946. The area of wasteland in the city centre was itself the size of a whole city. "One walks through it as if walking in a dream through Sodom and Gomorrah. Occasional trams pass, ringing their bells. No one has any business in this stony desert, he only has to get across it. From one shore of life to the other. [. . .] On the edges of this desert, which takes hours to travel, there begin those quarters of the city whose ruins allow a little life and breathing. Here it looks as it does in other devastated cities." Erich Kästner, ". . . und dann fuhr ich nach Dresden," *Die Neue Zeitung*, 30 September 1946. • 11 Cf. Roland Ander, "Ich war auch eine Trümmerfrau," *Enttrümmerung und Abrisswahn in Dresden 1945–1989* (Dresden 2010), p.179. • 12 Cf. on the rubble clearance strategy in Frankfurt: Werner Bendix, *Die Hauptstadt des Wirtschaftswunders. Frankfurt am*

Main 1945–1956. Studien zur Frankfurter Wirtschaftsgeschichte, vol. 49 (Frankfurt am Main, 2002), p.208 ff. • 13 Quoted from Treber, p.160. • 14 Kurt Worig, "Und über uns der Himmel," *Filmpost* 157 (1947). • 15 Otto Bartning, *Mensch ohne Raum. Baukunst und Werkform,* 1948. Quoted from Ulrich Conrads (ed.), *Die Städte himmeloffen. Reden über den Wiederaufbau des Untergegangenen und die Wiederkehr des Neuen Bauens 1948/49* (Basel, 2002), p.23. • 16 Quoted from the excellent dissertation by Sylvia Ziegner: *Der Bildband "Dresden—eine Kamera klagt an" von Richard Peter senior. Teil der Erinnerungskultur Dresdens* (Marburg, 2010), available at: http://archiv.ub.uni-marburg.de/diss/z2012/0083/pdf/dsz.pdf. Here you will also find information about the Bonitas sculpture. • 17 *Hessische/Niedersächsische Allgemeine,* 19 January 2011. • 18 Introduction by Franz A. Hoyer in Hermann Claasen, *Gesang im Feuerofen. Überreste einer alten deutschen Stadt,* 2nd edn (Düsseldorf, 1947, this edition 1949), p.10. • 19 Ibid. • 20 Eberhard Hempel, "Ruinenschönheit," in *Zeitschrift für Kunst* Year 1 2 (1948), p.76. • 21 Quoted from Wolfgang Kil, "Mondlandschaften, Baugrundstücke," in *So weit kein Auge reicht. Berliner Panoramafotografien aus den Jahren 1949–1952. Aufgenommen vom Fotografen Tiedemann, rekonstruiert und interpretiert von Arwed Messmer. Ausstellungskatalog der Berlinischen Galerie* (Berlin, 2008), p. 116. • 22 Quoted from *60 Jahre Kriegsende. Wiederaufbaupläne der Städte. Bundeszentrale für politische Bildung,* available at http://www.bpb.de/geschichte/deutsche-geschichte/wiederaufbau-der-staedte, [last retrieved 2 February 2018]. • 23 Quoted from Lucius Grisebach (ed.), *Werner Heldt: Ausstellungskatalog der Berlinischen Galerie* (Berlin, 1989), p.33. • 24 Military service in France had also been one of the few phases in Heldt's life when his depressions seemed to have been blown away. This otherwise highly sensitive painter, who did not have the slightest sympathy for the Nazis, had written in summer 1941: "We are firing industriously at the Tommies, and that must surely comfort one through an unproductive time." • 25 Quoted from Grisebach, p.49. • 26 It may in fact have been in the Galerie Bremer; it is impossible to say exactly, as he had solo exhibitions in both galleries. • 27 Quoted from Grisebach, p.54.

III: The Great Migration

1 With regard to the figures cf. Ulrich Herbert, *Geschichte Deutschlands im 20. Jahrhundert,* p.551 ff. and Hans-Ulrich Wehler, *Deutsche Gesellschaftsgeschichte. Vom Beginn des Ersten Weltkriegs bis zur Gründung der beiden deutschen Staaten 1914–1949* (Munich, 2003), p.942 ff. • 2 Ursula von Kardorff, *Berliner Aufzeichnungen 1942–1945* (Munich, 1992), p.351. • 3 Cf. Friedrich Prinz and Marita Krauss (eds), *Trümmerleben. Texte, Dokumente, Bilder aus den Münchner Nachkriegsjahren* (Munich, 1985), p.55. • 4 "The Kötzschenbroda-Express" is a quite brilliant transposition of a swing number by Mack Gordon and Harry Warren to

post-war conditions in Germany. "Chattanooga Choo Choo" is about a jour-
ney on a steam train from New York to Chattanooga, Tennessee, and the
Glenn Miller version of the song was number one in the American charts for
weeks in 1941. "Pardon me boy, is that the Chattanooga Choo Choo?" turns in
Bully Buhlan's version into "Verzeihen Sie, mein Herr, fährt dieser Zug nach
Kötzschenbroda?" ("Pardon me sir, is this the train for Kötzschenbroda?")
Kötzschenbroda was the only functioning railway station near Dresden. • 5
Hans Habe, *Off Limits*, trans. Ewald Osers (London, 1956), pp.32–3. • 6 Accord-
ing to a widespread definition by Wolfgang Jacobmeyer, the author of what
remains the main reference work on displaced persons, they were the "popu-
lation and labour policy remnants of National Socialist rule in the Second
World War, the great bulk of them forced labourers and forced deportees,
whose home regions lay principally in Eastern Europe." Cf. Wolfgang Jacobmeyer, *Vom Zwangsarbeiter zum Heimatlosen Ausländer. Die Displaced Persons in
Westdeutschland 1945–1951* (Göttingen, 1985), p.15. • 7 Cf. Ulrich Herbert: "In
March and April there were massacres of foreigners all over Germany. Often
these were the last official action of members of the Gestapo or the forces of
law and order, shooting groups of foreigners waiting for the Allies in forests
or on stretches of rubble-strewn land, before throwing their uniforms away."
Ulrich Herbert, *Geschichte Deutschlands im 20. Jahrhundert* (Munich, 2014),
p.540. • 8 Ibid., p.541. • 9 "Particularly characteristic of post-war criminality is
murder by armed gangs. This form of offence can practically be identified as
the rule for the years 1945 and 1946. Perpetrators seek out especially isolated
farmyards or individual properties remote from towns or villages, such as
mills. [. . .] The perpetrators tend to be foreigners who have come together
for the purposes of robbery and burglary." So said the legal expert Karl
S. Bader, an opponent of the Nazis whom the French military administration
had appointed attorney general in Freiburg. His assessment is formulated
without any racist hysteria. Bader found it reassuring that there were many
displaced persons among the perpetrators, on the grounds that both the populace and the law enforcement agencies could rely on the fact that the problem
would soon solve itself with the repatriation of the former forced labourers.
He was much more concerned about his investigations into the typical post-
war crimes committed by Germans. In Karl S. Bader, *Soziologie der deutschen
Nachkriegskriminalität* (Tübingen, 1949), p.28. • 10 Cf. Jacobmeyer, p.47: "It was
entirely characteristic of the profound damage to socialisation that the DPs
had suffered during their life as forced labourers, that after liberation there
was no automatic recourse to those legal norms that form a part of the
fundamental prohibition on killing in every constitutional society." • 11 Jacobmeyer, p.29. • 12 Cf. ibid., p.262. • 13 Cf. ibid., p.39. • 14 William Forrest: "You
will stand fast and not move," *London News Chronicle*, 11 April 1945, quoted

from Jacobmeyer, p.37. • 15 The French author and teacher Georges Hyvernaud gives an impression of the kind of dehumanisation and brutalisation
that went on in the camps. He spent five years in German imprisonment and
was able to observe the treatment of Russian prisoners of war, who were
treated even worse than the French. In his 1949 book *La peau et les os* (*Skin and
Bones*) he wrote: "The camp for Russians is three hundred metres away from
ours. Our pastime during that summer consisted in watching the Russians
having funerals. A very monotonous task. Hauling the cart full of bodies.
Unloading the bodies. Throwing the bodies into the grave. And then starting
over again. All day long. Scrabbling around in death all day long. On this
sunny, sandy plain. All day long, back and forth with the rattling cart between
camp and grave. The living who did that were not much more alive than the
dead; just as much life as one needs to walk, to push a little, to pull a little.
Men with unseeing eyes, weightless men. Entirely absent. And as guards of
the dead two whistling guards. Two fellows who didn't care about anything.
[. . .] Back and forth they roared their threats. In between they lashed out at
random with their rifle butts. Not out of malice, but because it was their job.
And because life is so sweet, blows and insults bounce off the Russians. That's
what they are like. One really wonders what could still hurt them. They put
one foot in front of the other. They perform certain hand gestures. But they
are no longer on this side of things." Georges Hyvernaud, *La peau et les os*
(Paris, 1949), p.138. • 16 Accessible as a facsimile at: https://www.eisenhower
.archives.gov/research/online_documents/holocaust/Report_Harrison.pdf
• 17 Ibid. • 18 Cf. Juliane Wetzel. "'Mir szeinen doh.' München und Umgebung
als Zuflucht von Überlebenden des Holocaust 1945–1948" in Martin Broszat,
Klaus-Dietmar Henke und Hans Woller (eds), *Von Stalingrad zur Währungsreform. Zur Sozialgeschichte des Umbruchs in Deutschland* (Munich, 1988), p.341. • 19
Cf. Tamar Lewinsky, "Jüdische Displaced Persons im Nachkriegsmünchen."
Münchner Beiträge zur jüdischen Geschichte und Kultur 1 (2010), p.19. Nalewki
Street in Warsaw is for many Jews a nostalgic place of memory, not only
because the first shots of the Warsaw Ghetto uprising were fired from its
rooftops. Nalewki Street was a cultural and economic centre of Jewish everyday life. "Authors such as Moshe Zonszain, Abraham Teitelbaum, Bernhard
Singer and many others remembered everyday life on Nalewki Street, the
noise and bustle, pickpockets and petty criminals, of attending school, of barter and trade 'shaped by its own rules, which were not to be found in any
school books.'" Katrin Steffen, in Dan Diner (ed.), *Enzyklopädie jüdischer
Geschichte und Kultur*, vol. 4 (Stuttgart, 2013), p.307. • 20 Quoted from the exhibition catalogue of the Jewish Museum in Hohenems: Esther Haber (ed.),
Displaced Persons. Jüdische Flüchtlinge nach 1945 in Hohenems und Bregenz (Innsbruck, 1998), p.66. • 21 Quoted from Lewinsky, p.20. • 22 Quoted from ibid.,

p.21. • 23 Ibid., p.335. • 24 Dan Diner speaks of "ultimately dramatic questions of Jewish belonging," behind which there also lies a conflict concerning the legal right to the heirless property of those who had been murdered. "Alongside the ostracism of the Jews who attempted to stay in Germany, which resembled an excommunication, there was a contrast with the authority of the 'Jewish people' as legal successors to those who had been murdered, with a collective of which they themselves were a part and to which they strove under all circumstances to belong." Dan Diner, "Skizze zu einer jüdischen Geschichte der Juden in Deutschland nach '45," in *Münchner Beiträge zur jüdischen Geschichte und Kultur* 1 (2010), p.13. • 25 Angelika Königseder and Juliane Wetzel, *Lebensmut im Wartesaal. Die jüdischen DPs im Nachkriegsdeutschland* (Frankfurt, 1994), p.101. • 26 Quoted from ibid., p.127. • 27 An important role was played by the educator Jacob Oleiski from Lithuania, who had studied in Halle and run a vocational college in Lithuania. After liberation from Dachau concentration camp he worked on setting up a professional school system for all the Jewish DP camps in the American zone. The meaning of life was to be made available once more through creative work, as soon as the survivors had to some extent recovered from the physical consequences of concentration camp detention. He was convinced that "the pulse of activity must be felt everywhere" in order to "avoid a further demoralisation and atrophy of thought and feeling among our companions in suffering." But the desire to rebuild was focused entirely on the prospect of Palestine. In a speech in Föhrenwald Oleiski said: "We have a great deal of building work to do in future. Eretz Israel is waiting for physically and mentally healthy people who know how to turn their muscle-power into purposeful and creative work." Quoted from Königseder and Wetzel, p.115. • 28 Quoted from ibid., p.167. • 29 George Vida, *From Doom to Dawn: A Jewish Chaplain's Story of Displaced Persons* (New York, 1967), quoted from Königseder and Wetzel, p.167. • 30 Jacobmeyer, p.122. • 31 Wolfgang Jacobmeyer, who wrote the first and still undisputed standard work on the fate of DPs, saw the well-meaning but partly suspicious attitude towards the DPs as a continuity of their treatment as "other." The "remaining DPs had finally come to terms with their life in the camp in a way that cannot be adequately described as apathy" (Jacobmeyer, p.255). • 32 From the US Army newspaper *Stars and Stripes*, quoted from Jacobmeyer, p.134. • 33 Ruth Andreas-Friedrich, *Der Schattenmann. Tagebuchaufzeichnungen 1938–1948* (Berlin, 2000), p.349. • 34 Ibid., p.350. • 35 She tells her story in Ulrich Völklein, *"Mitleid war von niemandem zu erwarten." Das Schicksal der deutschen Vertriebenen* (Munich, 2005), p.79 ff. The book contains 14 life stories, almost all based on interviews with the author. • 36 Ibid., p.91. • 37 Quoted from Andreas Kossert, *Kalte Heimat. Die Geschichte der deutschen Vertriebenen nach 1945* (Munich, 2008), p.63. • 38 Most expellees avoided the term "refugees" because they were afraid they might lose their claim to return or compensation, since the word implied that they had left their homes voluntarily. Recently, however, the appropriate term "flight" is used more often, along with "exile." • 39 Walter Kolbenhoff, "Ein kleines oberbayrisches Dorf," *Die Neue Zeitung*, 20 December 1946. • 40 Quoted from Kossert. The author also quotes the Flensburg member of parliament Johannes Tiedje, with the observation that "we Lower Germans and Schleswig-Holsteiners lead a life of our own that seeks to have nothing to do with the breeding of mulattos, as practiced by the East Prussian with his mingling of the peoples." (Ibid., p.73) • 41 Quoted from ibid., p.75. • 42 It is also part of the overall picture, however, that the hard-heartedness of the locals only represents one side of the picture. There were certainly people who welcomed the expellees with open arms and helped them as much as they could. Some families who lived on the refugee routes in Vorpommern and the Mark Brandenburg, stood by the side of the road and ladled soup from big pots for the people drifting by. They did so until their own supplies had run out. The expellees said time and again that it was the poorest who shared the little that they had, while the affluent kept their doors and pockets closed. To what extent selective experiences have been used to form an effective cliché, or whether the miserliness of the better-off was actually the rule, is hard to say. • 43 Paul Erker, "Landbevölkerung und Flüchtlingszustrom," in Martin Broszat et al., *Deutschlands Weg in die Diktatur. Internationale Konferenz zur nationalsozialistischen Machtübernahme im Reichstagsgebäude zu Berlin. Referate und Diskussionen. Ein Protokoll* (Berlin, 1983), p.398. • 44 Quoted from Kossert, p.82. • 45 *Der Spiegel* 16 (1947). • 46 Quoted from Kossert, p.82. • 47 Quoted from Klaus R. Scherpe (ed.), *In Deutschland unterwegs. 1945–1948. Reportagen, Skizzen, Berichte* (Stuttgart, 1982), p.287. • 48 Cf. *Der Spiegel* 15 (1977), p.41. • 49 In some instances, expellees turned former foreign-worker camps into their own small towns, and some of these quickly prospered; such successes as Espelkamp in East Westphalia, on the territory of a former army munitions factory, and Neugablonz in Bavaria, which became home to 18,000 people exiled from Gablonz on the Neisse in Bohemia (today Jablonec nad Nisou in the Czech Republic). Many of them remained together and moved into the grounds of the former explosives factory of Dynamit Nobel AG near Kaufbeuren, of which Neugablonz forms a part. The economic heart of Neugablonz was jewellery-making, an industry through which the expellees from Gablonz in Bohemia had made a name for themselves in their old home. Even today Gablonzer Bijouterie, which is divided into a large number of small businesses, is one of the most important businesses in the Allgäu, and competes with its Czech place of origin for the tradition of the old Gablonz fashion jewellery workshops. Its most successful descendant, however, is based in Austria: the Swarovski jewellery company.

• 50 Mau-Mau was the name given in the 1950s to the resistance movement against British colonial rule in Kenya. The Mau-Mau were defeated at the end of the decade, but in 1963 Kenya was granted independence after continuing unrest. • 51 Prinz and Krauss, p.13. Prinz goes on: "It is almost a miracle that the 'social contract' survived, and the nation did not tear itself apart. We cannot say to what extent that is down to the occupying power, which was always present and acted as sole ruler: but at least we were spared civil war." (Ibid., p.13.) • 52 Habe, p.33. • 53 Wolfgang Borchert, "Stadt, Stadt: Mutter zwischen Himmel und Erde," in *idem*, *Das Gesamtwerk* (Hamburg, 1949), p.72. • 54 Ibid., p.97. • 55 Quoted from Heinz Ludwig Arnold (ed.), *Die deutsche Literatur 1945–1960*, vol. 1 (Munich, 1995), p.39. • 56 Ibid., p.94. • 57 Ursula Herking, *Danke für die Blumen. Erinnerungen* (Munich, 1973). • 58 https://www.youtube.com /watch?v=4Vq3HTLyo4Y [last retrieved on 4 March 2018]. • 59 Jörg Andrees Elten, *Zwischen Bahnhof und Messe* (Hannover, 1947). Quoted from Scherpe, p.84. • 60 Prinz and Krauss, p.51. • 61 Von Kardorff, p.351. • 62 *Neue Illustrierte*, July 1947.

IV: Dancing Frenzy

1 Friedrich Prinz and Marita Krauss (eds.), *Trümmerleben. Texte, Dokumente, Bilder aus den Münchner Nachkriegsjahren* (Munich, 1985), p.56. • 2 Barbara Felsmann, Annett Gröschner and Grischa Meyer (eds.), *Backfisch im Bombenkrieg. Notizen in Steno* (Berlin, 2013), pp.280–311. • 3 Quoted from Prinz, Krauss, p.56 ff. • 4 Wolfgang Borchert, *Das Gesamtwerk* (Hamburg, 1959), p.309. • 5 Quoted from Herbert and Elke Schwedt, "Leben in Trümmern. Alltag, Bräuche, Feste—Zur Volkskultur," in Franz-Josef Heyen and Anton M. Keim (eds.), *Auf der Suche nach neuer Identität. Kultur in Rheinland-Pfalz im Nachkriegsjahrzehnt* (Mainz, 1996), p.23. • 6 Anton M. Keim, *11 Mal politischer Karneval. Weltgeschichte aus der Bütt. Geschichte der demokratischen Narrentradition vom Rhein* (Mainz, 1981), p.216. • 7 Ibid. • 8 Schwedt, p.24. • 9 Quoted from Keim, p.218. • 10 Quoted from Armin Heinen, "Narrenschau. Karneval als Zeitzeuge," in Edwin Dillmann and Richard van Dülmen (eds.), *Lebenserfahrungen an der Saar. Studien zur Alltagskultur 1945–1955* (St. Ingbert, 1996), p.303. • 11 Newspaper report quoted from Michael Euler-Schmidt and Marcus Leifeld (eds.), *Die Prinzen-Garde Köln. Eine Geschichte mit Rang und Namen 1906–2006* (Cologne, 2005), p.121. • 12 Quoted from Schwedt, p.26. *Der Spiegel* described the procession through Cologne thus: "The carnival society 'Kölsche Funke rutwiess' moved through the ruined streets to the front of the mayor's house, followed by thousands of people dressed in carnival costume and the elephants of the Williams Circus. The band played the Loyal Hussar and the hit of this year's carnival: 'If the gnomes come and take our jobs.' The Kölner Funken were

celebrating their own 125th birthday in red and white Prussian army uniform jackets with the traditional parade dance, the 'Stippelfötje,' and the military government had no objection to this militant form of dressing-up, or indeed to the Frederician pointed helmet, wooden rifles or recruits' swearing-in ceremony" (*Der Spiegel* 7 [1948]). • 13 Liessem's Nazi past was later put into perspective with reference to the so-called fools' revolt. In 1934 he had managed to prevent the carnival committees being taken over by the Nazi organisation Strength Through Joy. But he did not use the formal independence of carnival to affect its content in any way—on the contrary, until the processions were halted after the outbreak of war, the carnival had become more and more anti-Semitic, and the procession happily sang songs like the cynical "The Jews Are Emigrating." Admittedly the people of Cologne later claimed that they had let the anti-Semitic carnival floats pass them by in icy silence. In fact, however, during Liessem's tenure the Nazis had managed to remove any carnival traditions that were critical of authority, and under the motto "Stop complaining, join in," turn it into a largely anti-Semitic popular celebration. • 14 And businesses were in good shape. For the 1947 carnival season *Der Spiegel* reported from Cologne: "The Cologne fools' guild is on the scene again. Even though the city councillors had decided unanimously on 28 December not to permit carnival events and fourteen days later the main committee spoke of unimaginable hardship among the starving, freezing populace, of ten carnival societies, for the period between 15 January and 17 February (Rose Monday) 32 closed but large events were reported. We are justified in asking whether Cologne has another hall where such a festivity could be put on with the world-famous feverish quality of Cologne carnival. Half of all sessions will be held in the 'Atlantik' in Waisenhausgasse. The others in makeshift improvised quarters" (*Der Spiegel* 5 [1947]). • 15 One could tell from the chevrons and lanyards of the Princely Guard to which rank one had risen through service and donations. "Do you think everybody should take part in the Rose Monday procession and show off his furbelows?" Liessem replied to a critic who asked for more spontaneity. "There must be discipline and order. Even at carnival. Especially at carnival." Quoted from Euler-Schmid, Leifeld, p.139. • 16 Quoted from ibid., p.125. In contrast to the widespread hardship, the sums spent on carnival were actually exorbitant. *Der Spiegel* gave an account in its carnival report the previous year, 1947, of the activity in Munich. There, "for ten days, in about 1,200 hotels, bars and clubs, there was dancing and partying from eight till eight. Here were countless house balls at the same time. [. . .] Up to 500 Marks was spent at studio parties in Schwabing, which were celebrated as in the past with sometimes as many as 200 guests between Siegeltor and Feilitzchplatz, among nude paintings, screeching gramophones and inviting couches. But then one could also eat and drink whatever one liked all evening for 500 Marks (*Der Spiegel* 7 [1948]). • 17 Quoted from an internet publication produced by the Konrad-Adenauer-Stiftung political foundation: https://www.konrad-adenauer.de/dokumente/presse konferenzen/1950-04-19-pressekonferenz-berlin • 18 When Adenauer had the audience sing the future national anthem after delivering a speech in Berlin's Titania-Palast in 1950 (he had ensured that lyric sheets were laid out on the rows of seats, a typical piece of Adenauer cunning), the SPD spoke of being ambushed. President Theodor Heuss, who wanted more time to decide on an anthem for the young Republic—personally he was in favour of "Land des Glaubens, deutsches Land, Land der Väter und der Erben" ("Land of Faith, German Land, Land of Fathers and Heirs") by Hermann Reutter—did not give into Adenauer's urgings until 1952. The national anthem "Einigkeit und Recht und Freiheit" ("Unity and Right and Freedom") was never formerly laid down in the constitution. Instead the Federal press office simply followed the correspondence between Adenauer and the finally compliant Heuss, and the anthem was accepted. The young state sometimes established itself in rather unconventional ways. • 19 Quoted from Heinz Ludwig Arnold (ed.), *Die deutsche Literatur 1945–1960*, vol. 1 (Munich, 1995), p.79. • 20 Helene Klausner, *Kölner Karneval zwischen Uniform und Lebensform* (Münster, 2007), p.311. • 21 *Der Spiegel* 8 (1947). • 22 Quoted from Schoeller, *Diese merkwürdige Zeit. Leben nach der Stunde Null. Ein Textbuch aus der "Neuen Zeitung"* (Frankfurt am Main, 2005), p.333 • 23 For the "Bathtub" Heldt wrote a monologue with partly sung passages to the tune of the song "La Paloma." Under the title "Saint Lenchen," an actress stepped out in front of a backdrop of Heldt's wobbly house façades and sang: "I'm Saint Lenchen / I'm not a whore / I do it for free / because I like it / I fight you with love / you who give me nothing / because you yourselves are too cowardly to make a move." • 24 Prinz and Krauss, p.9.

V: Love Amidst the Rubble

1 The prototype for this was the "homecomer" Beckmann in the play *The Man Outside* by Wolfgang Borchert, the most famous of the so-called homecoming dramas which in a way forms a genre of its own. It is, as the prologue has it, "about a man who comes to Germany, one of those. One of those who come home and then don't come home because there is no longer a home there." • 2 Sibylle Meyer and Eva Schulze, *Von Liebe sprach damals keiner. Familienalltag in der Nachkriegszeit* (Munich, 1985), p.128. • 3 Cf. ibid., pp.161–206. • 4 Ibid. • 5 *Der Spiegel* 41 (1953). • 6 Meyer and Schulze, p.204. • 7 Anonymous, p.62. • 8 Quoted from Wilfried E. Schoeller, *Diese merkwürdige Zeit. Leben nach der Stunde Null. Ein Textbuch aus der "Neuen Zeitung,"* Frankfurt am Main, 2005, p.52. • 9 The full quote also contains the following passage: "The 180 Mark

wages are not much more than nothing. Previously, Herr Müller could have 'demanded' something from his wife in return (and demand he did). Now he has to stay nice and quiet. For three years husband and wife have been struggling with the bitterest material hardship. The man threw the 180 Marks at hardship. And he would have died there, had his wife not parried that hardship with stronger weapons. With her whole great unshakeable nature, her instinct for practicalities and for the nearest solution, with the deftness required to play 'by heart' on the keyboard of the household, with all the technique, refined over centuries of practice, of mastering the everyday. The seemingly indomitable and unspoilt power of women rises out of the breakdown of men. And it is the sign of the healthier sex: while many different kinds of burdens are placed upon it, its physicality is better maintained than that of men which, according to medical investigations, is in rapid physical decline (underweight!)." *Constanze—die Zeitschrift für die Frau und für jedermann*, vol. 1, no. 2 (1948). • 10 Annette Kuhn (ed.), *Frauen in der deutschen Nachkriegszeit*, vol. 2 (Düsseldorf, 1986), p.158. • 11 Cf. Nori Möding, *"Die Stunde der Frauen?,"* in Martin Broszat, Klaus-Dietmar Henke and Hans Woller (eds.), *Von Stalingrad zur Währungsreform. Zur Sozialgeschichte des Umbruchs in Deutschland* (Munich, 1988), p.623 ff. • 12 In the Civil Code of the Federal Republic, however, there were many regulations that contradicted the principle of equality. For example, paragraph 1354, "The decision in all matters concerning married life rests with the husband," was only deleted in 1958. In the GDR the legal position of women was one of equality from the beginning, however the proportion of women on the highest political committees was similarly low to the Federal Republic. • 13 Quoted from Tamara Domentat, *Hallo Fräulein. Deutsche Frauen und amerikanische Soldaten* (Berlin, 1998), p.162. • 14 This was the assessment of the film critic Fred Gehler. He wrote that the film was "one of the finest filmic revelations of post-war German cinema." Peter Pewas had, he wrote, skilfully undermined the task of making an educational film. Instead he showed "the authentic picture of a young post-war generation in all its helplessness and perplexity. It is hungry for life, thirsty for love. The dramatic construction of the film is surprisingly open: stories and faces appear and are forgotten again. A stalk-hunt through spiritual landscapes." Fred Gehler, "Straßenbekanntschaft," *Film und Fernsehen* 5 (1991), p.15. • 15 Wolfgang Weyrauch (ed.), *Tausend Gramm. Ein deutsches Bekenntnis in dreißig Geschichten aus dem Jahr 1949* (Reinbek bei Hamburg, 1989), p.86. The quotation has been slightly cut. • 16 The historian Alexander von Plato interviewed, for the archive "Deutsches Gedächtnis," a man who had come back from a Russian POW camp to his wife and a house where, as well as her and his now widowed father-in-law, a bombed-out family lived, consisting of a mother and a son with his wife. The homecoming husband tried to explain the convoluted relationships to the historian: "It was an attic flat, there wasn't much room. All of a sudden the husband, the son of the bombed-out mother, moved in with my wife on the first floor. He lived there. And then as things worked out he ended up having his dinner with my wife in the evening—and so on. And then my father-in-law went upstairs because the woman was five years older than her real husband. Do you see? So in the evening my father-in-law went up to the woman whose husband was sleeping with my wife at night, you see?" Cf. Alexander von Plato and Almut Leh, *"Ein unglaublicher Frühling." Erfahrene Geschichte im Nachkriegsdeutschland 1945–1948* (Bonn, 1997), p.240. • 17 *Constanze*, vol. 1, no. 11 (1948). • 18 Cf. Hans-Ulrich Wehler, *Deutsche Gesellschaftsgeschichte. Vol. 4. Vom Beginn des Ersten Weltkrieges bis zur Gründung der beiden deutschen Staaten 1914–1949* (Munich, 2003), p.945 ff. • 19 Robert A. Stemmle's film is a satirical musical, also known as a "cabaret film," with a budget as thin as Fröbe himself was at the time, but because of its many stylistic jumps and experiments it is one of the most interesting productions of those early years. It contains surreal dream sequences and is told from the Berlin of 2048, from which we look out onto the post-war era. For the design of futuristic Berlin Stemmle used models made for an architectural competition in 1948. • 20 Quoted from Karin Böke, Frank Liedtke and Martin Wengeler, *Politische Leitvokabeln in der Adenauer-Ära* (Berlin, 1996), p.214. • 21 Christina Thürmer-Rohr in Helga Hirsch: *Endlich wieder leben. Die fünfziger Jahre im Rückblick von Frauen* (Berlin, 2012), p. 14. • 22 Barbara Willenbacher, "Die Nachkriegsfamilie," in Broszat et al., p.599. • 23 Ibid., p.604. • 24 Cf. Norman M. Naimark, *Die Russen in Deutschland. Die sowjetische Besatzungszone 1945–1949* (Berlin, 1997); Ilko-Sascha Kowalczuk, *Stefan Wolle: Roter Stern über Deutschland. Sowjetische Truppen in der DDR* (Berlin, 2010); Ingeborg Jacobs, *Freiwild. Das Schicksal deutscher Frauen 1945* (Berlin, 2008). • 25 Margret Boveri, *Tage des Überlebens* (Berlin, 1945; Munich, Zürich, 1968), p.116. • 26 Jens Bisky, editor of the *Süddeutsche Zeitung*, revealed the author's identity shortly after the republication of the diary in Hans Magnus Enzensberger's "Andere Bibliothek" (*Süddeutsche Zeitung*, 24 September 2003). There was an often heated debate about this, and about Bisky's critical caveats about the value of the diary as a historical document. Bisky correctly pointed out that the author's work as a journalist was significant with regard to the ordering of the diary, and demonstrated that the original text had had to be improved and altered by her close friend, colleague and publisher Kurt Marek, better known as C. W. Ceram. From a philological point of view the objections are justified with regard to the assessment of the Russians in general, questions of war guilt, retrospective self-distancing from the Nazi regime, etc. But there are no reasons to doubt the depiction of the rapes themselves and ways of coming to terms with them. For this reason the diary is quoted here in spite of the aforementioned reservations. • 27 Anonymous, p.105. • 28 Ibid., p.184. • 29 For example in his speech to 200 Wehrmacht generals on 30 March 1941 in the Reich Chancellery. • 30 Quoted from Keith Lowe, *Savage Continent: Europe in the Aftermath of World War II* (London, 2012), p.104. • 31 Charlotte Wagner, quoted from Sibylle Meyer and Eva Schulze, *Wie wir das alles geschafft haben. Alleinstehende Frauen berichten über ihr Leben nach 1945* (Munich, 1984), p.51. • 32 Ruth Andreas-Friedrich, *Der Schattenmann. Tagebuchaufzeichnungen 1938–1948* (Berlin, 2000), p.332. • 33 Anonyma, *A Woman in Berlin*, p.305. • 34 In the June 1947 issue of *Ja. Zeitschrift der Jungen Generation* there is a poem that addresses the problems faced by couples after the wave of rapes. Named "Heimkehr" ("Homecoming") and signed by the community college teacher and author Dietrich Warnesius, it is only a few lines long. In a somewhat affected minimalism, he describes a husband and wife meeting up again after several years. After the wife has "prepared three carrots" for the man, the poem goes on: "Night. / No one sleeps. / 'You . . . you don't need to tell me anything, Maria . . .' / Someone takes a deep breath. / 'No,' says the woman. / Silence. / No breathing now. / Years pass. / 'Shall we try . . . Maria?' / Someone breathes deeply. / 'Yes,' says the woman." • 35 *Tagesspiegel* of 6 December 1959, quoted from Matthias Sträßner, "Erzähl mir vom Krieg!," Ruth Andreas-Friedrich, Ursula von Kardorff, Margret Boveri and Anonyma, *Wie vier Journalistinnen 1945 ihre Berliner Tagebücher schreiben* (Würzburg, 2014), p.181. • 36 Winfried Weiss, *A Nazi Childhood* (Santa Barbara, 1983), p.173. • 37 Ibid., p.171. • 38 Cf. Thomas Faltin, "Drei furchtbare Tage im April. Das Ende des Zweiten Weltkriegs in Stuttgart," *Stuttgarter Zeitung*, 18 April 2015. The historian Norman M. Naimark wrote: "Where bad discipline and acts of rape were concerned, in the West only the troops from French Morocco came close to the Soviet soldiers; particularly in the early days of the occupation women in Baden and Württemberg were victims of random attacks by occupying soldiers similar to those in the Eastern zone. In spite of these reservations it remains the case that the phenomenon of rapes became part of the social history of the Soviet zone of occupation on a scale unknown in the West." (Naimark, p.137.) • 39 Cf. Andreas Förschler, *Stuttgart 1945. Kriegsende und Neubeginn* (Gudensberg-Gleichen, 2004), p.8 ff. • 40 In her book *Als die Soldaten kamen*, the historian Miriam Gebhardt attempts to make such an equation. She carried out an in-depth study of the sexually motivated crimes of the Western Allies. Unfortunately she succumbed to the temptation to sensationalise the results of her research by equating the behaviour of the Western Allies and that of the Red Army. That only works if one dismisses the countless and more loving relationships between German women and Americans as "rape, sweetened by chocolate," and also simply ignores contradictory studies about the "GI Fräuleins," including those written from a feminist perspective. In his discussion of the book in the *Frankfurter Allgemeine Zeitung* Klaus-Dietmar Henke even went so far as to recall Goebbels's equation of "General Eisenhower's Jewish plutocratic band of soldiers" with the "Bolshevik hordes of the Asian Steppes." Miriam Gebhardt, *Als die Soldaten kamen. Die Vergewaltigung deutscher Frauen am Ende des Zweiten Weltkriegs* (Munich, 2015). • 41 Quoted from Klaus-Jörg Ruhl (ed.), *Deutschland 1945. Alltag zwischen Krieg und Frieden* (Neuwied, 1984), p.92 ff. • 42 Hildegard Knef, *Der geschenkte Gaul* (Vienna, Munich, Zürich, 1970), p.III. • 43 "Are these not proper saloon soldiers?" the school student Maxi-Lore E. wrote in her diary. "Everything about them looks so weak and sloppy." Looking at this soft crowd, she can't help "thinking about our boys." These Americans "aren't real soldiers, and they don't know the upright attitude that our ones have." Quoted from Benjamin Möckel, *Erfahrungsbruch und Generationsbehauptung. Die Kriegsjugendgeneration in den beiden deutschen Nachkriegsgesellschaften* (Göttingen, 2014), p.197. • 44 In July 1945, the British and the Americans occupied the two sectors assigned to them by the Yalta Agreement in February 1945. The French occupied their sector a little later. Even before this, Great Britain, the US and the Soviet Union had agreed to divide Germany into occupied zones but to treat the Reich capital of Berlin as a special case and place it under shared responsibility. When the French were accepted into the circle of the victorious powers, Berlin became a four-sector city. • 45 *Der Spiegel* reported on this on 15 February 1947. Clearly the author had visited the place where the process occurred: "They come from all levels of society and some of them, particularly Americanised from nail polish to language, emphasise that they are engaged to an American, and try 'to go dancing without doing anything forbidden.' Most of the girls see the passport as an opportunity to be together with their friends in pleasant surroundings. Some want to intensify their hitherto fleeting contact with American citizens and products by visiting a club. A few are also invited out by American women with whom they share offices. With the introduction of social passes, the American sector of Berlin follows the cities in the American zone which began this organisation of social life with Germans in Germany some months ago. [. . .] So far 600 women in Berlin have applied. The minimum age is 18. The 'oldest girl' so far was 47. On average the social pass candidates are 19 or 20. Applications from married women are not permitted" (*Der Spiegel* 7 [1947], p.6). • 46 Annette Brauerhoch, *"Fräuleins" und GIs. Geschichte und Filmgeschichte* (Frankfurt am Main, Basel, 2006). • 47 Tamara Domentat, *"Hallo Fräulein." Deutsche Frauen und amerikanische Soldaten* (Berlin, 1998), p.73. • 48 Ibid., p.77. • 49 Ibid., p.190. • 50 The anti-authoritarian potential of soldiers' brides is completely ignored in the historiography and self-perception of the generation of 1968. Perhaps the feeling of shame felt by their fathers was still at work 20 years later. In addition, there was the fact that revulsion over the Vietnam War was also transferred to the soldiers stationed in the Federal Republic. Women could happily get together with a hippie from San Francisco, but a girl who went out with a GI from Bamberg in the 1970s was finished as far as the left were concerned. So for vague political reasons there is also little sympathy for GI brides in the academic treatment of the post-war era. • 51 The film provoked violent unrest, and a member of the voluntary self-regulation committee that had passed the film resigned in protest; Church ministers called for demonstrations, disrupted cinema screenings and ended up in front of the judges because the cinema owners reported them; *Der Spiegel* quoted whole pages from the screenplay; critics got very worked up about the "repellent prettification with so-called art and aesthetic fuss" and spoke of "neo-prostitution." The queues at the cinema box offices grew longer and longer.

VI: Robbing, Rationing, Black-market Trading—Lessons for the Market Economy

1 The story is told in Rainer Gries, *Die Rationengesellschaft. Versorgungskampf und Vergleichsmentalität: Leipzig, München und Köln nach dem Kriege* (Münster, 1991), p.148. • 2 Barbara Felsmann, Annett Gröschner and Grischa Meyer (eds.), *Backfisch im Bombenkrieg. Notizen in Steno* (Berlin, 2013), p.268 ff. • 3 *Süddeutsche Zeitung*, 30 April 1946. • 4 Wolfgang Leonhard, *Die Revolution entlässt ihre Kinder*, quoted from Hermann Glaser, *1945. Beginn einer Zukunft. Bericht und Dokumentation* (Frankfurt am Main, 2005), p.194. • 5 Cf. Klaus-Jörg Ruhl (ed.), *Deutschland 1945. Alltag zwischen Krieg und Frieden* (Neuwied, 1984), p.161. • 6 Ibid., p.178. • 7 Cf. Jörg Roesler, *Momente deutsch-deutscher Wirtschafts- und Sozialgeschichte 1945–1990* (Leipzig, 2006), p.41. • 8 *Rheinische Zeitung*, 18 December 1946. • 9 Gries, p.290. • 10 Quoted from Annette Kuhn (ed.), *Frauen in der deutschen Nachkriegszeit*, Vol. 2: *Frauenpolitik 1945–1949. Quellen und Materialien* (Düsseldorf, 1989), p.198. • 11 Quoted from Ruhl, p.138. • 12 We can tell how serious the situation was by the fact that Adenauer, at that time the leader of the CDU faction in the NRW (North Rhine–Westphalia) regional parliament, does not neglect in this letter about the political situation to ask for a private package: "I don't know if it will be easy for you to send us a package again. If that is the case, I would be grateful to you if you would in fact think of a tonic for my wife and Georg, and coffee for me, particularly Nescafé. I always take it with me on my many travels. It gives me the necessary freshness at the many gatherings and conferences that I have to chair. You will thus also be indirectly supporting the CDU, whose goals I am sure are sympathetic to you!" Quoted from the web page of the Konrad-Adenauer-Stiftung: www.konrad-adenauer .de/dokumente/briefe/1946-12-10-brief-silver berg. • 13 Quoted from Günter

J. Trittel, *Hunger und Politik. Die Ernährungs-krise in der Bizone 1945–1949* (Frankfurt, New York, 1990), p.47. • 14 Quoted from Trittel, p.285. • 15 Cf. Gries, p.305. • 16 Margret Boveri, *Tage des Überlebens* (Berlin, 1945; Munich, Zürich, 1968), p.93. • 17 Ibid., p.124. • 18 Quoted from Werner Schäfke, *Kölns schwarzer Markt 1939 bis 1949. Ein Jahrzehnt asoziale Marktwirtschaft* (Cologne, 2014), p.65 ff. • 19 Cf. Roland Ander, "Ich war auch eine Trümmerfrau," *Enttrümmerung und Abrisswahn in Dresden 1945–1989* (Dresden, 2010), p.182. • 20 Cf. Stefan Mörchen, *Schwarzer Markt. Kriminalität, Ordnung und Moral in Bremen 1939–1949* (Frankfurt am Main, 2011). Many such statements are collected in the volume, including recorded memories from the research project "Leben in den Jahren 1945–49" by the Archiv für Volkskunde in the Focke-Museum. • 21 *Ja—Zeitung der jungen Generation* was published biweekly in Berlin from 1947 until 1948 and was edited by H. Kielgast and H. Keul. • 22 Heinrich Böll, *Heimat und keine. Schriften und Reden 1964–1968* (Munich, 1985), p.112. The passage continues: "Everyone owned a bare life and, besides that,whatever they could get their hands on: coal, books, building materials. [. . .] Anyone who wasn't shivering in a ruined city must have stolen their wood or their coal, and anyone who wasn't starving must have acquired their food illegally, or had it acquired for them." • 23 Karl Kromer (ed.), *Schwarzmarkt, Tausch-und Schleichhandel. In Frage und Antwort mit 500 Beispielen*, Recht für jeden 1 (Hamburg, 1947). • 24 Hans von Hentig, "Die Kriminalität des Zusammenbruchs." *Schweizerische Zeitschrift für Strafrecht* 62 (1947), p.337. • 25 Ruth Andreas-Friedrich, *Der Schattenmann. Tagebuchaufzeichnungen 1938–1948* (Berlin, 2000) p.338. • 26 Kuno Kusenberg, "Nichts ist selbstverständlich," in Schoeller, *Diese merkwürdige Zeit. Leben nach der Stunde Null. Ein Textbuch aus der "Neuen Zeitung"* (Frankfurt am Main, 2005), p.445. • 27 Von Hentig, p.340. • 28 Andreas-Friedrich, p.408. • 29 Jörg Lau, *Hans Magnus Enzensberger. Ein öffentliches Leben* (Berlin, 1999), p.20. • 30 Hans Magnus Enzensberger was always proud of his business skills, which he also demonstrated as an author. Anyone who wanted to have him as a speaker at an event, for example, would have to brace themselves for some tough negotiations. *Der Spiegel* asked during an interview in 2008 at what point Enzensberger had grasped how capitalism worked: "Enzensberger: I think it was after the war, and on the black market. Like many others I traded in cigarettes, butter and the Nazi weapons that the Americans wanted to have as trophies. It was a crash course in capital increase. But as a career or even as a source of income it seemed far too modest to me, so I soon bade farewell to that activity. Spiegel: As a banker you'd have qualified for a bonus these days. Enzensberger: Quite possibly. By the standards of the time I was quite rich for a while. The cigarettes were stacked in palettes of 10,000, and I had four of those in the cellar, which meant 40,000 cigarettes. Each box was worth 200 Reichsmark. So I was on the way to being a millionaire. But I had no intention of spending my life as a kind of Scrooge McDuck. Money's nice, but it's also a bit boring" *Der Spiegel* 45 (2008). • 31 It contains the title poem "Defence of the Lambs against the Wolves" and represents a provocative attack on the silent majority, the passive and the *Mitläufer* who make themselves guilty by tolerating the crimes of the rulers. The "lambs" who constantly feel like victims, "disinclined from learning, leaving the thinking up to the wolves," are in every respect guilty themselves. The last two sections read: "You lambs, sisters are / Compared to you, crows: / you each blind the others. / Fraternity rules among the wolves: / they go in packs. / Praised by the robbers: you / inviting to rape / throw yourselves on the rotten bed / of obedience. Still whining / you lie. You want / to be torn. You / won't change the world." Hans Magnus Enzensberger, *Gedichte 1950–1955* (Frankfurt am Main, 1996), p.11. • 32 Lau, p.20. • 33 Cf. Schäfke, p.69. • 34 Cf. Malte Zierenberg, *Stadt der Schieber. Der Berliner Schwarzmarkt 1939–1950* (Göttingen, 2008). In this ethnology-tinged study the author subjects the bartering arenas to a thorough investigation, from modes of distribution and trading practices to physical postures and dress codes. • 35 Siegfried Lenz, *Lehmanns Erzählungen oder So schön war mein Markt* (Hamburg, 1964), p.35. • 36 Cf. ibid., p.317. • 37 The myth of the post-war cigarette-butt lives on. The most recent example is the novel *Ikarien* by Uwe Timm. It relates a particularly touching variation: a German boy runs after an American officer with the cigarette butt that he threw away deliberately, because he thinks he has lost it. Uwe Timm, *Ikarien* (Köln, 2017), p.38. • 38 Zierenberg, p.287: "The black market was the symbol and experiential space of an intolerable lawlessness and a social event. It was the unjust redistributor that rewarded the cunning and punished the weak, and the place of creative ingenuity after the months of the final battle." • 39 Willi A. Boelcke, *Der Schwarzmarkt 1945–1948. Vom Überleben nach dem Kriege* (Braunschweig, 1986), p.6. • 40 Lenz, pp.35, 59, 67.

VII: The Economic Miracle and the Fear of Immorality

1 Chris Howland relates the episode in the TV documentary *Hamburg damals* (Episode 1, 1945–1948, directed by Christian Mangels, first broadcast on NDR, 25 April 2009). Howland later became one of the most popular entertainers of the early Federal Republic as "Mr. Pumpernickel." His first record was released in 1958: *Fräulein* sang of the love between German women and occupying soldiers. "You are true and hard-working / You kiss like a dream, I know / Little Fräulein from Isar and Rhine." His greatest success was the WDR radio programme "Musik aus Studio B," broadcast between 1961 and 1968. • 2 Ulrich Herbert, *Geschichte Deutschlands im 20. Jahrhundert* (Munich, 2014), p.596. • 3 Quoted from Werner Schäfke, *Kölns schwarzer Markt 1939 bis*

1949. Ein Jahrzehnt asoziale Marktwirtschaft (Cologne, 2014), p.43. • 4 Cf. Werner Abelshauser, *Deutsche Wirtschaftsgeschichte. Von 1945 bis zur Gegenwart* (Munich, 2011), p.123. Research shows variable figures. • 5 Herbert, p. 98 • 6 "No other event is inscribed quite so compellingly in the experiences of the West German population as the currency reform of 20 June 1948. It is the only event after 1945 that is introduced as a way of dating other experiences; there is no other event of which we could be sure that our partner in conversation is familiar with it and interprets its significance identically," Lutz Niethammer wrote on the basis of his experiences with eyewitness interviews. Cf. Niethammer, "Hinterher merkt man, daß es richtig war, daß es schiefgegangen ist." *Nachkriegserfahrungen im Ruhrgebiet* (Berlin, Bonn, 1983), p.79. • 7 Quoted from Rainer Gries, *Die Rationengesellschaft. Versorgungskampf und Vergleichsmentalität: Leipzig, München und Köln nach dem Kriege* (Münster, 1991), p.331. • 8 Ibid., p.332. • 9 The caption is a kind of doggerel that places the girl in the context of flourishing hopes and worries: "Diese Nette Dame/her name unknown/without Western money, Eastern money/cash or expenses/IDs of any kind/Residence papers/Denazification oaths/Rent money interest adjustments/Without personal allowance quotas/Old and new banknotes/Ah, the camera can't tell it straight:/Summer of forty-eight!" • 10 Presumably the first three post-war years, in spite of the enormous condensation of events, are hard to access in the collective memory because they are wedged in between two powerful foundation narratives. The stylised caesura of currency reform gave them the nebulous status of a prehistoric era that darkened as the economic miracle painted itself ever more brightly. • 11 Cf. Hans-Ulrich Wehler: "By equating all recipients of wages and salaries, in a pseudo-egalitarian form, with the same small 60 DM budget, currency reform devalued all savings in a proportion of 10:1m but favoured companies and property owners, it acquired the halo of an impressive new beginning that pushed open the door to economic revival." Hans-Ulrich Wehler, *Deutsche Gesellschaftsgeschichte*. Vol. 4. *Vom Beginn des Ersten Weltkrieges bis zur Gründung der beiden deutschen Staaten 1914–1949* (Munich, 2003), p.971. • 12 Christoph Stölzl, *Die Wolfsburg-Saga* (Stuttgart, 2008), p.197. • 13 *Katalog der Erinnerungsstätte an die Zwangsarbeit auf dem Gelände des Volkswagenwerks*, ed. Historische Kommunikation der Volkswagen AG (Wolfsburg, 1999; this ed. 2014), p.58. The catalogue provides a sophisticated look at the living conditions of the various groups of forced labourers in the factory. It is based on extensive research into the Nazi past of the company which VW-AG commissioned from Hans Mommsen in the mid-1990s. Cf. Hans Mommsen, *Das Volkswagenwerk und seine Arbeiter im Dritten Reich* (Düsseldorf, 1996). • 14 Horst Mönnich, *Die Autostadt. Abenteuer einer technischen Idee*. Quoted from the new edition (Munich, 1958), p.245. • 15 An American company commander reported that Wolfsburg forced labourers had broken into an arsenal and taken weapons from it. To celebrate their liberation they had got blind drunk and fired into the air standing on roofs and embankments, before being disarmed by soldiers. "When they fired the rifles, it threw them flat on their backs." Cf. Keith Lowe, *Savage Continent: Europe in the Aftermath of World War II* (London, 2012), p.130. • 16 For the author Western forces and Germans were natural allies, because they potentially shared a goal: to resume production as quickly as possible. The Allies only had to be deterred from dismantling the factory with a view to reparations. One particular scene typifies Mönnich's view of the situation, in which a German foreman installed by the Americans wants to persuade a general to protect the Germans and remove the Displaced Persons from the Wolfsburg camps. The camp was the "canker of the factory": "Until it is removed there will be no calm, no industrial peace." Mönnich, p.246. • 17 The Chicago episode isn't as implausible as all that, however. Some of the original VW workers had previously worked at Ford in Detroit. So it is theoretically quite conceivable that the engineer would have been able to recite Carl Sandburg's poem by heart: "Chicago! / Hog Butcher for the World, / Tool Maker, Stacker of Wheat, / Player with Railroads and the Nation's Freight Handler; / Stormy, husky, brawling / City of the Big Shoulders." The words rang out through the factory hall. Ibid., p.249. • 18 Ibid., p.305. • 19 File memo quoted from Günter Riederer, "Die Barackenstadt. Wolfsburg und seine Lager nach 1945," in *Deutschlandarchiv 2013. Bundes zentrale für politische Bildung* (Bonn, 2013), p.112. • 20 Quoted from ibid., p.112. • 21 Quoted from *Der Spiegel* 22 (1950). • 22 *Der Spiegel* 11 (1949). • 23 Cf. Hans Mommsen, "Das Volkswagenwerk und die "Stunde Null": Kontinuität und Diskontinuität," in Rosmarie Beier (ed.), *Aufbau West—Aufbau Ost. Die Planstädte Wolfsburg und Eisenhüttenstadt in der Nachkriegszeit. Buch zur Ausstellung des Deutschen Historischen Museums* (Ostfildern-Ruit, 1997), p.136. • 24 Karl W. Böttcher and Rüdiger Proske, "Präriestädte in Deutschland." *Frankfurter Hefte. Zeitschrift für Kultur und Politik* 5 (1950), p.503. • 25 Heidrun Edelmann, "'König Nordhoff' und die 'Wirtschaftswunderzeit,'" in Beier, p.184. • 26 Quoted from Beier, p.184. The wheeling and dealing between board and management later yielded the strangest fruits, such as the generous and corrupt financing of prostitution services by the company including first-class flights to Brazil. The profound connections between state and business are obvious even today, including the fact that one of the most fateful reform measures of the German government under Chancellor Gerhard Schröder, the reform of the social welfare system and the unemployment assistance laid out in "Agenda 2010," was named after the chief human resources officer for Volkswagen, Peter Hartz. The VW manager Hartz was the head of a governmental commission, which worked out the legislative reforms of the social system. The unemployment benefit is called "Hartz 4." • 27 Cf. Ulfert Herlyn, Wulf Tessin, Annette Harth and Gitta Scheller, *Faszination Wolfsburg 1938–2012* (Wiesbaden, 2012), p.20. • 28 Cf. Stölzl, p.104: "The fact that in the 'integration machine' of Wolfsburg a 'motley crew' should have become a new kind of industrial citizen was the precondition for the rise of the Volkswagen works to become the prototype of the social market economy. Its controller, Heinrich Nordhoff, embodied the switch from traditional owner-manager to social engineer, the sole decision-maker, yet demonstratively stressing the common purpose—an ideal figure in the Federal Republic on its conciliatory journey between capital and labour. What the whole country experienced, the tamed social-state form of modern industrialism—appeared very early on in Wolfsburg as a complete artwork in itself." • 29 One exception was the wildcat strike by Italian VW employees in 1962. • 30 Quoted from *Der Spiegel* 33 (1955), front-page story about the delivery of the millionth Volkswagen. • 31 This figure, corresponding to an income of 64,000 Reichsmark, comes from Uta van Steen, *Liebesperlen. Beate Uhse—eine deutsche Karriere* (Hamburg, 2003), p.101. Other sources put the figure as slightly lower. • 32 Figures for 2015 (profit) and 2017. However digitalisation has also been a worry for the market in erotica and in December 2017 the holding company of Beate Uhse AG voluntarily opened insolvency proceedings. • 33 Quoted from Sybille Steinbacher, *Wie der Sex nach Deutschland kam. Der Kampf um Sittlichkeit und Anstand in der frühen Bundesrepublik* (Berlin, 2011), p.247. • 34 Quoted from Alexander von Plato and Almut Leh, *"Ein unglaublicher Frühling." Erfahrene Geschichte im Nachkriegsdeutschland 1945–1948* (Bonn, 1997), p.238. • 35 Cf. van Steen, p.129. • 36 Quoted from Steinbacher, p.259. • 37 Mariam Lau, Beate Uhse obituary in *Die Welt*, 19 July 2001. • 38 Van Steen, p.130. • 39 Ibid., p.260. • 40 Cf. Steinbacher, p.255. • 41 These and other anti-comic invectives appear in Björn Laser, "Heftchenflut und Bildersturm—Die westdeutsche Comic-Debatte in den 50ern," in Georg Bollenbeck and Gerhard Kaiser, *Die janusköpfigen 50er Jahre*, Kulturelle Moderne und bildungsbürgerliche Semantik 3 (Wiesbaden, 2000), p.63 ff. • 42 Ibid., p.78. • 43 Hans Seidel, "Jugendgefährdung heute" (Hamburg, 1953), quoted from Julia Ubbelohde, "Der Umgang mit jugendlichen Normverstößen," in Ulrich Herbert (ed.), *Wandlungsprozesse in Westdeutschland 1945–1980* (Göttingen, 2002), p.404. • 44 Quoted from ibid. • 45 Helma Engels, "Jugendschutz," in *Jugendschutz* 1, vols 7–8 (1956), quoted from ibid. • 46 Alexander Mitscherlich, "Aktuelles zum Problem der Verwahrlosung," first published in *Psyche* 1 (1947–48), quoted from *idem, Gesammelte Schriften*, vol. 6 (Frankfurt, 1986), p.618. • 47 Alexander Mitscherlich, "Jugend ohne Bilder," first published in *Du. Schweizer Monatsschrift* 4 (1947), quoted from *idem, Gesammelte Schriften*, vol. 6, p.609. • 48 Cf. Eva Gehltomholt and Sabine Hering, *Das verwahrloste Mädchen. Diagnostik und Fürsorge in der Jugendhilfe zwischen Kriegsende und*

Reform (1945–1965) (Opladen, 2006). • 49 However even boys were not exempt from the demonisation of sexual impulses. The *Bildhefte der Jugend*, for example, showed a wildly desperate, naked giant, painted in the style of one of Goya's nightmarish visions, racked by inner furies under the heading "Lewd behaviour destroys." The accompanying text reads: "Lewd behaviour impedes. Prevents. Breaks. Takes joy away. But discipline and moderation sweep obstacles away. Think in good time before it's too late. You know of young people around you who have turned into deserts in the fire of lewd behaviour, greed and lust. [. . .] and finally you sense very clearly that in you too the wasteland is growing, the bacteria of the general plague are getting to work—what do you plan to do? Flee from reality into the intoxication of cinemas, of schnapps glasses, of sexual excess? Know this: every intoxication is followed by a rude awakening.—And what then? Howling with wolves? Reaching an agreement with the plague? [Metaphor for lax and decadent behaviour.] Know this: one day they will tear you to pieces. Soon they will destroy you entirely." Quoted from the internet collection "Wirtschaftswundermuseum.de" by Jörg Bohn. • 50 Quoted from Gehltomholt, p.41. • 51 Cf. Steinbacher, p.252. • 52 Cf. Dieter Schenk, *Auf dem rechten Auge blind. Die braunen Wurzeln des BKA* (Cologne, 2001). • 53 *Die Zeit*, 25 September 1952. • 54 *Der Spiegel* 42 (1952), in a report on the political situation in France, which tellingly begins with resistance against the introduction of a "modesty law." • 55 Quoted from Steinbacher, p.110. • 56 Ibid., p.115.

VIII: The Re-educators

1 The handbook, entitled *Post Utilities Planning Handbook on Policy and Procedure for the Military Occupation of Western Europe and Norway following the Surrender of Germany*, was released on 9 September as an order in book form. Quoted from Uta Gerhardt, *Soziologie der Stunde Null. Zur Gesellschaftskonzeption des amerikanischen Besatzungsregimes in Deutschland 1944–1945/46* (Frankfurt am Main, 2005), p.150 ff. • 2 Ibid. • 3 Cf. Ina Merkel, *Kapitulation im Kino: Zur Kultur der Besatzung im Jahr 1945* (Berlin, 2016), p.79. • 4 Ibid. • 5 Hildegard Hamm-Brücher, 2002, in an interview with Marita Krauss, quoted from Marita Krauss, "Deutsch-amerikanische Kultur- und Presseoffiziere," in Arnd Bauerkämper, Konrad H. Jarausch and Marcus M. Payk (eds.), *Demokratiewunder. Transatlantische Mittler und die kulturelle Öffnung Westdeutschlands 1945–1970* (Göttingen, 2005), p.149. • 6 Many Germans feared that after the end of the war they would have to atone collectively for Nazi crimes. These anxieties were fed among other things by US Treasury Secretary Henry Morgenthau's plan, announced in September 1944, to roll Germany back to the status of an agrarian state so that it could never again fight an aggressive war.

However, President Franklin D. Roosevelt expressly rejected the plan, which was never intended to be put into action. The fear of collective punishment was further confirmed by posters which were displayed everywhere in the American zone in the summer of 1945. They included shocking pictures from the Bergen-Belsen concentration camp. Under the heading: "These atrocities: your fault" they included the words: "You looked on quietly and put up with this in silence. Why did you not wake up the German conscience with a cry of rage? That is your grievous fault. You share responsibility for these dreadful crimes" (cf. Klaus-Jörg Ruhl, *Die Besatzer und die Deutschen. Amerikanische Zone 1945-48* [Bindlach/Düsseldorf, 1989]). Here they were clearly talking about shared responsibility. But the Allies never seriously considered collective guilt in terms of law, international law and politics. No war crimes trial waived the demonstration of personal guilt. Rather the theory of collective guilt supported by the Allies led many incriminated Germans to disavow the denazification measures as "victors' justice." • 7 *Die Neue Zeitung*, 25 October 1945. • 8 *Die Neue Zeitung*, 4 November 1945. Jaspers's concept of guilt, however, is significantly more complicated than he could have shown in a short newspaper article. In January and February he delivered lectures on "Germany's political accountability," in which collective guilt, not legally pursuable but palpable to the individual, had a large part to play. In 1946 it was published as a book entitled *The Question of Guilt*. In it he confessed "that I feel a shared responsibility, in a manner that is not rationally comprehensible, indeed which can be rationally contradicted, for what Germans do or have done. I feel closer to the Germans who feel similarly, and further from those whose souls seem to deny this connection. And this closeness means above all the shared, exhilarating task of not being German as one is, but as one should be, and as we hear from the call of our ancestors, not from the history of national idols." Karl Jaspers, *Die Schuldfrage* (Munich, 2012), p.60 ff. • 9 Quoted from Marcus Hajdu, *"Du hast einen anderen Geist als wir!" Die "große Kontroverse" um Thomas Mann 1945-1949*, dissertation (Giessen, 2002), p.15. • 10 Quoted from ibid., p.20. • 11 Quoted from Schoeller, *Diese merkwürdige Zeit. Leben nach der Stunde Null. Ein Textbuch aus der "Neuen Zeitung"* (Frankfurt am Main, 2005), p.50. • 12 Alfred Döblin, *Ausgewählte Werke in Einzelbänden*, vol. 19 (Olten, 1980), p.497. • 13 Günther Weisenborn, *Döblins Rückkehr*. Quoted from Harald Jähner and Krista Tebbe (eds.), *Alfred Döblin zum Beispiel. Stadt und Literatur* (Berlin, 1987), p.132. • 14 *Neues Deutschland*, 19 November 1949. • 15 Irina Liebmann, *Wäre es schön? Es wäre schön. Mein Vater Rudolf Herrnstadt* (Berlin, 2008), p.398. • 16 Ibid., pp.320, 322, 358. • 17 *Der Stern* 25 (1952), quoted from Tim Tolsdorff, *Von der Sternschnuppe zum Fixstern: Zwei deutsche Illustrierte und ihre gemeinsame Geschichte vor und nach 1945* (Cologne, 2014), p.415. • 18 The title of Nannen's article was particularly perfidious. The headline GET THIS VILLAIN

OUT OF GERMANY! uses almost exactly the same words with which Karl Kraus invited Hans Habe's father Imre Békessy to leave Austria: GET THIS VILLAIN OUT OF VIENNA! Békessy, publisher of Vienna's afternoon paper *Die Stimme,* was suspected of demanding money if one wanted to be mentioned in his paper or, conversely, if one wanted to prevent such a mention. The Hungarian is supposed to have presented his victims with "revelation texts," which he threw into the waste-paper basket in return for payment. His son János Békessy had to endure abuse and scandal which then extended to the rest of his family, and they had to move temporarily back to Hungary. Returning to Austria, he preferred to change his name, and to form his name out of the double initials: "Ha" (H) for Hans, the German equivalent to János, and "Be" (B) for Békessy. That was how Hans Habe came into being. This was a family tradition: his father Imre Békessy had renamed himself in his youth; his father's name had been Meyer Friedleber. • 19 Cf. Hermann Schreiber, *Henri Nannen. Drei Leben* (Munich, 1999). • 20 Cf. Henning Röhl, "'Freundliche Grüße von Feind zu Feind.' Henri Nannen und Hans Habe," *Spiegel Online,* 18 December 2013. http://www.spiegel.de/einestages/henri-nannen-und-hans-habe-journalisten-freund-schaft-zwischen-feinden-a-951334.html, last retrieved on 9 December 2017. • 21 *Der Spiegel* 44 (1954). • 22 Quoted from ibid. • 23 After years of disputes with the German Compensation Office he received a total of 28,000 DM for the "period of damage," as forced exile was then known to the authorities. Cf. Schoeller, p.782. • 24 Quoted from ibid. • 25 Alfred Döblin, "Schicksalsreise," in *idem, Autobiographische Schriften und letzte Aufzeichnungen* (Olten und Freiburg im Breisgau, 1977), p.376. • 26 Ludwig Marcuse, "Gebt Döblin den Nobelpreis," in *Aufbau,* 4 September 1953, quoted from Jähner and Tebbe, p.139. • 27 Quoted from Jähner and Tebbe, p.142.

IX: The Cold War of Art and the Design of Democracy

1 One example of many: "We don't need to be ashamed of the tears that were shed in those first concerts after the war, in bare, cold halls, in bombed-out churches, when we heard Beethoven or Mozart again for the first time, as for example by the Wilhelm Stross Quartet, or Fischer-Dieskau's first *Winterreise.* How many people were shaken to discover that there was now fundamentally one necessity only: to live again from within." Gustav Rudolf Sellner in Heinz Friedrich (ed.), *Mein Kopfgeld—Rückblicke nach vier Jahrzehnten* (Munich, 1988), p.111. • 2 Cf. Henning Ritschbieter, "Bühnenhunger," in Hermann Glaser, Lutz von Pufendorf and Michael Schöneich (eds.), *So viel Anfang war nie. Deutsche Städte 1945–1949* (Berlin, 1989), p.226. • 3 Ruth Andreas-Friedrich, *Der Schattenmann. Tagebuchaufzeichnungen 1938–1948* (Berlin, 2000), p.385. • 4 Quoted from Ina Merkel, *Kapitulation im Kino: Zur Kultur der Besatzung im Jahr 1945*

(Berlin, 2016), p.250. • 5 Quoted from Niels Kadritzke, "Führer befiel, wir lachen!" in *Süddeutsche Zeitung*, 19 May 2010. • 6 Ibid. • 7 Quoted from Thomas Brandlmeier, "Von Hitler zu Adenauer. Deutsche Trümmerfilme," in Deutsches Filmmuseum (ed.), *Zwischen Gestern und Morgen, Westdeutscher Nachkriegsfilm 1946–1962* (Frankfurt am Main, 1989), p. 44. • 8 Ulrike Weckel has tried to illuminate this most thoroughly in the form of "qualitatively historic reception research." Ulrike Weckel, "Zeichen der Scham. Reaktionen auf alliierte *atrocity*-Filme im Nachkriegsdeutschland," in *Mittelweg 36*, vol. 1 (2014), p.3 ff. • 9 Cf. Merkel, p.262 ff. • 10 Quoted from Markus Krause, *Galerie Gerd Rosen. Die Avantgarde in Berlin 1945–1950* (Berlin, 1995), p.42. • 11 Cf. Kathleen Schröter, "Kunst zwischen den Systemen. Die Allgemeine Deutsche Kunstausstellung 1946 in Dresden," in Nikola Doll, Ruth Heftrig, Olaf Peters and Ulrich Rehm, *Kunstgeschichte nach 1945. Kontinuität und Neubeginn in Deutschland* (Cologne, Weimar, Vienna, 2006), p.229. • 12 Cf. Glaser, von Pufendorf and Schöneich, p.61. • 13 *Die Frau—Ihr Kleid, ihre Arbeit, ihre Freude* 4 (1946). • 14 *Der Standpunkt—Die Zeitschrift für die Gegenwart* (1946). • 15 "Dictatorship by consent" is a central concept from Götz Aly's rich investigations into the mass character of the National Socialist ethnic state, which enjoyed a great following on a broad basis as long as it spoiled the population with social benefits at the expense of the plundered Jews and the occupied countries. Götz Aly, *Hitlers Volksstaat. Raub, Rassenkrieg und nationaler Sozialismus* (Frankfurt am Main, 2005). • 16 Hans Habe, "Freiheit des Geschmacks," in *Die Neue Zeitung*, 17 December 1945. • 17 Quoted from Krause, p.41. • 18 Cf. Christian Borngräber, "Nierentisch und Schrippendale. Hinweise auf Architektur und Design," in Dieter Bänsch (ed.), *Die fünfziger Jahre. Beiträge zu Politik und Kultur* (Tübingen, 1985), p.222. • 19 Quoted from Alfred Nemeczek, "Der Ursprung der Abstraktion. Der große Bilderstreit," in *art—das Kunstmagazin* 5 (2002). • 20 Dieter Honisch, "Der Beitrag Willi Baumeisters zur Neubestimmung der Kunst in Deutschland," in Angela Schneider (ed.), *Willi Baumeister. Katalog zur Ausstellung in der Nationalgalerie Berlin*, Staatliche Museen Preußischer Kulturbesitz (Berlin, 1989), p.82. • 21 Ibid. • 22 Cf. Martin Warnke, "Von der Gegenständlichkeit und der Ausbreitung der Abstrakten," in Bänsch, p.214. • 23 Alexander Dymschitz, "Über die formalistische Richtung in der deutschen Malerei. Bemerkungen eines Außenstehenden," in *Tägliche Rundschau*, 19 November 1948, p.11. The curious combination of precise knowledge of the art scene, a sensitive gift for description and unpleasant dogmatism is clear in a passage in which Dymschitz describes the plight in which the artist Karl Hofer, Director of the Berlin Academy of Fine Art from July 1945, found himself as a result of the gradual dominance of abstract art in the West which was already making its presence felt in 1947: "The rejection of realism leads to a boundless impoverishment of artistic creativity. We can observe this quite easily by studying the works of a master, as Professor Karl Hofer indubitably is. We need only to cast a glance at the paintings and prints of his last exhibitions to persuade ourselves that the formalistic positions plunged this outstanding artist into a tragic crisis. The world and humanity, the main thing, the most important subject of art, are impoverished by him to an incredible degree because he allows himself to be governed by a constantly and monotonously repeated style. The complex richness of the world is simplified, the diversity of human characters are swept aside by certain constantly employed masks that the artist runs through the brightly coloured scale of emotions. In place of vivid life Professor Hofer's paintings offer us a kind of mask theatre, a masquerade of passions, what we might call a Hoffmanniade [sic] in painting. But what person who really lives in and with the times recognizes himself in the contemplation of this carnival of monsters in Karl Hofer's tragic masks? The stubbornness with which this painter cultivates the forms of the falsification of reality is proof that in his art he is turning his back on life and moving into a world of fantasies which, like all subjectivist fantasies, do not survive the test of life." • 24 Quoted from Frances Stonor Saunders, *Who Paid the Piper? The CIA and the Cultural Cold War* (London, 2000), p.260. • 25 Cf. Niklas Becker: *Juro Kubicek. Metamorphosen der Linie*, dissertation at FU Berlin (Berlin, 2007). • 26 Cf. Stonor Saunders, p. 253. • 27 The book by Frances Stonor Saunders gives a precise insight into the cultural interventions of the CIA. • 28 The extent to which Kubicek had become the front man for the Cold War becomes clear from the fact that apart from Karl Hofer and Pablo Picasso he is the only painter that Alexandr Dymschitz mentions by name in his article on Formalism in German art in November 1948, even though he was not one of the most prominent German artists. Clearly America's commitment to Kubicek's career had not escaped the Soviets, which was why Dymschitz also introduced a sideswipe at the Western conduct of war: "Most of his [Kubicek's] paintings are a complete denial of reality, an unbounded caprice of the imagination, a play with empty forms and artificial constructions. Even where Kubitschek [sic] makes at least an attempt to address the material of reality, he immediately destroys the truth of life and presents his subjective idea of it as reality. This applies, for example, to one of his paintings depicting ruins after a bombing raid: the Formalist Kubitschek abstracts his depiction of reality and introduces a compositional order into chaos, as if the Anglo-American pilots, before their attacks on Berlin, had been something like pedantic geometry teachers." Alexander Dymschitz, "Über die formalistische Richtung in der deutschen Malerei. Bemerkungen eines Außenstehenden," in *Tägliche Rundschau*, 19 November 1948. • 29 Cf. Frank Möller, *Das Buch Witsch. Das schwindelerregende Leben des Verlegers Joseph Caspar Witsch* (Cologne, 2014). • 30 Borngräber, p.241. • 31 Christian de

Nuys-Henkelmann complains: "Its pseudo-organic form is, in its flatness, reduced to a two-dimensional optic, a synthesis of conformity (don't rub people up the wrong way), dynamic vigour (outraged optimism) and apparent openness (form and spread legs grant the viewer a view of the—clean—floor): "'Wir haben nichts zu verbergen.' Christian de Nuys-Henkelmann: Im milden Licht der Tütenlampe," in Hilmar Hoffmann and Heinrich Klotz (eds.), *Die Kultur unseres Jahrhunderts 1945–1960* (Düsseldorf, Vienna, New York, 1991), p.194. • 32 Alexander Koch, *Die Wohnung für mich* (Stuttgart, 1952). Quoted from Paul Maenz, *Die 50er Jahre* (Köln, 1984), p.130. • 33 *Die Frau—Ihr Kleid, ihre Arbeit, ihre Freude* (1946). • 34 Quoted from Jutta Beder, *Zwischen Blümchen und Picasso. Textildesign der fünfziger Jahre in Westdeutschland* (Münster, 2002), p.20. • 35 This is also given voice in the dedication found inside the building, a quotation from Benjamin Franklin: "God grant that not only the love of liberty but a thorough knowledge of the rights of man may pervade all the nations of the earth, so that a philosopher may set his foot anywhere on its surface and say: This is my country."

X: The Sound of Repression

1 Cf. Carl Zuckmayer, *Deutschlandbericht für das Kriegsministerium der Vereinigten Staaten* (Göttingen, 2004), p.228. • 2 Cord Arendes, *Schrecken aus dem Untergrund: Endphaseverbrechen des "Werwolf,"* in Cord Arendes, Edgar Wolfrum and Jörg Zedler (eds.), *Terror nach innen: Verbrechen am Ende des Zweiten Weltkrieges* (Wallstein, Göttingen, 2006), p.150. • 3 Stefan Heym, *Nachruf* (Berlin, 1990), p.388. • 4 Erika Neuhäußer, "Was ist deutsch? Das deutsche Problem und die Welt," in *Der Standpunkt. Die Zeitschrift für die Gegenwart*, vol. 1, year 2 (1947). • 5 Heinrich Schacht, "Vom neuen Geist des Lehramts," in *Der Standpunkt. Die Zeitschrift für die Gegenwart*, vol. 2, year 1 (1946). • 6 Wolfgang Rothermel, "Ist es noch zu früh," in *Der Standpunkt. Die Zeitschrift für die Gegenwart*, vol. 6–7, year 2 (1947). • 7 "Wo stehen wir heute?" in *Die Zeit*, 28 February 1946. • 8 Hans Schwippert, "Theorie und Praxis," in *Die Städte himmeloffen. Reden und Reflexionen über den Wiederaufbau des Untergegangenen und die Wiederkehr des Neuen Bauens, 1948–49. Ausgewählt aus den ersten beiden Heften der Vierteljahreshefte "Baukunst und Werkform" von Ulrich Conrads* (Basel, 2002), p.15. • 9 Theodor W. Adorno, "Auferstehung der Kultur in Deutschland?" in *Frankfurter Hefte. Zeitschrift für Kultur und Politik*, vol. 5, no. 5, May 1950, pp. 469–72. • 10 The lively intellectual life of his students even reminded Adorno of that of the murdered Jews. In a letter to Thomas Mann at the end of December 1949 he remarked that in his Frankfurt Seminar he sometimes felt as if he were in a Talmud school: "Sometimes I feel as if the spirits of the murdered Jews had entered the German intellectuals." Theodor W. Adorno /

Thomas Mann, *Briefwechsel 1943–1955* (Frankfurt am Main, 2002), p.46. Adorno's comparison seemed quite macabre even to himself. Shortly afterwards he told Leo Löwenthal about his letter to Thomas Mann: "I wrote to LA that it was as if the spirits of the Jewish intellectuals had entered the German students. Quietly uncanny. But for that very reason, in the authentically Freudian sense, also infinitely familiar." Quoted from Ansgar Martins, *Adorno und die Kabbala* (Potsdam, 2016), p.52. • 11 Hannah Arendt's duties as an official with the organisation Jewish Cultural Reconstruction consisted of securing what remained of the ruins of Jewish culture. She had to view Jewish cultural assets stolen by the Nazis that had been stored in library archives and museum storerooms and to begin negotiations concerning the transfer of the objects to Jewish cultural organisations. In many cases one could not talk about "returning" the items, because the former owners had been murdered or could no longer be found. Hannah Arendt was convinced, like the majority of Jews around the world, that Jewish cultural assets, particularly what was called heirless property, belonged in the hands of the Jewish people, as represented among other things by the World Jewish Congress. The small remaining Jewish communities in Germany were, understandably, of another opinion and claimed the stolen cultural assets either entirely or partly for themselves. This gave rise to a painful conflict which was not primarily concerned with material values, but with questions of self-assertion, Jewish identity and the future of Jewish community life in Germany. Hannah Arendt considered the latter impossible after the Holocaust; the degree to which that was a question of honour for her is reflected in her harsh assessment about the German Jews who had survived and decided to stay in Germany. She was still in contact with most of the Germans she had known before, and wrote to her husband, Heinrich Blücher, in New York: "They trust me, I still speak their language. The only terrible ones are the so-called German Jews, the communities are thieving communities, everything has run to seed and is extremely mean and vulgar. If I can't do it any more I will flee to the American Jewish organisations." Hannah Arendt, Heinrich Blücher, *Briefe 1936–1968* (Munich, Zürich, 1996), p.185. • 12 For example the German translation of her essay "Aftermath of the Nazi Rule. Report from Germany," which was published in 1950 in the US and only 36 years later in Germany, under the title "Ein Besuch in Deutschland" ("A Visit to Germany"). • 13 Hannah Arendt, "Ein Besuch in Deutschland," in *idem., Zur Zeit. Politische Essays* (Berlin, 1986), pp.44–52. • 14 In Hannah Arendt's work the sense of "living ghosts" is a distant echo of her depiction of the "living dead" in the concentration camps in her book *The Origins of Totalitarianism*, published in New York in 1951, in which she describes how people were killed even if they physically remained alive. The end result is "inanimate men, i.e., men who can no longer be psychologically understood, whose return to the psychologically or otherwise intelligibly human world closely resembles the resurrection of Lazarus" (p.442). "The real horror of the concentration and extermination camps lies in the fact that the inmates, even if they happen to keep alive, are more effectively cut off from the world of the living than if they had died" (p.444). Elsewhere she speaks of the systematic dehumanisation that preceded extermination in the camps. She writes about the "preparation of living corpses" that was preceded by the "insane mass manufacture of corpses," when millions of people were rendered homeless, stateless, deprived of their rights and rendered economically superfluous and socially undesirable (p.448). The dehumanisation practised on the victims also has an effect on the nature of the perpetrators. They, too, become inhuman. • 15 Arendt, *Aftermath of Nazi Rule*, p.xx. • 16 Theodor W. Adorno, Thomas Mann, *Correspondence 1943–1955*. Adorno felt the pull of repression even on himself: "That these events elude all adequate experience also has the paradoxical results that one hardly realises this fact. If I am honest I must confess I always need a moment of reflection to remember that my neighbour on the tram might have been an executioner" (ibid.). • 17 This is one example among many, from Erich Müller-Gangloff, "Die Erscheinungsformen des Bösen," in: *Merkur* 3 (1949), p.1182. • 18 An abbreviated quotation from Friedrich Kießling, *Die undeutschen Deutschen. Eine ideengeschichtliche Archäologie der alten Bundesrepublik* (Paderborn, 2012), p.87. It was trimmed for the sake of better readability from the following passage: "New thoughts are spreading across Europe. The bearers of this European reawakening are mostly young and unknown. They do not come from the silence of studies—they have had no time for that—but straight from the armed battle for Europe, from action. From here there stretches a thin, very daring rope across the abyss to another group of young Europeans who have deployed the whole of their persons in reckless devotion over the last few years. We mean young Germany. It stood for a wrong cause. But it stood." • 19 The text begins questionably enough with the depiction of Europe as an "anthill," moving on to a soldierly disdain for the quiet world of learning, to an understanding of the martial attitude as the shared quality in which the enemies of the past could be respected as the like-minded associates of the present. • 20 Wolfdietrich Schnurre, "Unterm Fallbeil der Freiheit," in *Neue Zeitung*, 9 January 1948. • 21 Quoted from Benjamin Möckel, *Erfahrungsbruch und Generationsbehauptung. Die "Kriegsjugendgeneration" in den beiden deutschen Nachkriegsgesellschaften* (Göttingen, 2014), p.330. • 22 Ruth Andreas-Friedrich, *Der Schattenmann. Tagebuchaufzeichnungen 1938–1948* (Berlin, 2000), p.399. • 23 Arendt, *The Aftermath of Nazi Rule*, p.xx. • 24 Jan Philipp Reemtsma, *200 Tage und ein Jahrhundert*, quoted from Steffen Radlmaier (ed.), *Der Nürnberger Lernprozess. Von Kriegsverbrechern und Starreportern* (Frankfurt am Main, 2001). • 25 *Süddeutsche Zeitung*, 30 November 1945, quoted from Klaus R. Scherpe (ed.), *In Deutschland unterwegs. 1945–1948. Reportagen, Skizzen, Berichte* (Stuttgart, 1982), p.308. • 26 Hans Fiedeler (the pseudonym of Alfred Döblin), *Der Nürnberger Lehrprozess* (Baden-Baden, 1946), quoted from Radlmaier, p.47. • 27 Cf. Alfred Döblin, *Journal 1952/53*, in *Schriften zu Leben und Werk* (Olten und Freiburg im Breisgau, 1986), p.386. • 28 The historian Ulrich Herbert's account of the success of the denazification process is ambivalent, and consequently a lot more telling than some produced over the following decades: "For all of the inadequacies and injustices—and given the scale of this massive experiment affecting the whole of society these were presumably inevitable—it [the denazification process] made a considerable contribution towards holding German society and its leadership groups responsible for the politics of National Socialist Germany: this applied to both active National Socialists and those who took part in the Nazi crimes. It named them, isolated them and, at least for a time, kept them out of office and away from public influence. For most Germans their own experiences, the Allied educational campaigns, the denazification process or even just the instinct towards political conformity did not just block National Socialism but rendered it taboo as a system of rule; which is not to say that some parts of the ideological and political legacy of the dictatorship did not continue to have an effect." • Ulrich Herbert (ed.), *Wandlungsprozesse in Westdeutschland 1945–1980* (Göttingen, 2002), p.571. • 29 Quoted from Martin Broszat et al. (eds.), *Deutschlands Weg in die Diktatur. Internationale Konferenz zur nationalsozialistischen Machtübernahme im Reichstagsgebäude zu Berlin. Referate und Diskussionen. Ein Protokoll* (Berlin, 1983), p.351. • 30 Cf. reflections on the subject by the young historian Hanne Leßau during the Fifth International Conference on Holocaust Research in Berlin: "For example where the *Persilschein* was concerned I was primarily interested in really asking: How did that work? Nobody had done it before. How did people go to other people and ask, how do you do that? How do you ask for your testimony? And that's very interesting overall because very current prejudices—and for that reason I'm not going to call it a *Perslischein*—simply can't be confirmed. It's complicated for people. It's not pleasant to ask people for something like that. And there are many limits to the testifiable, as I call it. So there are absolute limits on what one would be willing to say for the other person. And that simply doesn't match the familiar picture of 'There was bartering, buying and lying.' I think we have to differentiate." Hanne Leßau verbally on the radio feature "Umgang mit den Verbrechen der Nachkriegszeit" by Bettina Mittelstrauß, accessible at: http://www.deutschland funk.de/konferenz-umgang-mit-den-ns-verbrechen-in-der-nachkriegszeit .1148.de.html?dram:article_id=310158; last retrieved 10 February 2018. • 31 Hermann Lübbe, "Der Nationalsozialismus im politischen Bewußtsein der

Gegenwart. Abschlußvortrag," in Martin Broszat et al. (eds.), *Deutschlands Weg in die Diktatur. Internationale Konferenz zur nationalsozialistischen Machtübernahme im Reichstagsgebäude zu Berlin. Referate und Diskussionen. Ein Protokoll* (Berlin, 1983), p.334. • 32 Norbert Frei, *Vergangenheitspolitik. Die Anfänge der Bundesrepublik und die NS-Vergangenheit* (Munich, 1996), p.15. • 33 Konrad Adenauer in the German Bundestag on 20 September 1949, in *Stenographische Berichte, 1st Term of Office, 5th Session.* p.27. • 34 Egon Bahr in an interview with Thomas Schmid and Jacques Schuster, published as "Wir hatten ein bisschen was anderes zu tun" in *Die Welt*, 29 October 2010. • 35 Quoted from Klaus Behling, *Die Kriminalgeschichte der DDR* (Berlin, 2017). • 36 Here we should particularly mention Benjamin Möckel, who describes the social negotiation process behind the individual and collective post-war silences on the basis of Jay Winter's concept of a "Social Construction of Silence." Philipp Gassert provides a good overview of the state of research in "Zwischen 'Beschweigen' und 'Bewältigen': Die Auseinandersetzung mit dem Nationalsozialismus der Ära Adenauer," in Michael Hochgeschwender, *Epoche im Widerspruch. Ideelle und kulturelle Umbrüche der Adenauerzeit* (Bonn, 2011). • 37 Cf. Frei, p.16.

Afterword

1 Cf. Schoeller, *Döblin. Eine Biographie* (Munich, 2011), p.656. • 2 Hans Habe, *Off Limits*, trans. Ewald Osers (London, 1956), p.119. • 3 Flyer from the collection of Hannes Schwenger, quoted from Ulrich Ott and Friedrich Pfäfflin (eds.), *Protest! Literatur um 1968*, Marbacher Kataloge 51 (Marbach am Neckar, 1998), p.43. • 4 Hans Magnus Enzensberger, *Berliner Gemeinplätze II, Kursbuch 13* (Frankfurt am Main, 1968), p.191. • 5 Edgar Wolfrum, "Geschichte der Erinnerungskultur in der BRD und DDR," in *Dossier Geschichte und Erinnerung der Bundeszentrale für politische Bildung* (2008). Downloadable at: https:// www.bpb.de/geschichte/zeitgeschichte/geschichte-und-erinnerung/39814 /geschichte-der-erinnerungskultur?p=all • 6 Ibid. • 7 Karl Jaspers, *Die Schuldfrage. Von der politischen Haftung Deutschlands* (Munich, Berlin, 2012), p.15. • 8 Ibid., p.8.

Bibliography

Abelshauser, Werner, *Deutsche Wirtschaftsgeschichte. Von 1945 bis zur Gegenwart* (Munich, 2011)

Adorno, Theodor W., "Auferstehung der Kultur in Deutschland?," in *Frankfurter Hefte. Zeitschrift für Kultur und Politik*, vol. 5 (May 1950)

Adorno, Theodor W., and Thomas Mann, *Briefwechsel 1943–1955* (Frankfurt am Main, 2002)

Aly, Götz, *Hitlers Volksstaat. Raub, Rassenkrieg und nationaler Sozialismus* (Frankfurt am Main, 2005)

———, *Volk ohne Mitte. Die Deutschen zwischen Freiheitsangst und Kollektivismus* (Frankfurt am Main, 2015)

Ander, Roland, *"Ich war auch eine Trümmerfrau, darum bin ich verärgert." Enttrümmerung und Abrisswahn in Dresden 1945–1989. Ein Beitrag zur ostdeutschen Baugeschichte* (Dresden, 2010)

Andreas-Friedrich, Ruth, *Der Schattenmann. Tagebuchaufzeichnungen 1938–1948* (Berlin, 2000)

Anonymous, *A Woman In Berlin*, trans. Philip Boehm (London, 2018)

Arendt, Hannah, *The Origins of Totalitarianism* (New York, 1973)

———, *Essays in Understanding 1930–1954* (New York, 1994)

——— and Heinrich Blücher, *Within Four Walls: The Correspondence between Hannah Arendt and Heinrich Blücher, 1936–1968*, trans. Peter Constantine (New York, 2000)

Arnold, Heinz Ludwig (ed.), *Die deutsche Literatur 1945–1960*, vol. 1 (Munich, 1995)

Bader, Karl S., *Soziologie der deutschen Nachkriegskriminalität* (Tübingen, 1949)

Bänsch, Dieter (ed.), *Die fünfziger Jahre. Beiträge zu Politik und Kultur* (Tübingen, 1985)

Bauerkämper, Arnd, Konrad H. Jarausch and Marcus M. Payk (eds.), *Demokratiewunder. Transatlantische Mittler und die kulturelle Öffnung Westdeutschlands 1945–1970* (Göttingen, 2005)

Baumeister, Willi, *Das Unbekannte in der Kunst* (Cologne, 1988)

————, *Werke 1945–1955. Katalog zur Ausstellung des Kunstvereins Göttingen* (Göttingen, 2000)

Becker, Niklas, *Juro Kubicek. Metamorphosen der Linie, Dissertation an der FU Berlin* (Berlin, 2007)

Beder, Jutta, *Zwischen Blümchen und Picasso. Textildesign der fünfziger Jahre in Westdeutschland* (Münster, 2002)

Behling, Klaus, *Die Kriminalgeschichte der DDR* (Berlin, 2017)

Beier, Rosmarie (ed.), *Aufbau West—Aufbau Ost. Die Planstädte Wolfsburg und Eisenhüttenstadt in der Nachkriegszeit. Buch zur Ausstellung des Deutschen Historischen Museums* (Ostfildern-Ruit, 1997)

Beil, Ralf (ed.), *Wolfsburg unlimited. Eine Stadt als Weltlabor* (Stuttgart, 2016)

Bendix, Werner, *Die Hauptstadt des Wirtschaftswunders. Frankfurt am Main 1945–1956*, Studien zur Frankfurter Geschichte 49 (Frankfurt am Main, 2002)

Bessen, Ursula, *Trümmer und Träume. Nachkriegszeit und fünfziger Jahre auf Zelluloid. Deutsche Spielfilme als Zeugnisse ihrer Zeit. Eine Dokumentation* (Bochum, 1989)

Bienert, René, Manfred Grieger and Susanne Urban, *Nachkriegswege nach Volkswagen. Jüdische Überlebende zwischen Befreiung und neuer Identität. Schriften zur Unternehmensgeschichte von Volkswagen*, vol. 5 (Wolfsburg, 2014)

Boehling, Rebecca, Susanne Urban and René Bienert (eds.), *Freilegungen. Überlebende—Erinnerungen Transformationen* (Göttingen, 2013)

Boelcke, Willi A., *Der Schwarzmarkt 1945–1948. Vom Überleben nach dem Kriege* (Braunschweig, 1986)

Böke, Karin, Frank Liedtke and Martin Wengeler, *Politische Leitvokabeln in der Adenauer-Ära* (Berlin, 1996)

Böll, Heinrich, *Heimat und keine. Schriften und Reden 1964–1968* (Munich, 1985)

Bollenbeck, Georg, and Gerhard Kaiser (eds.), *Die janusköpfigen 50er Jahre*, Kulturelle Moderne und bildungsbürgerliche Semantik 3 (Wiesbaden, 2000)

Bommarius, Christian, *Das Grundgesetz. Eine Biographie* (Berlin, 2009)

Borchert, Wolfgang, *Das Gesamtwerk* (Hamburg, 1959)

Borngräber, Christian, *Stil novo. Design in den 50er Jahren. Phantasie und Phantastik* (Frankfurt am Main, 1979)

Boveri, Margret, *Tage des Überlebens* (Berlin, 1945; Munich, Zürich, 1968)

Brauerhoch, Annette, *"Fräuleins" und GIs. Geschichte und Filmgeschichte* (Frankfurt am Main, Basel, 2006)

Breuer, Gerda, *Die Zähmung der Avantgarde. Zur Rezeption der Moderne in den 50er Jahren* (Frankfurt am Main, 1997)

Broszat, Martin, et al. (eds.), *Deutschlands Weg in die Diktatur. Internationale Konferenz zur nationalsozialistischen Machtübernahme im Reichstagsgebäude zu Berlin. Referate und Diskussionen. Ein Protokoll* (Berlin, 1983)

Broszat, Martin, Klaus-Dietmar Henke and Hans Woller (eds.), *Von Stalingrad zur Währungsreform. Zur Sozialgeschichte des Umbruchs in Deutschland* (Munich, 1988)

Burk, Henning, *Fremde Heimat. Das Schicksal der Vertriebenen nach 1945* (Bonn, 2011)

Buruma, Ian, *Year Zero: A History of 1945* (London, 2013)

Claasen, Hermann, *Gesang im Feuerofen. Überreste einer alten deutschen Stadt*, 2nd ed. (Düsseldorf, 1947, this ed. 1949)

Conrads, Ulrich (ed.), *Die Städte himmeloffen. Reden über den Wiederaufbau des Untergegangenen und die Wiederkehr des Neuen Bauens 1948/49* (Basel, 2002)

Dillmann, Claudia and Olaf Möller (eds.), *Geliebt und verdrängt. Das Kino der jungen Bundesrepublik von 1949 bis 1963* (Frankfurt am Main, 2016)

Diner, Dan (ed.), *Zivilisationsbruch. Denken nach Auschwitz* (Frankfurt am Main, 1988)

———, "Skizze zu einer jüdischen Geschichte der Juden in Deutschland nach '45." *Münchner Beiträge zur jüdischen Geschichte und Kultur* 1 (2010)

——— (ed.), *Enzyklopädie jüdischer Geschichte und Kultur*, vol. 4 (Stuttgart, 2013)

———, *Rituelle Distanz. Israels deutsche Frage* (Munich, 2015)

Döblin, Alfred, *Schicksalsreise*, in ders.: *Autobiographische Schriften und letzte Aufzeichnungen. Olten* (Freiburg im Breisgau, 1977)

Doll, Nikola, et al., *Kunstgeschichte nach 1945. Kontinuität und Neubeginn in Deutschland* (Cologne, Weimar, Vienna, 2006)

Domentat, Tamara, *"Hallo Fräulein." Deutsche Frauen und amerikanische Soldaten* (Berlin, 1998)

Ebner, Florian, and Ursula Müller (eds.), *So weit kein Auge reicht. Berliner Panoramafotografien aus den Jahren 1949–1952, aufgenommen vom Fotografen Tiedemann, rekonstruiert und interpretiert von Arwed Messmer. Ausstellungskatalog der Berlinischen Galerie* (Berlin, 2008)

Enzensberger, Hans Magnus, "Berliner Gemeinplätze II." *Kursbuch* 13 (1968)

———, *Gedichte 1950–1955* (Frankfurt am Main, 1996)

Euler-Schmidt, Michael, and Marcus Leifeld, *Der Kölner Rosenmontagszug*, 2 vols. (Cologne, 2007 and 2009)

Felsmann, Barbara, Annett Gröschner and Grischa Meyer (eds.), *Backfisch im Bombenkrieg. Notizen in Steno* (Berlin, 2013)

Förschler, Andreas, *Stuttgart 1945. Kriegsende und Neubeginn* (Gudensberg, 2004)

Frei, Norbert, *Vergangenheitspolitik. Die Anfänge der Bundesrepublik und die NS-Vergangenheit* (Munich, 1996)

Friedrich, Heinz (ed.), *Mein Kopfgeld—Rückblicke nach vier Jahrzehnten* (Munich, 1988)

Gebhardt, Miriam, *Als die Soldaten kamen. Die Vergewaltigung deutscher Frauen am Ende des Zweiten Weltkriegs* (Munich, 2015)

Gehltomholt, Eva, and Sabine Hering, *Das verwahrloste Mädchen. Diagnostik und Fürsorge in der Jugendhilfe zwischen Kriegsende und Reform (1945–1965)* (Opladen, 2006)

Gerhardt, Uta, *Soziologie der Stunde Null. Zur Gesellschaftskonzeption des amerikanischen Besatzungsregimes in Deutschland 1944–1945/46* (Frankfurt am Main, 2005)

Glaser, Hermann, *1945. Beginn einer Zukunft. Bericht und Dokumentation* (Frankfurt am Main, 2005)

Glaser, Hermann, Lutz von Pufendorf and Michael Schöneich (eds.), *So viel Anfang war nie. Deutsche Städte 1945–1949* (Berlin, 1989)

Greven, Michael Th., *Politisches Denken in Deutschland nach 1945. Erfahrungen und Umgang mit der Kontingenz in der unmittelbaren Nachkriegszeit* (Opladen, 2007)

Gries, Rainer, *Die Rationengesellschaft. Versorgungskampf und Vergleichsmentalität: Leipzig, München und Köln nach dem Kriege* (Münster, 1991)

Grisebach, Lucius (ed.), *Werner Heldt. Ausstellungskatalog der Berlinischen Galerie* (Berlin, 1989)

Grohmann, Will, *Willi Baumeister* (Stuttgart, 1952)

Habe, Hans, *Ich stelle mich* (Vienna, Munich, Basel, 1954)

———, *Off Limits*, trans. Ewald Osers (London, 1956)

———, *Im Jahre Null. Ein Beitrag zur Geschichte der deutschen Presse* (Munich, 1966)

Haber, Esther (ed.), *Displaced Persons. Jüdische Flüchtlinge nach 1945 in Hohenems und Bregenz* (Innsbruck, 1998)

Hajdu, Marcus, *"Du hast einen anderen Geist als wir!" Die "große Kontroverse" um Thomas Mann 1945–1949*, dissertation (Gießen, 2002)

Hein, Verena, *Werner Heldt (1904–1954). Leben und Werk* (Munich, 2016)

Henkel, Anne-Katrin, and Thomas Rahe, *Publizistik in jüdischen Displaced Persons Camps im Nachkriegsdeutschland*, Charakteristika, Medientypen und bibliothekarische Überlieferung (Frankfurt am Main, 2014)

Hentig, Hans von, *Die Kriminalität des Zusammenbruchs. Schweizerische Zeitschrift für Strafrecht* 62 (1947)

Herbert, Ulrich, *Geschichte Deutschlands im 20. Jahrhundert* (Munich, 2014)

——— (ed.), *Wandlungsprozesse in Westdeutschland 1945–1980* (Göttingen, 2002)

Herlyn, Ulfert, et al., *Faszination Wolfsburg 1938–2012* (Wiesbaden, 2012)

Hermlin, Stephan, *Bestimmungsorte. Fünf Erzählungen* (Berlin, 1985)

Heukenkamp, Ursula, *Unterm Notdach. Nachkriegsliteratur in Berlin 1945–1949* (Berlin, 1996)

Heyen, Franz-Josef, and Anton M. Keim (eds.), *Auf der Suche nach neuer Identität. Kultur in Rheinland-Pfalz im Nachkriegsjahrzehnt* (Mainz, 1996)

Heym, Stefan, *Nachruf* (Berlin, 1990)

Hirsch, Helga, *Endlich wieder leben. Die fünfziger Jahre im Rückblick von Frauen* (Berlin, 2012)

Hobrecht, Jürgen, *Beate Uhse. Chronik eines Lebens* (Flensburg, 2003)

Hochgeschwender, Michael (ed.), *Epoche im Widerspruch. Ideelle und kulturelle Umbrüche der Adenauerzeit*, Rhöndorfer Gespräche 25 (Bonn, 2011)

Höfling, Helmut, *Flucht ins Leben. Roman einer verführten Jugend* (Kindle, 2014)

Hyvernaud, Georges, *Haut und Knochen* (Berlin, 2010)

Jacobmeyer, Wolfgang, *Vom Zwangsarbeiter zum Heimatlosen Ausländer. Die Displaced Persons in Westdeutschland 1945–1951* (Göttingen, 1985)

Jacobs, Ingeborg, *Freiwild. Das Schicksal deutscher Frauen 1945* (Berlin, 2008)

Jarausch, Konrad, and Hannes Siegrist (eds.), *Amerikanisierung und Sowjetisierung in Deutschland 1945–1970* (Frankfurt am Main, New York, 1997)

Jaspers, Karl, *Die Schuldfrage* (Munich, 2012)

Judt, Tony, *Geschichte Europas von 1945 bis zur Gegenwart* (Munich, 2006)

Kardorff, Ursula von, *Berliner Aufzeichnungen 1942–1945* (Munich, 1992)

Kästner, Erich, *Notabene 45. Ein Tagebuch* (Hamburg, 2012)

Kießling, Friedrich, *Die undeutschen Deutschen. Eine ideengeschichtliche Archäologie der alten Bundesrepublik* (Paderborn, 2012)

Klausner, Helene, *Kölner Karneval zwischen Uniform und Lebensform* (Münster, 2007)

Knef, Hildegard, *Der geschenkte Gaul. Bericht aus einem Leben* (Vienna, Munich, Zürich, 1970)

Koeppen, Wolfgang, *Tauben im Gras* (Frankfurt am Main, 1974)

Königseder, Angelika, and Juliane Wetzel, *Lebensmut im Wartesaal. Die jüdischen DPs im Nachkriegsdeutschland* (Frankfurt am Main, 1994)

Koop, Volker, *Tagebuch der Berliner Blockade. Von Schwarzmarkt und Rollkommandos, Bergbau und Bienenzucht* (Bonn, 1999)

———, *Besetzt. Amerikanische Besatzungspolitik in Deutschland* (Berlin, 2006)

Kossert, Andreas, *Kalte Heimat. Die Geschichte der deutschen Vertriebenen nach 1945* (Munich, 2008)

Kowalczuk, Ilko-Sascha, and Stefan Wolle, *Roter Stern über Deutschland. Sowjetische Truppen in der DDR* (Berlin, 2010)

Krause, Markus, *Galerie Gerd Rosen. Die Avantgarde in Berlin 1945–1950* (Berlin, 1995)

Krauss, Marita, *Heimkehr in ein fremdes Land. Geschichte der Remigration nach 1945* (Munich, 2001)

Krauss, Marita, "Trümmerfrauen. Visuelles Konstrukt und Realität," in Paul Gerhard, (ed.), *Das Jahrhundert der Bilder 1900–1949* (Göttingen, 2009)

Kromer, Karl (ed.), *Schwarzmarkt, Tausch und Schleichhandel. In Frage und Antwort mit 500 Beispielen*, Recht für jeden 1 (Hamburg, 1947)

Kuhn, Annette (ed.), *Vol 2* (Düsseldorf, 1986)

Lau, Jörg, *Hans Magnus Enzensberger. Ein öffentliches Leben* (Berlin, 1999)

Lenz, Siegfried, *Lehmanns Erzählungen oder So schön war mein Markt* (Hamburg, 1964)

Lewinsky, Tamar, "Jüdische Displaced Persons im Nachkriegsmünchen." *Münchner Beiträge zur jüdischen Geschichte und Kultur* 1 (2010)

Liebmann, Irina, *Wäre es schön? Es wäre schön. Mein Vater Rudolf Herrnstadt* (Berlin, 2008)

Link, Alexander, *"Schrottelzeit"—Nachkriegsalltag in Mainz. Ein Beitrag zur subjektorientierten Betrachtung lokaler Vergangenheit*, Studien zur Volkskultur in Rheinland-Pfalz 8 (Mainz, 1990)

Lowe, Keith, *Savage Continent: Europe in the Aftermath of World War II* (London, 2012)

Lübbe, Hermann, "Der Nationalsozialismus im politischen Bewusstsein der Gegenwart," in Martin Broszat et al. (eds.), *Deutschlands Weg in die Diktatur. Internationale Konferenz zur nationalsozialistischen Machtübernahme* (Berlin, 1983)

Lüdtke, Alf, Inge Marßolek, and Adelheid von Saldern, *Amerikanisierung. Traum und Albtraum im Deutschland des 20. Jahrhunderts* (Stuttgart, 1996)

Maenz, Paul, *Die 50er Jahre* (Köln, 1984)

Manthey, Jürgen, *Hans Fallada* (Reinbek bei Hamburg, 1963)

Martin, Marko, "Die einzigen Wellen, auf denen ich reite, sind die des Lago Maggiore. Wer war Hans Habe? Eine Spurensuche," online at http://www.oeko-net.de/kommune/kommune1-98/KHABE.html, last retrieved December 2017

Martins, Ansgar, *Adorno und die Kabbala* (Potsdam, 2016)

McGovern, James, *Fräulein* (London, 1957)

Merkel, Ina, *Kapitulation im Kino: Zur Kultur der Besatzung im Jahr 1945* (Berlin, 2016)

Meyer, Sibylle, and Eva Schulze, *Wie wir das alles geschafft haben. Alleinstehende Frauen berichten über ihr Leben nach 1945* (Munich, 1984)

———, *Von Liebe sprach damals keiner. Familienalltag in der Nachkriegszeit* (Munich, 1985)

Mitscherlich, Alexander, *Gesammelte Schriften*, vol. 6 (Frankfurt am Main, 1986)

Mitscherlich, Alexander, and Margarete Mitscherlich, *Die Unfähigkeit zu trauern. Grundlagen kollektiven Verhaltens* (Munich, 1977)

Möckel, Benjamin, *Erfahrungsbruch und Generationsbehauptung. Die Kriegsjugendgeneration in den beiden deutschen Nachkriegsgesellschaften* (Göttingen, 2014)

Möller, Frank, *Das Buch Witsch. Das schwindelerregende Leben des Verlegers Joseph Caspar Witsch* (Cologne, 2014)

Mommsen, Hans, *Das Volkswagenwerk und seine Arbeiter im Dritten Reich* (Düsseldorf, 1996)

Mönnich, Horst, *Die Autostadt. Abenteuer einer technischen Idee* (Munich, 1958)

Mörchen, Stefan, *Schwarzer Markt. Kriminalität, Ordnung und Moral in Bremen 1939–1949* (Frankfurt am Main, 2011)

Müller-Enbergs, Helmut, *Der Fall Rudolf Herrnstadt. Tauwetterpolitik vor dem 17. Juni* (Berlin, 1991)

Naimark, Norman M., *Die Russen in Deutschland. Die sowjetische Besatzungszone 1945–1949* (Berlin, 1997)

Nemeczek, Alfred, "Der Ursprung der Abstraktion. Der große Bilderstreit." *art—das Kunstmagazin* 5 (2002)

Niethammer, Lutz, "*Hinterher merkt man, daß es richtig war, daß es schiefgegangen ist.*" *Nachkriegserfahrungen im Ruhrgebiet* (Berlin, Bonn, 1983)

———, *Deutschland danach. Postfaschistische Gesellschaft und nationales Gedächtnis,* ed. Ulrich Herbert and Dirk van Laak (Bonn, 1999)

Nuys-Henkelmann, Christian de, "Im milden Licht der Tütenlampe," in Hilmar Hoffmann and Heinrich Klotz (eds.), *Die Kultur unseres Jahrhunderts 1945–1960* (Düsseldorf, Vienna, New York, 1991)

Osses, Dietmar, *Zwischen Ungewissheit und Zuversicht. Kultur und Alltag polnischer Displaced Persons in Deutschland 1945–1955* (Essen, 2016)

Ott, Ulrich, and Friedrich Pfäfflin (eds.), *Protest! Literatur um 1968,* Marbacher Kataloge 51 (Marbach am Neckar, 1998)

Plato, Alexander von, and Almut Leh, "*Ein unglaublicher Frühling.*" *Erfahrene Geschichte im Nachkriegsdeutschland 1945–1948* (Bonn, 1997)

Pletzing, Christian, and Marcus Velke (eds.), *Lager—Repatriierung—Integration. Beiträge zur Displaced Persons-Forschung* (Leipzig, 2016)

Prinz, Friedrich, and Marita Krauss (eds.), *Trümmerleben. Texte, Dokumente, Bilder aus den Münchner Nachkriegsjahren* (Munich, 1985)

Radlmaier, Steffen (ed.), *Der Nürnberger Lernprozess. Von Kriegsverbrechern und Starreportern* (Frankfurt am Main, 2001)

Rathke, Christian, *Die 50er Jahre. Aspekte und Tendenzen* (Wuppertal, 1977)

Reese, Beate (ed.), *Befreite Moderne. Kunst in Deutschland 1945 bis 1949, anlässlich der gleichnamigen Ausstellung im Kunstmuseum Mülheim an der Ruhr* (Berlin, Munich, 2015)

Riederer, Günter, "Die Barackenstadt. Wolfsburg und seine Lager nach 1945," in *Deutschland Archiv, Bundeszentrale für politische Bildung* (Bonn, 2013)

Roesler, Jörg, *Momente deutsch-deutscher Wirtschafts und Sozialgeschichte 1945–1990* (Leipzig, 2006)

Ruhl, Klaus-Jörg (ed.), *Deutschland 1945. Alltag zwischen Krieg und Frieden* (Neuwied, 1984)

———, *Die Besatzer und die Deutschen. Amerikanische Zone 1945–1948* (Bindlach, Düsseldorf, 1989)

Schäfke, Werner, *Kölns schwarzer Markt 1939 bis 1949. Ein Jahrzehnt asoziale Marktwirtschaft* (Cologne, 2014)

Schelsky, Helmut, *Die skeptische Generation. Eine Soziologie der deutschen Jugend* (Düsseldorf, Cologne, 1957)

———, *Auf der Suche nach Wirklichkeit* (Cologne, 1965)

Schenk, Dieter, *Auf dem rechten Auge blind. Die braunen Wurzeln des BKA* (Cologne, 2001)

Scherpe, Klaus R. (ed.), *In Deutschland unterwegs 1945–1948. Reportagen, Skizzen, Berichte* (Stuttgart, 1982)

Schildt, Axel, *Moderne Zeiten. Freizeit, Massenmedien und "Zeitgeist" in der Bundesrepublik der 50er Jahre* (Hamburg, 1995)

Schneider, Angela (ed.), *Willi Baumeister. Katalog zur Ausstellung in der Nationalgalerie Berlin* (Berlin, 1989)

Schoeller, Wilfried F. (ed.), *Diese merkwürdige Zeit. Leben nach der Stunde Null. Ein Textbuch aus der "Neuen Zeitung"* (Frankfurt am Main, 2005)

———, *Döblin. Eine Biographie* (Munich, 2011)

Schörken, Rolf, *Jugend 1945. Politisches Denken und Lebensgeschichte* (Frankfurt am Main, 1990)

———, *Die Niederlage als Generationserfahrung. Jugendliche nach dem Zusammenbruch der NS-Herrschaft* (Weinheim, 2004)

Schreiber, Hermann, *Henri Nannen. Drei Leben* (Munich, 1999)

Schulz, Bernhard, *Grauzonen Farbwelten—Kunst und Zeitbilder 1945–1955* (Berlin, 1983)

Seidl, Claudius, *Der deutsche Film der fünfziger Jahre* (Munich, 1987)

Sieburg, Friedrich, *Abmarsch in die Barbarei* (Stuttgart, 1983)

Steen, Uta van, *Liebesperlen. Beate Uhse—eine deutsche Karriere* (Hamburg, 2003)

Steinbacher, Sybille, *Wie der Sex nach Deutschland kam. Der Kampf um Sittlichkeit und Anstand in der frühen Bundesrepublik* (Berlin, 2011)

Stölzl, Christoph (ed.), *Die Wolfsburg-Saga. Stuttgart 2008. Stonor Saunders, Frances: Wer die Zeche zahlt . . . Der CIA und die Kultur im Kalten Krieg* (Berlin, 2001)

Sträßner, Matthias, *"Erzähl mir vom Krieg!" Ruth Andreas-Friedrich, Ursula von Kardorff, Margret Boveri und Anonyma: Wie vier Journalistinnen 1945 ihre Berliner Tagebücher schreiben* (Würzburg, 2014)

Strelka, Joseph P., *Hans Habe. Autor der Menschlichkeit* (Tübingen, 2017)

Tebbe, Krista, and Harald Jähner (eds.), *Alfred Döblin zum Beispiel. Stadt und Literatur* (Berlin, 1987)

Tewes, Frank, *125 Jahre Große Kölner. 125 Jahre Karnevals geschichte* (Cologne, 2007)

Timm, Uwe, *Ikarien* (Cologne, 2017)

Tischler, Carola, *Flucht in die Verfolgung. Deutsche Emigranten im sowjetischen Exil 1933 bis 1945* (Münster, 1996)

Tolsdorff, Tim, *Von der Sternschnuppe zum Fixstern: Zwei deutsche Illustrierte und ihre gemeinsame Geschichte vor und nach 1945* (Cologne, 2014)

Treber, Leonie, *Mythos Trümmerfrauen. Von der Trümmerbeseitigung in der Kriegs- und Nachkriegszeit und der Entstehung eines deutschen Erinnerungsortes* (Essen, 2014)

Trittel, Günter J., *Hunger und Politik. Die Ernährungskrise in der Bizone 1945–1949* (Frankfurt am Main, New York, 1990)

Uhse, Beate (with Ilonka Kunow), *Lustvoll in den Markt. Strategien für schwierige Märkte* (Planegg, 2000)

Völklein, Ulrich, *"Mitleid war von niemandem zu erwarten." Das Schicksal der deutschen Vertriebenen* (Munich, 2005)

Weckel, Ulrike, *"Zeichen der Scham. Reaktionen auf alliierte atro-city-Filme im Nachkriegsdeutschland." Mittelweg 36*, vol. 1 (2014)

Wehler, Hans-Ulrich, *Deutsche Gesellschaftsgeschichte. Vom Beginn des Ersten Weltkriegs bis zur Gründung der beiden deutschen Staaten 1914–1949* (Munich, 2003)

Weiss, Winfried, *A Nazi Childhood* (Santa Barbara, 1983)

Weyrauch, Wolfgang (ed.), *Tausend Gramm. Ein deutsches Bekenntnis in dreißig Geschichten aus dem Jahr 1949* (Reinbek bei Hamburg, 1989)

Wolfrum, Edgar, *"Geschichte der Erinnerungskultur in der BRD und DDR,"* in *Dossier Geschichte und Erinnerung der Bundeszentrale für politische Bildung*, 26 August 2008, available at: https://www.bpb.de/geschichte/zeitgeschichte/geschichte-und-erinnerung/39814/geschichte-der-erinnerungskultur?p=all, last retrieved September 2018

Ziegner, Sylvia, *Der Bildband "Dresden—eine Kamera klagt an" von Richard Peter senior. Teil der Erinnerungskultur Dresdens* (Marburg, 2010)

Zierenberg, Malte, *Stadt der Schieber. Der Berliner Schwarzmarkt 1939–1950* (Göttingen, 2008)

Zuckmayer, Carl, *Deutschlandbericht für das Kriegsministerium der Vereinigten Staaten* (Göttingen, 2004)

Periodicals

Bildhefte der Jugend, 1950

Constanze—die Zeitschrift für die Frau und für jedermann, 1948–52

Der Regenbogen. Zeitschrift für die Frau, 1946–52

Der Spiegel, 1947–55

Der Standpunkt. Zeitschrift für die Gegenwart, 1946–48

Die Frau—Ihr Kleid, ihre Arbeit, ihre Freude, 1946–49

Die Wandlung, 1945–49

Die Zeit, 1946–55

DND—Die Neue Demokratie. Illustrierte Wochenschrift in der französischen Zone, 1946–48

Ende und Anfang. Zeitung der jungen Generation, 1946–49

Er—Die Zeitschrift für den Herrn, 1950–55

Filmpost, 1947

Frankfurter Hefte. Zeitschrift für Kultur und Politik, 1946–50

Ja—Zeitung der jungen Generation, 1947–48

Lilith—Zeitschrift für junge Mädchen und Frauen, 1946–47

Magnum—Die Zeitschrift für das moderne Leben, 1954–59

Merkur 3, 1949

Neue Berliner Illustrierte, 1945–55

Neue Illustrierte, 1946–55

Sie, 1946

Zeitschrift für Kunst, 1948

Index

Page numbers of photographs and their captions appear in italics.

Illustration Credits

Frontispiece: in Reinhard Matz, and Wolfgang Vollmer: *Köln und der Krieg: Leben, Kultur, Stadt. 1940–1950*. Köln, 2016

p. 4: ullstein bild—Röhnert

p. 10: Sueddeutsche Zeitung Photo / Alamy Stock Photo

p. 21: SLUB / Deutsche Fotothek, Richard Peter sen.

p. 25: picture alliance / ZB / Richard Peter Jun

pp. 30-1: Hermann Claasen, *Fronleichnamsprozession, Köln 1945*. Fotografische Sammlung LVR—landesmuseum Bonn, photo: Jürgen Vogel

p. 32: Münchner Stadtmuseum, Sammlung Fotografie, Archiv Relang

p. 35: Josef Stoffels / Fotoarchiv Ruhr Museum

p. 37: Anja Elisabeth Witte / Berlinische Galerie (© DACS 2021)

p. 41: Public domain, from *United States Army Preventive Medicine in World War II*; Office of the Surgeon General, Department of the Army, Washington, D.C. (1969)

p. 47: dpa-Bildarchiv

p. 58: *Landsberger Lager-Cajtung*, 8 October 1945

p. 60: Stadtarchiv Geretsried, photo by Günther Fechner

p. 71: Fred Ramage / Hulton Archive: Getty Images

p. 85: Bundesarchiv, Bild 183-P0506-507 / Herbert Blunck

p. 93: Heinrich Sanden Sr. / AP / Shutterstock

p. 99: Hermann Claasen, *Die überfüllte Straße, Karneval 1949*. Fotografische Sammlung LVR—landesmuseum Bonn, photo: Jürgen Vogel

p. 102: in *Neue Illustrierte*, vol. 3, no. 3 (6 February 1948)

p. 106: dpa-Report

p. 111: bpk/Hanns Hubmann

p. 122: picture alliance/akg-images

p. 128: *Neue Illustrierte*, vol. 2, no. 21 (7 October 1947), photo: Jörg Bohn

p. 129: *Neue Illustrierte*, vol. 2, no. 34 (16 December 1948), photo: Jörg Bohn

p. 133: bpk/Hanns Hubmann

p. 151: akg-images/Sammlung Berliner Verlag/Archiv

p. 154: akg-images/Tony Vaccaro

p. 174: picture alliance/dpa-Zentralbild

p. 178: akg-images

p. 190: ullstein bild—Georg Schmidt

p. 203: *DND*, vol. 3, no. 9, 3–4 (1948–49)

p. 211: Archive Willi Luther

p. 217: ullstein bild—Röhnert

p. 222: bpk/Benno Wundshammer

p. 239: in *Der Spiegel* 44, 1954

p. 256: ullstein bild—Abraham Pisarek

p. 265: akg-images

p. 278: *Der Spiegel* 44, 1947 (© DACS 2021)

p. 281: akg-images/Willi Baumeister (© DACS 2021)

p. 289: documenta archiv/photo: Werner Lengemann (© The Pollock-Krasner Foundation ARS, NY and DACS, London 2021)

p. 291: ullstein bild—Röhnert

p. 293: Berlinische Galerie/Sergius Ruegenberg

p. 312: National Archives, College Park, MD, USA

p. 314: Bundesarchiv, Bild 183-V00197-3

p. 319: Office of Military Government for Germany, US (OMGUS)/Haus der Geschichte, Bonn